LINQ

FOR

DUMMIES®

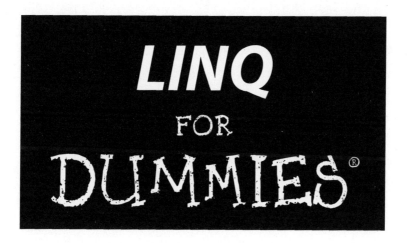

by John Paul Mueller

Wiley Publishing, Inc.

LINQ For Dummies®

Published by
Wiley Publishing, Inc.
111 River Street
Hoboken, NJ 07030-5774
www.wiley.com

WILEY

About the Author

John Paul Mueller is a freelance author and technical editor. He has writing in his blood, having produced 80 books and over 300 articles to date. The topics range from networking to artificial intelligence and from database management to heads-down programming. Some of his current books include a Windows power optimization book, books on both Windows Server 2008 GUI and Windows Server 2008 Server Core, and a programmer's guide that discusses the new Office Fluent User Interface (RibbonX). His technical editing skills have helped more than 56 authors refine the content of their manuscripts. John has provided technical editing services to both *Data Based Advisor* and *Coast Compute* magazines. He's also contributed articles to the following magazines: *CIO.com, DevSource, InformIT, Informant, DevX, SQL Server Professional, Visual C++ Developer, Hard Core Visual Basic, asp.netPRO, Software Test and Performance*, and *Visual Basic Developer*.

When John isn't working at the computer, you can find him in his workshop crafting wood projects or making candles. On any given afternoon, you can find him working at a lathe or putting the finishing touches on a bookcase. He also likes making glycerin soap, which comes in handy for gift baskets. You can reach John on the Internet at JMueller@mwt.net. John is also setting up a Web site and blog at http://www.johnmuellerbooks.com/; feel free to look and make suggestions on how he can improve it.

Dedication

This book is dedicated to my friend Osvaldo Téllez Almirall (Chicho). We've had many conversations about music and life in general and I've always felt that I came away a better person for them.

Author's Acknowledgments

Thanks to my wife, Rebecca, for working with me to get this book completed. I really don't know what I would have done without her help in researching and compiling some of the information that appears in this book. She also did a fine job of proofreading my rough draft.

Russ Mullen deserves thanks for his technical edit of this book. He added greatly to the accuracy and depth of the material that you see here. I appreciated the time he devoted to checking my code for accuracy. As I wrote this book, I also spent a good deal of time bouncing ideas off Russ, which is a valuable aid to any author.

Matt Wagner, my agent, deserves credit for helping me get the contract in the first place and taking care of all the details that most authors don't consider. I always appreciate his assistance. It's good to know that someone wants to help.

A number of people read all or part of this book to help me refine the approach, test the examples, and generally provide input that every reader wishes they could have. These unpaid volunteers helped in ways too numerous to mention here. I especially appreciate the efforts of Osvaldo Téllez Almirall, who provided me with some interesting bits of information. Bill Salkin gave me some good ideas. Andrew Matthews provided me with significant help and coding examples for the LINQ to RDF provider. In fact, a number of people made suggestions on how to improve my coding technique. I'd like to thank each person who wrote me with an idea by name, but there are simply too many.

Finally, I would like to thank Katie Feltman, Susan Pink, and the rest of the editorial and production staff for their assistance in bringing this book to print. It's always nice to work with such a great group of professionals.

Publisher's Acknowledgments

We're proud of this book; please send us your comments through our online registration form located at www.dummies.com/register/.

Some of the people who helped bring this book to market include the following:

Acquisitions, Editorial, and Media Development

Project Editor: Susan Pink

Acquisitions Editor: Katie Feltman

Copy Editor: Susan Pink

Technical Editor: Russ Mullen

Editorial Manager: Jodi Jensen

Assistant Project Manager: Jenny Swisher

Assistant Producer: Shawn Patrick

Editorial Assistant: Amanda Foxworth

Sr. Editorial Assistant: Cherie Case

Cartoons: Rich Tennant (www.the5thwave.com)

Composition Services

Project Coordinator: Katherine Key

Layout and Graphics: Stacie Brooks, Reuben W. Davis, Melissa K. Jester, Christin Swinford

Proofreaders: Linda Seifert, Amanda Steiner

Indexer: Sharon Shock

Publishing and Editorial for Technology Dummies

Richard Swadley, Vice President and Executive Group Publisher

Andy Cummings, Vice President and Publisher

Mary Bednarek, Executive Acquisitions Director

Mary C. Corder, Editorial Director

Publishing for Consumer Dummies

Diane Graves Steele, Vice President and Publisher

Joyce Pepple, Acquisitions Director

Composition Services

Gerry Fahey, Vice President of Production Services

Debbie Stailey, Director of Composition Services

Contents at a Glance

Introduction 1

Part I: An Overview of LINQ 7
Chapter 1: Getting to Know LINQ 9
Chapter 2: Creating Simple LINQ Queries 23
Chapter 3: Considering the .NET Language Extensions 47
Chapter 4: Working with LINQ in Visual Basic .NET 69
Chapter 5: Working with LINQ in Visual Studio 2005 91

Part II: Using Standard LINQ to Technologies 105
Chapter 6: LINQ to Object 107
Chapter 7: LINQ to DataSet 133
Chapter 8: LINQ to SQL Server 157
Chapter 9: LINQ to XML 181

Part III: Extending LINQ to New Horizons 211
Chapter 10: Using LINQ with Office 2007 213
Chapter 11: Advanced LINQ to SQL Server 233
Chapter 12: LINQ to Active Directory 253
Chapter 13: Other LINQ to Strategies 271

Part IV: The Part of Tens 299
Chapter 14: Ten Ways to Improve LINQ Development 301
Chapter 15: Ten Ways to Reduce Application Support Costs 321
Chapter 16: Ten LINQ Resources 335

Index 347

Table of Contents

Introduction *1*

About This Book 1
Conventions Used in This Book 2
What You Should Read 2
What You Don't Have to Read 3
Foolish Assumptions 3
How This Book Is Organized 4
    Part I: An Overview of LINQ 4
    Part II: Using Standard LINQ to Technologies 4
    Part III: Extending LINQ to New Horizons 5
    Part IV: The Part of Tens 5
    The accompanying Web site 5
Icons Used in This Book 5
Where to Go from Here 6

Part I: An Overview of LINQ *7*

Chapter 1: Getting to Know LINQ **9**

Considering LINQ 10
    Understanding the task that LINQ performs 10
    Contemplating why you need LINQ 11
    Defining the LINQ design goals 14
    Understanding the LINQ requirements 16
Using LINQ in the Real World 17
Understanding Declarative Programming 18
An Overview of the LINQ Namespaces 19
    System.Linq namespace 19
    System.Linq.Expressions namespace 19
    System.Data.Linq namespace 20
    System.Data.Linq.Mapping namespace 21
    System.Data.SqlClient namespace 21
    System.Data.SqlClient.Implementation namespace 22
    System.Xml.Linq namespace 22

Chapter 2: Creating Simple LINQ Queries **23**

Defining the LINQ Keywords 24
    Working with from 24
    Working with where 25

Working with orderby 26
Working with join 27
Working with let 28
Creating a Simple from Query 29
Understanding the simple query application code 29
Using the debugger to see the simple query in action................31
Filtering a Query 34
Grouping Queries 35
Creating Queries from Multiple Sources 36
Understanding the multiple-source application code................37
Working with the alternative multiple-source example................38
Using calculated values in multiple-source queries.......................39
Working with the Standard Query Operators 41
Mapping Keywords to Methods 43

Chapter 3: Considering the .NET Language Extensions 47

An Overview of the Language Extensions 48
Working with Lambda Expressions 51
Understanding the Role of the IEnumerable and IEnumerable<T>
Interfaces 54
Understanding Object Initializers 57
Understanding Collection Initializers 58
Working with Extension Methods 61
Working with Partial Methods 62
An Overview of Expression Trees 64
Working with Query Expressions 67

Chapter 4: Working with LINQ in Visual Basic .NET 69

Understanding the Visual Basic Differences 70
Creating the Simple Visual Basic Example 72
Working with From 72
Working with Where..75
Working with Order By 78
Working with Join 79
Working with Let...81
Using the Additional Visual Basic Keywords 82
Working with Aggregate..83
Working with Distinct...84
Working with Skip...85
Working with Take...87
Working with Lambda Functions in Visual Basic 88

Chapter 5: Working with LINQ in Visual Studio 2005 91

Obtaining LINQ Support for Visual Studio 2005 92
Installing LINQ Support...92

Creating the Simple Visual Studio 2005 Project...........................93
   Defining the project 94
   Working with from 95
   Working with join 98
   Working with where 100
   Working with orderby 102
   Working with let 103

Part II: Using Standard LINQ to Technologies.............. 105

Chapter 6: LINQ to Object 107
Considering the Use of Objects with LINQ.............................108
Creating the Simple Object Query Example............................109
Understanding the Role of Deferred Operators........................112
Creating the Deferred Operator Examples.............................113
   Working with Concat 113
   Working with AsEnumerable, AsQueryable, Cast, and Of Type 114
   Working with OfType and Where 115
   Working with DefaultIfEmpty, Empty, Range, and Repeat............116
   Working with GroupBy and ToLookup 118
   Working with GroupJoin and Join 120
   Working with Skip, SkipWhile, Take, and TakeWhile 120
   Working with Select and SelectMany 121
   Working with Distinct, Except, Intersect, and Union 123
   Working with OrderBy, OrderByDescending, Reverse,
      ThenBy, and ThenByDescending 124
Understanding the Role of Nondeferred Operators.....................125
Creating the Nondeferred Operator Examples 126
   Working with Aggregate, Average, Count, LongCount,
      Max, Min, and Sum 127
   Working with ToArray, ToDictionary, ToList, and ToLookup 128
   Working with ElementAt, ElementAtOrDefault, First, First
      OrDefault, Last, LastOrDefault, Single, and SingleOrDefault 128
   Working with SequenceEqual...129
   Working with All, Any, and Contains 130

Chapter 7: LINQ to DataSet....................................133
Considering the Use of DataSets with LINQ 134
Creating the Simple DataSet Example.................................136
   Defining the test tables 136
   Outputting the results 139
   Exploring the connection...139
Understanding the LINQ to DataSet Operators 141

Creating the Filtered Output Example 142
 Creating a simple display...143
 Modifying the filtered output 144
 Using the CopyToDataTable operator 146
 Working with typed DataSets 148
 Working with Multiple DataSet Tables 152

Chapter 8: LINQ to SQL Server **157**
 Considering the Use of SQL Server with LINQ.............................158
 Obtaining and Installing the Northwind Database 160
 Downloading the database 161
 Installing the database 162
 Testing the Visual Studio connection 164
 Generating the Northwind entity classes
  and XML mapping files 165
 Creating the Simple SQL Server Query Example 168
 Overcoming the Visual Studio 2008 connectivity issues.............168
 Defining the project 170
 Adding the code 171
 Viewing the debugger output 173
 Using Object Relational Designer 175
 Understanding the LINQ to SQL Server Operators 178

Chapter 9: LINQ to XML **181**
 Considering the Use of XML with LINQ 182
 Working with the LINQ to XML API...184
 Understanding the LINQ to XML Operators...................................186
 Working with XDeclaration, XElement, and XDocument.............186
 Working with XNamespace...188
 Working with XProcessingInstruction 190
 Working with XAttribute...191
 Working with XComment and XText 192
 Working with XCData 194
 Working with XDocumentType..195
 Working with XNodeDocumentOrderComparer............................197
 Working with XNodeEqualityComparer......................................199
 Working with Remove 201
 Working with XName...202
 Creating the Simple XML File Example 204
 Creating the project..204
 Building an XML document 205
 Saving an XML document 207
 Loading an XML document...208

Part III: Extending LINQ to New Horizons 211

Chapter 10: Using LINQ with Office 2007 213

Understanding the Office Document Structure 214
Understanding LINQ Interaction with Office 216
Obtaining the Required Library 218
Creating the Office 2007 Document Example 219
    Creating the project 220
    Understanding the custom properties 221
    Reading document properties 225
    Writing document properties 228

Chapter 11: Advanced LINQ to SQL Server 233

Considering SQL Server Issues 234
    Understanding concurrency problems 234
    Overcoming performance issues 238
Creating the Database Modification Example 240
    Performing an insert 241
    Performing an update 243
    Performing a delete 245
Using Concurrency Checks and Resolving Errors 247
    Resolving conflicts at the object level 248
    Resolving conflicts at the member level 251

Chapter 12: LINQ to Active Directory 253

Working with Specific Active Directory Objects 254
Defining Active Directory Variables 256
Obtaining the LINQ to Active Directory Provider 257
Creating the Simple Active Directory Query Example 260
    Performing the project setup 260
    Defining an Active Directory object class 262
    Creating a root node pointer 264
    Reading user information 265
    Writing user information 266
Understanding the Limitations of Active Directory Interaction 268
    Some LINQ methods aren't implemented 268
    Defining the need for LDAP patience 269

Chapter 13: Other LINQ to Strategies 271

Understanding the Qualifications for a LINQ to Solution 271
Accessing COM+ Using LINQ 273
    COM+ accessed as a Web service 276
    COM+ accessed using interop functionality 281

Creating the Resource Description Format (RDF) Files Example..........282
   A quick overview of RDF..283
   A quick overview of SPARQL...283
   Starting the project..284
   Configuring the project...285
   Creating the host application...288
   Creating the application class definition.............................292
   Reading RDF files...293
Creating the MySQL Example...294
   Getting the MySQL ADO.NET connector...................................295
   Compiling the DbLinq.DLL and DbLinq.MySQL.DLL files...................295
   Configuring the database..296
   Defining the MySQL project..296
   Developing the query code...297

Part IV: The Part of Tens 299

Chapter 14: Ten Ways to Improve LINQ Development. 301
   Using LINQ Tools to Simplify Coding...................................302
      Getting the VLinq add-in application...............................302
      Creating a VLinq query...303
      Using a VLinq query in an application..............................308
   Using LINQ to Create Self Documenting Code............................309
   Analyzing Code Patterns...311
   Querying a Code Snippet Database......................................314
   Locating Other Development Resources..................................316
   Using LINQ to Query Data Formats......................................316
   Finding Usage Trends..317
   Developing a LINQ Library...318
   Sharing LINQ Queries with Others......................................319
   Analyzing Compiler and IDE Output.....................................319

Chapter 15: Ten Ways to Reduce Application Support Costs 321
   Creating Self-Modifying Queries.......................................322
   Using LINQ to Create Reports..323
   Addressing User Search Needs..325
   Creating User-Friendly Mashups..326
   Making Help More Accessible...326
   Organizing and Querying Support Requests and Responses................327
   Developing Fast Searches from Multiple Sources........................328
   Helping Users Locate Existing Resources...............................331
   Performing Support Task Automation....................................331
   Improving Application and System Management...........................333

Chapter 16: Ten LINQ Resources 335
    Starting with the Microsoft Developer Network.....................................336
    Getting Tips from the Microsoft Blogs...338
    Finding Help in Third-Party Web Sites...339
    Finding Help in Third-Party Newsletters and Blogs 340
    Using Other Sources for LINQ to Objects Projects 342
    Using Other Sources for LINQ to SQL Server Projects 342
    Using Other Sources for LINQ to XML Projects....................................343
    Considering Other LINQ to Sources Projects 344
    Getting Help with Visual Basic Projects 345
    Getting Help with C# Projects...346

Index *347*

Introduction

L anguage INtegrated Query (LINQ) sounds like some kind of formless question that depends on how someone speaks. Of course, your queries are integrated with your language! How can you make them otherwise?

LINQ is actually a new feature of .NET Framework that expands your grasp well beyond things Microsoft. In fact, after playing with LINQ for quite some time I thought I'd start to run out of new data sources to query, but it hasn't happened yet. You can use LINQ to query just about anything (and I only say "just about" because I'm sure there is something LINQ can't reach).

The thing that should excite you most about LINQ is that it helps you access technologies that you couldn't ordinarily access or couldn't do so with ease. For example, you can use LINQ to access MySQL easily, without considering a workaround. You can also access Resource Description Framework (RDF) files, something that would be tough without LINQ. You get all of these additional opportunities to access varied data sources and you'll write less code, not more, to do it. LINQ is truly one of the most interesting features that Microsoft has ever added to .NET Framework, and you'd miss out on a lot if you didn't explore the LINQ technology for your own programming needs.

About This Book

LINQ For Dummies is your gateway to a new world — one in which you can ask questions (programmatically) of literally anything. This book starts with the basics. You need to discover the LINQ basics before you can begin pulling information from Active Directory, but LINQ is so small compared to many technologies that the basics require only a few pages. Most of this book is about getting serious work accomplished.

After working with LINQ for a while, I discovered that there are inequities in the LINQ world. For one thing, it seems as if Microsoft is avoiding Visual Basic .NET because their Web site has a decided lack of Visual Basic .NET materials. It was hard to find Visual Basic .NET examples on third-party Web sites too. I hope that this situation will change, but for now you have Chapter 4, which tells you the Visual Basic .NET side of the story, and Chapter 16, which provides you with a host of Visual Basic .NET resources.

The second inequity that *LINQ For Dummies* addresses is the needs of the Visual Studio 2005 developer. It appears that everyone assumes you have Visual Studio 2008. Although most of this book was written with Visual Studio

2008 in mind, there isn't any reason you can't write LINQ applications using Visual Studio 2005, and Chapter 5 provides the information you need. The remaining examples in the book will even work with Visual Studio 2005 with a little tweaking.

You'll also find a host of example types in *LINQ For Dummies*. For example, did you know that you can access the content of Office 2007 documents using LINQ? Chapter 10 tells you about all of the interesting things you can do with Office 2007 once you have LINQ at your disposal. The astonishing thing is that you can perform these tasks with little code. Using LINQ, it's possible to both read and write Office 2007 documents without resorting to odd programming strategies.

LINQ can also make your life as a developer considerably easier. Chapter 14 provides an array of interesting techniques you can use to obtain information about your applications that you might not have even thought available. Only in *LINQ For Dummies* can you find all of these mind-boggling techniques in one place.

Conventions Used in This Book

I always try to show you the fastest way to accomplish any task. In many cases, this means using a menu command such as File➪New➪Project. When working with LINQ, I'll tell you which dialog box tab to access first, and then which feature to use on that tab.

This book also uses special type to emphasize some information. For example, entries that you need to type appear in **bold**. All code, Web site URLs, and on-screen messages appear in `monofont type`. When I define a new word, you'll see that word in *italics*.

Because you use multiple applications when you're working with LINQ, I always point out when to move from one application to the next. When a chapter begins, I introduce the main application for that chapter. All the commands in that chapter are for the main application until I specifically tell you to move to another application. I also tell you when it's time to move back to the main application.

What You Should Read

Anyone who doesn't have any LINQ experience should read all of Part I. It's possible to skip Chapter 1 if you don't want to know about the array of LINQ providers already on the market or the other interesting things you can do with LINQ, but most people have a number of special needs and Chapter 1 is where you discover how to fulfill them.

Someone who's been exposed to LINQ but hasn't worked with it can probably skip Part I and begin with Part II. Make sure you read the chapters in turn. No, the chapters don't provide interlocked information, forcing you to grind through one chapter at a time, but the LINQ to DataSet provider does build on the LINQ to Objects provider, so you need to know both to create a LINQ to Objects application.

If you're familiar with the basic LINQ to providers (you have written programs using them) and just want to see the other things that LINQ can do, you'll want to start with Part III. In some cases, you may have questions about a particular technique and you can refer to Parts I and II when you need to answer such questions. Part III doesn't provide quite as much hand holding, so you do need to know how LINQ works to use it.

What You Don't Have to Read

Most of the chapters contain some advanced material that will interest only some readers. When you see one of these specialized topics (such as the requirements for using COM+ in Vista and Windows Server 2008 in Chapter 13), feel free to skip it. Most of this advanced material appears in sidebars and some of it applies only when you use a specific operating system. The sidebar title will always indicate the special nature of the advanced material.

You can also skip any material marked with a Technical Stuff icon. This material is helpful, but you don't have to know it to work with LINQ. I include this material because I find it helpful in my programming efforts and hope that you will, too.

Foolish Assumptions

You might find it difficult to believe that I've assumed anything about you — after all, I haven't even met you yet! Although most assumptions are indeed foolish, I made these assumptions to provide a starting point for the book.

I'm assuming that you've worked with Windows long enough to know how the keyboard and mouse work. You should also know how to use menus and other basic Windows features. It's also essential to know how to use the Visual Studio IDE and that you know at least one .NET language. This book doesn't provide any instruction on how to write applications outside the instructions needed to write LINQ applications. If you don't know what a `foreach` loop is, you definitely require a different book.

Some portions of the book work with Web pages and others use XML; you need to know at least a little about these technologies to use those sections.

You don't have to be an expert in any of these areas, but more knowledge is better. You must also have a very good knowledge of the programming language you use to work with LINQ.

This is a book for someone who has development experience. I'm assuming that you have a very good knowledge of either Visual Basic .NET or C#. You must also know how to work with any extension technology you want to access. For example, if you want to write a LINQ query to access COM+, you need to know something about COM+ before you can read about it in this book. The same holds true for Active Directory, RDF, MySQL, Office 2007, or any of the other extension technologies described in the book.

How This Book Is Organized

This book contains several parts. Each part demonstrates a particular LINQ concept. In each chapter, I discuss a particular topic and include example programs that you can use to discover more about LINQ on your own. You can find the source code for this book on the Dummies.com Web site at `http://www.dummies.com/go/linqfd`.

Part I: An Overview of LINQ

Part I looks at LINQ as a technology and introduces you to essential concepts such as the operators used to create a LINQ query. In addition, this part reviews the .NET Framework technologies that make LINQ queries possible. This is also the part of the book that helps you use LINQ with both Visual Basic .NET and Visual Studio 2005. One of the central themes of this part of *LINQ For Dummies* is helping you discover all the tasks that LINQ can perform.

Part II: Using Standard LINQ to Technologies

.NET Framework comes with four providers. A *provider* is a link between your application and the data source it requires. Each of the four LINQ providers that come with .NET Framework appear in a separate chapter in Part II. Using just these four providers, you can query any object, any data set, any kind of XML, and SQL Server. These four providers cover a lot of ground. Just knowing them will give you access to a considerable range of data, much of which isn't even hosted on Windows.

Part III: Extending LINQ to New Horizons

The four basic LINQ providers can perform quite a few tasks, but they have limits. Sometimes it isn't a matter of being able to access the data, but merely one of accessing the data without a lot of extra programming. Part III shows how you can combine third-party providers with LINQ to create some remarkable applications. Because the applications in this part of the book are unique, you'll want to skip around a bit and read about the technologies that interest you the most first.

Part IV: The Part of Tens

The final part of the book provides you with some helpful tips and resources you can use to make your LINQ development experience even better. Chapter 14 shows how you can use LINQ to create a better development environment for yourself. Chapter 15 helps you discover ways to use LINQ to make the application environment better for users and support staff, while reducing your workload. Chapter 16 provides ten truly useful resources that will help reduce your development time. If you have the idea by now that LINQ is all about making things easier, you have understood the intent of this book.

The accompanying Web site

This book contains a lot of code, and you might not want to type it. In fact, it's probably better if you don't attempt to type this code manually. Fortunately, you can find the source code for this book on the Dummies.com Web site at `http://www.dummies.com/go/linqfd`. The source code is organized by chapter, and I'll always tell you about the example files in the text. The best way to work with a chapter is to download all the source code for it at one time.

Icons Used in This Book

As you read this book, you'll see icons in the margins that indicate material of interest (or not, as the case may be).This section briefly describes each icon in this book.

Tips are nice because they help you save time or perform some task without a lot of extra work. The tips in this book are timesaving techniques or pointers to resources that you should try to get the maximum benefit from LINQ.

I don't want to sound like an angry parent or some kind of maniac, but you should avoid doing anything marked with a Warning icon. Otherwise, you could find that your program melts down and takes your data with it.

 Whenever you see this icon, think *advanced* tip or technique. You might find these tidbits of useful information just too boring for words, or they could contain the solution you need to get a program running. Skip these bits of information whenever you like.

 If you don't get anything else out of a particular chapter or section, remember the material marked by this icon. This text usually contains an essential process or bit of information that you must know to write LINQ programs successfully.

Where to Go from Here

It's time to start your LINQ adventure! I recommend that anyone who has only a passing knowledge of LINQ go right to Chapter 1. This chapter contains essential, get-started information that you need for writing your first LINQ program.

If you already have some LINQ experience, move right to Chapter 6. It is important to know about the four LINQ providers that come with .NET Framework. Otherwise, you might find that it's hard to understand how the third-party LINQ providers described in Part III work. If you desperately need LINQ on your next project, read through Chapter 6 first before you move on to Part III because every LINQ provider available today builds on the LINQ to Objects provider.

Part I
An Overview of LINQ

The 5th Wave   By Rich Tennant

"Yes, I know how to query information from the program, but what if I just want to leak it instead?"

In this part . . .

Someone once said that the beginning is a good place to start; well, this is the beginning. Chapter 1 introduces you to LINQ — it clears up any questions you might have about what LINQ is and what it can do. Most importantly, it introduces you to a considerably larger view of LINQ than you might have at the outset. Chapter 2 takes what you discover in Chapter 1 and shows you how to apply it in the form of practical LINQ queries.

Chapter 3 is special — it tells you about the unique features in .NET Framework that make LINQ a workable solution. You'll probably find yourself referring to this chapter as you read the rest of the book.

Chapters 4 and 5 provide exclusive information for Visual Basic.NET and Visual Studio 2005 developers. It seems as if these two groups get left out of most books, but you'll find them here.

Chapter 1

Getting to Know LINQ

In This Chapter

▶ Defining LINQ uses, benefits, and design goals

▶ Considering the real world uses of LINQ

▶ Defining declarative programming languages

▶ Understanding the LINQ namespaces

The Language INtegrated Query (LINQ) feature of Visual Studio 2008 provides you with a new way to interact with data of all types. In fact, this new feature provides you with tools that make it easier to create queries using less code. The resulting queries are often easier to understand than other techniques for deriving information from both standard (think databases) nonstandard (think memory data structures) data sources. In addition, you gain a measure of flexibility that most developers associate with using a database, not lists provided internally as part of applications.

The easiest way to think of LINQ at the outset is as a means of looking for something — a specialized kind of search. Because most people are inundated with information today, providing a fast means of locating specific data is important. LINQ provides the means to perform a search without writing a lot of code. Everything is built in to the development environment so all you need to consider is what to find, not how to find it. Unlike other kinds of searches, however, LINQ provides the means to look inside data structures that you normally can't search, such as objects. It can also standardize the methods you use to perform searches within Web services. In short, LINQ

- ✓ Provides access to a huge range of data
- ✓ Lets you simplify searches to locate just what you need
- ✓ Reduces the code required to perform a search
- ✓ Enables you to focus on the search instead of writing search routines
- ✓ Interacts with all kinds of data sources using a standardized approach

This chapter serves as an introduction to LINQ. You discover how LINQ will make your coding experience better, reduce real world complexity, and make searches more accurate. As part of discovering LINQ, you also need to know about declarative languages, and this chapter provides the information you need. Finally, since LINQ is part of the .NET Framework, you need to know which namespaces support it, so this chapter provides an introduction to these new namespaces.

Considering LINQ

LINQ is possibly the most exciting new feature Microsoft has added to Visual Studio 2008. Sure, the other features that Microsoft added are important, but they don't have the overwhelming reach of LINQ to change the way developers write applications. Anyone can use LINQ to create a better application — one that works more efficiently and uses less code. In addition, you no longer have to write custom search routines that differ from developer to developer. By using LINQ to perform searches of all types, you can standardize another part of your code base and incrementally improve overall developer productivity. The following sections describe LINQ in greater detail.

Understanding the task that LINQ performs

LINQ is all about searching efficiently and consistently. Your application searches efficiently by performing the task using less code and obtaining the results faster. Consistency comes from using the same code pattern to perform a search no matter what source of data you want to work with. From a pattern perspective, a search of an array looks the same as a search of a Web service or SQL Server database. Using LINQ, it no longer matters whether the data resides in SQL Server or MySQL, or even both. LINQ does divide queries into four common types (using different providers) that augment the basic patterns described in Chapter 2:

- LINQ to Object
- LINQ to DataSet
- LINQ to SQL
- LINQ to XML

It's possible to have other kinds of "LINQ to" scenarios by adding other libraries. For example, you can find a LINQ to Active Directory library at `http://www.codeplex.com/LINQtoAD`. The goal, however, is to perform as many tasks as possible using the four basic LINQ to strategies provided with .NET Framework 3.5.

The most important thing to remember about LINQ is that it isn't technology specific. This book shows you how to "LINQ to" any number of data sources, some of which you'll find unusual because you may not have thought to search them before. For example, you may have an assortment of data in an object that you need to search — LINQ is the perfect tool for performing this task.

In addition to finding data, LINQ can also help organize it so that you present the user with only the data needed as output. Using special features of LINQ, you can filter data so that the user sees just the desired elements. You can also group and sort the data so that the user sees it in an order that makes it easier to use the data. The essential task that LINQ performs, therefore, is to make the data accessible. The user sees only the data needed and in the most productive way.

However, LINQ goes beyond searching for and ordering data. In many cases, you can also use LINQ to create a query that manipulates data in various ways, assuming the data source allows such manipulation. For example, you can use LINQ to change the content of a SQL Server database. Some unusual data sources such as Active Directory also allow modification. In fact, you can modify any configuration database that relies on the Lightweight Directory Access Protocol (LDAP). Consequently, the techniques in this book show you how to work with mainstream products, but you can easily modify them to meet any need.

Contemplating why you need LINQ

With feature bloat running rampant and developer time in ever limited quantity, you may wonder whether LINQ is the right choice for you. In most cases, you'd look for a list of qualifiers describing the technology and use these qualifiers to decide whether a technology is the right one for you. LINQ is a well-designed technology that can apply to anyone's search needs — no qualifiers needed. You won't have to wait for drivers or additional software to use it. In short, anyone who searches for data can use LINQ to meet that need.

Of course, now you're thinking that this book is offering you the fabled silver bullet solution. LINQ isn't a silver bullet. The other tools you have for searching are still useful and you'll need to employ them. For example, even Microsoft admits that LINQ can have performance problems when searching SQL Server databases. You can read the five-part blog series about performance issues at `http://blogs.msdn.com/ricom/archive/2007/06/22/dlinq-linq-to-sql-performance-part-1.aspx` to obtain a good overview of the problems (but not any significant solutions). Chapter 11 provides you with information about how you can overcome performance issues (here's where you find the solutions), so make sure to check it out as well.

It's important to understand that LINQ works with most data sources but not all of them. For example, you can easily use LINQ with most public Web services and some private Web services. However, even though you can use LINQ with the Amazon, Google, and AOL Web services, it doesn't work with the eBay Web services due to security concerns. In short, specific Web service requirements can prevent LINQ from working properly. You can find a complete list of LINQ providers (LINQ to solutions) at `http://blogs.msdn.com/charlie/archive/2006/10/05/Links-to-LINQ.aspx`. Table 1-1 shows a list of the providers as of this writing.

Table 1-1	LINQ Providers
LINQ to Solution	**URL**
LINQ Extender (toolkit for building LINQ providers)	`http://www.codeplex.com/LinqExtender`
LINQ over C# project	`http://www.codeplex.com/LinqOverCSharp`
LINQ to Active Directory	`http://www.codeplex.com/LINQtoAD`
LINQ to Amazon	`http://weblogs.asp.net/fmarguerie/archive/2006/06/26/Introducing-Linq-to-Amazon.aspx`
LINQ to Bindable Sources (SyncLINQ)	`http://paulstovell.net/blog/index.php/why-synclinq-should-matter-to-you/`
LINQ to CRM (Customer Relationship Management)	`http://www.codeplex.com/LinqtoCRM`
LINQ to Excel	`http://www.codeplex.com/xlslinq`
LINQ to Expressions (MetaLinq)	`http://www.codeplex.com/metalinq`
LINQ to Flickr	`http://www.codeplex.com/LINQFlickr`
LINQ to Geo (geospatial data)	`http://www.codeplex.com/LinqToGeo`
LINQ to Google	`http://www.codeplex.com/glinq`
LINQ to Indexes	`http://www.codeplex.com/i4o/Release/ProjectReleases.aspx?ReleaseId=3519`

LINQ to Solution	URL
LINQ to IQueryable	`http://blogs.msdn.com/mattwar/archive/2007/08/09/linq-building-an-iqueryable-provider-part-vi.aspx`
LINQ to JavaScript	`http://www.codeplex.com/JSLINQ`
LINQ to JSON (JavaScript Object Notation)	`http://james.newtonking.com/archive/2008/02/11/linq-to-json-beta.aspx`
LINQ to LDAP (Lightweight Directory Access Protocol)	`http://community.bartdesmet.net/blogs/bart/archive/2007/04/05/the-iqueryable-tales-linq-to-ldap-part-0.aspx`
LINQ to Lucene	`http://www.codeplex.com/linqtolucene`
LINQ to Metaweb (freebase)	`http://www.codeplex.com/metawebToLinQ`
LINQ to MySQL, Oracle, and PostgreSql	`http://code2code.net/DB_Linq/`
LINQ to NHibernate	`http://www.ayende.com/Blog/archive/2007/03/17/Implementing-Linq-for-NHibernate-A-How-To-Guide--Part.aspx`
LINQ to RDF (Resource Description Framework) Files	`http://blogs.msdn.com/hartmutm/archive/2006/07/24/677200.aspx`
LINQ to SharePoint	`http://www.codeplex.com/LINQtoSharePoint`
LINQ to SimpleDB	`http://www.codeplex.com/LinqToSimpleDB`
LINQ to Streams	`http://www.codeplex.com/Slinq/`
LINQ to WebQueries	`http://blogs.msdn.com/hartmutm/archive/2006/06/12/628382.aspx`
LINQ to WMI (Windows Management Instrumentation)	`http://bloggingabout.net/blogs/emile/archive/2005/12/12/10514.aspx`, `http://tomasp.net/blog/linq-expand.aspx`, and `http://tomasp.net/blog/linq-expand-update.aspx`
LINQ to XtraGrid	`http://cs.rthand.com/blogs/blog_with_righthand/archive/2008/02/23/LINQ-to-XtraGrid.aspx`

Don't get the idea that LINQ always requires a provider. The provider does make it easier to perform tasks, but you can also create your own interface using the generic providers. For example, you can interact with Office 2007 files without using a specific provider. Chapter 10 shows you how to perform this task.

Even with these few warts, however, LINQ is a good solution for many search needs and you should at least try it. You need LINQ because it has so much to offer and doesn't require a lot of time to master or use. LINQ provides the experimental platform that most developers crave. In those few situations where LINQ can't do a good job for you, experimentation can at least help you understand the data source better.

Defining the LINQ design goals

Microsoft had a number of design goals in mind when it created LINQ. These design goals affect how you view LINQ today and how you can use it to solve specific application development problems. The following list describes the design goals.

- **Data source access simplification:** One of the major issues of working with any data source is that the developer must know several disciplines to perform the task of accessing the data. For example, when working with SQL Server, the developer must understand the nuances of the base programming language, a database provider, and a language such as SQL to obtain access to the data. If the developer decides to access XML data, it's necessary to master an entirely different set of disciplines. LINQ overcomes this problem by providing a single method of accessing data.

- **Data manipulation simplification:** When you make a query using C# or Visual Basic .NET, you have to worry about the structure of the data source. For example, when you query SQL Server, you must consider the tables, indexes, views, and other structural elements of the database. The use of these structural elements is necessary but not helpful. You end up thinking about the data structure and not the data. Consequently, many developers create convoluted and difficult to understand data-manipulation code when what they really wanted was the data (the underlying structure isn't important).

- **Data translation:** In most cases, you must write special routines to move data from one data source to another. For example, if you want to move data from an XML file to SQL Server, you must perform some special tasks to do it. In addition, moving the data doesn't always provide the results you expected. Differences in data source capabilities make the translation less than perfect. LINQ reduces the complexity of data translation significantly. It doesn't always provide a perfect translation either, but you'll find that the translation is usually better because each provider performs the required translation for you.

✔ **Object mapping:** Most programming languages today rely on some form of object orientation. Objects have special characteristics that you won't find in many data sources. For example, an object doesn't respect the tables, indexes, and other data structures found in SQL Server. Consequently, you need a means of mapping the object to the data source and vice versa. In the past, the developer had to rely on complex objects that Visual Studio generated for them. Using LINQ provides object mapping without the complexity.

✔ **Language extensibility:** Microsoft provides a limited number of "LINQ to" providers as part of the .NET Framework. These providers are capable, but they don't address every need. Consequently, one of the design goals for LINQ is to provide language extensibility so that third parties can create other providers. Table 1-1 shows an example of just how many providers have already been created by third parties, and you can expect more in the future.

✔ **Multiple data source extensibility:** Because one of the goals for LINQ is data translation, it's important to have providers that can work with multiple data sources. The goal is to make it possible to move data from any data source to any other data source. In addition, Microsoft wants LINQ to be able to use data from any data source and combine it with data from any other data source to create a composite output.

✔ **Type safety:** A major problem with many data source usage scenarios today is that data problems are discovered only at run time, often without any help from the language product or the application. A developer may not discover a problem until someone complains about mangled data. The type safety features of LINQ help you discover potential data problems during compile time, when they're easy to fix, rather than getting your bad news later.

✔ **IntelliSense support:** Creating a query using standard development tools can be hit or miss. LINQ provides IntelliSense support so that you can see how to create the query as you create it.

✔ **Debugger support:** Due to strong typing and other features of LINQ, you get full debugger support, which makes finding a particular problem considerably easier. No longer do you have to look for that errant bit of code in a loop or the missed type issue in a custom class. LINQ helps you diagnose problems quickly and easily.

✔ **Older product support:** Even though most of this book uses new technology that Microsoft provides, you can use LINQ with older products as well. Obviously, the support isn't built in to these older products, so LINQ doesn't work as seamlessly. (You must use at least the .NET Framework 2.0.)

✔ **Backward compatibility:** One of Microsoft's major goals was to ensure that you could continue using all the data structures you used in the past. LINQ simply provides a different way to interact with those data structures.

Using LINQ with other languages

Don't get the idea that LINQ is going to remain a solution for C# and Visual Basic .NET developers alone. Using LINQ does require the use of a different compiler, but that won't stop other languages from employing it. You can already find support for LINQ in Microsoft's new F# language and you'll probably find it in use with C++ as well.

LINQ will appear as part of other language packages in the future. There are rumors that Borland Delphi will also have LINQ support at some time (read more at `http://www.eweek.com/c/a/Application-Development/Borland-Plans-to-Support-MS-LINQ-in-Delphi-Platform/`), and you can expect that other languages such as PHP will have it as well. If you want to find out more about languages that will support LINQ, check out Charlie Calvert's Community Blog at `http://blogs.msdn.com/charlie/archive/2006/10/05/Links-to-LINQ.aspx`.

Understanding the LINQ requirements

LINQ is part of .NET Framework 3.5. Consequently, you need Visual Studio 2008 to work with LINQ effectively. This book assumes that you have a copy of Visual Studio 2008 installed on your system. The examples rely on Visual Studio 2008 Professional Edition and you may not get precisely the same results when you use a different edition of the product. Theoretically, you could use LINQ with Visual Studio 2005 (Chapter 5 discusses this technique), but the bulk of this book relies on Visual Studio 2008.

Microsoft has also decided to focus attention on C# as the programming language of choice when using LINQ. C# provides a few extensions and features that make working with LINQ easier. However, you can use Visual Basic .NET quite well with LINQ, too. Although most of the techniques in this book work with any language you want to use, the example code appears in C#. The exception is Chapter 4, which shows how to work with LINQ with Visual Basic .NET. These examples will help you to apply any of the examples to the Visual Basic .NET environment.

The use of C# begs the question of what makes it so special. Chapter 3 describes the .NET Framework extensions that make working with LINQ considerably easier. Some of these language extensions are found only in C# and others are easier to work with in C#. You find a complete description of the features and how to use them in the chapter. For now, all you need to know is that this book will help you use LINQ no matter which language you choose and what platform you have. It's also important to know that the majority of the book is focused on Visual Studio 2008 C# developers because this is the group that Microsoft has chosen as its target group for LINQ.

Using LINQ in the Real World

Realistically, using LINQ is possibly overkill if your goal is to search through a short list of items found in a control. Most developers will use LINQ for something a little more complex than simple lists (then again, nothing stops you from using LINQ even for simple tasks — it's that fast and easy). You know from previous sections of the chapter that LINQ isn't a silver bullet solution. The technology has problems with security and you may not always find the performance stellar, so it's important to weigh the cost of using LINQ against the benefits it provides, which are substantial.

Many developers will likely begin using LINQ in places where they don't currently have a good solution, such as with Web services, or in situations where they already know how to perform a search, such as with SQL Server. The starting goal is to discover how well LINQ works to perform a basic query and then move on to something more complicated. Developers will want to kick the tires for a while and then discover that LINQ really does do powerful things with only a little code.

LINQ query testing is required

LINQ is a new technology. As such, it's tempting to look at the benefits and say that it's the new perfect tool or to look at the deficiencies and proclaim another Microsoft failure. However, after you begin working with LINQ, you begin to understand that LINQ is neither of these viewpoints — it's simply a new tool to put in your arsenal. Many developers will find that LINQ is one very good answer to specific needs, but as with any tool, it has limitations.

The problem now is that because LINQ is a new tool, you don't know anything about its limitations. This book presents a considerable number of examples, and it's a good idea to try them all. However, at some point, you're going to have to test LINQ against the tools you currently use or should use. For example, you should probably test LINQ against your current .NET code and the SQL Server stored procedures that you use. In some cases, LINQ is most definitely a winner, but in other cases, you'll want to stick with existing technologies.

A rule of thumb for LINQ is that it simplifies queries. If your goal is to simplify the task of querying a data source, LINQ is normally going to come out ahead. Because LINQ uses a standardized method to create a query, it's simple to learn, and that can also make it considerably much more reliable than existing technologies. Developers are less likely to make errors when they have a tool that makes writing code easy. The fact that LINQ queries are generally shorter than any code you can write also tends to reduce errors and make code more reliable. However, because you're depending on LINQ to determine how to perform a particular task, LINQ doesn't always provide the required performance, which is why you must test any solution you create against the existing model (when one exists).

The most exciting use of LINQ is to perform data translation. Currently, a query of Amazon's Web service, interpretation, and translation into a form that SQL Server will use can require several hundred lines of code. I know this from experience because I've written such code in the past. It's nice to make two queries with LINQ that require perhaps twenty lines of code to perform the same task. As development environments become more complex and the number of data sources increase, developers will need the special talents of LINQ to perform their data translation for them.

It doesn't take long to realize that LINQ in the real world is all about getting the job done fast, reliably, and with fewer lines of code. In addition, the simplification that LINQ provides makes it possible to use data sources even when you aren't completely familiar with them. For example, a developer who normally works with SQL Server would need training to work with MySQL because the two products have differences. Because LINQ hides the differences between these two products, a SQL Server developer could possibly work with MySQL with little, if any, training. All that the developer would need to do is to ensure that the query is formed correctly — and IntelliSense even helps with that issue. In short, the real world view of LINQ is that it makes developers incredibly productive.

Understanding Declarative Programming

Most Visual Studio developers already understand imperative languages because C# and Visual Basic .NET are imperative languages. An *imperative* language describes how to solve a particular problem. You use an imperative language to write a procedure to answer a specific need. A user clicks a button and the button click event handler provides a procedure to respond.

Imperative languages assume that you know how to solve a problem, and in most cases, you do. However, sometimes you don't know how to solve a problem or the language itself has gaps that make a solution difficult. Obtaining data from a data source is one of those problems. In this case, you need a declarative language such as LINQ. When using a *declarative* language, you state the problem and let the language decide how to solve the problem. Other kinds of declarative languages include the Structured Query Language (SQL) used in SQL Server. In fact, you'll find that LINQ has similarities to SQL, even though the two languages aren't directly compatible.

Declarative languages can be divided into several groups, including logic, functional, and query languages. LINQ is in the query language group. Microsoft's new F# language is in the functional group (see my article at `http://www.devsource.com/cp/bio/John-Paul-Mueller/`). No matter which group a declarative language is in, the basic assumption is the same: A developer provides a problem and the language provides the method for solving that problem. In short, a declarative language defines a relationship between a problem and its solution.

Part of the strength of LINQ is that you can combine it with an imperative language such as C# or Visual Basic .NET to create a stronger whole. Using LINQ lets you rely on the language itself to solve certain problems, such as how to obtain the data you specify from a particular data source.

Despite Microsoft's declarations to the opposite, LINQ, like SQL, isn't a pure declarative language. For example, you can include functions as part of a LINQ query, so the language doesn't necessarily define a pure relationship between a problem and its solution — you can tweak the solution using the function. In addition, the order in which you define the problem affects the solution. These deviations from a pure declarative language are necessary to ensure that you receive the proper outcome of a query. For the purposes of this book, LINQ is a declarative language in the query language group that interacts with the C# or Visual Basic .NET imperative languages.

An Overview of the LINQ Namespaces

Microsoft chose not to provide a single LINQ namespace. The .NET Framework has a number of LINQ namespaces, each of which creates a different kind of data connection. The following sections describe the higher level LINQ namespaces in .NET Framework 3.5. You could find other LINQ libraries on the Internet for use with other connection types. Chapter 12 discusses one such library that you can use for accessing Active Directory.

System.Linq namespace

The `System.Linq` namespace contains all basic classes and interfaces that you use to work with LINQ. Every LINQ to solution relies on this namespace for basic support. As you'll see in later chapters, this is the one namespace that you always include when you want to use LINQ. The samples in Chapter 2 show initial usage of this namespace and you'll also see it in Chapters 3 through 5. Chapter 6 begins the full examination of this namespace as part of working with LINQ to objects. You can find out more about this namespace at `http://msdn2.microsoft.com/en-us/library/system.linq.aspx`.

System.Linq.Expressions namespace

The `System.Linq.Expressions` namespace contains the classes, interfaces, and enumerations used to create expressions. An expression is essentially a tree of nodes that define how a query works. For example, you can create a binary expression that defines how to subtract one number from another. A constant expression can define a constant value, and a named parameter expression can define a value that receives data of a particular type. The essential expression types are

- BinaryExpression
- ConditionalExpression
- ConstantExpression
- InvocationExpression
- LambdaExpression
- ListInitExpression
- MemberExpression
- MemberInitExpression
- MethodCallExpression
- NewArrayExpression
- NewExpression
- ParameterExpression
- TypeBinaryExpression
- UnaryExpression

Chapter 3 begins the discussion of several expression types, but you'll find expressions used throughout this book. You can find out more about this namespace at http://msdn2.microsoft.com/en-us/library/system.linq.expressions.aspx.

System.Data.Linq namespace

The System.Data.Linq namespace contains the classes, structures, interfaces, and enumerations used for SQL database interactions. This is the basic namespace used for LINQ to SQL scenarios. It's important to remember that this is LINQ to SQL and not LINQ to SQL Server. The classes in this namespace help you perform a number of data manipulation tasks, including:

- SELECT data from the database
- UPDATE data found in the database
- DELETE records as needed in the database
- Interact with binary data
- Use and implement referential integrity rules
- Work with a particular table or other database objects (such as indexes)
- Translate the data from one data source to another

You'll find that you use this namespace for a number of LINQ to SQL scenarios. Chapter 8 begins the discussion of working with LINQ to SQL Server. Chapter 11 discusses a number of advanced LINQ to SQL Server topics.

This namespace comes into play also when you work with `DataSet` objects. A `DataSet` needs to work exclusively with an external data source; you can also use it to work with internal data sources, so this is an extremely flexible namespace. Discussions in Chapter 7 show how you can use LINQ to DataSet to work with `DataSet` objects in your application. Look at Chapter 13 if you want to see how this namespace can affect other LINQ to scenarios, such as LINQ to MySQL. You can find out more about this namespace at `http://msdn2.microsoft.com/en-us/library/system.data.linq.aspx`.

System.Data.Linq.Mapping namespace

The `System.Data.Linq.Mapping` namespace contains the classes and enumerations to map data between an imperative language such as C# or Visual Basic .NET and a declarative language such as SQL. It also comes into play when working with technologies such as XML. In short, you'll use this class when working with any external data source that has a different representation from the standard object-oriented view of data found in the .NET Framework. Coverage of this namespace begins in Chapter 7, but you'll find it used throughout the book. You can find out more about this namespace at `http://msdn2.microsoft.com/en-us/library/system.data.linq.mapping.aspx`.

System.Data.SqlClient namespace

The `System.Data.SqlClient` namespace contains the classes used to create a basic connection with SQL Server. Although you might use this namespace in a number of scenarios, you'll generally use it exclusively with SQL Server. The classes in this namespace help you perform the following tasks:

- Interact with SQL Server 2000
- Interact with SQL Server 2005
- Perform string pattern matching
- Perform data manipulation, especially with dates
- Create a basic SQL Server connection

The coverage of this namespace begins in Chapter 8, but you'll also find advanced features described in Chapter 11. You can find out more about this namespace at `http://msdn2.microsoft.com/en-us/library/system.data.linq.sqlclient.aspx`.

System.Data.SqlClient.Implementation namespace

The `System.Data.SqlClient.Implementation` namespace contains the class used to implement the SQL Server client functionality found in the `System.Data.SqlClient` namespace. You generally won't use the classes found in this namespace directly. The coverage of this namespace begins in Chapter 8, but you'll also find advanced features described in Chapter 11. You can find out more about this namespace at `http://msdn2.microsoft.com/en-us/library/system.data.linq.sqlclient.implementation.aspx`.

System.Xml.Linq namespace

The `System.Xml.Linq` namespace contains classes and enumerations used to interact with XML data of all type. When you think about the number of ways in which modern computer systems use XML data, this namespace covers a significant amount of ground. As with SQL Server, you can use the classes of this namespace to interact with XML files in a number of ways. The following list provides an overview of the kinds of interaction you can perform:

- Load XML from files or streams (basic input functionality)
- Serialize XML to files or streams (basic output functionality)
- Create XML trees from scratch using functional construction (data translation)
- Query XML trees using LINQ queries (basic data viewing and manipulation)
- Manipulate in-memory XML trees (advanced data manipulation)
- Validate XML trees using XSD (data verification)
- Combine all of these features to perform advanced data translation tasks and even move data to other data sources

Chapter 9 begins the discussion of this particular namespace. However, you'll also see it in other parts of the book, such as when working with Office 2007 files in Chapter 10. You can find out more about this namespace at `http://msdn2.microsoft.com/en-us/library/system.xml.linq.aspx`.

Chapter 2

Creating Simple LINQ Queries

- -

In This Chapter

▶ Working with the LINQ keywords

▶ Creating a simple query using the `from` keyword

▶ Using the `where` keyword to filter the query

▶ Using the `orderby` keyword to group the query output

▶ Defining and using multiple query sources

▶ Using the standard query operators

▶ Using methods in a query

- -

*L*INQ is amazing in one respect: few keywords are associated with it. In fact, LINQ is quite terse for the tasks it performs. A keyword is a special word that tells LINQ the parameters of the query, such as which data source to use. The focus of this chapter is to acquaint you with the standard keywords, those that you'll use most often to create queries. In fact, the keywords found in this chapter may be all that you have in some LINQ to scenarios. Nothing stops a provider vendor from adding other keywords, but if you know the few found in this chapter, you'll have a considerable head start on using LINQ to perform most basic tasks.

Beside keywords, LINQ also uses an amazing array of operators. An *operator* is a special word that tells LINQ what kind of query to perform, such as checking whether two values are equal. Unlike keywords, operators can run into the hundreds. In most cases, you'll perform the majority of tasks using only a few standard operators. Most other operators provide special functionality that you may never need. This chapter reviews the standard operators available to all LINQ to providers. You'll find other operators discussed in chapters that describe a specific provider.

By combining keywords and operators, you can query, file, and group data from one or more data sources. In some cases, you can also manipulate the data in some way — a topic discussed in later chapters (starting with Chapter 6) because data manipulation is provider specific. This chapter helps you understand how to perform all basic LINQ tasks.

Finally, you can use a special technique called method mapping to influence the way LINQ performs its work. Using this technique is one way that you can nudge LINQ to perform a task in a certain way. This chapter shows some basic ways to use this technique. You'll see more advanced examples as the book progresses.

Defining the LINQ Keywords

The LINQ keywords provide the basis for making a query. In some respects, these keywords work and act like the keywords in SQL. As mentioned, the keywords provide parameters that tell LINQ what to find. At a minimum, you must define a `from` keyword. The `where`, `orderby`, `join`, and `let` keywords provide additional conditions. The following sections describe each of the LINQ keywords.

Working with from

The `from` keyword is the only keyword that you must include as part of a LINQ query. The `from` keyword determines the data source used to `select` information. You add one `from` keyword for each data source you want to include in a query. Here's an example of the `from` keyword in use.

```
var ThisQuery =
    from StringValue
    in QueryString
    select StringValue;
```

The query requires four lines, each of which has a different purpose. The first line is a variable that eventually holds the query. Even a simple query includes an `IEnumerator` object that you can use to select individual query values. Don't worry too much about how this works for now — you'll see a description of the technique that LINQ uses in the "Creating a Simple from Query" section of the chapter. The "Using the var Keyword" section of Chapter 3 describes the `var` keyword in greater detail.

The second line contains the `from` keyword and a variable used to hold the current enumerated value. For example, if you define an array like this one:

```
String[] QueryString =
    { "One", "Two", "Three", "Four", "Five" };
```

`StringValue` will contain, in turn, the values One, Two, Three, Four, and Five. It's important to note that we're using a simple string here. The variable can end up holding any kind of value depending on the kind of query you're making, so it's never safe to assume that the variable has a specific value in it.

The third line has the `in` keyword and defines where to find the data. In this case, you're querying `QueryString`. However, you can use any source that LINQ supports. All you need is a provider to access the data source.

The fourth line has the `select` keyword, followed by a definition of what to select. In this case, the code selects the entire value. However, the selection can include just about anything. For example, you could add a carriage return and linefeed at the end of each value. It's possible to add constants to the values, analyze the values in specific ways, and perform other tasks using the selection. Using operators, you can manipulate the selection in other ways. For now, just work with the idea of interacting with the string. The "Working with the Standard Query Operators" section of the chapter describes a few of the more complicated tasks you can perform.

Working with where

The `where` keyword performs filtering. Most queries will require filtering of some sort because you won't normally want to look at the entire data set. The kind of filtering you perform depends on the data source you're using, but generally, you can work with the `where` keyword variable using the methods that you would when working with a variable of that type alone. For example, when working with a `String`, you can choose to filter the data by length, substring, or comparison as needed.

In some cases, a developer will retrieve the entire data set even when the application won't use it under the assumption that using the entire data set will reduce code complications later. In fact, retrieving the entire data set has many undesirable side effects such as making the application perform poorly and use resources inefficiently, which in turn can affect the application's reliability. Having the entire data set available can also open potential security issues. In short, retrieve only what you need to ensure that the application performs properly.

A `where` keyword can appear anywhere after the `from` keyword and before the `select` keyword. The placement of a `where` keyword can affect how it filters the query. LINQ processes each `where` keyword in turn and uses it to filter the current selection. You'll see how filtering works as the book progresses. For now, look at this simple example of a query with the `where` keyword.

```
var ThisQuery =
    from StringValue
    in QueryString
    where StringValue.Length > 3
    select StringValue;
```

As you can see, this query contains all the elements described in the "Working with from" section of the chapter. The `where` keyword interacts with the `StringValue.Length` property. Any string longer than three characters appears as part of the selection. Consequently, if you use the same array as before to test this query, the values Three, Four, and Five appear in the output, but One and Two don't because they aren't longer than three characters.

Working with orderby

Data will often appear in an order other than the one you need to obtain useful output. The `orderby` keyword changes the order of the data to meet specific needs. As with the `where` keyword, you can use any of the native methods provided by a data type to perform the ordering. You can also use operators and other methods to order the data. The following example shows one way to order a LINQ query:

```
var ThisQuery =
    from StringValue
    in QueryString
    orderby StringValue
    orderby StringValue.Length
    select StringValue;
```

The query uses two `orderby` keywords. The first `orderby` keyword sorts the entries alphabetically, and the second sorts them by length. The effects are cumulative, so order is important. Let's say you begin with an array containing the words *one* through *six*. The output of this query is One, Six, Two, Five, Four, and Six. To see how order is important, you could try this query.

```
var ThisQuery =
    from StringValue
    in QueryString
    orderby StringValue.Length
    orderby StringValue
    select StringValue;
```

In this case, the output is Five, Four, One, Six, Three, and Two. The alphabetical sort ends up overwriting the length sort, even though the two sorts are equal. Of course, this begs the question of whether the sorts really are cumulative. When you try this query

```
var ThisQuery =
    from StringValue
    in QueryString
    orderby StringValue.Length
    select StringValue;
```

the output is One, Two, Six, Four, Five, and Three. This sort order reflects the original order of the data elements grouped by length. Consequently, the two-phase `orderby` shown initially really does change how LINQ orders the data.

You may also wonder whether you can combine the two-phase `orderby` into a single `orderby`. If you were working with two numeric values, LINQ would allow you to combine the two sorts using the `&&` operator. However, because this ordering relies on a `string` and an `int` value, you can't combine them.

Working with join

The `join` keyword performs the same task as join does in SQL. It combines two data sources into a single data source using some criterion. A `join` can have all the variations found in SQL, but the default is an inner join. Don't worry about the specifics of this keyword for now; you discover more in Chapters 7, 8, 11, and 13. For now, it does pay to look at how `join` functions.

Rather than make join difficult to understand, consider the basics of using it with two arrays. Normally, you'll use two `from` queries to work with arrays. For example, the following query shows how to obtain matching values from two arrays no matter where those values appear:

```
var TwoFroms = from QueryA in ArrayA
               from QueryB in ArrayB
               where QueryA == QueryB
               select new { QueryA, QueryB };
```

The output of this query is a new value that contains the matching values from the two arrays. The array elements `QueryA` and `QueryB` both contain the same value because that's the requirement of the `where` clause of the query. If you use the following two arrays

```
Int32[] ArrayA = { 1, 2, 3, 4, 8 };
Int32[] ArrayB = { 1, 3, 5, 7, 8 };
```

the output will contain three array elements. These array elements will contain two integers each and the output values will include 1, 3, and 8. To see how this works in more detail, see the "Creating Queries from Multiple Sources" section of the chapter. The goal right now is to see how a `join` will compare to using two `from` parameters. The following query produces the same output as the first query, but it uses a `join` instead:

```
var Joined = from QueryA in ArrayA
             join QueryB in ArrayB
             on QueryA equals QueryB
             select new { QueryA, QueryB };
```

Notice that the `join` version of the query varies in three important ways. First, you use a `join` instead of the second `from`. Second, you use the word `on` in place of `where` because a `join` creates a single physical element to replace the multiple elements. Third, `equals` replaces the `==` operator. This is your first example of an operator. The amazing thing is that IntelliSense tells you that you need to use `equals` in place of the `==` operator, so you can't make a mistake.

The examples in this section do point out an important feature of LINQ — you can usually perform a task using multiple approaches. The approach you use should reflect your personal coding style, the clearest query, and the best performance. In many cases, this means experimenting with several forms of the query to test it out. Experience will eventually show you which approach to use in a given situation.

Working with let

Sometimes a query will involve a calculation or an analysis that you must perform multiple times to obtain the desired information. Creating a query that performs the calculation multiple times wastes time and resources, so Microsoft has included the `let` keyword to provide a means of storing calculated values. You can even pass these calculated values outside the query to save additional time processing the data later. Here's an example of a query that uses the `let` keyword to create a calculated value:

```
var Squares =
    from QueryA in ArrayA
    from QueryB in ArrayB
    let TheSquare = QueryA * QueryB
    where TheSquare > 4
    select new { QueryA, QueryB, TheSquare };
```

The query creates a calculated value named `TheSquare`. It then uses this value to perform a comparison of the calculated value to a constant to determine which values to include in the output. Finally, `TheSquare` appears as part of the output so that the application doesn't have to compute the value again later. Given two arrays like this:

```
Int32[] ArrayA = { 1, 2, 3, 4 };
Int32[] ArrayB = { 1, 2, 3, 4 };
```

the output for this example will include these output values:

```
2 * 3 = 6
2 * 4 = 8
3 * 2 = 6
3 * 3 = 9
3 * 4 = 12
4 * 2 = 8
4 * 3 = 12
4 * 4 = 16
```

As you can see, the query examines each of the possible square values, determines which ones are greater than 4, and then outputs only those that exceed 4. Using `let` as part of the query doesn't make the output any different — you can achieve the same effect using other means. However, using `let` does tend to improve application performance and make the query itself easier to understand.

Creating a Simple from Query

The best way to start working with LINQ is to access simple data sources and then move on to accessing data sources you normally work with. Don't complicate queries at the outset because the connection you create is important. This section demonstrates how to create a simple connection to an array. In this section, the code creates a very simple array, shows how to build a LINQ query to access it, and then shows how to display the result on screen.

The second half of the discussion shows how this process works using the debugger. You should employ the debugger often when working with LINQ to see how things work. This is a novel experience for many developers who have used SQL because normally you see the result of a query but not necessarily how it works. LINQ makes it possible to trace the inner workings of the query to truly understand what you're doing when you create and execute the query.

Understanding the simple query application code

The example doesn't do a lot, but you can begin using this example as a basis for code of your own. Listing 2-1 shows the code you'll need. You'll also find this example in the \Chapter 02\SimpleFromQuery folder of the source code for this book.

Listing 2-1 Performing a Simple Query

```
private void btnTest_Click(object sender, EventArgs e)
{
    // Create an array as a data source.
    String[] QueryString =
        { "One", "Two", "Three", "Four", "Five" };

    // Define the query.
    var ThisQuery =
        from StringValue in QueryString
        select StringValue + "\r\n";

    // Display the result.
    foreach (var ThisValue in ThisQuery)
        txtResult.Text = txtResult.Text + ThisValue;
}
```

The example begins by creating an array containing some simple text. The query defines the required elements, including a temporary variable for the selection storage, the source of the data, and what to select. Because you'll probably want to display each of the entries on a single line, the code adds the carriage return and linefeed combination, "\r\n".

The code ends by using a simple `foreach` loop to display each of the elements. Notice how you use the `ThisQuery` query as the source of the `foreach` loop.

You must also use `var`, rather than a specific data type, for `ThisValue`. Although the code will compile, in this case, if you use string as the data type it won't compile in many other cases. You'll receive an anonymous type error message if you attempt to use a specific data type in some cases. For example, if this example relied on an array and you tried to declare `ThisValue` as a specific array type, you'd receive an error message such as

```
Cannot convert type 'AnonymousType#1' to 'System.Array'
```

Normally, you'd also need to provide a LINQ namespace to perform LINQ queries in your application. Objects are one exception to the rule because Visual Studio 2008 automatically includes the required reference and associated `using` or `Imports` statement for you. Look at the top of the application and you'll see a line of code like this:

```
using System.Linq;
```

The `using` statement provides only limited LINQ support for objects in your code. If you want to work with external data sources, you must include the required references and `using` or `Imports` statements. The provider-specific sections of this book discuss specific requirements for the discussed provider (such as LINQ to SQL). Figure 2-1 shows the output of this example.

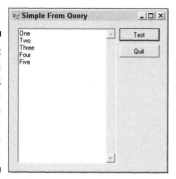

Figure 2-1:
Creating a
from LINQ
query dis-
plays the
entire con-
tent of the
data source.

Using the debugger to see the simple query in action

The debugger is your best friend when it comes to working with LINQ because you can use it to trace exactly what happens during a query. In some cases, you'll want to use the debugger just to see how the query works to improve performance or to make the query easier to understand. Of course, you can also use the debugger to locate query errors. To begin this example, place a break point at the following line of code.

```
var ThisQuery =
    from StringValue in QueryString
    select StringValue + "\r\n";
```

Start the application and click Test. The following steps show what happens next.

1. **Click Step Over.**

   The application creates the `ThisQuery` query.

2. **Select the Locals windows.**

   The query consists of a number of elements, as shown in Figure 2-2. The query itself is `System.Collections.Generic.IEnumerable <string>` type, which tells you that LINQ knows that it's working with a string array despite the fact that you never told it that it was using a string array. The `System.Collections.Generic.IEnumerator <TResult>.Current` and `System.Collections.IEnumerator. Current` properties tell you which values LINQ currently has selected. Now, look at `Results View`. You can use this method to enumerate the query without doing anything else. The output consists of five strings, as shown in Figure 2-2.

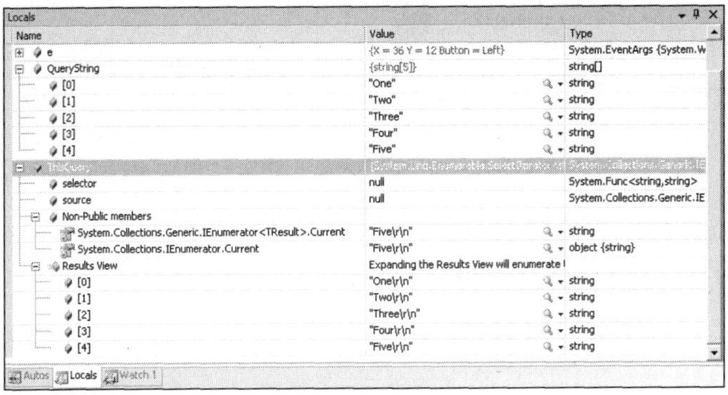

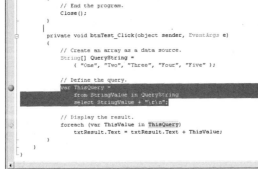

Figure 2-2:
A query
contains a
number of
useful infor-
mational
elements.

3. Click Step Into.

Visual Studio selects `ThisQuery`, as shown in Figure 2-3. If you look at the Locals window you'll see that the `Results View` is now inaccessible because `ThisQuery` is in use. The `selector` property now contains a value of type `System.Func`, which tells you that the return type from each query element is type `System.String`. The source property also contains a value now of type `System.Collections.Generic.IEnumerable<string>`. You can view the individual elements in the resulting array.

Figure 2-3:
The
application
creates a
selector and
source for
the query.

4. Click Step Into twice.

Visual Studio first selects the `in` keyword, followed by the `select` keyword argument, as shown in Figure 2-4. If you look at the Locals window now, you'll see that all the other variables are gone. The only variable you see is `StringValue`. It has a value of "One" and has a data type of `string`. Remember that the code adds the "\r\n" portion of the output separately.

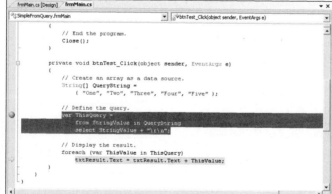

Figure 2-4:
The pro-
cessing loop
chooses
a value
based on
the select
portion of
the query.

5. **Click Step Into three times.**

Visual Studio first selects the in keyword, followed by var ThisValue,
followed by the processing statement for the foreach loop, as shown in
Figure 2-5. This sequence of events takes the output of the select portion of the query and places it in ThisValue. If you look at the Locals
window, you'll see that ThisValue is no longer null but contains the
first output value from the query.

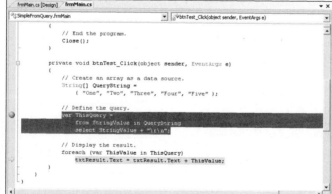

Figure 2-5:
At this point,
the output
variable
contains the
first query
output.

6. **Click Step Into.**

You go back to Step 4 of this procedure. The process keeps repeating
itself until the foreach loop processes every one of the query outputs.
Eventually, you see the output shown in Figure 2-1.

Filtering a Query

After you work with `from` queries for a while, you'll want to begin manipulating the output of those queries. Listing 2-2 shows the next version of the code you worked with in Listing 1-1. In this case, you select only the strings that have a length greater than three characters. Of course, you can experiment with the code to try a number of other filtering criteria. You'll also find this example in the `\Chapter 02\AddedWhereQuery` folder of the source code for this book.

Listing 2-2   Filtering a Query by Length

```
private void btnTest_Click(object sender, EventArgs e)
{
    // Create an array as a data source.
    String[] QueryString =
        { "One", "Two", "Three", "Four", "Five" };

    // Define the query.
    var ThisQuery =
        from StringValue in QueryString
        where StringValue.Length > 3
        select StringValue + "\r\n";

    // Display the result.
    foreach (var ThisValue in ThisQuery)
        txtResult.Text = txtResult.Text + ThisValue;
}
```

It's helpful to go through this example using the same debugger technique found in the "Using the debugger to see the simple query in action" section of the chapter. You'll notice a subtle change in the processing sequence. The code will go to the `where` part of the query first, before it goes to the `select` part of the query as in Step 4. When the `where` part of the query is satisfied, the code then moves onto the `select` part of the query. Otherwise, the code continues to look at one data source element after another until it finds the match that it needs. Figure 2-6 shows the output from this example.

If the code doesn't find a match in the `where` part of the query, you'll see the debugger return to the `in` keyword of the `foreach` statement and then exit the `foreach` statement without doing any more processing. In short, the move to the `in` keyword is where the `foreach` statement determines whether there's anything more to process. To test this for yourself, change the > sign to a < sign in Listing 2-2. You'll see the query test all five values, find them lacking, and then exit the `foreach` statement.

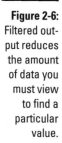

Figure 2-6:
Filtered out-
put reduces
the amount
of data you
must view
to find a
particular
value.

Grouping Queries

Grouping doesn't change the actual data, but it does change the order in which you see it. It's possible to group data in a lot of ways using built-in methods and operators. The example shown in Listing 2-3 builds on the example shown in Listing 2-1. In this case, the example orders the output first alphabetically and then by length. You'll find this example also in the \Chapter 02\AddedOrderByQuery folder of the source code for this book.

Listing 2-3 Grouping a Query Using Multiple Values

```
private void btnTest_Click(object sender, EventArgs e)
{
    // Create an array as a data source.
    String[] QueryString =
        { "One", "Two", "Three", "Four", "Five", "Six" };

    // Define the query.
    var ThisQuery =
        from StringValue
        in QueryString
        orderby StringValue
        orderby StringValue.Length
        select StringValue + "\r\n";

    // Display the result.
    foreach (var ThisValue in ThisQuery)
        txtResult.Text = txtResult.Text + ThisValue;
}
```

Using the debugger to view this query at work is revealing. Use the technique shown in the "Using the debugger to see the simple query in action" section of the chapter to see this query in action. When you get to Step 4, the query goes to the `orderby StringValue` part of the query first. You then click Step Into five times, once for each value in the array. This process is the application ordering the data. The application moves to the `orderby StringValue.Length` part of the query next and performs the same five steps to order the data.

This series of processing steps tells you that you should use as few ordering steps as possible because the code will perform all the ordering up front and for each element in the data source for each level of grouping. Careful selection of ordering criteria and reducing the number of ordering steps can significantly affect application performance.

Only after the ordering is complete does the application move on to the `select` part of the query, where it picks up the first value. Now the question you must be asking is whether the code goes through the entire ordering process for each element. The answer is in your debugger. The next time the debugger works with the query, it goes directly to the `select` part of the query instead of returning to the `orderby` portion of the query. Figure 2-7 shows the output from this example.

Figure 2-7: Grouped output makes it easier to find a particular value.

Creating Queries from Multiple Sources

Most developers aren't going to perform single-source queries, especially when working with databases. You can create queries from any number of sources when working with LINQ. In addition, the sources need not be of the same type. It's possible to perform tasks such as combining Web service data from several Web sources, along with data from your own database, and internal application sources as well. The possibilities are endless. However, it's important to start out simple because multiple source queries can quickly become unmanageable. The following sections discuss simple multiple-source queries.

Understanding the multiple-source application code

In most cases, you'll use the `join` keyword to create a multiple-source query (LINQ also supports a group join you use for special situations). Listing 2-4 shows the code you use for this multiple-source example. You'll find this example also in the `\Chapter 02\SimpleJoin` folder of the source code for this book.

Listing 2-4   A Simple Example of Multiple Sources

```
private void btnTest_Click(object sender, EventArgs e)
{
    // Define two test arrays.
    Int32[] ArrayA = { 1, 2, 3, 4, 8 };
    Int32[] ArrayB = { 1, 3, 5, 7, 8 };

    // Create the query.
    var Joined = from QueryA in ArrayA
                 join QueryB in ArrayB
                 on QueryA equals QueryB
                 select new { QueryA, QueryB };

    // Display the results.
    txtResult.Text = txtResult.Text +
        "\r\nJoin Results:\r\n\r\n";

    foreach (var OutPair in Joined)
        txtResult.Text = txtResult.Text +
            OutPair.QueryA.ToString() + " - " +
            OutPair.QueryB.ToString() + "\r\n";
}
```

This example uses two data sources and combines them to create a specific result. Even though the example looks a lot more complex than anything you've seen in the chapter so far, it really isn't. The same principles are in effect as when you create a simple `from` query. Use the technique shown in the "Using the debugger to see the simple query in action" section of the chapter to see this query in action.

When you begin debugging the example, you'll notice that instead of going directly to the `select` keyword in the query in Step 4, the program goes to the `on` keyword instead. It loads all five elements of QueryB first, and then just one QueryA element. The next step is to go to the `select` part of the query, create an array out of the QueryA and QueryB elements, and return to the `foreach` statement.

The code visits the QueryB portion of the on part of the query only once. However, each loop begins by obtaining another QueryA element. When a QueryA element doesn't match a QueryB element, the code goes to the next QueryA element until it runs out of QueryA elements to process. If there aren't any matching elements, the code goes back to the in part of the foreach statement and immediately exits the loop.

Working with the alternative multiple-source example

As mentioned, you normally have multiple options when queries become more complex. Listing 2-5 shows an alternative to the code in Listing 2-4 that produces the same result. You'll find this example also in the \Chapter 02\ SimpleJoin folder of the source code for this book.

Listing 2-5   An Alternative Multiple-Source Example

```
private void btnAlternative_Click(object sender,
                                  EventArgs e)
{
    // Define two test arrays.
    Int32[] ArrayA = { 1, 2, 3, 4, 8 };
    Int32[] ArrayB = { 1, 3, 5, 7, 8 };

    // Create the query.
    var TwoFroms = from QueryA in ArrayA
                   from QueryB in ArrayB
                   where QueryA == QueryB
                   select new { QueryA, QueryB };

    // Display the results.
    txtResult.Text = txtResult.Text +
        "\r\nTwo From Results:\r\n\r\n";

    foreach (var OutPair in TwoFroms)
        txtResult.Text = txtResult.Text +
            OutPair.QueryA.ToString() + " - " +
            OutPair.QueryB.ToString() + "\r\n";
}
```

Interestingly enough, the debugger will show you that these two queries work differently. Use the technique shown in the "Using the debugger to see the simple query in action" section of the chapter to see this query in action.

In this case, the query begins by going to the second `from` part of the query to work with `ArrayB`. However, it's actually working with both arrays. The code loads the first element from each array and then proceeds to the `where` part of the query, where it tests the equality of the two array elements. When the two array elements are equal, the code proceeds to the `select` part of the query, where it outputs the array.

On the next loop, the code loads the next `ArrayB` element, performs the comparison, and outputs the two values as an array when the `where` condition is true. This loop continues until the code has examined all the `ArrayB` elements. It then loads the next `ArrayA` element and begins again with the first `ArrayB` element.

If you're getting the idea that the two from method uses a considerably greater number of loops to perform the same task as the join method, you're right. Using the two from approach can result in poorer performance in some conditions. However, you'd never know about the extra processing without examining the two techniques using the debugger. Figure 2-8 shows the output from both methods of working with multiple sources.

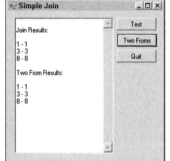

Figure 2-8:
The result is the same, no matter which technique you choose.

Using calculated values in multiple-source queries

As your queries become more complex, they'll likely contain calculated values. It's always more efficient to perform the calculation once. Using the `let` keyword provides one method for handling calculated values. Listing 2-6 shows how to use this technique both as part of a query and within the output of the application. You'll find this example also in the `\Chapter 02\ SimpleLetExample` folder of the source code for this book.

Listing 2-6   Using Let to Create Calculated Values

```
private void btnTest_Click(object sender, EventArgs e)
{
    // Create an array as a data source.
    Int32[] ArrayA = { 1, 2, 3, 4 };
    Int32[] ArrayB = { 1, 2, 3, 4 };

    // Define the query.
    var Squares =
        from QueryA in ArrayA
        from QueryB in ArrayB
        let TheSquare = QueryA * QueryB
        where TheSquare > 4
        select new { QueryA, QueryB, TheSquare };

    // Display the result.
    foreach (var ThisSquare in Squares)
        txtResult.Text = txtResult.Text +
            ThisSquare.QueryA.ToString() + " * " +
            ThisSquare.QueryB.ToString() + " = " +
            ThisSquare.TheSquare.ToString() + "\r\n";
}
```

The question is how the application uses the calculated value. As with the two from query in the "Working with the alternative multiple source example" section of the chapter, the example begins by loading the first ArrayA value into QueryA and the first ArrayB value into QueryB. If you look in the Locals window at this point, all you'll see are the two query values.

After the code loads the two values, you'll see it move to the let part of the query. At this point, you suddenly see TheSquare in the Locals window — the value doesn't exist before you read the let part of the query. This points out the need to place the let keyword in the correct position in the query; otherwise, you may find that the query experiences errors.

At this point, the code moves on to the where part of the query and performs the comparison using TheSquare. When the value of TheSquare is greater then 4, the code moves on to the select part of the query and finally outputs a value.

The next thing that happens is revealing. The value TheSquare doesn't exist outside the query, so you may wonder how it moves to the processing portion of the foreach loop. LINQ obviously creates the three-member array and copies the value to it. You can't see this action in the debugger, but it's the only way to explain how the transfer takes place. Consequently, you must consider the additional resource usage you'll encounter when using a calculated value outside a query. Figure 2-9 shows the output of this application.

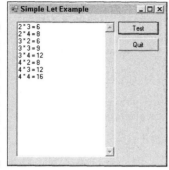

Figure 2-9:
Using calcu-
lated values
can improve
the perfor-
mance of
your appli-
cation.

Working with the Standard
Query Operators

This section isn't designed to tell you about every standard query operator because there are hundreds of them. However, you'll discover how standard query operators make working with LINQ considerably easier. In many ways, you've already worked with some simple query operators. For example, when you use the `orderby` keyword, you're using a query operator in the sorting group of standard query operators. When you use the `where` keyword, you're using another query operator, but this time it's in the filtering group.

Microsoft provides a considerable number of query operators, some of which are complex. For example, the filtering group also supports an `OfType` opera-tor. However, if you want to use this operator, you must create a special method to do so (see the examples at `http://msdn2.microsoft.com/en-us/library/bb360913.aspx` for details). Using the `OfType` operator lets you search for data of a particular custom type, so this is a useful filter-ing criteria but one that requires special programming on your part.

It's also important to consider the language you use to work with the stan-dard query operators. Sometimes one language will support an operator and another won't. For example, Visual Basic .NET supports the `Distinct` opera-tor directory, but you must write special code to perform the same task using C# (see the example at `http://msdn2.microsoft.com/en-us/library/bb546153.aspx` for details). Table 2-1 provides a list of the standard query operator groups and where you can find additional information about them.

Table 2-1	Standard Query Operators	
Group	*Included Operators*	*Additional Information*
Aggregation Operations	Aggregate, Average, Count, LongCount, Max, Min, and Sum	http://msdn2. microsoft.com/ en-us/library/ bb546138.aspx
Concatenation Operations	Concat	http://msdn2. microsoft.com/ en-us/library/ bb546141.aspx
Converting Data Types	AsEnumerable, AsQueryable, Cast, OfType, ToArray, ToDictionary, ToList, and ToLookup	http://msdn2. microsoft.com/ en-us/library/ bb546162.aspx
Element Operations	ElementAt, ElementAtOrDefault, First, FirstOrDefault, Last, LastOrDefault, Single, and SingleOrDefault	http://msdn2. microsoft.com/ en-us/library/ bb546140.aspx
Equality Operations	SequenceEqual	http://msdn2. microsoft.com/ en-us/library/ bb546160.aspx
Filtering Data	OfType and Where	http://msdn2. microsoft.com/ en-us/library/ bb546161.aspx
Generation Operations	DefaultIfEmpty, Empty, Range, and Repeat	http://msdn2. microsoft.com/ en-us/library/ bb546129.aspx
Grouping Data	GroupBy and ToLookup	http://msdn2. microsoft.com/ en-us/library/ bb546139.aspx
Join Operations	Join and GroupJoin	http://msdn2. microsoft.com/ en-us/library/ bb397908.aspx

Group	Included Operators	Additional Information
Partitioning Data	`Skip`, `SkipWhile`, `Take`, and `TakeWhile`	`http://msdn2.` `microsoft.com/` `en-us/library/` `bb546164.aspx`
Projection Operations	`Select` and `SelectMany`	`http://msdn2.` `microsoft.com/` `en-us/library/` `bb546168.aspx`
Quantifier Operations	`All`, `Any`, and `Contains`	`http://msdn2.` `microsoft.com/` `en-us/library/` `bb546128.aspx`
Set Operations	`Distinct`, `Except`, `Intersect`, and `Union`	`http://msdn2.` `microsoft.com/` `en-us/library/` `bb546153.aspx`
Sorting Data	`OrderBy`, `OrderByDescending`, `ThenBy`, `ThenByDescending`, and `Reverse`	`http://msdn2.` `microsoft.com/` `en-us/library/` `bb546145.aspx`

Mapping Keywords to Methods

Although the examples in this chapter are simple, you might already wonder what happens if the functionality that LINQ provides isn't sufficient for a particular requirement. For example, you may find that you want to tweak how the `where` keyword works. It turns out that each of the keywords has a matching method that you can override. In short, you can change the behavior of LINQ to meet specific needs.

The example in this section demonstrates a simple technique for modifying the behavior of the `where` keyword. Listing 2-7 shows the code you need for this example. You'll find this example also in the `\Chapter 02\` `ModifyingWhereBehavior` folder of the source code for this book.

Listing 2-7   Modifying the Behavior of where

```
// The extension method must appear in a public static
// class.
public static class MyWhere
{
    // Define the new version of where.
    // The definition must match precisely.
    public static IEnumerable<TSource> Where<TSource>(
        this IEnumerable<TSource> source,
        Func<TSource, bool> predicate)
    {
        // Obtain the number of elements in the source
        // array.
        int ThisCount = source.Count<TSource>();

        // Create a new array of the correct type.
        TSource[] Results = new TSource[ThisCount];

        // Initialize the array.
        Results.Initialize();

        // Create a counter to track the current results
        // element.
        int ArrayCount = 0;

        // Process the source array.
        foreach (TSource ThisValue in source)
        {
            // When the source array element meets the
            // required value...
            if (ThisValue.ToString().Length > 3)
            {
                // add it to the results array and increment
                // the array counter.
                Results[ArrayCount] = ThisValue;
                ArrayCount++;
            }
        }

        // Return the matching elements.
        return Results;
    }
}
```

The basic example is the same as the one in Listing 2-2. However, this example ignores the where part of the query. Try it out with the debugger and you'll find that the moment the debugger gets to the query, it creates the query and then moves to the extension class shown in Listing 2-7. The application recognizes this custom class as containing a new version of the Where() method.

The custom version isn't elegant, but it does the job. It begins by creating a new array that matches the data type of the `source` data. The code initializes the array and a counter used to track the current `Results` array element.

The `foreach` loop processes the `source` array. Whenever the `source` array contains a value that matches the criteria, it places the value in the `Results` array. When the processing is complete, the code passes the array back to the caller.

This example demonstrates a new aspect of LINQ. The processing of the `source` array occurs before the code calls the `foreach` loop in the main code block. Just in case you wondered how LINQ creates the query, you now have a better idea of what happens. The processing occurs immediately, during the creation of the query. You'll see more examples of how LINQ works internally as the book progresses.

Chapter 3

Considering the .NET Language Extensions

In This Chapter

▶ Understanding the language extensions

▶ Using lambda expressions

▶ Working with the `IEnumerable` and `IEnumerable<T>` interfaces

▶ Considering object initializers

▶ Considering collection initializers

▶ Using extension methods

▶ Using partial methods

▶ Understanding expression trees

▶ Defining query extensions

*L*INQ doesn't appear as part of older versions of Visual Studio. Yes, you can use LINQ in these older versions, but you must use special techniques to do it — not much is automatic (see Chapter 5 for details). Part of the reason that LINQ works the way it does is the addition of language extensions to .NET Framework. The language extensions make it possible for .NET Framework to support LINQ and for you to create queries of various types.

This chapter provides an overview of the major .NET language extensions from the C# developer's perspective. Chapter 4 provides information about the differences between C# and Visual Basic .NET from the Visual Basic .NET developer's perspective. Although the two languages do support the same basic features, you'll find that Visual Basic .NET provides some additional automation that C# doesn't and C# provides flexibility that Visual Basic .NET doesn't. Either language will perform all basic queries and most complex queries without any problem.

The chapter begins with an overview of the extensions in .NET Framework 3.5. The sections that follow provide additional details on each of these extensions. In many cases, you won't use the advanced extensions, but some extensions, such as the var keyword, appear in every query you make. The individual sections tell you which extensions are most common and those that you'll use a little less often. The best idea is to scan this chapter now and then use it as a reference later as you work through the other examples in the book.

An Overview of the Language Extensions

As mentioned in Chapter 1 and demonstrated in Chapter 2, LINQ provides a new way of looking at the problem of searching. Instead of using imperative methods found in older languages, it relies on declarative query methods to perform a task. Because of this difference between native C# and LINQ, Microsoft had to provide language extensions to C# to help the two languages work together. A *language extension* is a new feature that augments basic language functionality. The following list provides an overview of the LINQ-related language extensions found in C#.

✔ **var keyword:** The var keyword is actually a new data type. When you use the var keyword, you tell the compiler to infer the correct data type to use based on the contents on the right side of an equation. As shown in the examples in Chapter 2, a var data type can contain anything from a specific data type to an expression. For example, if you type var Hello = "Hello"; the variable Hello contains a string data type after the compiler performs its task. The var keyword has the following limitations:

   • You can use the var keyword for local variables only and you must initialize the var variable within the same statement.

   • Never initialize a variable of the var type to null.

   • The compiler will display an error message when you try to initialize variables using variables of the var type, such as Num = Num++;.

   • You can initialize only one variable of the var type in a statement.

   • Be careful about creating variables named var. If you have a variable named var within a local scope, you can't create variables of the var type.

Don't associate the var data type with the Variant data type. A Variant data type is loosely typed and late bound; using var simply tells the compiler to assign the correct data type during compile time.

✔ **Anonymous types:** The `var` keyword actually has two purposes. In the first case, you define a variable of the `var` type to hold a value, reference, or expression. The second purpose is within a `foreach` statement when you retrieve data from a data source. In this case, the compiler doesn't know the data type the application will receive, so it assigns an anonymous type to the variable within the `foreach` statement. Chapter 2 describes how this feature works in detail.

✔ **Extension methods:** Extension methods let you add new methods to an existing type without deriving a new type, recompiling the type, or modifying the original type in any way. This technique can save a lot of time when working with your own types, but you'll use it most often with types that you haven't created. LINQ applications use this feature to perform custom handling of expressions, as shown in the "Mapping Keywords to Methods" section of Chapter 2.

✔ **Partial methods:** A partial method is one in which the declaration for the method appears in one partial class, while the implementation of that method appears in another partial class. You can create as many declarations as needed to fill out your class. However, unless the implementation also appears as part of another partial class, the compiler doesn't produce any Intermediate Language (IL) output. In other words, it doesn't cost you anything from an application size or resource usage perspective to create the declaration. The partial method has a lot of different uses, but for LINQ developers, the major use for partial methods is to work with events such as `OnChange()`, `OnCreated()`, or `On[PropertyName]Change()`. You see functional examples of partial methods in Chapters 8 and 9. However, to see a simple example of how this feature works, look at the example in the "Working with Partial Methods" section of this chapter.

✔ **Object initializers:** With the introduction of anonymous data types, C# needed a way to initialize variables without specifying a type. In addition, using object initializers relieves some of the tedium of working with structures in C#. When working with older versions of C#, you had to work with the members of a structure or other data source separately. Using object initializers lets you treat the structure as a single object, without using specialized constructors or any other code. This feature has a number of uses, so you'll see it in use throughout the book. The "Understanding Object Initializers" section of this chapter provides a basic object initializer example to get you started.

✔ **Collection initializers:** A collection initializer performs the same task for collections as object initializers do for objects. The resulting code creates and initializes the collection in a single step. You can use collection initializers with standard data types such as strings or with custom objects. This feature has a number of uses, so you'll see it in use throughout the book. The "Understanding Collection Initializers" section of this chapter provides a basic collection initializer example to get you started.

✔ **IEnumerable and IEnumerable<T> interfaces:** The IEnumerable and IEnumerable<T> interfaces aren't new, but they do have new functionality to work with LINQ. The original intent of the IEnumerable interface is to make it possible to enumerate (itemize) a collection or an array. The IEnumerable<T> interface adds the ability to work with a specific type. LINQ relies on the IEnumerable and IEnumerable<T> interfaces to provide a method for moving through a list of values, references, or objects as part of a query. Chapter 2 shows many simple examples of the IEnumerable interface at work, and you'll see it in just about every other chapter in this book.

IEnumerable normally applies only to generic collections. However, you can use the Cast or OfType operators to use IEnumerable with custom collections and LINQ.

✔ **IQueryable and IQueryable<T> interfaces:** The IQueryable and IQueryable<T> interfaces provide an efficient means to work with large data sources. When working with a default LINQ setup, you see these interfaces only as part of the LINQ to SQL provider described in Chapter 11. In general, you'll interact with these interfaces only during output unless you create a LINQ to provider of your own. See the material at http://msdn2.microsoft.com/en-us/library/bb546158.aspx for more information about building your own provider.

✔ **Lambda expressions:** The lambda expression isn't a new idea. In fact, it's been around since Alonzo Church and Stephen Cole Kleene conceived it in 1936 and appears in languages such as LISP (LISt Processing), Scheme, and Haskell. You use lambda expressions as a means of defining an algorithm. In C#, you use lambda expressions to pass an algorithm to a method to perform tasks based on the algorithm, rather than using static values, lists, objects, or other means.

✔ **Query expressions:** It's important to understand that the SQL-like syntax used for most of the examples in this book requires translation because C# doesn't support this syntax natively as part of the language. A query expression is a SQL-like statement that begins with from and ends with either select or group. Between these two statements, you find the where, orderby, join, let, and additional from clauses. The alternative to using a query expression is the dot notation syntax. Both forms of LINQ query end up as the same IL output, so there's no benefit to using one syntax or the other. Using either query expression or dot notation syntax is entirely up to the developer.

✔ **Expression trees:** An expression tree is an efficiency mechanism in LINQ. It helps an application make efficient use of a data source such as a database. The examples in Chapter 2 show that LINQ normally examines each operator individually. Using this approach with a large data source, such as a database, would prove incredibly inefficient. LINQ commonly uses expression trees in three instances:

- **IQuerable data sources:** Using the `IQueryable` interface, LINQ creates a single expression to perform the entire query at once and place the result in an expression tree. This is the approach used by the LINQ to SQL provider to obtain information without undo performance issues.

- **Special lambda expressions:** A lambda expression of type `Expression<(Of <(TDelegate>)>)` uses expression trees to obtain results faster.

- **Dynamic LINQ queries:** In some cases, you'll want to create a dynamic LINQ query. For example, you need to build dynamic queries when you build your own provider. This book doesn't show how to build a custom LINQ provider, but you can find the information needed to do so at `http://msdn2.microsoft.com/en-us/library/bb546158.aspx`.

Working with Lambda Expressions

There are many uses for lambda expressions for the C# developer, but for the purposes of this book, the main use is as a means of expressing a filter of some type in a concise manner. In previous versions of C#, a developer would create a library function to filter the data. The function would accept a list of values and a delegate to a filtering function as input. When the library function called the delegate, the associated function returned true or false, depending on whether the input value matched the filter criteria. The resulting named or anonymous method code worked, but it was bulky and could be difficult to read. Lambda expressions provide the same sort of functionality, but in a smaller and easier to read package.

IComparable?

C# doesn't use the symbols of the mathematical form of lambda expressions. Instead, it relies on a syntax that works better with the programming language. A basic lambda expression consists of a parameter, followed by the lambda operator `=>` followed by an expression to use to evaluate the parameter. For example, a simple lambda expression is

```
x => x
```

You read this statement as x goes into x. In this case, the lambda expression would simply return itself. However, you can do anything with the lambda expression that you'd normally do as part of a filter. The following statement

```
x => x.Length
```

returns the length of x. A lambda expression can include multiple parameters. In this case, you enclose the parameters within parentheses like this:

```
(x, y, z) => x + y + z
```

This example returns the sum of x + y + z. You can also perform evaluations that result in a Boolean value, such as x = y.

Don't get the idea that lambda expressions necessarily consist of a single evaluation. When working with complex expressions, you enclose the statements within curly braces like this:

```
(x, y) => {if (x > y)
            return (x);
        else
            return (y);}
```

Lambda expressions act as a delegate, so you wouldn't use them as a direct evaluation. You can't set a variable equal to the value of a lambda expression because the lambda expression doesn't work that way. What you need to do, instead, is provide a situation in which you'd normally use a delegate method to perform filtering. Listing 3-1 shows a simple example of how you could use a lambda expression to perform filtering. You'll find this example also in the \Chapter 03\LambdaExpression folder of the source code for this book.

Listing 3-1   Performing Filtering Tasks with Lambda Expressions

```
// Create the delegate used for filtering strings.
public delegate Boolean CheckString(String Str);

// This is a generic function that will accept any
// array of strings and filter it. The output is a
// filtered array of strings.
public static String[] FilterStrings(String[] Input,
                                    CheckString Filter)
{
   // Create an array to hold the output.
   ArrayList ResultList = new ArrayList();

   // Check each of the input array elements.
   foreach (String ThisString in Input)
   {

      // Determine whether the string meets the filtering
      // criteria.
      if (Filter(ThisString))

         // When the string meets the filtering criteria,
         // add the string to the output array.
         ResultList.Add(ThisString);
   }

   // Return the list as output.
```

```
      return (String[])ResultList.ToArray(typeof(String));
}

private void btnTest_Click(object sender, EventArgs e)
{
   // Create a string array.
   String[] TestArray =
      { "One", "Two", "Three", "Four", "Five" };

   // Filter the array.
   String[] OutputArray =
      FilterStrings(TestArray,
         TestStr => TestStr.Length > 3);

   // Display the results.
   foreach (String ThisString in OutputArray)
      txtResult.Text = txtResult.Text +
         ThisString + "\r\n";
}
```

The code begins by creating a delegate that will eventually accept the lambda expression for filtering purposes. In this case, the delegate defined a function that accepts a `String` as input and outputs a `Boolean` value based on some filtering criteria.

The `FilterStrings()` method provides a generic function to filter strings based on the filtering function you provide. There isn't anything special about this function — it's a generic method for performing the check. In fact, this method will accept a named function, an anonymous function, or a lambda expression as input as long as the delegate requirements are met. The `FilterStrings()` method simply checks the output for the filtering function and adds the current value to an output array when the input value matches the filtering requirements. You do need to perform a cast on `ArrayList`, `ResultList` to ensure it matches the expected output type.

The test method, `btnTest_Click()`, creates a simple array of strings. It then calls on `FilterStrings()` to create a filtered output array, `Output Array`. The lambda expression simply determines whether the string is at least three characters long. You can substitute any valid lambda expression here to perform filtering without changing any other part of the code. This is your chance to try out various expressions to see how they work. The `btn Test_Click()` method ends by outputting the result, as shown in Figure 3-1.

Lambda

This chapter provides a good overview of lambda expressions. Check the article at `http://msdn2.microsoft.com/en-us/library/bb397687. aspx` if you want additional details about working with lambda expressions. The remaining chapters of the book also discuss lambda expressions in various situations.

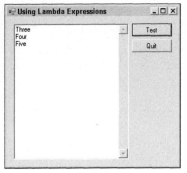

Figure 3-1:
Lambda
expressions
provide a
convenient
way of
expressing
relation-
ships.

Understanding the Role of the IEnumerable and IEnumerable <T> Interfaces

The essential role of the IEnumerable and IEnumerable<T> interfaces is to provide access to a sequence of items in an array or a collection. LINQ uses this functionality to create an iterator for performing queries on collections. For example, if you have a string array and create an enumerator to parse it, you can use a where query to locate specific values. The where query is part of the System.Linq.Enumerable.WhereIterator<T> class. Listing 3-2 shows an example of how you can perform this task. You'll find this example also in the \Chapter 03\IEnumberableExample folder of the source code for this book.

Listing 3-2   Using IEnumerator with LINQ

```
private void btnTest_Click(object sender, EventArgs e)
{
    // Create a string array.
    String[] TestArray =
        { "One", "Two", "Three", "Four", "Five" };

    // Create a query on TestArray.
    IEnumerable<String> Results =
        TestArray.Where(TheValue => TheValue.Length > 3);

    // Display the results.
    foreach (String ThisString in Results)
        txtResult.Text = txtResult.Text +
            ThisString + "\r\n";
}
```

The example begins by creating an array of strings. The next step is to create `Results`, which is actually of the `System.Linq.Enumerable.Where Iterator<T>` type. (You can verify the type by looking at `Results` in the debugger, as shown in Figure 3-2.) Notice how the example uses a lambda expression to create output that includes only the strings with a length greater than three.

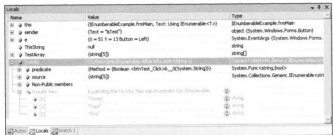

Figure 3-2:
Make sure you under-
stand the
data types
used by the
application.

The final step is to output the result using a `foreach` loop. The results look similar to those shown in Figure 3-1. If you follow this example using the debugger (as described in the "Using the debugger to see the simple query in action" section of Chapter 2), you'll see that it works very much like any other filtered query (see the "Filtering a Query" section of Chapter 2 for details).

You may find that you don't want to allow deferred evaluation of the `Where` query. Because of the deferred evaluation of the lambda expression, the output of this example can vary each time you provide a `foreach` loop. The deferred evaluation has the advantage of providing the latest results of any query but also makes it impossible to obtain consistent output. In this case, you can convert `Results` to an array, instead of an enumeration, by using the following code:

```
String[] Results =
   TestArray.Where(
      TheValue => TheValue.Length > 3).ToArray();
```

It's possible to achieve these results using the `ToArray()`, `ToList()`, `ToDictionary()`, and `ToLookup()` methods. Instead of the `System.Linq.Enumerable.WhereIterator<T>` type shown in Figure 3-2, you see an actual array when viewing `Results`, as shown in Figure 3-3. If you follow this form of the example using the debugger, you'll notice that the application no longer goes back to the `Where` query with each iteration of the `foreach` loop.

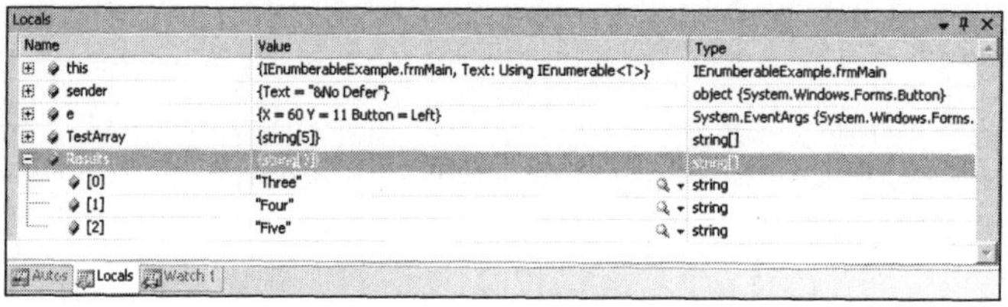

Figure 3-3:
Careful pro-
gramming
avoids
deferred
evaluations.

Understanding automatic properties

This chapter doesn't include every new feature you find in C# because some features don't relate specifically to LINQ. One such feature is automatic properties. An automatic property is helpful when working with LINQ because you can use it to create properties you need within a class using less code. For example, if you normally write code similar to the following example to create a property, you can use an automatic property instead. (You'll find this example also in the \Chapter 03AutomaticProperties folder of the source code for this book.)

```
public class MyName1
{
    string mFirstName;
    string mLastName;

    public string FirstName
    {
        get
        {
            return mFirstName;
        }

        set
        {
            mFirstName = value;
        }
    }

    public string LastName
    {
        get
        {
            return mLastName;
```

```
        }

        set
        {
            mLastName = value;
        }
    }
}
```

You can now write this same property using much less code, as shown here:

```
public class MyName2
{
    public String FirstName
    {
        get;
        set;
    }

    public String LastName
    {
        get;
        set;
    }
}
```

This second form is an automatic property. As you can see, it's considerably shorter and easier to use. However, you can use this new form only when the properties perform standardized tasks. If you want either the get or set method to do something special, you need to write the property code out as you did in previous versions of C#. In addition, automatic properties must always have both get and set accessors.

Understanding Object Initializers

Object initializers make it possible to work with objects without having to instantiate the object first and then work with the members individually. To see how this works, consider the structure shown in Listing 3-3. You'll find this example also in the `\Chapter 03\ObjectInitializer` folder of the source code for this book.

Listing 3-3   Defining the Structure

```
// Define a simple structure.
public struct MyAddress
{
    public String Name;
    public String Company;
    public String Address1;
    public String Address2;
    public String City;
    public String State;
    public String ZIP;
}
```

The data structure looks just like it would in past versions of C#. In fact, you can still work with it as you would have in past versions of C#, as shown in Listing 3-4.

Listing 3-4   Using the Old Method

```
private void btnOldMethod_Click(object sender,
                                EventArgs e)
{
    // Instantiate the object.
    MyAddress ThisAddress = new MyAddress();

    // Initialize the object.
    ThisAddress.Name = "George Samuels";
    ThisAddress.Address1 = "1234 Anywhere";
    ThisAddress.City = "Somewhere";
    ThisAddress.State = "WA";
    ThisAddress.ZIP = "12345-1234";

    // Output the data.
    txtResult.Text =
        ThisAddress.Name + "\r\n" +
        ThisAddress.Address1 + "\r\n" +
        ThisAddress.City + ", " +
        ThisAddress.State + "       " +
        ThisAddress.ZIP;
}
```

Notice that you have to instantiate the object first, and then initialize each object property. This technique requires several lines of code and can prove inconvenient or unusable when you need to work with lambda expressions (described in the "Working with Lambda Expressions" section of the chapter). It can also prove laborious when working with collections, which is a central part of using LINQ to make queries. C# 2008 provides object initializers, which are a different method for working with objects, as shown in Listing 3-5.

Listing 3-5   Creating a Structure Instance

```
private void btnTest_Click(object sender, EventArgs e)
{
   // Create a new structure.
   MyAddress ThisAddress = new MyAddress
   {
      Name = "George Samuels",
      Address1 = "1234 Anywhere",
      City = "Somewhere",
      State = "WA",
      ZIP = "12345-1234"
   };

   // Output the data.
   txtResult.Text =
      ThisAddress.Name + "\r\n" +
      ThisAddress.Address1 + "\r\n" +
      ThisAddress.City + ", " +
      ThisAddress.State + "      " +
      ThisAddress.ZIP;
}
```

In this case, the object is instantiated and initialized using a single statement. You've combined the multiple lines of code used in the past to create a new object into a single, easy-to-read, line of code. The results are the same, but you save time and effort by using the single line of code shown. It's important to remember to separate the individual object properties with commas; otherwise the code won't compile.

Understanding Collection Initializers

Collection initializers help you produce efficient code that relies on a single step to instantiate and initialize a collection. The concept is the same as working with an object initializer, except that you interact with a collection, as shown in Listing 3-6. You'll find this example also in the \Chapter 03\ ObjectInitializer folder of the source code for this book.

Listing 3-6   Initializing a Simple Collection

```
private void btnSimpleCollection_Click(object sender,
                                            EventArgs e)
{
    // Create and initialize the list.
    List<String> Names = new List<string>
    {
        "George",
        "Amy",
        "Zach",
        "Chris",
        "Renee"
    };

    // Display it on the screen.
    foreach (String ThisName in Names)
        txtResult.Text = txtResult.Text + ThisName + "\r\n";
}
```

In this case, the `List` contains `String` values. As with an object initializer, you separate individual elements using a comma. The `foreach` loop displays each of the names on the screen.

You can extend the principles in this section to apply to both object initializers and collection initializers, as shown in Listing 3-7. This code relies on the structure shown in Listing 3-3 as a starting point. What this example does is combine the object initializer shown in Listing 3-5 with a collection initializer.

Listing 3-7   Creating a Custom Object Collection

```
private void btnObjectCollection_Click(object sender,
                                            EventArgs e)
{
    // Create a collection of addresses.
    List<MyAddress> AddressCollection = new List<MyAddress>
    {
        new MyAddress
        {
            Name = "Sam Rugged",
            Address1 = "1234 Somewhere",
            Address2 = "Suite 3",
            City = "Anywhere",
            State = "WA",
            ZIP = "12345"
        },
        new MyAddress
        {
            Name = "Mary Wurth",
```

(continued)

Listing 3-7 *(continued)*

```
            Company = "Faxes Our Us",
            Address1 = "1414 21st Street",
            City = "Nowhere",
            State = "MI",
            ZIP = "99999"
        }
    };

    // Output the data.
    foreach (MyAddress ThisAddress in AddressCollection)
        txtResult.Text = txtResult.Text +
            ThisAddress.Name + "\r\n" +
            ThisAddress.Company + "\r\n" +
            ThisAddress.Address1 + "\r\n" +
            ThisAddress.Address2 + "\r\n" +
            ThisAddress.City + ", " +
            ThisAddress.State + "        " +
            ThisAddress.ZIP + "\r\n\r\n";
}
```

Interestingly enough, you're only looking at two lines of code here. The first line creates a list of `MyAddress` objects and places them in `Address Collection`. Notice that you pass the custom class name, rather than a generic class name. Each list entry is actually an object initializer. You don't have to initialize every property for every object. These structures may sound complex, but they look simple when you view them in the debugger, as shown in Figure 3-4. Notice that you also receive a complete set of collection statistics (which include the `Capacity` property that shows the size of the collection). It's often helpful to view the resulting structures to better understand how C# works with them.

The output `foreach` loop displays all available information for each of the objects in the `List`. When an entry is `null`, it appears as a blank in the output.

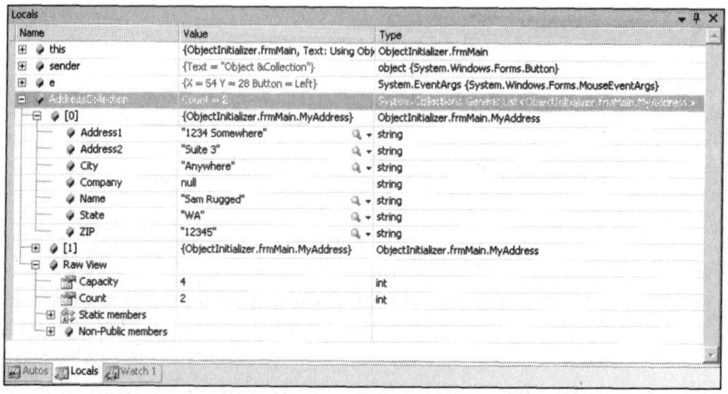

Figure 3-4: Collections that include objects need not appear complex in memory.

Working with Extension Methods

Extension methods are an important new feature for LINQ developers because this feature helps you map keywords to methods when you want to override the default expression handling functionality. The "Mapping Keywords to Methods" section of Chapter 2 shows a simple example of this technique.

It's important to remember that the relationship between extension methods and LINQ need not always be one where LINQ depends on extension methods for support. You can also use LINQ to extend common types. For example, you may want to count the special characters in a string. Using standard C# code, you'd need to write a loop and a rather large `switch` statement. When working with LINQ, you can create a small extension such as the one shown in Listing 3-8. You'll find this example also in the `\Chapter 03\ ExtensionMethods` folder of the source code for this book.

Listing 3-8   Creating an Extension Method with LINQ

```
public static class MyStrings
{
    public static int SpecialCharCount(this String Str)
    {
        // Define a LINQ Query for special characters.
        var CharQuery = from ThisCount
                        in Str
                        where ThisCount == '!'
                            || ThisCount == '@'
                            || ThisCount == ';'
                            || ThisCount == ','
                            || ThisCount == ':'
                            || ThisCount == '?'
                            || ThisCount == '+'
                            || ThisCount == ' '
                        select ThisCount;

        // Return the number of special characters.
        return CharQuery.Count<Char>();
    }
}
```

In this case, two lines of code are all you need to perform the task. The first line is a LINQ query that tells the compiler to review the input string one character at a time. Whenever the character matches any of the `where` criteria, the query should select that character and place it in the output enumeration, `CharQuery`. Notice that this is the first time the query contains multiple `where` cases and that the query relies on the `||` (or) operator. You can add as many entries as needed to capture all the special characters — spending a lot of time writing `switch` statements and special looping code.

The second line is equally simple. The code relies on the Count<of T> method to count the number of Char type entries in CharQuery. The result is the number of special characters. You can use the code shown in Listing 3-9 to test this extension.

Listing 3-9   Testing the LINQ-based Extension

```
private void btnTest_Click(object sender, EventArgs e)
{
   // Define a string with special characters.
   String MyString = "abcd;@abc,abc:abc?abc+ hello!";

   // Obtain the number of special characters.
   int CharCount = MyString.SpecialCharCount();

   // Display the result.
   txtResult.Text =
      "The number of special characters is: " +
      CharCount.ToString();
}
```

The code begins by creating a nonsense string with special characters. Because this is an extension method, you can access the SpecialCharCount() method as if it were part of the String type. The output of the call is an int value that tells you how many special characters the string contains. The final step outputs this value to txtResult.Text.

It pays to think about the order in which you add filters to a query. As shown in Listing 3-8, you can end up with a significant list of checks for a given query. By placing the characters (or other checks) that you expect to succeed most often at the top of the list, you reduce the number of comparisons that LINQ performs and improve application performance.

Working with Partial Methods

Partial methods are helpful when you want to define a complete class description, without necessarily implementing the class completely unless you really need to do so. You use partial methods differently than inheritance or virtual methods. The point of a partial method is to create a description of a particular method without generating the code for it unless necessary. An application can even call the partial method, but nothing will happen unless the code also includes an implementation. To see how this works, start with a partial class, as shown in Listing 3-10. You'll find this example also in the \Chapter 03\PartialMethods folder of the source code for this book.

Listing 3-10   Defining a Partial Method

```
public partial class PMethodTest
{
   // Create the method declarations.
   partial void DisplayMe(String Msg);
   partial void NoDisplayMe(String Msg);

   public PMethodTest(String Msg)
   {
      // Show that we're in the constructor.
      MessageBox.Show("Entering the Constructor.");

      // Perform the required tasks.
      DisplayMe(Msg);
      NoDisplayMe(Msg);

      // Show that we're exiting the constructor.
      MessageBox.Show("Leaving the Constructor.");
   }
}
```

This definition appears in `PMethodTest.CS`. Note that the constructor requires a string as input. You could use other methods or even define a default constructor that doesn't require any inputs, but for now accept the need of the constructor to accept a string as input. The constructor calls both `DisplayMe()` and `NoDisplayMe()`, both of which require a string as input. The method declarations don't include any implementation — just a declaration. At this point, compiling the code would create an IL file that doesn't have either method in it.

The example includes two message boxes that show when the application enters and leaves the constructor. These message boxes simply help you see how the example works when you run it. Depending on the implementation class, you should see an entering message, one or two display activities, and an exiting message. It's also interesting to follow this example in the debugger so you can see how the various pieces interact.

The other part of the `public partial class PMethodTest` class appears in the `frmMain.CS` file. This is the same file that contains the user interface code for the example. The code could just as easily appear in another file. However, the implementation code must appear in a different file from the declaration code. This requirement points out one of the nice features of partial methods — one group can maintain the class declaration while another maintains its implementation. The same structure could have multiple implementations, making it considerably more flexible than not using partial methods. Listing 3-11 shows the `PMethodTest` class implementation.

Listing 3-11 Implementing the PMethodTest Class

```
public partial class PMethodTest
{
   // Define an implementation for DisplayMe.
   partial void DisplayMe(String Msg)
   {
      // Display the message sent from frmMain.
      MessageBox.Show(Msg, "Display Me");
   }
}
```

Notice that this class defines the `DisplayMe()` method. When the compiler generates code, it creates code only for `DisplayMe()`, not `NoDisplayMe()`, even though the `PMethodTest()` constructor calls both of them. In this case, the code simply displays a message box showing the message.

Now it's time to show how you can use this combination of declaration and implementation to display a message. Listing 3-12 shows the user interface code for this example.

Listing 3-12 Displaying the PMethodTest Output

```
private void btnTest_Click(object sender, EventArgs e)
{
   // Define a string to display.
   String MyString = txtResult.Text;

   // Display the message.
   PMethodTest Test = new PMethodTest(MyString);
}
```

Note that there's no mention of the capabilities that `PMethodTest` provides — you simply call the constructor with the string you want to display. Given the implementation shown in Listing 3-11, you see the entering constructor message, followed by the custom message you provide in the text box, and ending with the exiting constructor message. The `NoDisplay Me()` call never shows up because the example lacks an implementation for it.

An Overview of Expression Trees

Expression trees answer a specific need — they provide an efficient means for working with large data sources such as a database. When you create a lambda expression, the compiler can create either IL code or an expression tree. In most cases, the compiler will create IL code because the provider you work with must provide the support required to create an expression tree. Consequently, unless you're using the LINQ to SQL provider in a generic LINQ setup, the compiler will likely create IL code from your lambda expression.

The prototype for a query determines whether the compiler creates an expression tree or IL code. For example, when working with a LINQ to SQL provider, the query will use the IQueryable<T> interface and rely on an expression of the System.Linq.Expressions.Expression class.

An expression tree is a compiled form of the query. It actually appears in a tree form. You can create a simple expression tree and view the various pieces that it contains. Listing 3-13 shows an example of how you might work with an expression tree. You'll find this example also in the \Chapter 03\ ExpressionTree folder of the source code for this book.

Listing 3-13   Creating an Expression Tree

```csharp
private void btnTest_Click(object sender, EventArgs e)
{
    // Create the expression tree.
    Expression<Func<String, bool>> MyLambdaExpression =
        MyString => MyString.Length > 3;

    // Obtain the expression tree elements.
    // Contains the list of parameters.
    ParameterExpression Parameters =
     (ParameterExpression)MyLambdaExpression.Parameters[0];
    // Contains the evaluation.
    BinaryExpression TheEvaluation =
        (BinaryExpression)MyLambdaExpression.Body;
    // Contains the left side of the evaluation.
    MemberExpression LeftSide =
        (MemberExpression)TheEvaluation.Left;
    // Contains the right side of the evaluation.
    ConstantExpression RightSide =
        (ConstantExpression)TheEvaluation.Right;

    // Output the elements of the expression tree.
    txtResult.Text = "The tree contains:\r\nParameters: " +
        Parameters.ToString() + "\r\nEvaluation: " +
        TheEvaluation.ToString() + "\r\nLeft Side: " +
        LeftSide.ToString() + "\r\nRight Side: " +
        RightSide.ToString();
}
```

The example begins by creating what looks like a complex piece of code, but it's not once you know how the code is put together. The Expression<T> class accepts a delegate prototype as input. You define the delegate using the Func<T, TResult> generic delegate. In this case, the generic delegate accepts a String as input and outputs a bool. However, you can provide any input or output types needed by your application.

The definition of the expression comes next. `MyLambdaExpression` contains a lambda expression that outputs a Boolean value that determines when a string is longer than three characters. At this point, `MyLambda Expression` actually contains a tree structure that includes all the elements required for the lambda expression `MyString => MyString.Length > 3`.

The next section of code takes the expression tree apart. It begins with the parameter, `MyString`. Next comes the expression, `MyString.Length > 3`. This expression contains a left side, `MyString.Length`, and a right side, `3`. All four of these elements have specific types:

- `ParameterExpression`: Contains `MyString`
- `BinaryExpression`: Contains `MyString => MyString.Length > 3`
- `MemberExpression`: Contains `MyString.Length`
- `ConstantExpression`: Contains `3`

Figure 3-5 shows the output from this program. If this expression tree contained additional elements, you could continue to move down the tree until you had looked at every element. The point is that the output from this example will show you a complete expression tree. You can also view all of this information using the debugger.

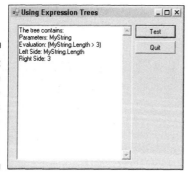

Figure 3-5:
Expression trees save your queries in a tree-formatted object.

You don't normally need to know whether a data source uses expression trees because it's the responsibility of the data provider vendor to determine whether the data provider uses expression trees. Because expression trees don't have much of an affect on your daily LINQ usage, they don't appear anywhere else in this book.

Working with Query Expressions

You have already seen a lot of query expressions in this book and you'll use a lot more as the book progresses. A query expression is the LINQ query you have used in the first three chapters of this book to obtain information from arrays and collections. A query expression has the following characteristics:

- Begins with the `from` keyword

- Contains zero or more instances of the `where`, `let`, or `from` keywords

- Remainder includes zero or more instances of the `orderby` keyword (which can include a direction of `ascending` or `descending`)

- Ends with the `select` or `group` keyword

- Optionally continues with zero or more instances of the `into` keyword, zero or more `join` keywords, or a sequence of numbered elements

C# also provides access to a dot notation syntax. The basic elements of this syntax are the same. The only difference is convenience to the developer. Listing 3-14 shows the same query as Listing 3-13 using a query expression and dot notation syntax. You'll find this example also in the `\Chapter 03\ QueryExpression` folder of the source code for this book.

Listing 3-14   Comparing Query Expressions to Dot Notation Syntax

```
private void btnTest_Click(object sender, EventArgs e)
{
    // Create an array as a data source.
    String[] QueryString =
        { "One", "Two", "Three", "Four", "Five" };

    // Define the query.
    var ThisQuery =
        from StringValue in QueryString
        where StringValue.Length > 3
        select StringValue + "\r\n";

    // Display the result.
    foreach (var ThisValue in ThisQuery)
        txtResult.Text = txtResult.Text + ThisValue;
}

private void btnDotNotation_Click(object sender, EventArgs
        e)
{
    // Create an array as a data source.
```

(continued)

Listing 3-7 *(continued)*

```
String[] QueryString =
    { "One", "Two", "Three", "Four", "Five" };

// Define the query.
var ThisQuery = QueryString
    .Where(StringValue => StringValue.Length > 3)
    .Select(StringValue => StringValue + "\r\n");

// Display the result.
foreach (var ThisValue in ThisQuery)
    txtResult.Text = txtResult.Text + ThisValue;
}
```

Both queries use `var` to define the query variable. Instead of providing the `from` and `in` keywords, the dot notation syntax simply includes the source name. Notice that both versions use `where`, but the dot notation syntax uses the `.Where` form. The same holds true for `select` and `.Select`. Finally, the dot notation syntax requires that you provide the evaluation criteria in the form of a lambda expression. The choice is a matter of personal taste.

Chapter 4

Working with LINQ in Visual Basic .NET

In This Chapter

▶ Considering how Visual Basic .NET applications differ

▶ Designing your first Visual Basic .NET LINQ application

▶ Creating applications with the additional Visual Basic keywords

▶ Using lambda functions

*Y*ou may get the idea in some circles that Visual Basic .NET (simply called Visual Basic for the rest of the book) is a second-class citizen when it comes to LINQ. However, nothing can be further from the truth. It's true that Microsoft and many third-party Web sites tend to emphasize the flexibility provided by C#, but you can create some great LINQ applications using Visual Basic as well. In fact, that's the reason for this chapter — to demonstrate to everyone that Visual Basic is a good LINQ language, too.

There are differences between Visual Basic and C# when it comes to using LINQ. In some respects, Visual Basic is less flexible than C# when it comes to using LINQ, but you'll also find that Visual Basic provides some additional automation you don't find in C#. Consequently, using LINQ in Visual Basic can prove less difficult than working with C#, so there are advantages.

This chapter also shows how Visual Basic handles LINQ in various environments and with different providers. Using the information in this chapter, you can make better use of the examples found throughout the book (which are mostly in C# to reflect general usage trends by the developer community). You'll find that most of the examples in the book translate with relative ease to use with Visual Basic.

LINQ on the cheap

If you simply want to experiment with LINQ, you don't have to go out and purchase an expensive copy of Visual Studio 2008 to do it. LINQ works just fine with your copy of Visual Studio 2005 (see Chapter 5). However, you may not want to deal with the limitations of using Visual Studio 2005 for LINQ. In this case, you have another alternative, using the Visual Studio 2008 Express Editions.

Microsoft provides access to both Visual Studio 2005 and Visual Studio 2008 as free downloadable Express Editions. You can find the main

Express Edition Web site at `http://www.microsoft.com/express/`. The download area is at `http://www.microsoft.com/express/download/default.aspx`. The downloads include Visual Basic 2008 Express Edition and Visual C# 2008 Express Edition as well as SQL Server 2005 Express Edition. This Web site contains downloads also for Visual Web Developer 2008 Express Edition and Visual C++ 2008 Express Edition. In short, you can download any or all of these products and end up with a useful LINQ test platform free of charge.

Understanding the Visual Basic Differences

Visual Basic supports all of the basic operations described in Chapter 2. However, it has some interesting differences. For example, you won't use the `var` keyword in Visual Basic; Microsoft has expanded use of the `Dim` keyword instead. All the other differences between C# and Visual Basic also apply. A Visual Basic LINQ query will have the same appearance as any other Visual Basic code you create. The "Creating the Simple Visual Basic Example" section of this chapter helps you discover how these operations work in Visual Basic. You can easily compare them with the same operations for C# in Chapter 2.

You may notice that the Microsoft documentation appears to use *keyword* and *operator* interchangeably. The two terms mean essentially the same thing when working with LINQ. A query expression consists of one or more *keywords* that define how the query works. These keywords are a kind of operator. The term *operator* expands to mean all kinds of special symbols, functions, and other LINQ features that modify a query. You also use the term operator with lambda expressions.

Like C#, Visual Basic includes a number of new features for supporting LINQ. The number of features isn't as extensive or as flexible as those in C#, but often you'll find that Visual Basic supports automation that C# doesn't provide. Visual Basic supports the following C# features explained and demonstrated in Chapter 3:

- ✔ Anonymous types

- ✔ Extension methods

- ✔ Partial methods

- ✔ Object initializers

- ✔ `IEnumerable` and `IEnumerable<T>` interfaces

- ✔ `IQueryable` and `IQueryable<T>` interfaces

- ✔ Lambda expressions

- ✔ Query expressions

- ✔ Expression trees

Microsoft doesn't provide the full list of C# features in Visual Basic. My research found that Visual Basic doesn't support the following C# features:

- ✔ Collection initializers

- ✔ Automatic properties

Many of the LINQ features in Visual Basic don't work the same as their counterparts in C#. Consequently, sometimes you can't directly port code from C# to Visual Basic (or vice versa). For example, the Visual Basic debugger doesn't show that Visual Basic defaults to using the deferred evaluation described in the "Understanding the Role of the IEnumerable and IEnumerable<T> Interfaces" section of Chapter 3. The "Working with From" section of this chapter describes this issue in greater detail. The remaining examples in the chapter discuss other differences that you should know about when working with Visual Basic.

All Visual Basic queries rely on query expressions. You can't create a query in Visual Basic that relies on the dot notation syntax described in the "Working with Query Expressions" section of Chapter 3. Because Visual Basic lacks this feature, this book will use the query expression format whenever possible.

It's interesting to note that Visual Basic provides a number of additional keywords (operators) not found in C#. There are the expected keywords such as `Or` and `And`, which are replaced with the `||` and `&&` operators in C#. However, Visual Basic also sports the following keywords that you don't automatically find when working with C#:

- ✔ `Aggregate`
- ✔ `Distinct`
- ✔ `Skip`
- ✔ `Take`

These special keywords add functionality that you'd have to program into C#, so Visual Basic provides a plus in this area. Unfortunately, you don't see a comparison of C# and Visual Basic anywhere that tells you these extra keywords exist, so you could easily miss them. I found these keywords during my research. The "Using the Additional Visual Basic Keywords" section of this chapter tells you how to use these special keywords to make your application better.

Creating the Simple Visual Basic Example

Chapter 2 contains a number of simple C# examples that you use to discover how C# works with LINQ. This section performs the same task for Visual Basic developers. The examples are precisely the same (or as close as possible), but some of the results aren't. The purpose of the following sections is twofold. First, you discover how to create basic queries in Visual Basic. Second, you see how these queries execute differently from their C# counterparts as a way to understand the Visual Basic differences. You'll find this example in the \Chapter 04\SimpleQueries folder of the source code for this book.

Working with From

The basic From query can tell you a lot about how Visual Basic works and show how it differs from C#. This example shows an extended form of the query shown in Listing 2-1. In this case, the From query not only demonstrates how Visual Basic performs the basic query but also examines how the query differs in the debugger. Interestingly enough, this section also shows that the results are the same, no matter which language you use.

Understanding the code

As with C#, the basic From query in Listing 4-1 selects all the values from the QueryString array and displays them on the screen. Normally, you wouldn't take this approach because this simple query doesn't search for anything — it displays the current contents of the array and you could just as easily work with the array directly. However, the example is useful for seeing how a basic LINQ query works.

Listing 4-1   Creating an Extended From Example

```vb
Private Sub btnFrom_Click(ByVal sender As System.Object, _
                          ByVal e As System.EventArgs) _
                          Handles btnFrom.Click

   ' Create an array as a data source.
   Dim QueryString As String() = _
      New String() {"One", "Two", "Three", "Four", "Five"}

   ' Define the query.
   Dim ThisQuery = _
      From StringValue In QueryString _
      Select StringValue + vbCrLf

   ' Display the result.
   For Each ThisValue In ThisQuery
      txtResult.Text = txtResult.Text + ThisValue
   Next

   ' Visual Basic does support deferred evaluation, but
   ' the debugger doesn't display it. To see this
   ' difference, the code changes the array and then
   ' performs the For Each loop again.
   QueryString(0) = vbCrLf + "Second Result"

   ' Display the second result.
   For Each ThisValue In ThisQuery
      txtResult.Text = txtResult.Text + ThisValue
   Next

End Sub
```

The example begins by creating the QueryString array and initializing its values. It then creates a query, ThisQuery. Except for the use of Dim in place of var, this query looks very much like its C# counterpart. The example then uses a For Each loop to display the contents of ThisQuery on the screen.

To demonstrate that Visual Basic uses deferred evaluation just like C#, the example makes a change to QueryString and then displays the result again using another For Each loop. Figure 4-1 shows the result of this test. If Visual Basic didn't support deferred evaluation, the results would be the same in both cases, but you can see the change made to the QueryString array.

Using the debugger to see the code execute

Unlike C#, you won't see a lot of how a query works when using the Visual Basic debugger. In fact, the results you receive often don't match what the debugger shows you. This lack of information is unfortunate because the debugger really should show you what takes place in the background. To begin this example, place a break point at the following line of code:

```
Dim ThisQuery = _
    From StringValue In QueryString _
    Select StringValue + vbCrLf
```

Figure 4-1:
Visual Basic
supports
deferred
evaluation.

Start the application and click From Query. The following steps show what happens next:

1. **Click Step Over.**

   The application creates the `ThisQuery` query and moves to the `For Each` statement.

2. **Select the Locals window.**

   You see the Locals window shown in Figure 4-2. Compare this Locals window with the same window for C# in Figure 2-2. As you can see, Visual Basic displays significantly less information about `ThisQuery`. The only information you receive is shown under the `Results` property. Just why Microsoft chose to show less information is unclear, but it does make debugging Visual Basic LINQ applications significantly more difficult.

3. **Click Step Into.**

   The debugger moves directly to the display code for the `For Each` code without showing you the inner workings of the query, as shown in Figure 4-3. Consequently, without additional testing, you won't know whether Visual Basic uses deferred evaluation.

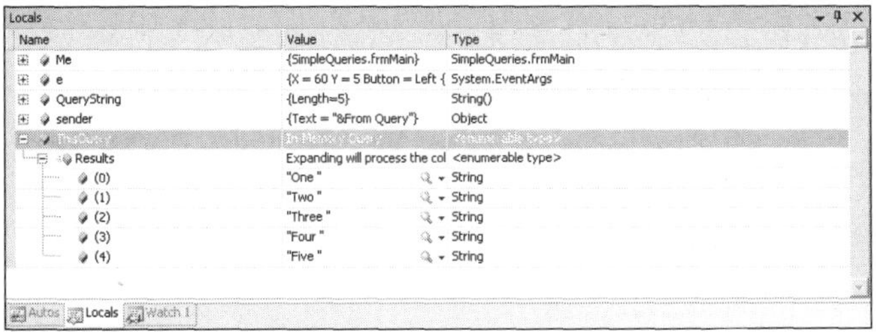

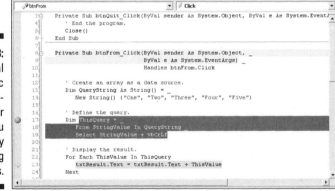

Figure 4-2:
The
debugger
indicates
that execu-
tion differs
in Visual
Basic.

4. **Click Step Into.**

   The debugger highlights the `Next` statement.

5. **Click Step Into.**

   The debugger moves back to the display code and begins the processing loop again.

Figure 4-3:
The Visual
Basic
debug-
ger never
shows you
the query
processing
steps.

Working with Where

Visual Basic makes it extremely easy to work with LINQ queries. It shows you all acceptable keywords when you press Space, as shown in Figure 4-4. As mentioned, Visual Basic also supports a number of special keywords, which are discussed in the "Using the Additional Visual Basic Keywords" section of this chapter.

Figure 4-4:
Selecting
the keyword
you need
is easy
in Visual
Basic.

The `Where` keyword provides filtering functionality in Visual Basic, just as it does in C#. Listing 4-2 shows a modified version of the basic `From` query in Listing 4-1.

Listing 4-2   Filtering a Query by Length

```vb
Private Sub btnWhere_Click( _
    ByVal sender As System.Object, _
    ByVal e As System.EventArgs) _
    Handles btnWhere.Click

  ' Create an array as a data source.
  Dim QueryString As String() = _
      New String() {"One", "Two", "Three", "Four", "Five"}

  ' Define the query.
  Dim ThisQuery = _
      From StringValue In QueryString _
      Where StringValue.Length > 3 _
      Select StringValue + vbCrLf

  ' Display the result.
  For Each ThisValue In ThisQuery
      txtResult.Text = txtResult.Text + ThisValue
  Next

End Sub
```

In this case, the `Where` keyword restricts the output to words that are longer than three characters, so the output is the same as the C# example in Chapter 2. You'll see Three, Four, and Five as output values, just as you do in Figure 2-6.

However, the difference between Visual Basic and C# is that you use a keyword to link multiple `Where` conditions. The problem is to determine which keyword to use because you have three from which to choose: `Or`, `And`, and `AndAlso`. The `Or` keyword simply means to select an output when one or the other condition is true. The difference between `And` and `AndAlso` is more subtle. The `AndAlso` keyword provides short-circuit evaluation, which means that your code could execute faster, but you can use it only when you don't want to evaluate the second expression when the first expression is false. Tables 4-1 and 4-2 show the logic behind the `And` and `AndAlso` keywords.

Table 4-1	**And Logic Table**	
First Value	*Second Value*	*Output*
True	True	True
True	False	False
False	True	False
False	False	False

Table 4-2	**AndAlso Logic Table**	
First Value	*Second Value*	*Output*
True	True	True
True	False	False
False	Not Evaluated	False

The moment that `AndAlso` sees a `False` value, it stops evaluating the statement. In many cases, you want precisely this action because using `AndAlso` can improve application performance. However, if the second statement is a function that you need to execute whether or not it's true, your application could suddenly fail for no apparent reason. Consequently, you must use `AndAlso` carefully. Listing 4-3 shows how you can use `And` or `AndAlso` to link multiple filtering statements together. To make this version functional, remove the comments from "Define the query (version 2)." in the source code.

Listing 4-3   Filtering a Query by Length and First Letter

```
Private Sub btnWhere_Click( _
    ByVal sender As System.Object, _
    ByVal e As System.EventArgs) _
    Handles btnWhere.Click

    ' Create an array as a data source.
    Dim QueryString As String() = _
        New String() {"One", "Two", "Three", "Four", "Five"}

    ' Define the query.
    Dim ThisQuery = _
        From StringValue In QueryString _
        Where StringValue.Length > 3 _
        AndAlso StringValue.StartsWith("F") _
        Select StringValue + vbCrLf

    ' Display the result.
    For Each ThisValue In ThisQuery
        txtResult.Text = txtResult.Text + ThisValue
    Next

End Sub
```

The example filters by both length and the initial character. As a result, the output is only Four and Five, as shown in Figure 4-5.

Figure 4-5:
Visual Basic
provides
several
methods of
filtering the
output.

Working with Order By

The Order By keyword is one of the few keywords that doesn't have a quirk when compared to C#. Even though Order By appears as two words, it acts as a single keyword in Visual Basic. Otherwise, you use it precisely as you use orderby in C#. Listing 4-4 shows how this keyword works in Visual Basic.

Listing 4-4   Grouping a Query Using Multiple Values

```
Private Sub btnOrderBy_Click( _
   ByVal sender As System.Object, _
   ByVal e As System.EventArgs) _
   Handles btnOrderBy.Click

   ' Create an array as a data source.
   Dim QueryString As String() = _
      New String() {"One", "Two", "Three", "Four", "Five"}

   ' Define the query.
   Dim ThisQuery = _
      From StringValue In QueryString _
      Order By StringValue _
      Order By StringValue.Length _
      Select StringValue + vbCrLf

   ' Display the result.
   For Each ThisValue In ThisQuery
      txtResult.Text = txtResult.Text + ThisValue
   Next

End Sub
```

As with C#, the order of the Order By keywords is important. This example produces the same output as its C# counterpart (see Figure 2-7): One, Two, Five, Four, and Three.

As with C#, you can change the order of the output by using the Descending keyword. Try it with the example code in Listing 4-4 to see the changes to your code.

Working with Join

A Visual Basic application has the same choices as C# when it comes to querying multiple sources. Depending on your needs, you can use a combination of a From and one or more Join keywords, or you can use multiple From keywords. Listing 4-5 shows both options at work.

Listing 4-5   A Simple Example of Using Multiple Sources

```
Private Sub btnJoin_Click(ByVal sender As System.Object, _
                  ByVal e As System.EventArgs) _
                  Handles btnJoin.Click
```

(continued)

Listing 4-5 *(continued)*

```
' Define two test arrays.
Dim ArrayA As Integer() = _
    New Integer() {1, 2, 3, 4, 8}
Dim ArrayB As Integer() = _
    New Integer() {1, 3, 5, 7, 8}

' Create the query.
Dim Joined = From QueryA In ArrayA _
        Join QueryB In ArrayB _
        On QueryA Equals QueryB _
        Select QueryA, QueryB

' Display the results.
txtResult.Text = txtResult.Text + _
    "Join Results:" + vbCrLf + vbCrLf

For Each OutPair In Joined
    txtResult.Text = txtResult.Text + _
        OutPair.QueryA.ToString() + " - " + _
        OutPair.QueryB.ToString() + vbCrLf
Next

' Create the second query.
Dim Joined2 = From QueryA In ArrayA _
        From QueryB In ArrayB _
        Where QueryA = QueryB _
        Select QueryA, QueryB

' Display the results.
txtResult.Text = txtResult.Text + _
    vbCrLf + "Two From Results:" + vbCrLf + vbCrLf

For Each OutPair In Joined2
    txtResult.Text = txtResult.Text + _
        OutPair.QueryA.ToString() + " - " + _
        OutPair.QueryB.ToString() + vbCrLf
Next

End Sub
```

As you can see, this example displays most of the same characteristics as the C# examples shown in Chapter 2. However, you need to pay special attention to a few nuances. Of course, the method for declaring and initializing the array is different from C#, but most developers will expect that requirement — it isn't anything new.

TIP

The second change might not be apparent at first. When you view the C# code in Listings 2-4 and 2-5, note that the `Select` statement relies on an array to output the values. You can do the same thing with Visual Basic if desired. In this case, you'd use

```
Select New Integer() {QueryA, QueryB}
```

Unfortunately, using this technique means that the value selection code also changes to

```
For Each OutPair In Joined
   txtResult.Text = txtResult.Text + _
      OutPair(0).ToString() + " - " + _
      OutPair(1).ToString() + vbCrLf
```

which isn't very readable. It's better to use the technique shown in Listing 4-5 so that you can address the array elements directly. This is one place where using the direct correlation between C# and Visual Basic doesn't provide the same results.

In all other respects, this application works like the C# equivalent and produces the same results shown in Figure 2-8. From a performance perspective, Visual Basic suffers from the same issues that C# does when working with a two `From` selection versus a combination of a `From` and a `Join`. Unfortunately, as in many other situations, the Visual Basic debugger won't demonstrate this deficiency. You must find it using large tests and timing the results.

Working with Let

Using Let to create a calculated value works the same in Visual Basic as it does with C#. As you can see in Listing 4-6, the differences between Visual Basic and C# are the same as when working with any multiple source application. You use a different technique to declare the arrays than in C#, and the `Select` statement must reflect the differences in working with Visual Basic.

Listing 4-6   Using Let to Create Calculated Values

```
Private Sub btnLet_Click(ByVal sender As System.Object, _
                         ByVal e As System.EventArgs) _
                         Handles btnLet.Click

   ' Create an array as a data source.
   Dim ArrayA As Integer() = _
      New Integer() {1, 2, 3, 4}
```

(continued)

Listing 4-6 *(continued)*

```
    Dim ArrayB As Integer() = _
      New Integer() {1, 2, 3, 4}

    ' Define the query.
    Dim Squares = _
      From QueryA In ArrayA _
      From QueryB In ArrayB _
      Let TheSquare = QueryA * QueryB _
      Where TheSquare > 4 _
      Select QueryA, QueryB, TheSquare

    ' Display the result.
    For Each ThisSquare In Squares
        txtResult.Text = txtResult.Text + _
          ThisSquare.QueryA.ToString() + " * " + _
          ThisSquare.QueryB.ToString() + " = " + _
          ThisSquare.TheSquare.ToString() + vbCrLf
    Next
End Sub
```

Behind the scenes, this Visual Basic example works the same as its C# counterpart in Listing 2-6. The output of this example is the same as the output shown in Figure 2-9.

By this point in the chapter, you should be getting the idea that Visual Basic provides good LINQ functionality — it's the small distinctions that will cause problems for you. Theoretically, you could test complex queries using C# and the advanced debugger support it provides before moving them to Visual Basic. However, when you do move the queries, make sure you consider the little differences.

Using the Additional Visual Basic Keywords

In its default setup, Visual Basic includes a number of additional keywords that provide added query functionality. C# does support a few of these keywords but only as part of specific providers, which means that you can't use them unless you're making a query using that provider. This section shows how to use the additional Visual Basic keywords in standard queries. You'll find this example in the \Chapter 04\AdditionalKeywords folder of the source code for this book.

Working with Aggregate

The `Aggregate` keyword helps you perform mathematical tasks with data, such as finding the sum of a group of numbers, counting the number of items, or creating an average. You use the `Aggregate` keyword as the first term in the query when working with lists and arrays, as shown in Listing 4-7.

Listing 4-7   Using Aggregate within a Query

```
Private Sub btnAggregate_Click( _
   ByVal sender As System.Object, _
   ByVal e As System.EventArgs) _
   Handles btnAggregate.Click

   ' Define a test array.
   Dim TestArray As Integer() = _
      New Integer() {1, 2, 3, 4}

   ' Define the query.
   Dim ThisQuery = Aggregate TheResult In TestArray _
                   Into Sum(TheResult)

   ' Display the result.
   txtResult.Text = "Sum: " + ThisQuery.ToString()

End Sub
```

In this case, the query sums the individual values in the array and places the result in `ThisQuery`. The wording of this query is different from other queries in this chapter — the query actually asks LINQ to look at the individual values in `TestArray` and sum them, rather than search for particular data in the array. Notice that `ThisQuery` is an `Integer` value, so you work with it as you would any other `Integer` value. Figure 4-6 shows the output from this example.

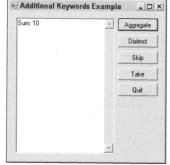

Figure 4-6:
Use the
Aggregate
keyword
to perform
math tasks
on data.

You combine the `Aggregate` keyword with the `From` keyword when working with a complex data source such as a `DataSet` or a database. The `From` keyword chooses individual records from the data source, while the `Aggregate` keyword chooses a particular field in that data source. The combination of the two keywords lets you perform analysis of individual database records. C# developers gain access to this keyword when working with the LINQ to SQL provider.

Working with Distinct

The `Distinct` keyword is exceptionally helpful when you have a list of values that include duplicates and you want to see only one copy of each value. This keyword lets you see the unique values in a collection, so that you don't have to consider needless duplication when trying to determine what the collection contains. Normally, you add the `Distinct` keyword after the `Select` keyword, as shown in Listing 4-8.

Listing 4-8   Viewing Unique Values in a Collection

```
Private Sub btnDistinct_Click( _
   ByVal sender As System.Object, _
   ByVal e As System.EventArgs) _
   Handles btnDistinct.Click

   ' Define a test array.
   Dim TestArray As Integer() = _
      New Integer() {2, 1, 2, 3, 4, 3, 1, 5}

   ' Define the query.
   Dim ThisQuery = From ThisElement In TestArray _
               Order By ThisElement _
               Select ThisElement Distinct

   ' Display the result.
   For Each TheResult In ThisQuery
      txtResult.Text = txtResult.Text + _
         TheResult.ToString() + vbCrLf
   Next
End Sub
```

The test array, `TestArray`, contains a series of numbers that are both unordered and duplicated. The query, `ThisQuery`, performs the standard sorting action using `Order By`, as you discovered in the "Working with Order By" section of this chapter. The difference is that the query also contains the `Distinct` keyword, which eliminates the duplicates. Figure 4-7 shows the results from this query.

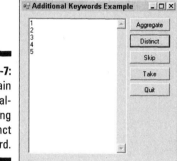

Figure 4-7:
Obtain
unique val-
ues by using
the Distinct
keyword.

You can use `Distinct` in Visual Basic applications wherever you expect to find duplicate values. Using `Distinct` means that you won't see every value in a collection, `DataSet`, or database unless these data sources contain unique values. You gain ease of viewing but could end up hiding some records in a complex data source. Normally, you'll want to run the query without `Distinct` first to ensure that you see everything you need to see, and then use `Distinct` to clean up the output. C# developers gain access to this keyword when working with the LINQ to SQL provider.

Working with Skip

Sometimes you need to skip a number of elements. For example, you may have already processed a number of elements in a collection, `DataSet`, or database. In some cases, you already know that you don't need the top elements and are interested only in the latter elements. A reverse search could choose the top elements and discard those on the bottom. No matter what the reason, using `Skip` lets you disregard a certain number of elements in a search. Listing 4-9 shows how you can use Skip to retrieve skip a certain number of elements in a result set.

This example begins by defining an array containing the numbers 1 through 8. It then uses a query to select those elements into `ThisQuery`. Notice how the query uses the `Skip` keyword to skip the first four numbers. The output contains the numbers 5 through 8, as you'd expect.

The second query shows one method you can use to display the numbers 1 through 4. In this case, the query sorts the array in reverse order and skips the first four numbers, which are now 5 through 8. This means that the output will show the result as the numbers 4 through 1, instead of the expected 1 through 4. To overcome this problem, the query includes a second `Order By` to reverse the result. This query shows that you can combine various keywords to produce a specific result. Figure 4-8 shows the result of this query.

Listing 4-9 Skipping Elements in a Result Set

```
Private Sub btnSkip_Click( _
   ByVal sender As System.Object, _
   ByVal e As System.EventArgs) _
   Handles btnSkip.Click

   ' Define a test array.
   Dim TestArray As Integer() = _
     New Integer() {1, 2, 3, 4, 5, 6, 7, 8}

   ' Define the query.
   Dim ThisQuery = From ThisElement In TestArray _

                     Select ThisElement Skip 4
   ' Display the result.
   txtResult.Text = "Standard Order" + vbCrLf
   For Each TheResult In ThisQuery
      txtResult.Text = txtResult.Text + _
         TheResult.ToString() + vbCrLf
   Next

   ' Define the reverse order query.
   ThisQuery = From ThisElement In TestArray _
               Order By ThisElement Descending _
               Select ThisElement Skip 4 _
               Order By ThisElement

   ' Display the result.
   txtResult.Text = txtResult.Text + _
      vbCrLf + "Reverse Order" + vbCrLf
   For Each TheResult In ThisQuery
      txtResult.Text = txtResult.Text + _
         TheResult.ToString() + vbCrLf
   Next

End Sub
```

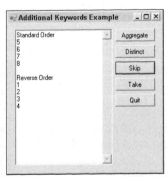

Figure 4-8:
The Skip keyword can help you retrieve just the elements you want.

Working with Take

Just as the `Skip` keyword skips a certain number of elements in a collection, `DataSet`, or database, the `Take` keyword returns the number of elements that you specify. Instead of outputting all the elements, the `Take` keyword lets you take just those that you want. In addition, you can combine `Skip` and `Take` to access specific elements without fancy coding. Listing 4-10 shows examples of both `Take` alone and `Take` used with `Skip`.

Listing 4-10   Taking Elements in a Result Set

```
Private Sub btnTake_Click( _
   ByVal sender As System.Object, _
   ByVal e As System.EventArgs) _
   Handles btnTake.Click

   ' Define a test array.
   Dim TestArray As Integer() = _
      New Integer() {1, 2, 3, 4, 5, 6, 7, 8}

   ' Define the query.
   Dim ThisQuery = From ThisElement In TestArray _
               Select ThisElement Take 4

   ' Display the result.
   txtResult.Text = "Simple Take" + vbCrLf
   For Each TheResult In ThisQuery
      txtResult.Text = txtResult.Text + _
         TheResult.ToString() + vbCrLf
   Next

   ' Define the query.
   ThisQuery = From ThisElement In TestArray _
               Select ThisElement Skip 2 Take 4

   ' Display the result.
   txtResult.Text = txtResult.Text + _
      vbCrLf + "Take And Skip Combined" + vbCrLf
   For Each TheResult In ThisQuery
      txtResult.Text = txtResult.Text + _
         TheResult.ToString() + vbCrLf
   Next

End Sub
```

The example begins by creating an array of numbers, `TestArray`, with the values 1 through 8. The first query simply takes the first four elements, 1 through 4. It then outputs these values using the usual `For Each` loop.

The second query shows how to combine Skip and Take. The order in which you define Skip and Take determines the output you see on the screen. For example, if you reversed Skip and Take in this query, you'd see the numbers 3 and 4 in the output. That's because Take would take the numbers 1 through 4, and then Skip would skip 1 and 2, leaving 3 and 4. As with all other keywords, Skip and Take work with the result left by previous keywords, so you can end up with the wrong results if you use these keywords in the wrong order. Figure 4-9 shows the output from this example.

Figure 4-9:
Combine
Skip and
Take as
needed to
produce
specific
results with-
out a lot of
coding.

As with the other special Visual Basic keywords, C# developers gain access to the Skip and Take keywords when working with the LINQ to SQL provider. Visual Basic is special, however, because these keywords are always available and you can use them in a number of ways with collections.

Working with Lambda Functions in Visual Basic

Lambda expressions are different in Visual Basic than they are in C#. In fact, this is one area where the difference is significant. Whereas C# uses an expression, Visual Basic uses a function. For example, the following query generates an error in Visual Basic:

```
Dim ThisQuery = From ThisElement In TestArray _
            Where Function(Num As Integer) Num > 3 _
            Select ThisElement
```

It pays to start simply with Visual Basic. You can use lambda expressions even for simple tasks. All you need to do is create a variable that contains the desired function, as shown in Listing 4-11. You'll find this example in the \Chapter 04\LambdaFunctions folder of the source code for this book.

Listing 4-11   Using a Simple Lambda Function

```
Private Sub btnSimple_Click( _
   ByVal sender As System.Object, _
   ByVal e As System.EventArgs) _
   Handles btnSimple.Click

   ' Define the expression.
   Dim Backwards = Function(Str As String) Str.Reverse()

   ' Display a result.
   For Each Output As String In Backwards("Hello")
      txtResult.Text = txtResult.Text + Output
   Next
End Sub
```

This example shows one of the oddities of working with Visual Basic. The output of Backwards is an enumeration of Char. Consequently, you need the For Each loop to put the string back together. In this case, the output is "olleH" — a reversed string.

Using lambda expressions in a query is significantly different, too. Listing 4-12 shows a typical example of a query.

Listing 4-12   Making a Query with a Lambda Function

```
Private Sub btnQuery_Click( _
   ByVal sender As System.Object, _
   ByVal e As System.EventArgs) _
   Handles btnQuery.Click

   ' Define a test array.
   Dim TestArray As Integer() = _
      New Integer() {1, 2, 3, 4, 5, 6, 7, 8}

   ' Define the query.
   Dim Filter = _
      TestArray.Where(Function(Num As Integer) Num > 3)
   Dim ThisQuery = From ThisElement In Filter _
                   Select ThisElement

   ' Display the result.
```

(continued)

Listi ng 4-12 *(continued)*

```
    For Each TheResult In ThisQuery
        txtResult.Text = txtResult.Text + _
            TheResult.ToString() + vbCrLf
    Next

End Sub
```

Notice that you first define `Filter` as a lambda function. The syntax is completely different from C#. You use the `Where()` method of `TestArray` to create the function. The function lacks any kind of name. It accepts an `Integer` as input and produces a `Boolean` value as output. The result of this filter is that it rejects any number less than or equal to 3.

You still haven't created a query. To create the query, you define `ThisQuery` in relation to `Filter`, rather than `TestArray` as you normally would. You can still perform all the usual manipulations in the query. The only difference is that `Filter` acts as your data source. The output from this example is the numbers 4 through 8.

Chapter 5

Working with LINQ in Visual Studio 2005

In This Chapter

▶ Getting LINQ for Visual Studio 2005

▶ Adding LINQ support to Visual Studio 2005

▶ Developing your first Visual Studio 2005 LINQ project

*A*lthough LINQ support comes with Visual Studio 2008, you won't find it natively in Visual Studio 2005. Yes, you can definitely use LINQ in your Visual Studio 2005 applications, but you'll end up working a bit harder to get it because you must download and install the required support. Even after you install the required support, you'll find that Visual Studio 2005 lacks the automation found in Visual Studio 2008. Consequently, writing a LINQ application in Visual Studio 2005 is a little more work than writing the same application in Visual Studio 2008.

Discovering how LINQ works in Visual Studio 2005 has some benefits if you want to see LINQ in action. Because you have to do more of the work, you'll uncover some issues that the Visual Studio 2008 automation tends to hide. Therefore, if you have the time, you should try working with Visual Studio 2005 even if you plan to do most of your development in Visual Studio 2008.

This chapter begins with a look at a simple LINQ application in Visual Studio 2005 so that you can compare development to the simple Visual Studio 2008 examples in Chapters 2 and 3. The chapter then progresses to common LINQ scenarios, including objects, `DataSets`, XML, and SQL Server. Understanding how these providers function in Visual Studio 2005 is helpful in understanding LINQ as a whole in this environment. In addition, the techniques you discover will help you transform Visual Studio 2008 application code into a Visual Studio 2005 counterpart as applicable.

You won't want to make the mistake of thinking that Visual Studio 2005 gives you everything that Visual Studio 2008 provides. This chapter helps you discover some of the issues that you'll encounter when working with LINQ in Visual Studio 2005. It also uncovers some of the limitations you should expect.

Obtaining LINQ Support for Visual Studio 2005

Microsoft is determined that you'll use LINQ with Visual Studio 2008. When you go to the LINQ Web site downloads at `http://msdn2.microsoft.com/en-us/netframework/aa569263.aspx`, you see .NET Framework 3.5, a link for the evaluation version of Visual Studio 2008, and a link for Visual Studio 2008 Express, but nothing for Visual Studio 2005.

Fortunately, you can still use LINQ with Visual Studio 2005, but you need to know where to look. Download the Visual Studio 2005 compatible product from `http://www.microsoft.com/downloads/details.aspx?familyid=1e902c21-340c-4d13-9f04-70eb5e3dceea`. In addition to the LINQ download, you also need a copy of the Visual Studio 2005 language product (including any of the Express editions). Make sure you have all the required updates installed on your system and that LINQ runs properly. LINQ for Visual Studio 2005 works fine with the .NET Framework 2.0 as long as you don't want to use any special WinFX features in your application.

You may also need some optional components. For example, if you want to work with any of the DLinq applications (the LINQ to SQL provider), you must have a copy of either SQL Server 2000 or SQL Server 2005 installed on your system. It's also possible to use SQL Server 2005 Express, which you can download free from `http://www.microsoft.com/downloads/details.aspx?familyid=220549b5-0b07-4448-8848-dcc397514b41`.

LINQ also provides support for the Windows Presentation Foundation (WPF) through WinFX. To obtain this support in Visual Studio 2005, you can download the WinFX Runtime components. However, all versions of this package currently found on the Internet are in a beta status. You'll probably get better results using the .NET Framework 3.5 download found at `http://www.microsoft.com/downloads/details.aspx?FamilyId=333325FD-AE52-4E35-B531-508D977D32A6`.

Installing LINQ Support

After you install all the required updates for your copy of Windows and have all the files downloaded, it's time to install LINQ support on your system. The following steps take you through the process:

1. **Double-click the LINQ Preview (May 2006).MSI file.**

   You see the welcome page.

2. **Click Next.**

The wizard displays the licensing information.

3. **Select I Agree after you read the licensing agreement and then click Next.**

   The wizard displays a dialog box asking whether you want to use the C# Language Service, as shown in Figure 5-1. The C# Language Service provides limited C# 3.0 support in Visual Studio 2005, making it considerably easier to write applications. This chapter assumes that you have this support installed.

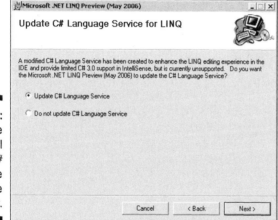

Figure 5-1: Make sure you install the C# Language Service support.

4. **Select Update C# Language Service and click Next.**

   You see a confirm installation page.

5. **Click Next.**

   The wizard performs the required installation tasks.

You can optionally install SQL Server 2005 Express and .NET Framework 3.5 on your system. The examples in this chapter won't use either technology, but they may be useful in your own projects. To obtain this support, download the required files, double-click the installation files, and follow the instructions that Microsoft provides for installing these two products.

Creating the Simple Visual Studio 2005 Project

You'll begin creating your first example, as you usually do, by opening Visual Studio 2005. The first message you'll see is one telling you that this is an unsupported product. This message is normal; don't worry about it. Click OK to clear the message and you're ready to go.

The examples in this section show basic query techniques and discuss potential limitations in Visual Studio 2005 when compared to the full features provided in Visual Studio 2008. Use the Chapter 2 examples as a comparison for the examples in the sections that follow. You'll find this example in the `\Chapter 05\SimpleQueries` folder of the source code for this book.

Defining the project

You start a LINQ project in Visual Studio 2005 the same as you would any other project. However, to obtain LINQ support, you must use the special LINQ template shown in Figure 5-2. Notice that you can build any of the following project types:

✔ LINQ Console application

✔ LINQ Windows application

✔ LINQ Library

✔ LINQ WinFX application

This book concentrates on the LINQ Windows application because it provides the most flexibility and easiest output options. Using the Visual Studio 2005 Express Edition will limit the number of choices you have when selecting a template.

Figure 5-2: Choose the LINQ template that matches the application you want to create.

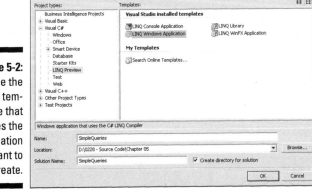

You could probably get a LINQ application to work with one of the standard templates, but you'll find it frustrating. None of the keywords will work properly and you'll have to do just about everything the hard way. Always use the LINQ templates to make it easier to create a LINQ application with Visual Studio 2005. You may find this fact difficult to remember if you move between Visual Studio 2005 and Visual Studio 2008 because Visual Studio 2008 doesn't require that you select any special projects.

Working with from

The basic `from` query can provide you with a good start when it comes to LINQ. Working with a `from` query in C# 2005 is slightly different than working with a C# 2008 query. Most of the differences are in not the code but the interface. This makes sense considering that Visual Studio 2005 has no built-in LINQ functionality. This section describes some of the differences you'll encounter when working with Visual Studio 2005. You'll find the examples in this section in the `\Chapter 05\SimpleQueries` folder of the source code for this book.

Understanding the code

This example provides a simple `from` query. It pays to start with a `from` query whenever you work with Visual Studio 2005. You want to be sure that you have access to the data source before you complicate matters by adding other keywords (operators) to the query. Listing 5-1 shows the source code for this example.

Listing 5-1   Defining a Simple from Query

```
private void btnFrom_Click(object sender, EventArgs e)
{
    // Create an array as a data source.
    String[] QueryString =
        { "One", "Two", "Three", "Four", "Five",
          "Six", "Seven", "Eight", "Nine", "Ten" };

    // Define the query.
    var ThisQuery =
        from StringValue in QueryString
        select StringValue + "\r\n";

    // Display the result.
    foreach (var ThisValue in ThisQuery)
        txtResult.Text = txtResult.Text + ThisValue;
}
```

Type this example, rather than use the source code provided with the book, so you can see how IntelliSense works in Visual Studio 2005. The first thing you'll notice is that there isn't any IntelliSense support for the LINQ portion of the query. When you type var and press the spacebar, you'll see var change color to indicate that it's a keyword, but you won't get any help from the IDE in making the next step. As you continue to type the query, the absence of any IntelliSense support is noticeable. Unfortunately, it doesn't appear that you'll receive much IntelliSense support, so it pays to put queries together carefully and in increments to reduce the complexity of working with Visual Studio 2005.

The sections that follow build on the example shown in Listing 5-1. In this case, the query, ThisQuery, selects all the entries in QueryString. The output contains strings from One through Ten.

Using the debugger

The debugging functionality provided by Visual Studio 2005 isn't nearly as helpful as that provided by Visual Studio 2008. This is hardly surprising considering you've bolted on the required support. To begin this example, place a break point at the following line of code:

```
var ThisQuery =
    from StringValue in QueryString
    select StringValue + "\r\n";
```

Start the application and click From. The following steps show what happens next:

1. **Click Step Over.**

   The application creates the ThisQuery query. Notice that a Step Into button isn't available. You can't step into a query as you can with C# 2008.

2. **Select the Locals windows.**

   The query consists of a number of elements, as shown in Figure 5-3. The query itself is System.Collections.Generic.IEnumerable <string> type, which tells you that LINQ knows that it's working with a string array despite the fact that you never told it that it was using a string array. The System.Collections.Generic.IEnumerator <TResult>.Current and System.Collections.IEnumerator. Current properties tell you which values LINQ currently has selected.

   Here's where you need to look closely at the capability that Visual Studio 2005 provides. Compare Figure 5-3 with Figure 2-2. Notice that Visual Studio 2005 doesn't provide a Results View, so you have no idea what the query contains. In addition, it's important to note that the This Query value is different from Visual Studio 2008. Instead of using a System.Linq. Enumerable.SelectIterator<string,string> value, Visual Studio uses a

System.Query.Sequence.Select Iterator<string,string>
value. This difference will affect how the application views the query and
interacts with it.

Figure 5-3:
A query
contains a
number of
useful infor-
mational
elements.

3. **Click Step Over.**

   Visual Studio selects ThisQuery. The changes you normally see in the
   Locals window in Visual Studio 2008 don't appear in the Visual Studio
   2005 Locals window.

4. **Click Step Over twice.**

   Visual Studio first selects the in keyword. Normally, you'd expect to see
   the debugger select the select keyword argument in the query.
   However, Visual Studio 2005 doesn't show you how the query works
   internally. It skips over the query and selects var ThisValue instead,
   as shown in Figure 5-4. The Locals window does show some interesting
   information. Notice that ThisQuery now has Selector and Source
   values. As shown in Figure 5-4, the Selector property shows the entire
   result set for the query. In addition, you can see the currently selected
   value in the System.Collections.Generic.IEnumerator
   <TResult>.Current and System.Collections.IEnumerator.
   Current properties.

5. **Click Step Over.**

   Visual Studio selects the processing statement for the foreach loop.
   This sequence of events takes the output of the select portion of the
   query and places it in ThisValue. If you look at the Locals window,
   you'll see that ThisValue is no longer null but contains the first
   output value from the query.

6. **At this point, if you click Step Over, you'll go back to Step 4 of this
   procedure.**

   The process keeps repeating itself until the foreach loop processes
   every one of the query outputs.

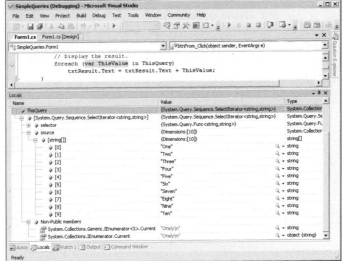

Figure 5-4:
The debug-
ger doesn't
show the
internals of
the query.

Working with join

Most business applications don't work with a single data source — you normally need to work with several data sources and combine them in some way.
Because Visual Studio 2005 doesn't tell you much about the internal workings
of your query, you'll want to focus your attention on accessing all of the data
sources you require at the outset to ensure that any bug you encounter later
isn't one of data source accessibility. Listing 5-2 shows an example of how you
might combine two data sources to create specific output.

Listing 5-2   Using Two Data Sources

```
private void btnJoin_Click(object sender, EventArgs e)
{
    // Create an array as a data source.
    String[] QueryString =
        { "One", "Two", "Three", "Four", "Five",
          "Six", "Seven", "Eight", "Nine", "Ten" };

    // Define a second array for the second data source.
    String[] IndexArray =
        { "A", "B", "C", "D", "E", "F", "G", "H", "I",
          "J", "K", "L", "M", "N", "O", "P", "Q", "R",
          "S", "T", "U", "V", "W", "X", "Y", "Z" };
```

```
// Define the query.
var ThisQuery =
    from StringValue in QueryString
    join IndexValue in IndexArray
    on StringValue.Substring(0, 1) equals IndexValue
    select new {StringValue, IndexValue};

// Display the result.
foreach (var ThisValue in ThisQuery)
    txtResult.Text = txtResult.Text +
        ThisValue.IndexValue + " - " +
        ThisValue.StringValue + "\r\n";
}
```

The two arrays, `QueryString` and `IndexArray`, provide the data sources for this example. The output will eventually match an index letter to the first letter of the selected string, as shown in Figure 5-5.

Figure 5-5:
This join shows how you can match an individual letter to a string for indexing.

The query, `ThisQuery`, begins by joining the two data sources. Note how the code uses `StringValue.Substring(0, 1)` to obtain the first letter of the string and compare it to the values within `IndexValue`. When the query finds a match, it generates a new array elements consisting of the `StringValue` and `IndexValue` variables.

The order in which you perform the `join` is important. If the query had used `IndexArray` first, as shown here

```
// Define the query using IndexArray first.
var ThisQuery =
    from IndexValue in IndexArray
    join StringValue in QueryString
    on IndexValue equals StringValue.Substring(0, 1)
    select new {StringValue, IndexValue};
```

the results would have shown the output in `IndexArray` order, as shown in Figure 5-6. The results are the same, but the order is different. Of course, you can always use a `where` keyword to change the order as needed.

Figure 5-6: Join order is important, especially with large data sets.

No matter which development environment you choose, you can always use two `from` keywords to create a particular result. The following query produces the same output as the query shown in Listing 5-2.

```
// Define the query using two from keywords.
var ThisQuery =
    from StringValue in QueryString
    from IndexValue in IndexArray
    where StringValue.Substring(0, 1) == IndexValue
    select new {StringValue, IndexValue};
```

As with C# 2008, the problem with this query is that it requires more time to execute. The query performs more steps to accomplish a given task. Unfortunately, the debugger doesn't show you how the query works, so you can't find this problem using the same techniques you use in C# 2008. You'll need to use timing tests to locate the problem instead.

Working with where

After you have one or more data sources to work with, it often becomes necessary to filter the result. Otherwise, you can quickly drown in unwanted data. Listing 5-3 takes the example shown in Listing 5-2 and filters it to show only a subset of the data.

Listing 5-3   Filtering Data to Meet Specific Criteria

```
private void btnWhere_Click(object sender, EventArgs e)
{
    // Create an array as a data source.
    String[] QueryString =
        { "One", "Two", "Three", "Four", "Five",
          "Six", "Seven", "Eight", "Nine", "Ten" };

    // Define a second array for the second data source.
    String[] IndexArray =
        { "A", "B", "C", "D", "E", "F", "G", "H", "I",
          "J", "K", "L", "M", "N", "O", "P", "Q", "R",
          "S", "T", "U", "V", "W", "X", "Y", "Z" };

    // Define the query.
    var ThisQuery =
        from StringValue in QueryString
        join IndexValue in IndexArray
        on StringValue.Substring(0, 1) equals IndexValue
        where Convert.ToChar(IndexValue) > 'F'
        select new {StringValue, IndexValue};

    // Display the result.
    foreach (var ThisValue in ThisQuery)
        txtResult.Text = txtResult.Text +
            ThisValue.IndexValue + " - " +
            ThisValue.StringValue + "\r\n";

}
```

The interesting point of this query is that you must convert the String to a Char before you can perform the required comparison. The compiler does complain when you attempt to use a String for comparison, but it doesn't always tell you about the source of the problem. Consequently, you should add this check to your list of issues to verify during the debugging process. In this case, the output contains strings that begin with G or greater, as shown in Figure 5-7.

Figure 5-7:
Filtering keeps you from drowning in too much data.

A matter of order for Visual Studio 2005

It is always important to work methodically when writing an application. However, using LINQ in Visual Studio 2005 presents some special challenges. As mentioned in several sections of this chapter, you should build your queries one step at a time and test between steps to ensure that the query output is moving in the direction you anticipated. Otherwise, you can end up with a query that's incredibly difficult to debug.

The first step is to create the `from` portion of your query. It's important to verify that you have access to the data source you want to use. When working with multiple data sources, add `join` or additional `from` keywords as needed to obtain full access to all the data sources you want to use for the query. In some cases, this portion of the query creation process can prove time consuming because the size of the resultant query can be huge and require a lot of time to transmit over network connections. However, making sure you have proper data source access is critical, so the time you spend now will save debugging time later.

The second step is to filter the query. You can use any combination of filtering steps to reduce the output to just the data items needed by the application. Add filtering criteria one at a time to reduce the risk of a bad filter producing an error or blocking data that you need in the output.

The third step is to sort the output so that it appears in the required form. Again, work one step at a time to ensure that the output is precisely what you expect.

Finally, use calculated values to improve query performance. At this point, you need to check both the output of the query and the time required to perform the query. Because Visual Studio 2005 does little to help you optimize queries, you may have to try several approaches to obtain the desired result. Don't be afraid to experiment! The time you spend optimizing the query at the output can make a significant difference in overall application performance.

Working with orderby

Outputting the data in order is important because most people don't want to search through an unordered list. Even if you can convince someone to search through such a list, the result is often erroneous because the person will miss needed information. The example code is the same as Listing 5-3 for this example — only the query changes. Here's the new query.

```
// Define the query.
var ThisQuery =
    from StringValue in QueryString
    join IndexValue in IndexArray
    on StringValue.Substring(0, 1) equals IndexValue
    where Convert.ToChar(IndexValue) > 'F'
    orderby IndexValue
    select new {StringValue, IndexValue};
```

If you've been following the evolution of this example, you can see that the output has changed quite a bit from that first `from` query. The output now appears in indexed order, as shown in Figure 5-8.

Figure 5-8:
Ordering the data makes it much easier to search.

You may wonder about the choice of index value. Indexing the output by a single letter is considerably faster than indexing by entire words. Consequently, the choice of `IndexValue` as the `orderby` argument makes the application perform faster.

Working with let

Using `let` can save significant time and effort when working with LINQ. The example shown in Listing 5-3 requires two data sources and a complex query to perform the task that it performs. It's always better to use less code when you can, and that's the purpose of the example in this section. This example shows how you can obtain the same results using significantly less code by employing the `let` keyword effectively. Listing 5-4 shows the code for this example.

Listing 5-4   Reducing Complexity with let

```
private void btnLet_Click(object sender, EventArgs e)
{
    // Create an array as a data source.
    String[] QueryString =
        { "One", "Two", "Three", "Four", "Five",
          "Six", "Seven", "Eight", "Nine", "Ten" };

    // Define the query.
    var ThisQuery =
```

(continued)

Listing 5-4 *(continued)*

```
        from StringValue in QueryString
        let IndexValue = StringValue.Substring(0, 1)
        where Convert.ToChar(IndexValue) > 'F'
        orderby IndexValue
        select new {StringValue, IndexValue};

    // Display the result.
    foreach (var ThisValue in ThisQuery)
        txtResult.Text = txtResult.Text +
            ThisValue.IndexValue + " - " +
            ThisValue.StringValue + "\r\n";

}
```

The code begins with a single array, QueryString. Because the first letter of each word already contains the required index value, all you really need to do is extract that first letter. The previous query had to perform this task anyway for the comparison, so you aren't adding any time to the old query.

Note how this example uses let to create the IndexValue shown in the previous query (see the example in the "Working with orderby" section of the chapter). The where and orderby keywords work as they did in the past. The output still contains IndexValue, but now IndexValue is a calculated value rather than using an index value from another array.

Using this approach helps the resulting application execute significantly faster, without any loss of functionality. The results look the same as shown in Figure 5-8. Always look for ways to use calculated values to improve the overall performance of your applications. In some cases, the combination of reduced network requirements and local execution time can make your application run orders of magnitude faster, using less memory and other resources.

Part II

Using Standard LINQ to Technologies

In this part . . .

LINQ comes with four standard providers (special software that makes LINQ work with particular kinds of data sources): LINQ to Objects, LINQ to DataSet, LINQ to SQL, and LINQ to XML. Chapters 6 through 9 discuss each of these providers in turn and help you understand how to use them within an application. These four providers give you access to a vast range of data — more than their names imply.

Chapter 6

LINQ to Object

In This Chapter

▶ Working with objects in LINQ

▶ Developing a simple object query

▶ Using deferred operators

▶ Developing a deferred operator application

▶ Using nondeferred operators

▶ Developing a nondeferred operator application

*O*bjects (from a LINQ perspective) can refer to any elements that implement the IEnumerable interface in your application. For example, an object can include an array, a DataSet, a database, or even a control when it supports the correct interface. You can even create custom classes to support the IEnumerable interface and interact with them as objects in LINQ. The LINQ to Object provider is the most generic provider that you'll use. You use this provider to perform any task with LINQ — the other providers add to the functionality provided by the LINQ to Object provider. Consequently, this is the most important provider to know about because it affects everything you do.

The examples in Chapters 1 through 5 rely on the LINQ to Object provider. However, these examples show only the basics of what you can do with this provider. The purpose of this chapter is to move from the basics into some more advanced examples of how you can use this provider to work with objects of various sorts.

Besides looking at some of the interesting tasks you can perform with the LINQ to Object provider, this chapter also begins a discussion of operators. *Operators* include keywords, such as `from` and `select`, and methods of interpreting the data. Table 2-1 provides a list of the standard query operators and where you can find additional information about them — this chapter goes considerably further in exploring the object operators.

This chapter also explores the role of deferred and nondeferred operators in your LINQ applications. *Deferred* operators refer to any keyword or method that LINQ interprets as it parses the result set. A deferred operator will always yield results that change with changes in the result set. *Nondeferred* operators refer to any keyword or method that LINQ interprets as it creates the query. Using nondeferred operators produces static results that don't change when the result set changes. Your programming toolbox requires both kinds of operators to create the full range of applications.

Considering the Use of Objects with LINQ

It's important to have a firm grasp of the LINQ to Object provider before you begin working with any of the other providers. Everything you discover in this chapter will help you create interesting and useful LINQ applications. The most important concept you can take from this chapter is that there isn't anything like a standard or default LINQ query. Any data you can access is fair game when it comes to LINQ.

LINQ uses a few generic terms for special purposes. A *sequence* is a list of elements from a given query. Each *element* is a specific piece of information and you can address it separately. For example, you can choose to display a specific array element. Try not to think of information as human readable data; LINQ can work with any form of data. You may also see sequences described as *result sets* or a *collection*. In all cases, these terms refer to a list of items that you retrieve as the result of making a query.

It may be possible that you'll think about LINQ objects in a specific way — a list, `DataSet`, database, or other data source. However, you need not consider objects of a specific type. Any object that provides an `IEnumerable` or `IQueryable` interface will normally work as a LINQ object.

.NET Framework and the real world in general provide access to a considerable number of data sequences that don't support either an `IEnumerable` or `IQueryable` interface. In this case, you can use a conversion operator — `AsEnumerable`, `AsQueryable`, `Cast`, `OfType`, `ToArray`, `ToDictionary`, `ToList`, or `ToLookup` — to convert the data sequence into a usable form. For example, you could use LINQ to query a graphic, music, or video file. All you need is a data sequence and some method of interpreting that sequence.

You also need not limit objects to standard data. For example, you can use LINQ to interact with controls. The control could act as a data sink for any data source — LINQ doesn't care. All LINQ needs is access to the data that the control is manipulating on behalf of the user. You can even use LINQ to help buffer the control data. For example, every time the control data changes, you could use code to read the new values, remove any replicated data, and then present the modified result in the same control — the user need not ever know the difference.

The goal of using LINQ to Object then is to interpret and optionally modify data of any type from any source using any object. By employing the operators discussed in this chapter carefully, you can create applications that modify data to create unique sequences at a speed you may not have envisioned in the past and with an ease you never thought possible.

Creating the Simple Object Query Example

If you haven't already reviewed the basic examples in Chapter 2, 4, or 5, you should do so now to understand the example in this section. The example here will do something not typical. It uses LINQ to order the data in a combo box. As you type data into the combo box, LINQ will automatically reorder it for you. In addition, LINQ will eliminate any duplicate values and present the input in a consistent format — all without complex programming on your part. Listing 6-1 shows this simple example of working with a combo box control. You'll find this example in the `\Chapter 06\ComboBoxDemo` folder of the source code for this book.

Listing 6-1   Using LINQ with Controls

```
private void cbResult_KeyPress(object sender,
                               KeyPressEventArgs e)
{
   // Check for an Enter keypress.
   if (e.KeyChar == (char)Keys.Return)
   {
      // Add the appropriate text to the list.
      cbResult.Items.Add(cbResult.Text);

      // Perform the required LINQ update.
      String[] CBQuery =
         cbResult.Items.Cast<String>().OrderBy(
         TheseItems => TheseItems).Select(
         TheseItems =>
            TheseItems.Substring(0, 1).ToUpper() +
```

(continued)

Listing 6-1 *(continued)*

```
            TheseItems.Substring(1,
                TheseItems.Length - 1).ToLower()).
                    ToArray();

        // Clear the current Items list.
        cbResult.Items.Clear();

        // Add the updated list to the Items property.
        foreach (String ThisString in CBQuery)
            cbResult.Items.Add(ThisString);
    }
}
```

A combo box control doesn't include code to add new entries automatically, so you add these new entries using the `KeyPress` event handler. Whenever the code detects that the user has pressed Enter, it adds the input, `cb Result.Text`, to the `cbResult.Items` property. At this point, you have an unordered list of items in `cbResult.Items`.

Now you have to think about the control update. At some point, you'll want to clear the control to add the ordered list to it. Otherwise, the control will display two lists — one ordered and another unordered. The "Understanding the Role of the IEnumerable and IEnumerable<T> Interfaces" discussion in Chapter 3 describes some of the differences between deferred and non-deferred LINQ queries. To make this query work, you must create it in such a way that the result is nondeferred; otherwise you'll end up with a blank output.

The LINQ query in this example using the lambda expression method to obtain a nondeferred array output. The query looks complicated, but it isn't if you take it apart one element at a time.

The `cbResult.Items` property doesn't provide the required functionality, so you must cast it as a `String` array before you can work with it using the `Cast<String>()` template. If you try to use the property directly, you receive an error message telling you that the `System.Windows.Forms.ComboBox.ObjectCollection` doesn't include a definition for `OrderBy`.

Now that you have access to `OrderBy`, you can use the `OrderBy` method to order the output with a lambda expression. In this case, you simply use `TheseItems` as the ordering mechanism, but you could use any expression desired. The ability to change the ordering by modifying a simple expression is one of the reasons you want to use LINQ to order the combo box output. You don't have to worry about any complex programming strategy to obtain the desired output.

Ordering the output is only the first step in the process. It's also important to define a specific selection criterion. In this case, the user can input the text in any form, but the combo box will display the text using initial uppercase. Consequently, the `Select()` method includes code that ensures the output appears in the correct form.

The final bit of code is the most important. You use the `ToArray()` method to convert the output to a standard array. This is the nondeferred part of the query — the part that makes the rest of the query work. The next step clears the `cbResult.Items` property, so a deferred query will see an empty data source at this point and fail to produce any output. The final step uses a `foreach` loop to add the items back into the list in the order you specified. Figure 6-1 shows the output from this example.

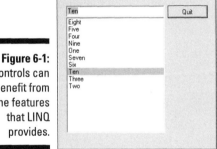

Figure 6-1:
Controls can benefit from the features that LINQ provides.

This example also provides the means to delete entries. Unfortunately, the `KeyPress` event doesn't detect the Delete key, so the example adds the required code to the `KeyDown` event handler. Unlike adding entries, deleting entries doesn't require you to modify the order of the list. Consequently, you can still address this portion of the example using straight code, as shown here:

```
private void cbResult_KeyDown(object sender,
                              KeyEventArgs e)
{
    // Check for a Delete key press.
    if (e.KeyValue == (int)Keys.Delete)

        // Remove an item when no longer needed.
        cbResult.Items.Remove(cbResult.SelectedItem);
}
```

In this case, whenever the code detects the Delete key, it removes the selected item from the list. Notice that this portion of the code uses an `int` for detection rather than a `char`. Otherwise, the code behaves as you'd expect.

Understanding the Role of Deferred Operators

Deferred operators let you interpret the results of a query dynamically. The results change as the data source content changes. You use this type of operator when you want to have results that match the data source all the time. In addition, you use this kind of operator for reusable data sources — those that you plan to query often using the same LINQ query. The following operators provide deferred interpretation:

- ✔ AsEnumerable
- ✔ AsQueryable
- ✔ Cast
- ✔ Concat
- ✔ DefaultIfEmpty
- ✔ Distinct
- ✔ Empty
- ✔ Except
- ✔ GroupBy
- ✔ GroupJoin
- ✔ Intersect
- ✔ Join
- ✔ OfType
- ✔ OrderBy
- ✔ OrderByDescending
- ✔ Range
- ✔ Repeat
- ✔ Reverse
- ✔ Select
- ✔ SelectMany
- ✔ Skip
- ✔ SkipWhile
- ✔ Take

✔ TakeWhile

✔ ThenBy

✔ ThenByDescending

✔ Union

✔ Where

Creating the Deferred Operator Examples

It's time to look at the various deferred operators. In this section, I provide simple examples of how you can use these operators. Going through the examples with the debugger as described in the "Using the debugger to see the simple query in action" section of Chapter 2 will illustrate how LINQ builds the query dynamically. As shown in Listing 6-1, you can create LINQ queries of any complexity as required by your application. This section examines the various operators by operator class as described in Table 2-1.

Working with Concat

The sole concatenation operator lets you combine two sequences. The resulting sequence contains all elements found in the two input sequences. Listing 6-2 shows an example of using the concatenation operator. You'll find this example in the \Chapter 06\Concatenation folder of the source code for this book.

Listing 6-2   Implementing the Concatenation Operator

```
private void btnTest_Click(object sender, EventArgs e)
{
   // Define two test arrays.
   String[] First = { "One", "Two", "Three" };
   String[] Second = { "Four", "Five", "Six" };

   // Create the query.
   var ThisQuery = First.Concat<String>(Second);

   // Display the output.
   foreach (String ThisElement in ThisQuery)
      txtResult.Text = txtResult.Text +
         ThisElement + "\r\n";
}
```

Remember that you could end up with a situation where you need to put together sequences from diverse sources. For example, you might have to add sequences from databases maintained by several satellite offices. The code shows two String arrays. As you might imagine, the output contains the concatenation of those two arrays: One, Two, Three, Four, Five, and Six.

Unlike the set operators described in the "Working with Distinct, Except, Intersect, and Union" section of the chapter, Concat() won't remove duplicates. It creates a true superset of the inputs you provide. If you need to combine two sources and remove duplicates, use one of the set operators instead of this operator.

Working with AsEnumerable, AsQueryable, Cast, and OfType

The deferred conversion operators convert the results of a query to a particular type as the code interprets the result set. (See the "Working with ToArray, ToDictionary, ToList, and ToLookup" section of the chapter for a list of the nondeferred conversion operators.) Listing 6-3 shows an example of using the conversion operators. You'll find this example in the \Chapter 06\Conversion1 folder of the source code for this book.

Listing 6-3   Implementing the Deferred Conversion Operators

```
private enum NumToWord
{
    Zero, One, Two, Three, Four, Five,
    Six, Seven, Eight, Nine, Ten
}

private void btnTest_Click(object sender, EventArgs e)
{
    // Create the query.
    var ThisQuery =
        lstSource.Items.Cast<String>().Where(
            ThisElement => Convert.ToInt32(ThisElement) > 3).
            Select(ThisElement =>
                (NumToWord)Convert.ToInt32(ThisElement));

    // Display the output.
    foreach (var ThisElement in ThisQuery)
        txtResult.Text = txtResult.Text +
            ThisElement.ToString() + "\r\n";
}
```

In some cases, you want to combine the techniques you've used in the past to create a particular output. This LINQ query begins with a list box filled with data as shown in Figure 6-2. Notice that this is just a list of numbers from 1 to 10.

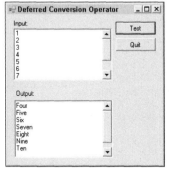

Figure 6-2:
Combining strategies can produce interesting results.

The query begins by converting the number strings into `Int32` values as part of a `Where()`. It then compares each of these values to 3 to determine whether the value is indeed greater than 3. When a value is greater than 3, the code moves to the next processing stage.

Data conversion is a requirement for many applications. This application uses a `Select()` to transform the data into another form with the help of an enumeration, `NumToWord`. The output appears at the bottom of Figure 6-2 as text equivalents of the numbers that met the `Where()` criterion.

Working with OfType and Where

The filtering operators help you exclude or include elements in a sequence based on specific criteria. Using a filter helps you eliminate unneeded information. The `OfType` operator is one of the few repeated operator names that LINQ uses. The "Working with AsEnumerable, AsQueryable, Cast, and OfType" section of the chapter describes the other use for the `OfType` operator. Listing 6-4 shows an example of using the filtering operators. You'll find this example in the `\Chapter 06\Filtering` folder of the source code for this book.

Listing 6-4   Implementing the Filtering Operators

```
private void btnTest_Click(object sender, EventArgs e)
{
```

(continued)

Listing 6-4 *(continued)*

```
    // Define a test object.
    Dictionary<String, Object> TestData =
        new Dictionary<string, object>();

    // Fill the test object with data.
    TestData.Add("One", 1);
    TestData.Add("Two", "Two");
    TestData.Add("Three", 3);
    TestData.Add("Four", "Four");
    TestData.Add("Five", 5);
    TestData.Add("Six", "Six");

    // Create the query.
    var ThisQuery = TestData.Values.OfType<String>();

    // Display the output.
    foreach (String ThisElement in ThisQuery)
        txtResult.Text = txtResult.Text +
            ThisElement + "\r\n";
}
```

Some objects hold data of mixed types. Use `OfType<T>()` when you need to work with a specific data type. As shown in this code, `OfType<String>()` lets the strings in `TestData` pass but rejects the `int` values. This technique works exceptionally well when you don't know what you'll receive as input, such as when you work with XML data. The output of this example is Two, Four, and Six.

Working with DefaultIfEmpty, Empty, Range, and Repeat

The generation operators create a new sequence based on the criteria you specify. Listing 6-5 shows an example of using the generation operators. You'll find this example in the `\Chapter 06\SimpleQueries` folder of the source code for this book.

Listing 6-5 Implementing the Generation Operators

```
private void btnTest_Click(object sender, EventArgs e)
{
    // Define a test object.
    List<String>   TestData = new List<String>();

    // Create the query.
```

```
      var ThisQuery = from TheData in TestData
                      select TheData;

      // Display the output.
      foreach (var ThisElement in ThisQuery.DefaultIfEmpty())
         txtResult.Text = txtResult.Text +
            ThisElement + "\r\n";

      // Fill the array with data.
      TestData.Add("One");
      TestData.Add("Two");
      TestData.Add("Three");

      // Display the output again.
      foreach (var ThisElement in ThisQuery.DefaultIfEmpty())
         txtResult.Text = txtResult.Text +
            ThisElement + "\r\n";
   }
```

It's possible that you'll make a query against an empty object and need to overcome this problem with the least possible application impairment. Rather than letting the application simply fail, you can provide a default value for the query, which is the purpose of the DefaultIfEmpty() method. In this case, the application begins with an empty List object. The foreach loop handles the problem by calling DefaultIfEmpty(). Unfortunately, if you rely on the default setup, DefaultIfEmpty returns a null result set, which isn't particularly helpful — you need to create a DefaultIfEmpty() handler. Listing 6-6 shows the DefaultIfEmpty() handler for this example.

Listing 6-6   Defining a DefaultIfEmpty() Handler

```
public static class MyStrings
{
   // The DefaultIfEmpty() function may use a specific
   // or generic data type.
   public static IEnumerable<string>
      DefaultIfEmpty(this IEnumerable<string> source)
   {
      // Pass the original data if the source isn't null.
      if (source.Count<String>() > 0)
         return source;
      else
      {
         // Create a new value to pass back to the caller.
         List<string> DefaultValue = new List<string>();

         // Fill the new value with data.
         DefaultValue.Add("Empty");
```

(continued)

Listing 6-6 *(continued)*

```
        // Return the value.
        return DefaultValue;
    }
  }
}
```

Logically, you may think that the code will only have to handle the situation where the application receives an empty object. However, reality is different. Trace the example with the debugger and you'll discover that LINQ calls the DefaultIfEmpty() handler for each query.

The first query is empty for this example, so the code returns a new List that contains a single string, Empty. At least this output tells the user that something is empty rather than completely missing.

The second query has a List that contains the values One, Two, and Three. In this case, the DefaultIfEmpty() handler must detect the presence of the values and return the original List to the caller. Otherwise, the application will still display the default value you provide. Note how the code uses Count<String>() to perform this task.

Working with GroupBy and ToLookup

The grouping operators help you sort data by a particular characteristic, such as the first letter in a group of strings. The output contains one group for each characteristic. For example, if you group a sequence by the first letter in each string, the groups would consist of sequences of strings that begin with the same letter, such as all strings that begin with the letter *A*. The ToLookup operator has a nondeferred counterpart described in the "Working with ToArray, ToDictionary, ToList, and ToLookup" section of the chapter. Listing 6-7 shows an example of using the grouping operators. You'll find this example in the \Chapter 06\Grouping folder of the source code for this book.

Listing 6-7   Implementing the Grouping Operators

```
private void btnTest_Click(object sender, EventArgs e)
{
    // Define a test object.
    String[] TestData = {"One", "Two", "Three", "Four",
                         "Five", "Six", "Seven", "Eight",
                         "Nine", "Ten"};
```

```
// Create the query.
var ThisQuery = from ThisElement in TestData
                group ThisElement
                by ThisElement.Substring(0, 1)
                into Groups
                orderby Groups.Key
                select Groups;

// Display the output.
foreach (var ThisElement in ThisQuery)
{
    txtResult.Text = txtResult.Text +
        ThisElement.Key + "\r\n";
    foreach (String ThisText in ThisElement)
        txtResult.Text = txtResult.Text +
            "   " + ThisText + "\r\n";
}
}
```

Grouping data comes in handy for reports or when you need to categorize the data in some way. This example groups the data by its first letter. Listing 6-7 shows the most flexible way to create a group. The code begins by creating the groups and then ordering them by the group key. Figure 6-3 shows the output from this example. As you can see, this approach would work well for any report that needs data grouped by a particular characteristic.

Figure 6-3:
Use groups
to cat-
egorize
sequences.

You always have options when creating a LINQ query. In this case, you could easily replace the query shown in Listing 6-7 with the one shown here:

```
var ThisQuery = TestData.GroupBy(
    ThisElement => ThisElement.Substring(0, 1));
```

Using a lambda expression makes the query considerably shorter and easier to read. However, you can lose a little flexibility with this approach and sometimes it isn't nearly as easy to discover what has gone wrong with your query when you use a lambda expression. But in the end, it comes down to a stylistic choice.

Working with GroupJoin and Join

The joining operators accept two or more sequences as input and create a single output sequence based on a specific join type and the join criteria. A join can help you create a single data set out of multiple data sources. For example, you can join a list of orders to associated lists of order details and customer details to create a complete set of invoices.

The output also depends on the kind of join you create. LINQ supports a number of join types, including these standard types:

- ✔ Inner
- ✔ Grouped inner
- ✔ Grouped left outer

The joins that LINQ supports don't directly correlate to those used in SQL, so you should assume that you could create precisely the same joins in both languages. Chapters 2, 4, 5, 7, 8, and 9 contain a number of join examples that you can use to discover more about these operators.

Working with Skip, SkipWhile, Take, and TakeWhile

The partitioning operators help you section a sequence to locate specific information. Listing 6-8 shows an example of using the partitioning operators. You'll find this example in the `\Chapter 06\Partitioning` folder of the source code for this book.

Listing 6-8   Implementing the Partitioning Operators

```
private void btnTest_Click(object sender, EventArgs e)
{
    // Define a test object.
    String[] TestData = {"One", "Two", "Three", "Four",
                         "Five", "Six", "Seven", "Eight",
```

```
                         "Nine", "Ten"};

   // Create the query.
   var ThisQuery =
      TestData.SkipWhile(
         ThisElement => ThisElement != "Four").
      TakeWhile(ThisElement => ThisElement != "Nine");

   // Display the output.
   foreach (var ThisElement in ThisQuery)
      txtResult.Text = txtResult.Text +
         ThisElement + "\r\n";
}
```

The partitioning operators have a lot of uses. For example, you can divide sequences for easier processing or to eliminate unnecessary elements. This example shows how you can partition a sequence based on the data values it contains. The application outputs the strings Four through Eight based on the two partitioning operators used in this case. The SkipWhile() method skips all of the elements until it reaches Four. The TakeWhile() method stops processing any additional elements when it reaches Nine (making Eight the last element processed).

Working with Select and SelectMany

The projection operators create a new type based on the query you create. The selection process transforms the original data into a new form.

You use Select when you want to create a single new type based on the query you create. The SelectMany operator creates a single output based on multiple, concatenated, input sequences using the criteria you provide. In some respects, SelectMany is a type of join in which you transform the data as part of the joining process. Listing 6-9 shows an example of using the projection operators. You'll find this example in the \Chapter 06\Projection folder of the source code for this book.

Listing 6-9   Implementing the Projection Operators

```
// A class describing favorite numbers.
class MyNumbers
{
   // Each number type name
   public String NumName { get; set; }

   // can have multiple values associated with it.
```

(continued)

Listing 6-9 *(continued)*

```
   public List<Int32> NumValue {get; set; }
}

private void btnTest_Click(object sender, EventArgs e)
{
   // Define a test object.
   List<MyNumbers> TestData =
      new List<MyNumbers>();

   // Fill the test object with data.
   TestData.Add(new MyNumbers
   {
      NumName = "Single Digit",
      NumValue = new List<Int32> {0, 1, 2}
   });
   TestData.Add(new MyNumbers
   {
      NumName = "Double Digit",
      NumValue = new List<Int32> { 10, 21, 32 }
   });
   TestData.Add(new MyNumbers
   {
      NumName = "Triple Digit",
      NumValue = new List<Int32> { 100, 211, 322 }
   });

   // Create the query.
   var ThisQuery =
      TestData.SelectMany(
         ThisElement => ThisElement.NumValue);

   // Display the output.
   foreach (var ThisElement in ThisQuery)
      txtResult.Text = txtResult.Text +
         ThisElement.ToString() + "\r\n";
}
```

You can find lots of examples of the one-to-many data set in the real world, which is the kind of data that `SelectMany()` is designed to handle. In this case, the data set contains a single word that describes a series of numbers. It then includes multiple numbers that fit in that category. It's possible to use this technique with a one-to-many relationship of any sort, but this example points out that you don't necessarily need a database as a data source. This technique is also useful for many XML data sets you must process.

The key to this example is the `MyNumbers` class, which contains a single `String` value and a `List` of numbers. During processing, the example extracts the numbers found in each of the `MyNumbers` objects found in `TestData`. The output from this example is a series of numbers: 0, 1, 2, 10, 21, 32, 100, 211, and 322.

Working with Distinct, Except, Intersect, and Union

The set operators create sets. Think of the set arithmetic you performed in school. The results reflect the kind of set you specify. Listing 6-10 shows an example of using the set operators. You'll find this example in the \Chapter 06\Sets folder of the source code for this book.

Listing 6-10   Implementing the Set Operators

```
private void btnTest_Click(object sender, EventArgs e)
{
    // Define two test arrays.
    String[] First =
        { "One", "Two", "Two", "Three", "Four" };
    String[] Second =
        { "Three", "Four", "Five", "Six" };

    // Create the Distinct query.
    var ShowDistinct = First.Distinct();

    // Display the output.
    txtResult.Text = "Distinct:\r\n";
    foreach (String ThisElement in ShowDistinct)
        txtResult.Text = txtResult.Text +
            ThisElement + "\r\n";

    // Create the Except query.
    var ShowExcept = First.Except(Second);

    // Display the output.
    txtResult.Text = txtResult.Text +
        "\r\n\r\nExcept:\r\n";
    foreach (String ThisElement in ShowExcept)
        txtResult.Text = txtResult.Text +
            ThisElement + "\r\n";

    // Create the Intersect query.
    var ShowIntersect = First.Intersect(Second);

    // Display the output.
    txtResult.Text = txtResult.Text +
        "\r\n\r\nIntersect:\r\n";
    foreach (String ThisElement in ShowIntersect)
        txtResult.Text = txtResult.Text +
            ThisElement + "\r\n";

    // Create the Union query.
```

(continued)

Listing 6-10 *(continued)*

```
var ShowUnion = First.Union(Second);

// Display the output.
txtResult.Text = txtResult.Text +
    "\r\n\r\nUnion:\r\n";
foreach (String ThisElement in ShowUnion)
    txtResult.Text = txtResult.Text +
        ThisElement + "\r\n";
}
```

Set theory may seem like something you last visited in college, but it's also a useful method for working with data of all sorts. This example relies on sets to obtain various results from two arrays, `First` and `Second`. Each array contains a combination of unique and common values so that you can easily see the action of the `Distinct()`, `Except()`, `Intersect()`, and `Union()` methods. Table 6-1 shows the output from this example.

Table 6-1	Set Operator Results
Set Operator	*Output*
Distinct	One, Two, Three, and Four
Except	One and Two
Intersect	Three and Four
Union	One, Two, Three, Four, Five, and Six

Working with OrderBy, OrderByDescending, Reverse, ThenBy, and ThenByDescending

The sorting operators help you put a sequence into a particular order. Ordering the data makes it easier to work with by reducing the difficulty a user encounters locating a particular value. Listing 6-11 shows an example of using the sorting operators. You'll find this example in the `\Chapter 06\ Sorting` folder of the source code for this book.

Listing 6-11   Implementing the Sorting Operators

```
private void btnTest_Click(object sender, EventArgs e)
{
    // Define a test object.
    String[] TestData = {"One", "Two", "Three", "Four",
                         "Five", "Six", "Seven", "Eight",
                         "Nine", "Ten"};

    // Create the query.
    var ThisQuery =
        TestData.OrderByDescending(
            ThisKey => ThisKey.Length).
        ThenBy(ThisKey => ThisKey.Substring(0, 1));

    // Display the output.
    foreach (var ThisElement in ThisQuery)
        txtResult.Text = txtResult.Text +
            ThisElement + "\r\n";
}
```

The code in Listing 6-11 begins with a simple array. It uses the
`OrderByDescending()` method to sort the array by length in descending
order, and then the `ThenBy()` method to sort the array by the first character
in each string.

An interesting result of the sorting criteria for this example is that the order
looks a bit odd until you think about how the strings are sorted. In this case,
the output is Eight, Seven, Three, Four, Five, Nine, One, Six, Two, and Ten. The
first thought you might have is that Five should appear before Four and Ten
should appear before Two. However, note that the code sorts by only the first
letter, so the output is correct. The value Ten originally appears after Two, so
it appears after Two in the output as well. For this reason, you need to exercise care in creating the sort criteria for your applications.

Understanding the Role of Nondeferred Operators

Nondeferred operators let you interpret the results of a query statically. The
results remain the same, even when the data source content changes. You
use these operators when you need consistent results in changing conditions. For example, the combo box control example in Listing 6-1 won't work
without nondeferred operators. Applications present many situations where
you must obtain consistent results despite changes in the data source. The
following operators provide nondeferred interpretation:

- Aggregate
- All
- Any
- Average
- Contains
- Count
- ElementAt
- ElementAtOrDefault
- First
- FirstOrDefault
- Last
- LastOrDefault
- LongCount
- Max
- Min
- SequenceEqual
- Single
- SingleOrDefault
- Sum
- ToArray
- ToDictionary
- ToList
- ToLookup

Creating the Nondeferred Operator Examples

It's time to look at the various nondeferred operators. These examples provide simple examples of how you can use the operators. Going through the examples with the debugger as described in the "Using the debugger to see the simple query in action" section of Chapter 2 will illustrate how LINQ builds an array or other static object. Pay close attention to the static data types that nondeferred queries use when compared to the dynamic queries of the deferred operators. Listing 6-1 actually ends up with a simple array as the output of the query. The following sections examine the various operators by operator class as described in Table 2-1.

Working with Aggregate, Average, Count, LongCount, Max, Min, and Sum

The aggregation operators all help you perform mathematical tasks with a data source. You use them to interpret a group of values in some way, such as finding the maximum of a list of numbers. The output is always a single value that represents the result of the interpretation. Listing 6-12 shows an example of using the aggregation operators. You'll find this example in the \Chapter 06\Aggregation folder of the source code for this book.

Listing 6-12   Implementing the Aggregation Operators

```
private void btnTest_Click(object sender, EventArgs e)
{
   // Define a test object.
   String[] TestData = {"One", "Two", "Three", "Four",
                        "Five", "Six", "Seven", "Eight",
                        "Nine", "Ten"};
   Int32[] TestData2 = { 1, 2, 3, 4, 5 };

   // Create the query.
   var ThisQuery =
      TestData.Aggregate(
         (ThisElement, Next) =>
            ThisElement + "\r\n" + Next);

   // Display the output.
   txtResult.Text = "Strings:\r\n";
   txtResult.Text = txtResult.Text + ThisQuery;

   // Create the query.
   var ThisQuery2 =
      TestData2.Aggregate(
         (ThisElement, Next) => ThisElement + Next);

   // Display the output.
   txtResult.Text =
      txtResult.Text + "\r\n\r\nNumbers:\r\n";
   txtResult.Text =
      txtResult.Text + ThisQuery2.ToString();
}
```

As with some of the other mathematical methods described in this chapter (such as the set operators), you can use the aggregation operators to work with both text and numbers. This example shows how to perform both tasks. In the first case, the code creates a single `String` that contains all the values in the `TestData` array separated by carriage return and linefeed characters.

The important issue is that you work with two elements, `TheElement`, which holds the current element, and `Next`, which holds the next element in the sequence. You can manipulate these two elements in any way needed to provide the output you require, but you must work with both elements. This is one place where tracing through the query sequence with the debugger can prove exceptionally helpful.

The numeric version of the `Aggregate()` method works more like you might expect. In this case, it adds all the numbers in `TestData2` and displays the sum on the screen.

Working with ToArray, ToDictionary, ToList, and ToLookup

The nondeferred conversion operators change the output of a query to a particular type. In all cases, the output represents a specific kind of collection. Different collections work better for specific purposes, so having the right kind of collection can save considerable time and effort as you write your application. (See the "Working with AsEnumerable, AsQueryable, Cast, and OfType" section of the chapter for a list of the deferred conversion operators.) Listing 6-1 shows an example of using the nondeferred conversion operators.

Working with ElementAt, ElementAtOr Default, First, FirstOrDefault, Last, LastOrDefault, Single, and SingleOrDefault

The element operators help you select a particular element in a sequence, even when you don't know any identifying information about that element, such as its name. Using these element operators can help in complex loop processing and make it easier to select data based solely on its position within the sequence. Listing 6-13 shows an example of using the element operators. You'll find this example in the `\Chapter 06\Elements` folder of the source code for this book.

Listing 6-13   Implementing the Element Operators

```
private void btnTest_Click(object sender, EventArgs e)
{
    // Define a test object.
    String[] TestData = {"Zero", "One", "Two", "Three",
                         "Four", "Five", "Six", "Seven",
                         "Eight", "Nine", "Ten"};
    // Create the query.
    var ThisQuery = TestData.First();

    // Display the output.
    txtResult.Text = "First Element: " + ThisQuery;

    // Get the last element.
    ThisQuery = TestData.Last();

    // Display the output.
    txtResult.Text = txtResult.Text +
        "\r\nLast Element: " + ThisQuery;

    // Get a particular element.
    ThisQuery = TestData.ElementAt(5);

    // Display the output.
    txtResult.Text = txtResult.Text +
        "\r\nFifth Element: " + ThisQuery;

}
```

This example shows how you can locate any piece of data in a sequence based on its position within the sequence. It's helpful to compare these operators with some of the other operators discussed in the chapter, such as the partitioning operators. In this case, you see the first, fifth, and last elements in the sequence as output. It doesn't matter what those values are; LINQ will find the element based solely on position.

Working with SequenceEqual

The sole equality operator helps you determine whether two sequences are equal. The sequences are equal when the number of elements and the content of each element are equal. Listing 6-14 shows an example of using the equity operator. You'll find this example in the \Chapter 06\Equality folder of the source code for this book.

Listing 6-14 Implementing the Equality Operator

```csharp
private void btnTest_Click(object sender, EventArgs e)
{
    // Define the test objects.
    String[] Array1 = { "Zero", "One", "Two", "Three"};
    String[] Array2 = { "Zero", "One", "Two", "Three" };
    String[] Array3 = { "Two", "Zero", "One", "Three" };
    String[] Array4 = { "One", "Two", "Three", "Four" };

    // Check Array1 and Array2.
    var ThisQuery = Array1.SequenceEqual(Array2);

    // Display the output.
    txtResult.Text = "Array1 = Array2: " + ThisQuery.
        ToString();

    // Check Array1 and Array3.
    ThisQuery = Array1.SequenceEqual(Array3);

    // Display the output.
    txtResult.Text = txtResult.Text +
        "\r\nArray1 = Array3: " + ThisQuery.ToString();

    // Check Array1 and Array4.
    ThisQuery = Array1.SequenceEqual(Array4);

    // Display the output.
    txtResult.Text = txtResult.Text +
        "\r\nArray1 = Array4: " + ThisQuery.ToString();
}
```

In some cases, you must answer the question of whether two sequences are equal. They may look equal, but not really provide equality. This example has four arrays that contain similar data. However, only Array1 and Array2 are truly equal. Array3 has one of the elements out of order and Array4 has some differences in the array content. Obviously, the equality operator is most useful when you work with complex sequences where comparison isn't easy.

Working with All, Any, and Contains

The quantifier operators help you select elements based on specific criteria. You use these operators to determine whether none, one, or more than one elements meet the selected criteria. All three of these operators output a Boolean value that tells you whether the required information appears anywhere in the sequence. Listing 6-15 shows an example of using the quantifier operators. You'll find this example in the \Chapter 06\Quantifier folder of the source code for this book.

Listing 6-15　Implementing the Quantifier Operators

```
private void btnTest_Click(object sender, EventArgs e)
{
    // Define a test object.
    String[] TestData = {"Zero", "One", "Two", "Three",
                         "Four", "Five", "Six", "Seven",
                         "Eight", "Nine", "Ten"};

    // Create the All query.
    var ThisQuery = TestData.All(
        ThisElement => ThisElement.Length == 4);

    // Display the output.
    txtResult.Text =
        "All elements have 4 characters: " + ThisQuery;

    // Create the Any query.
    ThisQuery = TestData.Any(
        ThisElement => ThisElement.Length == 4);

    // Display the output.
    txtResult.Text = txtResult.Text +
        "\r\n\r\nAt least one element has 4 characters: " +
        ThisQuery;

    // Create the Any query.
    ThisQuery =
        TestData.Contains("Four");

    // Display the output.
    txtResult.Text = txtResult.Text +
        "\r\n\r\nThe sequence contains 'Four': " +
        ThisQuery;
}
```

Quantifying a sequence is important when you need a fast answer regarding whether a sequence even contains the data you want. Rather than spend time reviewing the sequence, you can use the quantifier operators to ask LINQ to perform the task for you. In this case, the application asks LINQ about characteristics of TestData, such as whether all of the elements contain four characters — they don't. However, some of the elements contain four characters, so the Any() method test passes. It's also possible to look for at least one occurrence of a particular data value, such as Four, in this case, using the Contains() method.

hapter 7

to DataSet

• •

Q

t example

perators

bles

• •

s gone through many permutations. However, .NET
the DataSet as a kind of in-memory database. You
ng with a physical database, a Web service, or to
tabases. No matter how you work with the DataSet,
type of relational database model for storing your
data, so it does help you model more complicated scenarios involving data
within a physical database such as SQL Server or MySQL. Consequently, the
DataSet is probably one of the first uses you thought about when you learned
about LINQ. Querying a DataSet is a natural part of the LINQ experience.

This chapter describes both single and multiple table scenarios when using the
LINQ to DataSet provider. The goal of this chapter is to help you discover
the LINQ to DataSet provider, rather than explore specific methods of using the
DataSet control. The specific usage methods appear in other chapters of
this book. For example, you use the LINQ to DataSet provider as part of working with SQL Server in Chapter 8. Of course, Chapter 8 also helps you discover the LINQ to SQL provider. To reduce the complexity of the examples in
this chapter, most of the examples will rely on locally defined data sets.

As part of describing how the LINQ to DataSet provider works, this chapter
also helps you understand the various LINQ to DataSet operators. These
operators add to the capabilities of the standard operators and the deferred
and non-deferred operators used by the LINQ to Object provider. In other
words, the operators described in this chapter are cumulative with the operators you used in the past.

It's important to understand that the `DataSet` control provides considerable functionality. Consequently, you shouldn't view LINQ as a complete solution for your application needs, but rather as a means of augmenting the functionality that the `DataSet` control already provides. This chapter uses the native `DataSet` functionality wherever possible to demonstrate how to combine that functionality with the functionality that LINQ provides. Consequently, you may not see a lot of information about ordering data because the `DataSet` control already handles that need quite well, but you will see a lot about filtering data because this is an area in which the `DataSet` control is weak.

Considering the Use of DataSets with LINQ

You use a data set to organize data and make it easier to access. Consequently, the `DataSet` control includes many of the features of a relational database. However, from a LINQ perspective, the most important feature is that a `DataSet` stores all the data locally. Therefore you use a provider designed to work with local data. A database can also rely on a `DataReader` control. However, the `DataReader` relies on a live connection to the database — the dynamics are difference from the LINQ perspective.

Overall, ADO.NET controls the dynamics of `DataSet` behavior, so you must take this into account when working with the LINQ to DataSet provider. You can see a pictorial representation of the ADO.NET architecture at `http://msdn2.microsoft.com/en-us/library/27y4ybxw(VS.71).aspx`. Notice that the .NET Framework Data Provider only comes into play when working with a database — other data sources, such as XML, interact with the `DataSet` control directly. The direct interaction is important. While the LINQ to SQL provider only lets you interact with SQL Server, using LINQ to DataSet lets you interact with any database that you can access with ADO.NET, including those that rely on an Open DataBase Connectivity (ODBC) connection, such as MySQL.

You can use LINQ to interact with any of the organizational features of a `DataSet`, which provides you with access to the data itself. A `DataSet` contains a number of collections (each of which is represented by a class), including:

- ✔ `DataTableCollection`: Hosts one or more `DataTable` objects that hold the tables used to store the data. The `DataTable` is a container for the `DataRowCollection`, `DataColumnCollection`, and `ConstraintCollection` classes.

✔ `DataRowCollection`: Hosts one or more `DataRow` objects. Each `DataRow` is a single instance of data. When you need to discover an essential piece of information in the database, you se the `DataRowCollection` to do it and interpret the results by viewing the content of individual `DataRow` objects.

✔ `DataColumnCollection`: Hosts one or more `DataColumn` objects. The `DataColumnCollection` defines the schema for the database and each `DataColumn` object describes a single database field. When you want to uncover the database structure, you use a the `DataColumn Collection` to obtain an overview and the `DataColumn` objects to see the details.

✔ `ConstraintCollection`: Contains any number of `UniqueConstraint` and `ForeignKeyConstraint` objects. A table need not have any constraints at all. When it does have constraints, you rely on the `UniqueConstraint` object to interact with the primary key of the database and the `ForeignKeyConstraint` object to determine what will happen in related tables when your application adds, updates, or deletes data.

✔ `DataRelationCollection`: Contains any number of `DataRelation` objects. A `DataSet` need not contain more than one table, which means that you may not see any relations because you must have two or more tables to create a relation. Each `DataRelation` object can contain information about parent or child relation, so you must exercise care when querying this information with LINQ to ensure you establish the proper relationship.

A `DataSet` has a number of other objects connected with it that you won't find discussed in this book because the `DataSet` class already does an admirable job working with them. These classes include: `ExtendedProperties` and `DataView`. You can see a pictorial representation of the `DataSet` object model at `http://msdn2.microsoft.com/en-us/library/zb0sdh0b(VS.80).aspx`.

The overall goal of working with LINQ to DataSet is to add capabilities, not replicate capabilities. In most cases, the native functionality of the `DataSet` control will work more reliably and perform better than something you add to the `DataSet` control using LINQ. However, there are many opportunities to use LINQ to look for information within the `DataSet` or to augment `DataSet` capabilities in other ways. Avoid the potential problems of the gadget mentality — the new product on the block isn't always the right tool for the job, especially when it comes to working with data.

Configuring Visual Studio for LINQ to DataSet

The basic Visual Studio.NET 2008 setup provides LINQ to Object provider functionality with every project. However, if you want to work with LINQ to DataSet, you must perform a little additional work.

The first step is to add the required assembly references. The common assembly reference is `System.Data.DLL`. In addition to this common reference, you also normally need to add the `System.Data.DataSet Extensions.DLL` reference. Adding both of

these references will give your full LINQ to DataSet functionality.

The second step is to reference the namespaces you need. The most common reference is `System.Linq`, of course (such as `using System.Linq;`). You should also add the `System.Data` reference (such as using `System.Data;`). After you make these changes to your project, you should be ready to work with the LINQ to DataSet examples in this chapter.

Creating the Simple DataSet Example

This first example is going to examine an extremely simple scenario — accessing data within a `DataSet` that contains a single `DataTable`. The `DataTable` contains a number of records and the query will extract those matching specific criteria. You'll find this example in the `\Chapter 07\SimpleDataSet` folder of the source code for this book.

Defining the test tables

The examples in this chapter will use some common code to create the `DataSet`. You find this common code in the `CreateDataSet.CS` file included with every example. Using a common `DataSet` will help you make comparisons and reduce the example complexity so you can focus on LINQ. The `DataSet` entries rely on the `WeatherEntry` structure shown here.

```
public struct WeatherEntry
{
    public String Name;
    public DateTime Day;
    public Int16 Temp;
    public Boolean Sunny;
    public Int16 WindSpeed;
    public Double Barometer;
}
```

Real weather entries likely contain far more data than shown here, but the example entry provides a number of data types and makes it possible to create a number of query types. Listing 7-1 shows how the example works with the `WeatherEntry` structure to create a data table. Notice the use of individual methods so that you can use as little or as much of the sample data as required for an example.

Listing 7-1   Creating Test Tables Using a Common Class

```
public static DataSet CreateDS(String DSName,
                               String DTName)
{
   // Create some test data.
   WeatherEntry[] Data = CreateDataSet.CreateQuickData();

   // Create the data set.
   DataTable TestTable =
      CreateDataSet.CreateDT(Data, DTName);
   DataSet ThisDS = new DataSet(DSName);
   ThisDS.Tables.Add(TestTable);

   // Return the result.
   return ThisDS;
}

public static DataTable CreateDT(WeatherEntry[] Entries,
                                 String DTName)
{
   // Create the table.
   DataTable DT = new DataTable(DTName);

   // Add the columns.
   DT.Columns.Add("Name", typeof(String));
   DT.Columns.Add("Day", typeof(DateTime));
   DT.Columns.Add("Temp", typeof(Int16));
   DT.Columns.Add("Sunny", typeof(Boolean));
   DT.Columns.Add("Windspeed", typeof(Int16));
   DT.Columns.Add("Barometer", typeof(Double));

   // Add the data.
   foreach (WeatherEntry ThisEntry in Entries)
      DT.Rows.Add(ThisEntry.Name, ThisEntry.Day,
         ThisEntry.Temp, ThisEntry.Sunny,
         ThisEntry.WindSpeed, ThisEntry.Barometer);

   // Return the data table.
   return DT;
}
```

(continued)

Listing 7-1 *(continued)*

```
public static WeatherEntry[] CreateQuickData()
{
    // Create the weather data.
    WeatherEntry[] QuickData =
    {
        new WeatherEntry {Name = "Joe",
            Day = new DateTime(08, 09, 01),
            Temp = 75, Sunny = true,
            WindSpeed = 10, Barometer=30.02},
        new WeatherEntry {Name = "Ann",
            Day = new DateTime(08, 09, 02),
            Temp = 70, Sunny = false,
            WindSpeed = 25, Barometer=29.35},
        new WeatherEntry {Name = "Sally",
            Day = new DateTime(08, 09, 03),
            Temp = 89, Sunny = true,
            WindSpeed = 0, Barometer=30.15},
        new WeatherEntry {Name = "Irvin",
            Day = new DateTime(08, 09, 04),
            Temp = 84, Sunny = true,
            WindSpeed = 5, Barometer=29.98},
        new WeatherEntry {Name = "Nancy",
            Day = new DateTime(08, 09, 05),
            Temp = 72, Sunny = false,
            WindSpeed = 30, Barometer=29.41},
        new WeatherEntry {Name = "Joe",
            Day = new DateTime(08, 09, 06),
            Temp = 82, Sunny = false,
            WindSpeed = 10, Barometer=29.11}
    };

    // Return the weather data.
    return QuickData;
}
```

All the methods in this class are static so that you can call them directly from the code. The `CreateQuickData()` method defines an array of type `WeatherEntry`. This code relies on the object initializers and collection initializers feature described in Chapter 2. Older versions of C# don't have this feature, but you could easily create the array using the same methods you've employed in the past. When the `CreateQuickData()` method exits, it returns an array of test data — you can substitute your own data as desired to test specific LINQ features.

The `CreateDT()` method accepts an array of type `WeatherEntry`, along with the table name, as input. The code begins by adding columns of specific types to the table. It then uses a `foreach` loop to create the `DataTable` rows. Finally, the `CreateDT()` method returns a `DataTable` to the caller.

The CreateDS() method accepts the name of the DataSet and its associated DataTable as input. This code shows how to work with the other static methods in this class within your own test applications. The output is a DataSet that contains one table and is ready for use with your test applications. This class provides as much automation as is feasible for testing purposes in this chapter. A number of the examples will require a second table that the test code builds as needed.

Outputting the results

The examples all rely on a DataGridView control for display. As a minimum, you must define columns for the DataGridView control before you can fill it with data. Listing 7-2 shows the simple code that this example employs to create columns for each of the outputs.

Listing 7-2   Displaying the Results On Screen

```
public static void AddDGColumns(DataGridView ThisDGV)
{
    // Add the columns.
    ThisDGV.Columns.Add("Name", "Name");
    ThisDGV.Columns.Add("Day", "Day");
    ThisDGV.Columns.Add("Temp", "Temperature");
    ThisDGV.Columns.Add("Sunny", "Sunny?");
    ThisDGV.Columns.Add("WindSpeed", "Wind Speed");
    ThisDGV.Columns.Add("Barometer", "Barometer Reading");
}
```

Exploring the connection

If you've followed the previous sections about creating the test DataSet, it's finally time to define the first LINQ query. A single table DataSet isn't completely out of the question for many application uses, but when working with a database, you'll probably use more tables than shown in Listing 7-3. This example simply provides the basics using a simple DataTable.

Listing 7-3   Defining a Simple LINQ to DataSet Connection

```
private void btnTest_Click(object sender, EventArgs e)
{
    // Obtain a DataSet.
    DataSet TestMe = CreateDataSet.CreateDS("TestDS",
                                            "TestTable");
```

(continued)

Listing 7-3 *(continued)*

```
    // Perform a query.
    var DataOut =
        TestMe.Tables["TestTable"].Rows.Cast<DataRow>().
        Where(
            ThisEntry =>
                ThisEntry.ItemArray[0].ToString() == "Joe");

    // Configure the data grid.
    CreateDataSet.AddDGColumns(dgResult);

    // Display the results.
    foreach (DataRow ThisRow in DataOut)
        dgResult.Rows.Add(ThisRow.ItemArray);
}
```

The code creates a test `DataSet` using the `CreateDataSet` features. The "Defining the test tables" section of the chapter tells you how this class works.

Creating a LINQ query is only a little different from working with queries on arrays and other control types. As when you work with a control, you must begin with `Cast<DataRow>()` in the query or the `TestMe DataSet` won't provide the required functionality. After you perform the cast, you can begin using methods such as `Where()` to refine the query.

It's important to notice the difference in the lambda expression for this query. Look at how the lambda expression accesses a particular element of the `ItemArray` and converts it to a `String` from an object in order to perform the comparison. Another way to formulate this query is to perform the cast into a separate object and then work directly with that object, as shown here:

```
// Perform the cast.
IEnumerable<DataRow> Sequence =
    TestMe.Tables["TestTable"].AsEnumerable();

// Perform the query.
var DataOut = Sequence.Where(
    ThisEntry =>
        ThisEntry.ItemArray[0].ToString() == "Joe");
```

As you'll discover in the "Understanding the LINQ to DataSet Operators" section, LINQ provides some additional operators to make working with a `DataSet` easier. The "Creating the Filtered Output Example" example shows a method for working with fields with greater ease. For now, the example makes the query as needed using conventional methods and the special LINQ to DataSet extensions.

After the code makes the query, it adds the required headers to `dgResult`. It then displays the records returned as part of the query as part of a `foreach` look and displays them in `dgResult`. Notice that you must add the `ThisRow.ItemArray` property using the `dgResult.Rows.Add()` method. Figure 7-1 shows the output of this application.

Figure 7-1: LINQ DataSet queries are quite small and fast.

Name	Day	Temperature	Sunny?	Wind Speed	Barometer Reading
Joe	9/1/0008 12:00...	75	True	10	30.02
Joe	9/6/0008 12:00...	82	False	10	29.11

Simple DataSet — Test / Quit

Understanding the LINQ to DataSet Operators

As with LINQ to Object, you'll find that you work with certain operators when using the LINQ to DataSet provider. Some of these operators, such as the `DataRow` set operators, are common to those found in LINQ to Object and perform essentially the same tasks. Chapter 6 describes the following operators and tells you how to use them.

✔ Distinct

✔ Except

✔ Intersect

✔ Union

✔ SequenceEqual

The main difference in these five operators from what you discovered in Chapter 6 is that you must now consider the `IComparable` interface as part of the LINQ to DataSet provider. The `IComparable` interface makes it possible to work with databases. If you didn't have access to this interface, then LINQ would provide invalid comparisons because comparisons that don't rely in `IComparable` use a hash or other means to perform the comparison. A reference that includes multiple fields will produce the incorrect result in this situation. The examples in the "Working with Multiple DataSet Tables" section of the chapter demonstrate why you need the `IComparable` interface through code.

The `DataRow` field operators are new to LINQ to DataSet. These operators help you interact with database fields efficiently. The following list provides a brief description of each of the `DataRow` field operators.

- ✔ `Field<T>`: Creates a strongly typed connection to each field in a `DataTable`. You use this operator to make field access easier and more reliable, rather than using the `ItemArray` property (as shown in Listing 7-3). The `Field<T>` operator also handles boxing and unboxing of values, as well as `null` values within fields.

- ✔ `SetField<T>`: Sets the value of the specified field. You can use this operator to modify the data in a record as the result of a query. For example, you could create a query on XML input and output it to a SQL Server database. The `SetField<T>` operator ensures that translations occur properly and handles `null` values as needed.

LINQ to DataSet only includes one `DataRowComparer` operator, `Default`. The `Default` operator helps you perform comparisons on `DataRow` objects. This operator works by comparing the individual elements of the `DataRow` object, rather than viewing the `DataRow` object in its entirety (as a reference). None of the `DataSet` comparisons work properly without this operator, so you see it used a lot in this chapter and any chapter that works with databases or data organized as a database (including XML files in some cases).

The `DataTable` operators contain a combination of new and updated operators to help you interact with `DataTable` objects effectively. The purpose of these operators, for the most part, is to let you gain insights into the structure of the `DataTable` or extract the data that it contains. The following list provides a brief description of the `DataTable` operators.

- ✔ `AsDataView`: Reduces the need to perform conversions on a `Data Table` before outputting it. You can use the `DataTable` as a LINQ-enabled view instead.

- ✔ `AsEnumerable`: Provides an alterative to performing a cast on the `DataTable` objects. The "Exploring the connection" section of the chapter provides discussion of the two methods.

- ✔ `CopyToDataTable<DataRow>`: Outputs the specified `DataRow` objects as a `DataTable`. You can use this feature to create a subset of an original table using a LINQ query. The new `DataTable` contains only the rows specified by the query.

Creating the Filtered Output Example

In most cases, you don't display all the content of a data set because the data set usually contains more information than the user really wants. Filtering reduces the amount of data the user must view in order to find a particular piece of information — as the size of the data set increases, the need for filtering increases as well. The following sections demonstrate how to work with filtered output. You'll find this example in the \Chapter 07\FilteredData Set folder of the source code for this book.

Creating a simple display

The first task is to display the filtered output using a query. Listing 7-4 shows how to create a query that filters the data in a DataSet.

Listing 7-4   Filtering Data in a DataSet

```
private void btnTest_Click(object sender, EventArgs e)
{
   // Obtain a DataSet.
   DataSet TestMe = CreateDataSet.CreateDS("TestDS",
                                           "TestTable");

   // Perform the query.
   EnumerableRowCollection<DataRow> DataOut =
      TestMe.Tables["TestTable"].AsEnumerable().Where(
      ThisEntry =>
         ThisEntry.Field<Int16>("WindSpeed") > 9).OrderBy(
      ThisEntry =>
         ThisEntry.Field<String>("Name")).ThenBy(
      ThisEntry => ThisEntry.Field<Double>("Barometer"));

   // Create a view.
   DataView ThisView = DataOut.AsDataView();

   // Display the results.
   dgResult.DataSource = ThisView;
}
```

A DataSet acts as a container for one or more tables. When you access the table, you must do so using the Tables collection as shown in the code and provide an index for the desired table. In this case, the code accesses TestTable.

The query is output to an EnumerableRowCollection object, DataOut. A EnumerableRowCollection is a collection of DataRow objects that are in a form that LINQ can use. If you use var instead of the EnumerableRow Collection class, LINQ creates a generic enumeration that doesn't contain all the functionality required to process the resulting output without a lot of extra code.

Before you can make a query, you must perform the required cast using any of the methods described so far in the book. This example uses the `AsEnumerable()` method.

The query relies on lambda expressions. In this case, the query consists of the `Where()`, `OrderBy()`, and `ThenBy()` methods. Notice the use of the `Field` operator as part of the lambda expression. As you can see, you specify the field's data type and name as part of the input. The conditions work precisely as you've seen with other queries in the book so far.

Data output comes next. In this case, the application takes a two-step shortcut. It first converts the query to a `DataView` using the `AsDataView()` method. The second step uses the `ThisView`, `DataView` object, as the `Data Source` for `dgResult`. The results appear in Figure 7-2. Using this approach means that you give up a little flexibility for less programming. You would need to add code to change the column headings and so on if desired. The columns also appear in the same order as they do within the `DataSet`. Using the `Select()` method in the query would help you partially control the output.

Name	Day	Temp	Sunny	Windspeed	Barometer
Ann	9/2/0008	70	□	25	29.35
Joe	9/6/0008	82	□	10	29.11
Joe	9/1/0008	75	☑	10	30.02
Nancy	9/5/0008	72	□	30	29.41

Modifying the filtered output

It's possible to modify the filtered output that you create. The LINQ to Data Set provider includes the `SetField` operator for this purpose. However, you don't actually change the field as part of the query process. What you do is perform the task as part of post processing in most cases. Listing 7-5 shows one approach to using the `SetField` operator to modify `DataSet` content.

Listing 7-5   Modifying a Filtered DataSet

```
private void btnModify_Click(object sender, EventArgs e)
{
    // Make sure we have data to work with.
```

```
    if (dgResult.DataSource == null)

        btnTest_Click(this, null);

    // Get the data set.
    DataView ThisView = (DataView)dgResult.DataSource;

    // Modify the data.
    foreach (DataRow ThisRow in ThisView.Table.Rows)
        if (ThisRow.Field<Int16>("WindSpeed") > 9 &&
            ThisRow.Field<Boolean>("Sunny") == false)
        ThisRow.SetField<Int16>("WindSpeed", 100);
}
```

In this case, the example simply calls the code shown in Listing 7-4 to display the DataSet when dgResult.DataSource is null. At this point, the DataGridView contains data that you can see. The example changes the Windspeed field to 100 when the data meets specific conditions. The code begins by extracting the data from dgResult.DataSource into the ThisView DataView object. Notice that you must perform the proper cast to make this transfer work.

The DataView object you create from the DataSource property still includes all the rows of the original DataSet. Consequently, when you make a modification to the DataView, the rows filtered from the original query can still appear on screen. In this case, when you view the Table.Rows.Count property, you still see 6 rows, as shown in Figure 7-3. Therefore, to preserve the query results, the update must include logic to protect the original entries in the Where() clause of the query, which is ThisRow.Field<Int16> ("WindSpeed") > 9 for this example. If you suddenly start seeing data that you thought you had filtered out, you may have overwritten your filter during a SetField operator update. You can test the problem in this example by removing the if part of the code to make the foreach loop look like this:

```
foreach (DataRow ThisRow in ThisView.Table.Rows)
    ThisRow.SetField<Int16>("WindSpeed", 100);
```

The query portion of the if statement uses the Field operator. When the query conditions are met, the code relies on the SetField operator to change the data. The SetField requires two inputs. The first input is the name of the field that you want to change. The second input is the new value of that field. You can see the results in Figure 7-4. Compare these results with those shown in Figure 7-2 and you'll see that the Windspeed field now contains 100 when the Sunny field is false.

Figure 7-3:
The debugger shows you interesting facts about LINQ and the DataSet control.

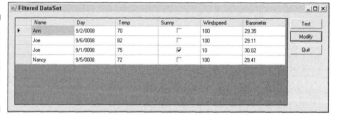

Figure 7-4:
Modifying a data set is easy with LINQ.

Using the CopyToDataTable operator

In some cases, you'll make a query on a source table and need to copy the result to another table. The reasons for performing this task are many. The new `DataTable` may act as a source for additional queries, you might choose to save the new `DataTable` for use by users who can't access all the information, or you may simply need the `DataTable` for extended use within your own application. No matter what your reason may be, the `CopyToDataTable` operator helps you create a new table based on a LINQ query you create. Listing 7-6 shows one example of this technique. You'll find this example in the `\Chapter 07\CopyToDataTableExample` folder of the source code for this book.

Listing 7-6   Copying a Query to a DataTable

```
private void btnTest_Click(object sender, EventArgs e)
{
    // Obtain a DataSet.
```

```
DataSet TestMe = CreateDataSet.CreateDS("TestDS",
                                        "TestTable");

// Perform the query.
EnumerableRowCollection<DataRow> DataOut =
   TestMe.Tables["TestTable"].AsEnumerable().Where(
   ThisEntry =>
      ThisEntry.Field<Boolean>("Sunny") == true).
   OrderBy(ThisEntry =>
      ThisEntry.Field<String>("Name")).ThenBy(
   ThisEntry =>
      ThisEntry.Field<Double>("Barometer"));

// Create a copy of the table.
DataTable SunnyDay = DataOut.CopyToDataTable();

// Modify the table content.
SunnyDay.Columns.Remove("Sunny");
SunnyDay.Columns["WindSpeed"].ColumnName =
   "Wind Speed";
SunnyDay.Columns["Temp"].ColumnName =
   "Temperature";

// Create a view.
DataView ThisView = SunnyDay.AsDataView();

// Display the results.
dgResult.DataSource = ThisView;

// Wait to display the original.
MessageBox.Show("Click OK to see the orignal",
                "See the Original");

// Display the original database.
ThisView = DataOut.AsDataView();
dgResult.DataSource = ThisView;
}
```

The example begins by creating the DataSet. It then defines a query much
like other queries in the chapter. In this case, the output contains a list of all
the sunny days in the DataTable, ordered by the enterer's name and then by
the barometer reading. The result is similar to the output shown in Figure 7-2.

Of course, you really don't need the Sunny column any longer since all the
entries are for sunny days. The code uses the DataOut.
CopyToDataTable() method to copy the table to the SunnyDay
DataTable. This is a true copy of the original DataTable, and not merely a
reference to it. Any changes you make to SunnyDay won't appear in DataOut
(and vice versa).

The code makes some changes to the content of SunnyDay. It removes the Sunny column and then changes the ColumnName properties for both WindSpeed and Temp. The code attaches the result to dgResult using the DataSource property as before. You can see the result in Figure 7-5.

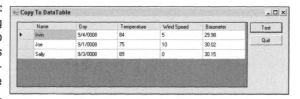

Figure 7-5:
Copying one table to another lets you customize the content.

A big question you may have at this point is whether the original DataSet really is unchanged. The code displays a message box telling you to click OK to see the original. Click OK, at this point, and you'll see that the original DataSet truly is unchanged.

Working with typed DataSets

A typed DataSet provides some significant advantages over using an untyped DataSet. The article at http://msdn2.microsoft.com/en-us/library/8bw9ksd6(VS.80).aspx provides a good overview of the general advantages. From a LINQ perspective, using a typed DataSet offers two main advantages:

✔ The strong typing provided by a typed DataSet tends to reduce application errors.

✔ A typed DataSet requires less code to create a query.

The example in this section shows how the weather database used for the other examples in this chapter would appear as a typed DataSet, which makes it considerably easier to perform a comparison of the various techniques. You'll find this example in the \Chapter 07\TypedDataSet folder of the source code for this book.

Defining the DataSet

Before you can do much with a typed DataSet, you have to create it. This example uses the same DataTable as all of the other examples in this chapter, but this time you use a method that helps you create the DataSet as a typed DataSet. The following steps get you started.

1. **Right-click the project entry in Solution Explorer and choose Add⇨New Item from the context menu.**

   Visual Studio displays the Add New Item dialog box shown in Figure 7-6. If you select the Data category as shown in the figure, it's easier to locate the right entry.

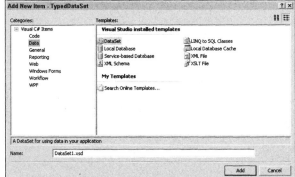

2. **In the Templates list, choose DataSet.**

3. **In the Name field, type a name for the DataSet (the example uses Weather) and click Add.**

   You see a new XSD file opened in Visual Studio. The XSD file is blank for now.

4. **Drag and drop a DataTable object from the Toolbox onto the Design window.**

   The `DataTable` is simply a rectangle that doesn't contain any information. Normally, you want to give the `DataTable` a meaningful name by changing the Name field entry in the Properties window. The example uses WeatherEntries.

5. **Right-click the DataTable object and choose Add⇨Column from the context menu.**

   You see a new column added to the DataTable.

6. **In the Properties window, configure the column as needed.**

   Figure 7-7 shows an example of the WeatherEntries DataTable for this example.

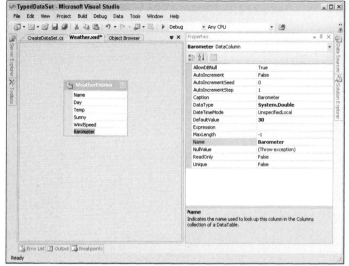

Figure 7-7:
Add columns and configure them to create your DataSet.

7. Repeat Steps 5 and 6 until you've completed the DataSet.

Figure 7-7 shows all the columns used for WeatherEntries.

Working with the typed DataSet

This example shows that it can be easier working with a typed `DataSet` than using the untyped `DataSet` objects found in the other examples in this chapter. Of course, the first step was to create the new `DataSet`. This section shows the second and third steps: filling the DataSet with data and making a query against it. Listing 7-7 shows how the example fills the `Data Set` with data.

Listing 7-7   Defining the DataSet Content

```
// A global typed DataSet.
Weather MyWeather;

public frmMain()
{
    InitializeComponent();

    // Create the DataSet.
    MyWeather = new Weather();
    MyWeather.WeatherEntries.AddWeatherEntriesRow(
        "Joe", new DateTime(08, 09, 01), 75, true, 10,
        30.02);
```

```
    MyWeather.WeatherEntries.AddWeatherEntriesRow(
        "Ann", new DateTime(08, 09, 02), 70, false, 25,
        29.35);
    MyWeather.WeatherEntries.AddWeatherEntriesRow(
        "Sally", new DateTime(08, 09, 03), 89, true, 0,
        30.15);
    MyWeather.WeatherEntries.AddWeatherEntriesRow(
        "Irvin", new DateTime(08, 09, 04), 84, true, 5,
        29.98);
    MyWeather.WeatherEntries.AddWeatherEntriesRow(
        "Nancy", new DateTime(08, 09, 05), 72, false, 30,
        29.41);
    MyWeather.WeatherEntries.AddWeatherEntriesRow(
        "Joe", new DateTime(08, 09, 06), 82, false, 10,
        29.11);
}
```

The difference in using a typed versus untyped `DataSet` makes it possible to reduce the amount of initial code you create (partly because the IDE creates a lot of the code for you). In this case, the example creates a global `Weather DataSet` named `MyWeather`. It then instantiates the object as part of the form constructor and fills it with data using the `AddWeatherEntries Row()` method.

The query phase of this example is incredibly short. Listing 7-8 shows the code you need to make a query that provides the same output as the example in the "Creating a simple display" section of the chapter.

Listing 7-8 Creating a Typed DataSet Query

```
private void btnTest_Click(object sender, EventArgs e)
{
    // Make the query.
    EnumerableRowCollection<Weather.WeatherEntriesRow>
        DataOut = MyWeather.WeatherEntries.
            Where(Condition => Condition.WindSpeed > 9).
            OrderBy(Order => Order.Name).
            ThenBy(Order => Order.Barometer);

    // Display the results.
    dgResult.DataSource = DataOut.AsDataView();
}
```

The example starts out by making the query because it has already created the required `DataSet`. Notice that the query begins with a typed `EnumerableRowCollection<Weather.WeatherEntriesRow>` object, rather than using the generic `EnumerableRowCollection<DataRow>`

object shown in Listing 7-4. The resulting typed object better defines the characteristics of the `DataTable` than using the generic object. As a result, you don't have to use the `Tables` collection to access the `DataTable` or perform a type cast using the `AsEnumerable()` method.

The second surprise is the lambda expressions. Notice that you access the fields directly — you don't need to use the `Field` operator because LINQ knows all about the fields in `MyWeather.WeatherEntries`. The resulting code is considerably shorter and easier to understand, yet performs precisely the same task.

The third change is that you don't have to convert the output to a `DataView` before you add it as a `DataSource` to `dgResult`. Instead of the two-step process shown in Listing 7-4, you can use a single step process that converts the query result directly to a `DataView` using the `AsDataView()` method. Figure 7-8 shows the output from this example.

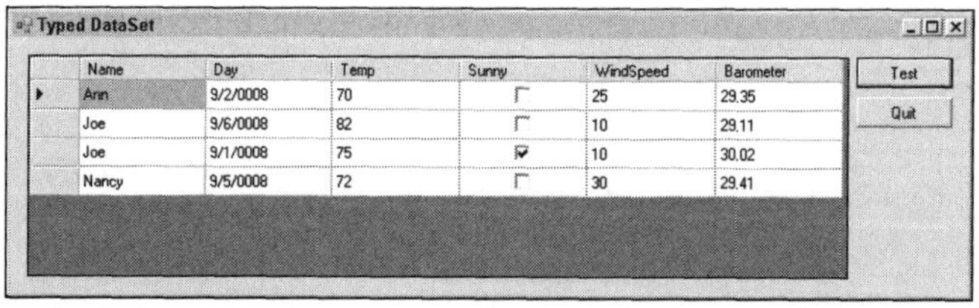

Figure 7-8:
Use typed DataSets to produce code faster when you know the database structure.

Name	Day	Temp	Sunny	WindSpeed	Barometer
Ann	9/2/0008	70	☐	25	29.35
Joe	9/6/0008	82	☐	10	29.11
Joe	9/1/0008	75	☑	10	30.02
Nancy	9/5/0008	72	☐	30	29.41

Both the typed and untyped `DataSets` have a particular place in your toolbox. This chapter won't discuss the intricacies of choosing a particular `DataSet` technology. However, from a LINQ perspective, the rule of thumb is that you use an untyped `DataSet` when you don't know the structure of your database before hand, such as when you access a Web service or ferret out the content of a file on your hard drive. The typed `DataSet` is better when you know how your data appears during design time. As the example in this section demonstrates, the use of a typed or untyped `DataSet` won't affect your ability to create a query. However, the untyped `DataSet` does require a little more work to create a successful query.

Working with Multiple DataSet Tables

As previously mentioned, you'll normally work with more than one table to model complex data in a `DataSet`. A single `DataSet` can hold multiple tables whether or not those tables are related. In some cases, you'll even take seemingly unrelated data, combine it, and create new data patterns. Of course, before you can create the next combination that signals a major scientific breakthrough, you need to consider how to work with multiple tables.

As mentioned earlier, the `IComparable` interface makes it possible to compare two `DataTable` objects in some way and produce a query based on that comparison. The five comparison operators include: `Distinct`, `Except`, `Intersect`, `Union`, and `SequenceEqual`. The examples in this section of the chapter creates two tables, places them in the same DataSet, and performs comparisons on them. You'll find this example in the `\Chapter 07\ MultipleTables` folder of the source code for this book.

The first example works with the `Distinct` operator. The example creates two tables, concatenates them, and then removes the extra entries, as shown in Listing 7-9.

Listing 7-9   Obtaining Distinct Results

```
private void btnDistinct_Click(object sender, EventArgs e)
{
    // Obtain a DataSet.
    DataSet TestMe = CreateDataSet.CreateDS("TestDS",
                                            "Table1");

    // Add a second table.
    TestMe.Tables.Add(
        CreateDataSet.CreateDT(
            CreateDataSet.CreateQuickData2(), "Table2"));

    // Concatenate the two tables.
    IEnumerable<DataRow> Combined =
        TestMe.Tables["Table1"].AsEnumerable().Concat(
            TestMe.Tables["Table2"].AsEnumerable()).
                OrderBy(ThisRow => ThisRow.
                    Field<DateTime>("Day"));

    // Perform the query.
    IEnumerable<DataRow> DataOut =
        Combined.Distinct(DataRowComparer.Default);

    // Add the headings.
    CreateDataSet.AddDGColumns(dgResult);

    // Display the results.
    foreach (DataRow ThisItem in DataOut)
        dgResult.Rows.Add(ThisItem.ItemArray);
}
```

This example begins by creating a `DataSet` using the same method as before. It adds a `CreateQuickData2()` method that works just like the `CreateQuickData()` method explained in Listing 7-1. The only difference is that `CreateQuickData2()` adds a few entries and modifies one for the comparison examples in this section of the chapter.

The next step is to concatenate the two tables in the `DataSet` into a single table named `Combined` using the `Concat()` method. The query also orders the entries by the `Day` field so that you can see them in order. Notice that you must include the `AsEnumerable()` method call for both tables or the compiler will display an error.

At this point, `Combined` has a number of duplicate entries in it. The code removes these duplicates using the `Distinct()` method. Notice the use of `DataRowComparer.Default`. If you don't include this `IEqualityComparer` reference, the output will display all the entries in `Combined`, not just the unique entries. Unlike collections, you must include an `IEquityComparer` for comparisons to work with a `DataSet` or database.

Now that `Combined` has distinct values in it, the code displays the results on screen. Figure 7-9 shows the output of this example. Notice that the first entry varies only by the Wind Speed column.

Figure 7-9:
Use Distinct to remove duplicate entries from the DataTable.

Name	Day	Temperature	Sunny?	Wind Speed	Barometer Reading
Joe	9/1/0008 12:00...	75	True	10	30.02
Joe	9/1/0008 12:00...	75	True	11	30.02
Ann	9/2/0008 12:00...	70	False	25	29.35
Sally	9/3/0008 12:00...	89	True	0	30.15
Irvin	9/4/0008 12:00...	84	True	5	29.98
Nancy	9/5/0008 12:00...	72	False	30	29.41
Joe	9/6/0008 12:00...	82	False	10	29.11
Amy	9/7/0008 12:00...	82	True	12	30.11

Using Multiple Tables — Buttons: Distinct, Except, Intersect, Union, Seq Equal, Quit

You use the `Except` operator to display the differences between two `DataTable` objects, just as you do when working with objects. Listing 7-10 shows an example of how you could use the `Except` operator for `DataTable` comparisons.

Listing 7-10   Using the Except Operator

```
private void btnExcept_Click(object sender, EventArgs e)
{
    // Obtain a DataSet.
```

```
        DataSet TestMe = CreateDataSet.CreateDS("TestDS",
                                                "Table1");

        // Add a second table.
        TestMe.Tables.Add(
            CreateDataSet.CreateDT(
                CreateDataSet.CreateQuickData2(), "Table2"));

        // Perform the query.
        IEnumerable<DataRow> DataOut =
            TestMe.Tables["Table1"].AsEnumerable().
                Except(TestMe.Tables["Table2"].AsEnumerable(),
                    DataRowComparer.Default);

        // Add the headings.
        CreateDataSet.AddDGColumns(dgResult);

        // Display the results.
        foreach (DataRow ThisItem in DataOut)
            dgResult.Rows.Add(ThisItem.ItemArray);
}
```

The code begins by creating the `DataSet` with the two `DataTable` objects as before. The next step is to create the query. The order of the `DataTable` entries in the query makes a big difference. Using the code shown in Listing 7-10, you see only one entry in the output because there's only one difference using this query. However, if you reverse the table names, you see two entries in the output because `Table2` contains two differences from `Table1`. In short, your query must consider the order of the `DataTable` entries or you'll obtain the wrong results. The output code for this example is the same as shown in Listing 7-9.

Intersection tells you which elements are the same between two tables. By combining the `Except` and `Intersect` queries, you can compare inputs from two different sources to troubleshoot specific problems. The first operator tells you about the differences between the two tables, while the second operator tells you about the common entries. You can use this output to locate errors between the two tables and repair them. As with the `Except` operator, the order of the `DataTable` entries matter when using the `Intersect` operator. Here's an example of using the `Intersect` operator for a query:

```
// Perform the query.
IEnumerable<DataRow> DataOut =
    TestMe.Tables["Table1"].AsEnumerable().
        Intersect(TestMe.Tables["Table2"].AsEnumerable(),
            DataRowComparer.Default);
```

In this case, you see five entries in the output. The `Table1 DataTable` contains six entries. The first entry differs from the corresponding entry in `Table2`, so you only see five rows in the output.

The `Union` operator produces a result that looks just like the `Distinct` operator results in Listing 7-9. However, you don't need to concatenate the tables. Using the `Union` operator outputs a list of unique elements in both tables. This is one operator where order doesn't matter. Here's an example of the `Union` operator in action:

```
// Perform the query.
IEnumerable<DataRow> DataOut =
    TestMe.Tables["Table1"].AsEnumerable().
        Union(TestMe.Tables["Table2"].AsEnumerable(),
            DataRowComparer.Default).
        OrderBy(ThisRow => ThisRow.Field<DateTime>("Day"));
```

The final operator, `SequenceEqual`, outputs a simple Boolean value that tells you whether two sequences are equal. In this case, the two `DataTable` objects must be equal in every way — structure and content. Obviously, the two references need not be equal. Here's an example of a `SequenceEqual` query:

```
// Perform the query.
Boolean DataOut =
    TestMe.Tables["Table1"].AsEnumerable().
        SequenceEqual(
            TestMe.Tables["Table2"].AsEnumerable(),
            DataRowComparer.Default);
```

Chapter 8

LINQ to SQL Server

In This Chapter

▶ Using SQL Server databases with LINQ

▶ Getting and installing the Northwind database

▶ Developing a simple SQL Server query

▶ Creating LINQ to SQL entity classes with Object Relational Designer

▶ Working with the SQL Server operators

*T*he LINQ to SQL provider helps you create the complex connections required by SQL Server databases and query those sources quickly. The use of LINQ to SQL as the name for this provider is a bit of a misnomer. You can use the provider only with SQL Server. If you want to create a connection to another kind of a database, you must use the LINQ to DataSet provider at this time. Microsoft may eventually update LINQ to SQL so that it lives up to its name.

Don't get the idea, however, that LINQ to SQL lacks functionality. This provider builds on the functionality of both LINQ to Object and LINQ to DataSet to provide a significant set of database query and manipulation features. As with LINQ to DataSet, you can use the features found in LINQ to SQL to modify database content, as well as work with structural elements. Of course, you still want to use the native functionality that Microsoft provides with Visual Studio to perform most maintenance tasks. LINQ to SQL augments this native functionality and makes SQL Server easier to work with.

Besides showing you how to create basic LINQ queries with SQL Server, this chapter also explores the operations, entity classes, and operators that LINQ provides to work with SQL Server. These features help you create complex queries with a minimum of code, so understanding them is essential. The chapter contains examples to demonstrate all the techniques you need to use these new features.

This chapter uses SQL Server 2008 for its examples. At the time of writing, SQL Server 2008 was still in late beta (as a Community Technology Preview, or CTP). The reason I used SQL Server 2008 is that it offers some opportunities for using LINQ not found in SQL Server 2005. You may find that a few details have changed when you read this book, but the SQL Server 2008 examples should still work fine.

LINQ to SQL differences for Visual Basic

Visual Basic presents a few differences when it comes to LINQ to SQL. You'll be able to use the material in this chapter without problem, but it pays to know about the small differences to avoid frustrating hours of trying to ferret out the minor problem in your code. The following list provides some articles you can consult to discover the small differences in LINQ to SQL for the Visual Basic developer:

✔ Query a Database by Using LINQ (Visual Basic): http://msdn2.microsoft.com/en-us/library/bb907138.aspx

✔ Call a Stored Procedure by Using LINQ (Visual Basic): http://msdn2.microsoft.com/en-us/library/bb918119.aspx

✔ Modify Data in a Database by Using LINQ (Visual Basic): http://msdn2.microsoft.com/en-us/library/bb907191.aspx

✔ Combine Data with LINQ by Using Joins (Visual Basic): http://msdn2.microsoft.com/en-us/library/bb918093.aspx

---

Considering the Use of SQL Server with LINQ

As mentioned, LINQ to SQL focuses on working with SQL Server, but it builds on the functionality provided by both LINQ to Object and LINQ to DataSet. One of the major features that LINQ to SQL provides is mapping. When you create an application, it creates objects that represent real world objects. The objects can nest data several levels deep depending on how the real world object is constructed. SQL Server is a relational database that represents the real world as a series of tables. Consequently, your application views data differently from SQL Server. LINQ to SQL seamlessly maps the object representation of data in your application to the relational table representation of data in SQL Server. The mismatch in representations that most developers experience when working with SQL Server is overcome mostly by LINQ to SQL through mapping. LINQ to SQL provides two methods for creating the required entity classes and associations:

✔ SQLMetal: A command line tool that works well for scripted and batched scenarios.

✔ Object Relational Designer: Also called O/R Designer, this tool provides an easy-to-use graphical interface for creating entity classes one at a time.

Part of the reason why you want to perform this mapping between your application and the SQL Server database during design time is to make the database transparent to the Visual Studio IDE. Creating the map means that you now have access to the same features when working with the database as you do when working with your code, such as IntelliSense to help you interact with the database more efficiently and with fewer errors. Fewer errors translate into fewer bugs, as well, and more time spent relaxing during the weekend.

Another reason to perform the mapping is to provide a means to handle certain problematic issues in the background. For example, concurrency issues are a major problem for most developers. You may already spend a considerable amount of time writing code to keep two users from butting heads over a piece of data. Using LINQ to SQL can help solve that problem, at least partially.

The secret of the ability of LINQ to SQL to do so much for you is in the `DataContext` class. To use this feature, you create a new class for the specific database and derive it from the `DataContext` class. The derived class normally has the same name as the database and contains all the details about the database structure. Consequently, when you want to access the Customers table in the Northwind database, you simply instantiate an object based on the `Northwind` class derived from the `DataContext` class and access the various members of the database by name. IntelliSense will even help you use the correct table, field, view, and other element names.

LINQ to SQL also relies on classes for specific entities, such as tables. These entity classes are part of the mapping process. In most cases, an entity class points to a particular table in the database. The entity class properties include the fields in the table, so you can access the table as if it were any other object in your application, rather than trying to think of the database as a combination of tables and fields.

An entity class also contains attributes for the primary and foreign keys in the database. These associations help you discover the parent/child relationships in the database. You find special properties in the entity class that point to a collection in a child relationship. For example, when working with the `Customer` entity class, you find an `Orders` property that points to a collection of orders made by that customer. The `Order` entity class also has a property named `Customer` that points to the parent of the relationship so that you can find which customer made a particular order.

You can do a lot with LINQ to SQL. However, this product isn't the end of the database line. For example, LINQ to SQL doesn't provide support for entity inheritance. You may find that some situations require more flexibility and more features than those provided in LINQ to SQL. In this case, you can also try LINQ to Entities (`http://msdn2.microsoft.com/en-us/library/bb386964.aspx`) to meet your database needs. LINQ to Entities is an order of magnitude more complex to use and therefore doesn't appear as part of this book. If you want help deciding which LINQ provider to use, check out the article at `http://dotnetaddict.dotnetdevelopersjournal.com/adoef_vs_linqsql.htm`.

Configuring Visual Studio for LINQ to SQL

The basic Visual Studio .NET 2008 setup provides LINQ to Object provider functionality with every project. However, if you want to work with LINQ to SQL, you must perform a little additional work.

The first step is to add the required assembly references. The common assembly references are `System.Data.DLL` and `System.Data.Linq.DLL`. You also normally need to add the `System.Data.DataSetExtensions.DLL` reference. Adding all three references will give you full LINQ to SQL functionality and also provide full LINQ to DataSet functionality.

The second step is to reference the namespaces you need. The most common reference is `System.Linq` (such as using `System.Linq;`). You should also add the `System.Data` reference (such as using `System.Data;`). After you make these changes to your project, you should be ready to work with the LINQ to SQL examples in this chapter.

This chapter also requires that you add a special using `NWind;` statement. This statement provides access to the entity classes file you create in the "Generating the Northwind entity classes and XML mapping files" section of the chapter. Depending on the database configuration for your application, you may need to add several of these entity classes statements to your application when working with LINQ for SQL.

Obtaining and Installing the Northwind Database

The examples in this chapter use the Northwind database. The Northwind and Pubs databases used to come with all Microsoft database products, but Microsoft recently replaced them with the AdventureWorks database. AdventureWorks is an interesting database, but it's complex and focuses more on demonstrating every possible SQL Server 2008 feature than on providing a good database, so this book uses the Northwind database that comes with all older versions of SQL Server. The reasons for using this database are threefold:

- ✔ The Northwind database is simple, making it a better choice than AdventureWorks when creating LINQ examples. Yes, LINQ works just fine with AdventureWorks, but the book would require more code to do it and the point is to make the examples useful to anyone.

- ✔ The Northwind database is familiar. You don't need a newer version of SQL Server to use it, and because LINQ works just find with SQL Server 2000, using Northwind is an advantage.

- ✔ It's easy to locate and download a copy of the Northwind database. Even if Microsoft decides to stop supporting Northwind at some point, you'll probably find it on other Web sites.

Everything you discover in this chapter also applies to any other database you work with, so you shouldn't feel that working with Northwind leaves you without practical skills for newer databases. The following sections describe how to download, install, and work with the Northwind database from LINQ.

Downloading the database

Unfortunately, you won't find either the Pubs or Northwind database installed as part of the default SQL Server 2008 installation — you won't find an option for installing them either. Consequently, you need to download and install these databases if you have a newer version of SQL Server. You can find scripts for creating these databases in SQL Server online at http://www.microsoft.com/downloads/details.aspx?familyid=06616212-0356-46a0-8da2-eebc53a68034. The name of the file you'll receive is SQL2000SampleDb.MSI. Even though Microsoft originally created this file for SQL Server 2000, it works just fine with SQL Server 2008. After you download the script files, you'll need to run them using the following steps:

1. **Right-click the file and choose Install from the context menu.**

   A Welcome dialog box tells you that this file contains the sample databases for SQL Server 2000.

2. **Click Next, read the licensing agreement, choose I Agree, and click Next.**

   You see a Choose Installation Options dialog box. The dialog box contains a single option and you really can't change anything here.

3. **Click Next.**

   The wizard displays a Confirm Installation dialog box.

4. **Click Next.**

   The wizard begins installing the scripts.

5. **If you're using Vista or Windows Server 2008 and have default security enabled, you see a UAC message. Click Continue.**

   When the installation completes, the wizard displays an Installation Complete dialog box.

6. **Click Close.**

   The installation program closes.

At this point, you have two scripts for creating the sample databases. If you used the default installation settings, these files appear in the \SQL Server 2000 Sample Databases folder of your machine. The InstNwnd.SQL file will create the Northwind database and the InstPubs.SQL file will create the Pubs database.

Installing the database

Installing the SQL Server 2000 sample databases didn't add the databases to your copy of SQL Server. Use the following steps to install the databases in SQL Server:

1. **Open an administrator command prompt by choosing Start➪Programs➪Accessories, right-clicking Command Prompt, and choosing Run As Administrator from the context menu.**

   An administrator command prompt has administrator privileges so you don't have to constantly grant permission to perform some tasks. If you're using Vista or Windows Server 2008 and have default security enabled, you see a UAC message. Click Continue to open the command prompt. The administrator command prompt has the word *Administrator* as part of the title bar, as shown in Figure 8-1.

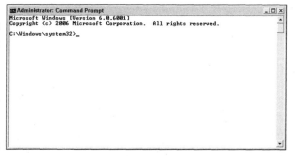

Figure 8-1:
Make sure you open an administrator command prompt.

2. **Type** CD "\SQL Server 2000 Sample Databases" **and press Enter.**

   You see the \SQL Server 2000 Sample Databases folder on your machine.

3. **Type** OSQL -E -i InstNwnd.SQL **and press Enter.**

   The case of the Object-oriented Structured Query Language (OSQL) utility command line switches is important. The -E and -e command line switches are different, as are the -I and -i command line switches. Make sure you use the correct case for the command line switches when installing the two databases.

   The -E command line switch tells OSQL to use a trusted connection. When you specify this command line switch, OSQL uses a Windows Authentication connection and supplies the credentials for the current user account. The -i command line switch provides OSQL with the name of the input (script) file, which is InstNwnd.SQL in this case. The OSQL utility is a powerful command line utility you use to interact with SQL Server. Discover more about this utility at `http://msdn2.microsoft.com/en-us/library/aa213090(SQL.80).aspx`.

The OSQL utility creates the Northwind database for you (this process can take quite some time). When the utility is finished, you'll see the command line along with what appears as nonsensical output, as shown in Figure 8-2.

Figure 8-2:
The OSQL utility runs for quite a while and displays output like this as it completes.

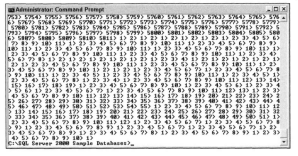

4. **Type** OSQL -E -i InstPubs.SQL **and press Enter.**

The process you saw for the Northwind database will repeat.

Verify that the installation worked as anticipated by opening a copy of SQL Server Management Studio. Open the `Databases` folder. You should see both the Northwind and Pubs databases shown in Figure 8-3.

Figure 8-3:
Verify that the databases installed as anticipated.

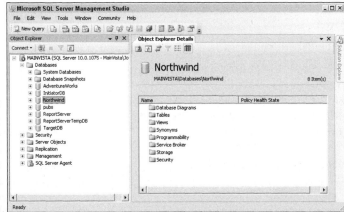

If you try to run the OSQL utility and find that you receive an error message at the command prompt, it means that the SQL Server installation didn't modify the path information for your system as it should have. In some cases, this makes your installation suspect and you should reinstall the product if you experience other problems. To use the installation scripts, add the SQL Server application path to the path statement. Type **Path = %PATH%;\Program Files\Microsoft SQL Server\100\Tools\Binn** and press Enter at the command line. (Older versions of SQL Server use either 90 or 80 for the path in place of 100, so you may need to change this command to match your version of SQL Server.) You can run the OSQL utility at the command prompt from this folder to create the two sample databases.

Testing the Visual Studio connection

You'll want to test the connection from Visual Studio. Open a copy of Visual Studio and use the following steps to test the database connection:

1. **Choose View➪Server Explorer.**

   You see the Server Explorer.

2. **Right-click Data Connections and choose Add Connection from the context menu.**

3. **If you haven't chosen a data source previously, you see the Choose Data Source dialog box. Select Microsoft SQL Server in the Data Source list and click Continue.**

   Server Explorer displays the Connection Properties dialog box shown in Figure 8-4 (this one already has all the information filled out).

4. **In the Select or Enter a Server Name field, type the name of your machine.**

5. **Click the down arrow in the Select or Enter a Database Name field.**

   You should see both the Northwind and Pubs databases, as shown in Figure 8-4. If you don't see these entries, it means an error occurred. Try running the scripts a second time. A second failure usually means there's a problem with your SQL Server setup and you might need to reinstall the product. At this point, you need to make sure you can access the database.

6. **Choose the Northwind database.**

7. **Click Test Connection.**

   When the scripts install the databases properly and you can access them, you'll see a success message.

8. **Click OK to clear the success message and Cancel to clear the Database Connection dialog box.**

9. **You can close Visual Studio if desired.**

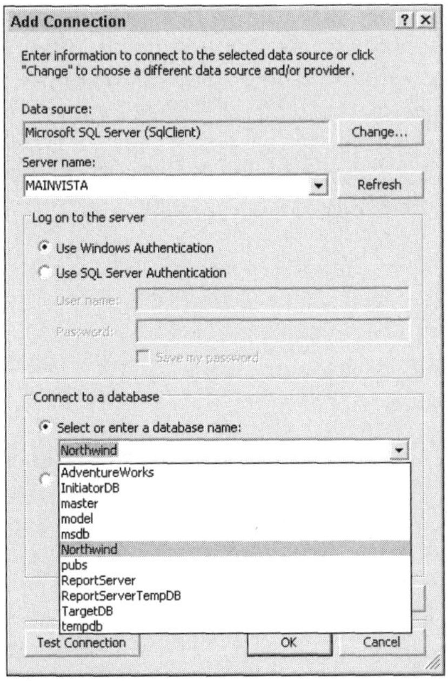

Figure 8-4:
Use the
Connection
Properties
dialog box
to check
for the two
databases.

Because you're the only one using SQL Server, you don't need to worry about
assigning login permissions for the test database. If you want to test any applications created in this book with the full version of SQL Server, you'll probably need to assign login permissions to the test database to ensure that they
work as anticipated.

Generating the Northwind entity classes and XML mapping files

Visual Studio 2008 includes a new tool called SQLMetal that helps you generate classes for your databases just like Object Relational Designer does.
The reason you need this tool is to create entity classes for the Northwind
database. The "Understanding the LINQ to SQL Entity Classes" section of
the chapter describes entity classes in detail. For now, you need to know
that you require these entity classes to use LINQ to SQL with the Northwind
database. If you have an older version of Visual Studio, you can download the
SQLMetal tool from `http://msdn2.microsoft.com/en-us/library/`
`bb386987.aspx`.

SQLMetal is a command line tool, so knowing how to work at the command line is a plus. However, some people find the command line daunting, so someone came up with a user interface for SQLMetal. You can download this tool at http://sourceforge.net/projects/sqlmetalbuilder/. This chapter uses the command line version to make things easier to understand and a little faster. It pays to try both the command line and the Windowed version of SQLMetal, however, to see which version you like better.

In addition to the entity classes, you may also need XML mapping files to use the Northwind database in some cases. The basic examples in this chapter don't use the XML mapping file, so you can skip creating the XML mapping file if you only plan to work with the basic examples (simply omit the /Map command line switch).

The following steps show how to create the Northwind entity classes and XML mapping files without telling you much about how entity classes work. The procedure assumes that you don't have a lot of experience at the command line. It's important to follow every step or you may end up with an unusable configuration. The procedure assumes also that you're working with Vista or Windows Server 2008 — some steps are overkill in Windows XP and Windows 2003 because these older versions of Windows lack the strict security of the newer versions:

1. **Choose Start➪Programs➪Microsoft Visual Studio 2008➪Visual Studio Tools. Right-click Visual Studio 2008 Command Prompt and choose Run As Administrator from the context menu.**

   Windows opens an administrator command prompt that looks similar to the one shown in Figure 8-1. However, this one has additional features for working with Visual Studio. The title bar also says *Administrator: Visual Studio 2008 Command Prompt.*

2. **Type** MD \Northwind **and press Enter.**

   Windows creates a new folder named Northwind.

3. **Type** CD \Northwind **and press Enter.**

   You see the Northwind folder you just created. This folder will hold the files you need to work with the Northwind database. You'll add these files to your project and add a using statement to use the generated classes within your application.

4. **Type** SQLMetal /Server:<Server Name> /User:<User Name> / Password:<Password> /Database:Northwind /Namespace:NWind / Code:Northwind.CS /Map:Northwindmap.XML /Pluralize /Functions / Sprocs /Views **and press Enter.**

The /Server command line switch tells SQLMetal which SQL Server instance to use. The /User and /Password command line switches provide your credentials for accessing the SQL Server instance. The / Database command line switch is the name of the database to use in SQL Server. The remaining command line switches affect the output files that SQLMetal creates for you. Use the /Namespace command line switch to determine the namespace for the C# code file specified with the / Code command line switch (always include the CS file extension). You create an XML mapping file using the /Map command line switch (always include the XML file extension). The /Pluralize command line switch tells SQLMetal to automatically pluralize or singularize class names based on their use in an object environment (such as Customer for a table or Orders for a collection). Adding the /Functions, Sprocs, and Views command line switches tell SQLMetal to extract the functions, stored procedures, and views, respectively, from the database file, in addition to the database structure. SQLMetal provides a number of other command line switches that you'll find explained at `http://msdn2.microsoft.com/en-us/library/bb386987.aspx`.

If your SQL Server setup uses Windows authentication, you can skip the /User and /Password command line switches. Some earlier documentation for SQLMetal shows that you can generate the code and mapping files separately. SQLMetal no longer allows this option — you must use the /Code and /Map command line switches together. You also have the option of using the /Code command line switch by itself.

SQLMetal connects to your SQL Server and opens the Northwind database for use. It then generates the files you need to work with the Northwind database, including all functions, stored procedures (sprocs), and views. All this code resides in the NWind namespace, so you need to add `using NWind` to your code files to access the resulting classes. All the code resides in the `Northwind.CS` file. The mapping information appears in the `Northwindmap.XML` file. Your output should look like the output in Figure 8-5 when the utility runs without error.

Figure 8-5: Create the entity classes you need when working with the sample applications.

```
Administrator: Visual Studio 2008 Command Prompt

C:\Northwind>SQLMetal /Server:MainVista /Database:Northwind /Namespace:NWind /Co
de:Northwind.CS /Map:Northwindmap.XML /Pluralize /Functions /Sprocs /Views
Microsoft (R) Database Mapping Generator 2008 version 1.00.21022
for Microsoft (R) .NET Framework version 3.5
Copyright (C) Microsoft Corporation. All rights reserved.

C:\Northwind>_
```

Creating the Simple SQL Server Query Example

The example in this section creates a simple connection to the Customers table in the Northwind database and displays the list of customers in Oregon. The following sections explore several issues in working with SQL Server 2008. The first is that, at the time of writing, you can't create an automatic connection to SQL Server 2008, but it's easy to overcome the problem. The examples will work with any version of SQL Server you own — the code doesn't do anything fancy. You'll find this example in the `\Chapter 08\ SimpleDataQuery` folder of the source code for this book.

Overcoming the Visual Studio 2008 connectivity issues

It seems odd, but you can't create an automatic connection to SQL Server 2008 with Visual Studio 2008 — at least not as of this writing. Microsoft will undoubtedly fix this problem with a future service pack, so you may not need to use this section at all. You can, however, use LINQ with SQL Server 2008 just fine. Follow these steps to see the problem yourself:

1. **Open Visual Studio.**

2. **Choose View⇨Server Explorer.**

   You see the Server Explorer pane.

3. **Right-click Data Connections and choose Add Connection from the context menu.**

4. **If you haven't chosen a data source previously, you see the Choose Data Source dialog box. Select Microsoft SQL Server in the Data Source list and click Continue.**

   Server Explorer displays the Connection Properties dialog box shown in Figure 8-4 (this one already has all the information filled out).

5. **In the Select or Enter a Server Name field, type the name of your machine.**

6. **Click the down arrow in the Select or Enter a Database Name field.**

   You should see both the Northwind and Pubs databases, as shown in Figure 8-4. If you don't see these entries, it means that an error occurred. Try running the scripts a second time. A second failure usually means that there's a problem with your SQL Server setup and you might need to reinstall the product. At this point, you need to make sure you can access the database.

7. Choose the Northwind database.

8. Click OK.

You'll see an error message at this point, if Microsoft hasn't fixed the problem, as shown in Figure 8-6. Otherwise, Microsoft has fixed the problem and you can exit this procedure. Click OK to clear the message box. Fortunately, you can still use the information provided by the connection in your application — you just have to do it in a roundabout manner.

Figure 8-6:
Visual
Studio 2008
can't
connect to
SQL Server
2008 in its
current
form.

Microsoft Visual Studio

This server version is not supported. Only servers up to Microsoft SQL Server 2005 are supported.

OK   Help

9. Click Advanced.

Visual Studio displays the Advanced Properties dialog box shown in Figure 8-7. Notice the connection string at the bottom of the display. You can use this connection string to connect to SQL Server 2008 using LINQ, despite the lack of functionality in Visual Studio.

10. Highlight the entire connection string and then press Ctrl+C.

Windows copies the connection string to the Clipboard.

Figure 8-7:
Use the
connection
string that
Visual
Studio
provides to
create your
connection.

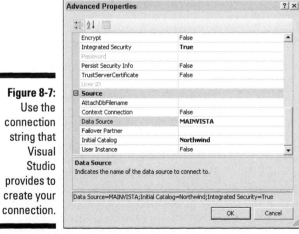

Advanced Properties

Encrypt	False
Integrated Security	**True**
Password	
Persist Security Info	False
TrustServerCertificate	False
User ID	
⊟ Source	
AttachDbFilename	
Context Connection	False
Data Source	**MAINVISTA**
Failover Partner	
Initial Catalog	**Northwind**
User Instance	False

Data Source
Indicates the name of the data source to connect to.

Data Source=MAINVISTA;Initial Catalog=Northwind;Integrated Security=True

OK   Cancel

11. **Click Cancel twice to close the Advanced Properties and Add Connection dialog boxes.**

12. **Open your source code or a copy of Notepad. Press Ctrl+V.**

    Windows pastes the connection string so that you can use it within your code. Using this approach may not be quite as nice as having Visual Studio record the information for you automatically, but it does work and will save you considerable time trying to discover how to make the connection using other techniques.

Defining the project

A typical LINQ to SQL project requires some additional configuration on your part. The following steps provide you with the basics you need to create a project:

1. **Create the basic project as you normally do.**

2. **Right-click the project entry and choose Add⇨Existing Item from the context menu.**

    Visual Studio displays the Add Existing Item dialog box.

3. **Select the All Files (*.*) option. Locate and highlight the Northwind. CS and Northwindmap.XML files in the Northwind folder that you created earlier.**

    Visual Studio selects both files, as shown in Figure 8-8.

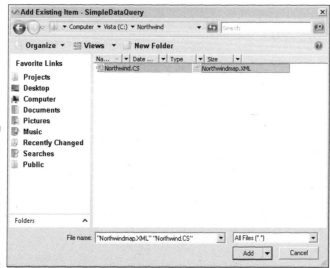

Figure 8-8: Select the entity class and XML mapping files that you created earlier.

4. **Click Add.**

   Visual Studio adds both files to your project.

5. **Right-click References and choose Add Reference from the context menu.**

   Visual Studio displays the Add Reference dialog box.

6. **Highlight the System.Data.DataSetExtensions, System.Data.Linq, and System.Xml.Linq entries (as needed). Click OK.**

   Solution Explorer displays the files and references you need to create a project.

7. **Type** using NWind; **and** using System.Data.Linq.Mapping; **in the main project file.**

   Adding these references provides access to the database and required mapping functionality.

Adding the code

You can finally add some code to your project to interact with the Northwind database. This example relies on a connection string. You could also rely on an existing connection, but the technique shown here works reliably. Listing 8-1 shows the code for this example.

Listing 8-1   Defining a Simple Data Query

```
private void btnTest_Click(object sender, EventArgs e)
{
    //Define the XML mapping source.
    XmlMappingSource MS;
    MS = XmlMappingSource.FromUrl(
        @"C:\Northwind\Northwindmap.XML");

    // Create the DataContext object.
    Northwind DB = new Northwind(
        @"Data Source=MAINVISTA;Initial Catalog=Northwind;"
            +
        "Integrated Security=True", MS);

    // Create the query.
    var ThisCust = from Custs in DB.Customers
                      where Custs.Region == "OR"
                      select Custs;

    // Display the results.
    dgResults.DataSource = ThisCust;
}
```

The example begins by creating an XmlMappingSource, MS. This XML file contains all the information required to map between the object-oriented environment of .NET and the tables in SQL Server. Because the XML mapping information appears in a file, you use the FromUrl() method to obtain it. You can also use FromReader() (when the source is from a remote location such as a Web service), FromStream() (when the source is from a remote location such as a network drive), and FromXml() (when using an embedded resource) as needed.

The next step is to create a data context. Essentially, this is an object that provides your application with access to the data source. The Northwind class derives from System.Data.Linq.DataContext and provides custom methods for working with the Northwind database. You must provide connection information, either an existing connection object or a connection string, and a mapping source as input to the constructor for the Northwind class as shown.

Don't make creating the string more difficult than necessary. Most database connections that rely on Windows Authentication require three elements in the connection string:

✔ The Data Source option, which is the name of the SQL server and instance.

✔ The Initial Catalog option, which is the name of the database you want to access.

✔ The Integrated Security option, which is always set to True for Windows Authentication.

Now that you have a connection to the database, you can use it to create a query. The code accesses the Customers table and retrieves the records where the Region field contains OR for Oregon. The LINQ feature that makes this query so easy to write and understand is XML mapping. As far as your code is concerned, it's working with any other object. The code places the results of the query in ThisCust.

You don't even have to perform any odd translation of the output. To display the results on the screen, simply make ThisCust the DataSource for dgResults. Figure 8-9 shows the output of this application (it assumes that you're using a pristine copy of Northwind — a modified copy may show different results due to changes in the Customers table content).

Figure 8-9:
LINQ
provides
an efficient
method for
extracting
information
from
databases.

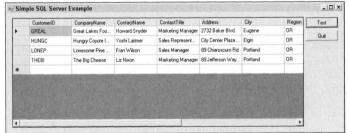

Viewing the debugger output

You've already viewed several examples of the Visual Studio 2008 debugger
at work. Chapter 2 describes basic debugger operation, Chapter 4 describes
debugger differences in Visual Basic.NET, and Chapter 5 describes debugger
differences in Visual Studio 2005. This section describes some differences in
how the debugger works with a database connection. To begin this example,
place a break point at the following line of code:

```
// Create the DataContext object.
Northwind DB = new Northwind(
    @"Data Source=MAINVISTA;Initial Catalog=Northwind;" +
    "Integrated Security=True", MS);
```

Start the application and click Test. The following steps show what happens
next:

1. **Click Step Into.**

   The debugger takes you to the `Northwind.CS` file where the code creates the `Northwind` object.

2. **Click Step Into four more times.**

   You return to the main project file and go to the next line of code. This
   is where you can see the first error. When SQL Server grants the connection, you see a listing of database tables and other objects as shown
   in Figure 8-10. It's possible to explore these tables and discover more
   about the database. As shown in the figure, you can even delve into the
   data held by various tables.

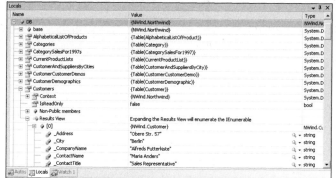

Figure 8-10:
A good
connection
helps you
discover
more
about the
database.

However, when SQL Server denies the connection, you see an error
message like the one shown in Figure 8-11. In this case, the example
fails because the login fails. The system even tells you about the error.
Notice the highlighted line in Figure 8-11 shows that the login failed.
The important aspect about this feature is that the error shows up in DB
long before you see the error displayed as an exception. Knowing where
to look for the information can help you find the bug earlier. When a
login error occurs, you won't even see the exception until you get to the
`dgResults.DataSource = ThisCust` line of code.

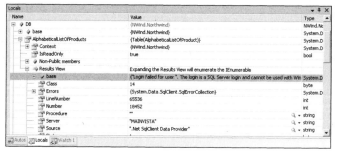

Figure 8-11:
Errors show
up relatively
early, but
you have to
look in
the Locals
window.

3. **Click Step Into.**

   The debugger takes you to the `Customers` property in the `Northwind.`
   `CS` file. Notice that all the tables are of type `System.Data.Linq.`
   `Table<>`.

4. **Click Step Into five more times.**

   You return to the main project file and go to the next line of code. It's
   time to display the data on the screen.

5. **Click Step Into.**

   The debugger takes you to the `Customers()` constructor in the `Northwind.CS` file. The constructor creates an action list for each of the results in the output. Consequently, you'll see the application loop through `Customers()` four times for this example.

6. **After you look through all the constructor code, click Step Into again.**

   The debugger takes you to the `CustomerID` property, where the application retrieves the customer identifier for the first record in the output.

7. **Continue stepping through the debugger.**

   You'll notice an interesting pattern of how the application retrieves data for each record. The code apparently begins with the key fields and then moves on to each of the detail fields in turn until the table is complete. If you single-step through the debugger long enough, the screen eventually flashes for a moment as it displays the data on the screen. The debugger then returns to this loop and begins the process again.

8. **Click Continue to see the application in action.**

Using Object Relational Designer

Object Relational (O/R) Designer helps you design a map between a database and your application using a graphical setup. The best way to discover O/R Designer is to create an application using it. This section shows how to create a basic application using O/R Designer. You'll find this example in the `\Chapter 08\ORDesign` folder of the source code for this book.

O/R Designer works with only SQL Server 2000 and 2005. You can't use O/R Designer with SQL Server 2008 in the current version of Visual Studio 2008. If you want to interact with SQL Server 2008, you must use the manual method described in the "Generating the Northwind entity classes and XML mapping files" and "Creating the Simple SQL Server Query Example" sections of the chapter.

Before you can do anything with O/R Designer, you need to add a new feature to your application, the LINQ to SQL Classes template. Begin by right-clicking the project entry and choosing Add⇨New Item from the context menu. Select the Data entry in the Add New Item dialog box. You'll see the LINQ to SQL Classes template as shown in Figure 8-12. Type a name for your template and click Add to add it to your application.

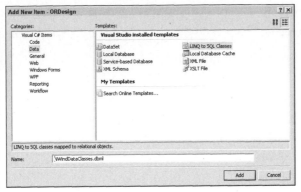

Figure 8-12:
Add the
LINQ to SQL
Classes
template as
the first step
in using O/R
Designer.

Now that you have the template in place, create a connection to the Northwind database using the same process you used to test the connection previously (see the "Testing the Visual Studio connection" section of the chapter). Instead of clicking Cancel after you test the connection, click OK to add the connection to Server Explorer.

At this point, you can begin creating the data classes and associated methods. Open the Data Connections⇨<Server>.Northwind.dbo⇨Tables folder as shown in Figure 8-13. You can choose any table, view, or sproc in the list.

Figure 8-13:
Use Server
Explorer to
view the
structure
of the
database.

The example works with the Customers table. Drag and drop the Customers table from Server Explorer to the left pane of the NWindDataClasses.dbml file as shown in Figure 8-14. If you'd wanted to work with a sproc, you'd place it in the right pane instead. The IDE shows where you should place the elements by displaying a plus sign in the correct pane.

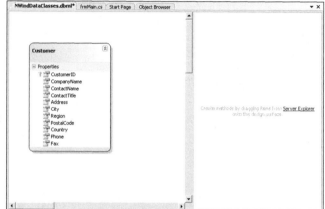

Figure 8-14: Place tables you want to use in the left pane.

The design is finished — at least for this example. You can add as many or as few items as you want from the Northwind database. Now it's time to create the query code. The output from this example looks the same as the manual method described in the "Creating the Simple SQL Server Query Example" section of the chapter. Listing 8-2 shows the code you need for this example.

Listing 8-2   Using O/R Designer for Database Access

```
private void btnTest_Click(object sender, EventArgs e)
{
   // Define the data context.
   NWindDataClassesDataContext DB =
      new NWindDataClassesDataContext();

   // Create the query.
   var DataOut = DB.Customers.Where(
      ThisArea => ThisArea.Region == "OR");

   // Display the results.
   dgResults.DataSource = DataOut;
}
```

When working with O/R Designer, you don't need to define an XML mapping source or specify a connection string because the system already has this information. The connection string you create as part of your connection to SQL Server and the visual design shown in Figure 8-14 contain the mapping source. Consequently, the code in Listing 8-2 is considerably shorter and even easier to understand than the code in Listing 8-1. You aren't getting anything free; you just define it in a different way.

The example still requires that you create a data context and this data context still defines the connection to the database for the query. After the code defines the data context, it creates a query, `DataOut`. The query still produces output that you can use directly with the `dgResults.DataSource` property. In this case, the query uses a lambda expression; you can also use the same syntax shown in Listing 8-1 if desired. When you run this example, you see the same output as shown in Figure 8-9.

An O/R Designer application doesn't require the entity classes or XML mapping files used by the manual method. In fact, you want to avoid adding these two files to prevent confusion. You need only the DBML file that O/R Designer creates for you.

Understanding the LINQ to SQL Server Operators

As with the other providers discussed in this book, LINQ to SQL Server includes some changes to standard operators. The changes modify how the standard operators work so that they perform better with databases.

One of the biggest issues to consider is that SQL Server generally deals with unordered sets of information. Ordering occurs as a post-processing function, rather than as part of defining the intermediate results. .NET Framework, on the other hand, relies on ordered sets of data. For example, if your query uses both the `Take` and `OrderBy` operators, the LINQ query will normally show the `OrderBy` operator first and the `Take` operator second. Due to limits in SQL, however, the translated SQL query will have the `SELECT TOP` (corresponding to `Take`) argument first and the `ORDER BY` argument second. The difference in the two environments means that LINQ must perform additional processing in some cases and won't support specific functionality in others.

SQL queries also produce multisets (bags), rather than sets as .NET Framework expects. The reason for this difference is that in SQL, identity is defined by value rather than position. Therefore, the identity of an element is different in LINQ than it is in SQL. Table 8-1 shows the differences in standard operator performance for LINQ to SQL Server.

Table 8-1		Standard Operator Differences for LINQ to SQL
Operator	*Supported?*	*Difference*
Concat	Yes	Does work with multisets where the order of the source (argument) and the target (receiver) are the same. The result is the same as performing a UNION ALL over the two sets. However, the query doesn't retain the ordering of the arguments because SQL automatically reorders them in the order specified by the table and you must therefore specifically order the output.
DefaultIf Empty	No	N/A
ElementAt	No	N/A
ElementAtOr Default	No	N/A
Except	Yes	Works only with sets. LINQ doesn't define an output for multisets.
Intersect	Yes	Works only with sets. LINQ doesn't define an output for multisets.
Last	No	Translation of this operator is possible, but the current LINQ to SQL provider doesn't support it. Microsoft may add functionality to future providers to support this operator.
LastOr Default	No	Translation of this operator is possible, but the current LINQ to SQL provider doesn't support it. Microsoft may add functionality to future providers to support this operator.
Reverse	No	Translation of this operator is possible, but the current LINQ to SQL provider doesn't support it. Microsoft may add functionality to future providers to support this operator.
Skip	Yes	Works only with ordered sets, which means you must use the Order By operator. The output from unordered sets or multisets is undefined.
SkipWhile	No	N/A
Take	Yes	Works only with ordered sets, which means you must use the Order By operator. The output from unordered sets or multisets is undefined.

(continued)

Table 8-1 *(continued)*

Operator	Supported?	Difference
TakeWhile	No	N/A
Union	Yes	Performs essentially the same task as UNION ALL on multisets. In essence, this operator performs the same as the Concat operator.

Chapter 9

LINQ to XML

In This Chapter

▶ Using XML with LINQ

▶ Considering the LINQ to XML API

▶ Working with the XML operators

▶ Developing a simple XML query

XML is one of those technologies that seem extremely simple to use once you overcome the learning curve to understand them. The uses of XML extend to everything from application settings storage to Web service data retrieval. In fact, XML often appears in files that don't have an XML extension — consider the CONFIG file used by .NET applications and all the settings files that Windows uses today. A number of databases even support XML directly — perhaps not as their native storage media, but as an option. You'd be hard pressed to find an application or a technology that doesn't include XML in some way, unless the application is so simple that it doesn't require anything more than extremely simple data storage (such as Notepad).

Because XML appears just about everywhere, it's possible that you'll find more use for the LINQ to XML provider than just about any other provider available today. In addition, because XML provides a hierarchical storage technology, the LINQ to XML applications you create will probably have more robust storage options than any other provider described in this book.

An interesting side effect of the LINQ to XML provider is that it offers a better method of manipulating XML data than more direct methods in many cases. LINQ provides an alternative to the kludge method of changing XML data element-by-element that you probably used in the past. The resulting data manipulation is both elegant and reliable. This chapter provides some information on using LINQ for XML database manipulation.

Even more interesting is an opportunity that LINQ to XML provides that you won't find with the other providers in this book — you can actually transform data from one presentation to another. In fact, you can create new kinds of presentations based on the content of an XML file. For example, given the right application and LINQ queries, you could possibly use an XML file to store an application specification and then transform it to application code. An application like this would require considerable time to create. The examples of transformation in this chapter are a little easier to understand.

Considering the Use of XML with LINQ

Of the default providers, LINQ to XML is perhaps the most complex because it includes the most functionality. XML data can come from a number of sources — everything from Web services to data files to configuration files on your machine. Any of these sources can rely on files, data streams, or specialized readers. An XML document can appear in a number of forms and LINQ to XML must handle them all. Developers using LINQ with XML also need to insert, update, and delete XML elements and attributes. Finally, you can transform XML to other document forms and transform other document forms to XML, making XML a sort of middle ground for data transformations.

Processing XML documents also adds to the complexity of the LINQ to XML provider. You can choose to parse the entire document, a part of the document, or even particular strings in the document. There's always the chance that your code will encounter a parsing error, so the LINQ to XML provider must also have the functionality required to handle parsing errors. Most providers handle these kinds of errors for you, but XML is an environment where your code must provide some of the required intelligence to handle errors of various sorts.

The primary task of LINQ is still performing a query to locate information, and LINQ to XML handles this task with aplomb. Depending on how you define a query, LINQ can locate specific bits of data no matter where they appear in the XML hierarchy. Letting LINQ do the work is definitely easier than attempting to locate the information yourself by looping through individual nodes one at a time. It's even possible to build queries that rely on XPath, although Microsoft doesn't recommend this course of action due to performance concerns.

To some extent, LINQ to XML is another kind of document model you can use to work with XML. Microsoft compares LINQ to XML to the Document Object Model (DOM) — you can read about this comparison at `http://msdn2.microsoft.com/en-us/library/bb387021.aspx`. (Microsoft also compares LINQ to XML to other technologies at `http://msdn2.microsoft.com/en-us/library/bb387048.aspx`.) LINQ to XML provides a full range of XML processing features, but it's probably better to view LINQ to XML as a specialized method of interacting with XML documents, rather than as an object model. The following list describes how you can use LINQ to XML to interact with XML:

🖊 Load XML documents into memory from files or streams

🖊 Serialize XML documents in memory to files or streams

🖊 Define your own XML documents using XML queries

🖊 Create simple XML queries that look like any other LINQ query

🖊 Create complex XML queries that use XPath-like axes to locate specific bits of data

🖊 Modify the in-memory presentation of an XML tree using methods such as `Add`, `Remove`, `ReplaceWith`, and `SetValue`

🖊 Validate the content of XML trees using XSD to eliminate potential database contamination

🖊 Transform data from one format to another using XML as the starting point, the end point, or as an intermediary between two dissimilar formats

---

Configuring Visual Studio for LINQ to XML

The basic Visual Studio.NET 2008 setup provides LINQ to Object provider functionality with every project. However, if you want to work with LINQ to XML, you must perform a little additional work.

The first step is to add the required assembly references. The common assembly references are `System.Linq.DLL`, `System.Xml.Linq.DLL`, and `System.Collections.Generic.DLL`. Adding all three of these references will give you full LINQ to XML functionality. If you want to interact with SQL or use a `DataSet` for transformations, make sure you add the appropriate references described in the "Configuring Visual Studio for LINQ to DataSet" sidebar in Chapter 7 or the "Configuring Visual Studio for LINQ to SQL" sidebar in Chapter 8.

The second step is to reference the namespaces you need. The most common reference is `System.Linq` (such as `using System.`

`Linq;`). You should also add the `System.Xml.Linq` reference (such as `using System.Xml.Linq;`). In some cases, you'll also want to add the `System.Diagnostics` and `System.IO` namespaces to provide the file handling functionality that your application requires. After you make these changes to your project, you will be ready to work with the LINQ to XML examples in this chapter.

LINQ to XML also has a number of supplemental references you should consider. If you want to verify the XML you create against XSD, you need to add a reference to `System.Xml.Schema.Extensions` (such as `using System.Xml.Schema.Extensions;`). Before you can evaluate XPath queries on an XML tree, you must add the `System.Xml.XPath.Extensions` reference (such as `using System.Xml.XPath.Extensions;`).

This chapter doesn't spend much time teaching you about XML. The best quick tutorial for discovering specific aspects of XML appears at http://www.w3schools.com/xml/. If you want to discover XML in detail, you'll want to check out *XML All-in-One Desk Reference For Dummies* by Richard Wagner and Richard Mansfield. This huge tome discusses everything you ever wanted to know about XML and possibly a few things you didn't even know existed. The reason an in-depth knowledge of XML is valuable with LINQ to XML is that you can finally create complex XML files without writing huge applications. LINQ to XML provides the missing piece for developers who have always wanted to use XML for more, but didn't want to invest time and resources in becoming skilled with the arcane XML programming rules in previous versions of Visual Studio.

Working with the LINQ to XML API

The System.Xml.Linq namespace is the focal point for the LINQ to XML API. This namespace is the source of the interesting manipulation functionality that LINQ to XML provides. Table 9-1 describes the various classes you need to consider when working with LINQ to XML. This chapter uses most of these classes somewhere in the examples.

Table 9-1	Classes of Concern for LINQ to XML	
Operator	**Base Class**	**Description**
Remove	Extensions	Provides the means for removing attributes or nodes from the XML tree. You must provide a reference to System.Xml.Linq.Extensions to use this feature.
XAttribute	XAttribute	Defines an XML attribute.
XCData	XCData	Defines a CDATA text node.
XComment	XNode	Defines a comment anywhere in the XML document.
XContainer	XNode	Provides an abstract class used for the XElement and XDocument operators. You won't use this class directly.

Operator	Base Class	Description
XDeclaration	XDeclaration	Specifies the XML version and encoding at the beginning of the document. You can use this operator also to define whether the document is standalone.
XDocument	XContainer	Provides an overall container for the XML document.
XDocumentType	XNode	Specifies the XML Document Type Definition (DTD).
XElement	XContainer	Provides an element container in the XML document.
XName	XName	Defines the names of elements and attributes. This LINQ to XML feature simplifies using names in XML documents by resolving all prefixes to their corresponding XML namespace.
XNamespace	XNamespace	Specifies the namespace for an element or attribute. This class is managed by XName within LINQ to XML.
XNodeDocument OrderComparer	XNodeDocument OrderComparer	Provides the means to compare nodes for their document order.
XNodeEquality Comparer	XNodeEquality Comparer	Provides the means to compare nodes for their equality.
XProcessing Instruction	XNode	Contains information that the application processing the XML uses to process the data in the XML document. For example, a processing instruction may specify which XSLT document to use to produce output from the XML document.
XText	XNode	Defines a text element, which is normally used for mixed content.

Table 9-1 leaves out a number of abstract classes. For example, it doesn't contain the XObject class, which forms the basis of the XNode (XText, XContainer, XComment, XProcessingInstruction, and XDocumentType operators), and XAttribute classes. You also use some classes for specific tasks when working with LINQ to XML, such as XObjectChange (signals an XObject event) and XObjectChangeEventArgs (provides data for the Changing and Changed events).

Understanding the LINQ to XML Operators

Most of the LINQ to XML operators provide axis manipulation features. *Axis manipulation* works on individual elements in a collection. You use axis manipulation methods to modify documents, elements, nodes, and attributes. The two Remove operators aren't axis methods.

Each of these operators performs a special task when working with XML. The following sections describe the operators in greater detail and provide usage examples. (The operators appear in the order in which you're most likely to use them.) You'll find this example in the \Chapter 09\Operators folder of the source code for this book.

Working with XDeclaration, XElement, and XDocument

The three operators that will form the basis of most of your XML applications are XDeclaration, XElement, and XDocument. You use these three operators to create any basic XML document. In addition, you often use them when reading existing documents. These three operators provide the basic containers you use to store and examine the data that an XML document contains.

One of the first things you'll notice in this first example is that the code doesn't perform the same sorts of queries that appear in past chapters. This chapter doesn't begin by looking for data. Instead, it creates data of its own. As mentioned, the LINQ to XML provider has more capabilities than the other providers examined in this book — you can do more with it than might initially appear possible. You can create all kinds of documents — well formed or not, with an XML extension or not — as long as the content uses some form of XML.

Listing 9-1 is an odd sort of example for this book. The code in the
`CreateDocument()` and `DisplayDocument()` methods is used for most
of the other examples, so I chose to place it in these separate methods for
easier access.

Listing 9-1   Creating a New XML Document

```
// Define a global XML document.
XDocument NewDoc;

private void btnDocument_Click(object sender, EventArgs e)
{
    // Create the new XML document.
    CreateDocument();

    // Display it.
    DisplayDocument();
}

private void CreateDocument()
{
    // Create the new XML document.
    NewDoc = new XDocument(
        new XDeclaration("1.0", "utf-8", "yes"),
        new XElement("Root", "MyDoc"));
}

private void DisplayDocument()
{
    // Display it on screen.
    txtResult.Text =
        NewDoc.Declaration.ToString() +
        "\r\n" + NewDoc.Document.ToString();
}
```

The code begins with a global `XDocument` object, `NewDoc`. An XML document doesn't contain anything. It simply acts as a container for whatever
you want to put there. Consequently, when `btnDocument_Click()` calls
`CreateDocument()`, the `CreateDocument()` method begins by creating a
new document with an `XDeclaration` object and an `XElement` object. The
`XDeclaration` object provides the XML declaration, while the `XElement`
obtain contains the root node for the document. The result is a well-formed
document that doesn't contain any real data.

Displaying this document requires that you display both the XML declaration and the root node. The `DisplayDocument()` method displays both
of them, as shown in Figure 9-1. Notice that the information appears in two
properties, `Declaration` and `Document`, and that you must convert them to
strings using the `ToString()` method. In most cases, you work with only the
`Document` property because it contains the root node and all its children.

Working with XNamespace

Namespaces provide unique identification of XML elements. The basic reason for using them is to avoid conflicts when a single XML file describes elements from more than one programming technology or software vendor. The namespace reference also provides additional information about the technology or software product in question in many cases. No matter what reason you have for using an XML namespace in an application, they're remarkably easy to create using LINQ to XML, as shown in Listing 9-2.

Listing 9-2   Defining a Namespace

```
private void btnNamespace_Click(object sender,
                                EventArgs e)
{
    // Create the XML Document if necessary.
    if (NewDoc == null)
        CreateDocument();

    // Define the namespace.
    XNamespace MyNS = "http://www.johnmuellerbooks.com/";

    // Add the namespace to the root node.
    NewDoc.Element("Root").Name = MyNS.GetName("Root");

    // Add an element that uses the namespace.
    NewDoc.Element(MyNS + "Root").Add(
        new XElement(MyNS + "Child1", "Some Data 1 "),
        new XElement(MyNS + "Child2",
```

```
        new XAttribute(
            XNamespace.Xmlns + "NewNS",
            "http://www.microsoft.com"),
        "Some Data 2"));

    // Display the document.
    DisplayDocument();
}
```

The code in this example begins by creating a default document. It then defines an overall XNamespace, named MyNS. Now, here's something important to note. The code accesses the Root node the first time using NewDoc.Element("Root"). However, after it adds MyNS to the Root node using the Name property, the code accesses this element using NewDoc.Element(MyNS + "Root") instead. If you attempt to access the Root node without the namespace after adding it, the code rightly reports that the value is null, which isn't what you were expecting.

The example creates two child elements. The first, Child1, is of the same namespace as the Root node. The second is also part of the namespace but adds a namespace of its own.

The method that the second child, Child2, uses to add a namespace is important. The namespace appears as an XAttribute object. To make the namespace addition, you provide the XNamespace.Xmlns property and a string name for the namespace. In addition, you provide the namespace URI as a value. The additional namespace always appears before any element value, and you can provide as many additional namespaces as needed for your application by adding more XAttribute objects. Figure 9-2 shows the output from this part of the example.

Figure 9-2:
Adding a namespace distinguishes data elements.

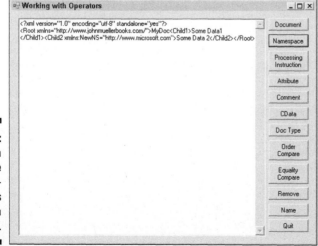

Note that the `<Child1>` element doesn't have a namespace listed. This is because `<Child1>` is in the same namespace as `<Root>`, which does have a namespace attached to it. Likewise, `<Child2>` only has the additional namespace attached to it. This additional namespace has a name attached to it, as you'd expect.

Working with XProcessingInstruction

Processing instructions perform a basic task: They tell the application viewing the XML file how to process the XML file content. In many cases, the processing instruction contains a reference to an XSLT file that transforms the XML data into another form, such as a Web page. However, you can find processing instructions for other purposes too. For example, a special processing instruction identifies an XML file as having Office document content. Listing 9-3 shows how to add a processing instruction to a basic file.

Listing 9-3   Adding a Processing Instruction

```
private void btnProcessingInstruction_Click(object sender,
                                            EventArgs e)
{
    // Create the XML Document if necessary.
    if (NewDoc == null)
        CreateDocument();

    // Add the processing instruction.
    NewDoc.AddFirst(new XProcessingInstruction(
        "xml-stylesheet",
        "type='text/xsl' href=' MyXSL.XSL'"));

    // Display the document.
    DisplayDocument();
}
```

The code begins by creating a basic XML document. It then adds the processing instruction. However, remember that the basic document has a root node. The processing instruction must appear as the first item in the document, so the example uses the `AddFirst()` method instead of `Add()` to add the new processing instruction. The code also adds the processing instruction to the document, not to the root node.

The processing instruction includes a target string and a data string. In this case, the target is an XSLT file and the data is the location of that file. Figure 9-3 shows the output from this example. If you saved this file to disk and opened it with a browser, the browser would look for a file named `MyXSL.XSL` and attempt to open it. After opening `MyXSL.XSL`, the browser would use the instructions found in this file to transform the XML data into another form.

Figure 9-3:
Processing
instructions
change
the way
applications
process
XML.

Working with XAttribute

Attributes commonly enhance elements in some way. For example, an attribute can contain a namespace used to identify and interpret the element or a data type used to identify the kind of information the element handles. In some cases, developers use attributes to hold specific types of document data as well. Listing 9-4 shows the code for this example.

Listing 9-4   Adding an Attribute

```
private void btnAttribute_Click(object sender,
                                EventArgs e)
{
   // Create the XML Document if necessary.
   if (NewDoc == null)
      CreateDocument();

   // Add an attribute to the root node.
   NewDoc.Element("Root").Add(
      new XAttribute("MyAttr", "Attribute Value"));

   // Display the document.
   DisplayDocument();
}
```

The code begins by creating a basic document. It then uses an XAttribute object to attach a new attribute to the Root node. The two input values are the attribute name, MyAttr, and its value. Figure 9-4 shows the output from this example.

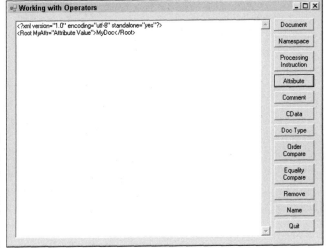

Figure 9-4:
Attributes
help define
elements
to a greater
level.

Working with XComment and XText

Comments and text can appear in an XML file. A comment commonly appears in documents that define a standard, such as an XSD file, or a configuration file, such as a CONFIG file. Text entries are rare, but you may see them used in mixed content elements. It's unlikely that you'll ever see comments or text in a pure data file because the designer will assume that everyone will view the file using the application designed to interact with it. Listing 9-5 shows the code used to add comments and text to a basic document.

Listing 9-5   Using Comments and Text

```
private void btnComment_Click(object sender,
                             EventArgs e)
{
   // Create the XML Document if necessary.
   if (NewDoc == null)
      CreateDocument();

   // Add a comment.
```

```
NewDoc.AddFirst(
   new XComment("This is a comment."));

// Add another comment.
NewDoc.Element("Root").Add(
   new XComment("This is another comment."));

// Add a third comment.
NewDoc.Add(
   new XComment("This is the third comment."));

// Add some text.
NewDoc.Element("Root").Add(
   new XText("This is some text."));

// Display the document.
DisplayDocument();
}
```

The example begins by creating a basic document. It then shows how to add comments in three locations:

✔ At the beginning of the file (where the comments identify the file creator and other pertinent information)

✔ Before or after elements (where the comments document the element's purpose and any special configuration requirements)

✔ At the end of the file (where the designer normally tells you how to find additional information or provides copyright information)

When a comment appears at the beginning of the file, you usually use the `AddFirst()` method to ensure there's no intervening content. A comment that appears as part of an element normally relies on the element's `Add()` method. In this case, the example uses the `NewDoc.Element("Root").Add()` method to add the comment to the `Root` node. Comments that appear at the end of the document normally rely on the document's `Add()` method.

After the code adds the comments, it adds some text using an `XText` object. The text appears as part of the `Root` node, but you can add it to any node desired. Generally, you avoid using the `XText` object, except when you need to add mixed content to a document. Working with the element directly is always a better strategy. Figure 9-5 shows the output from this example. The `XText` object appears simply as text in the output (without any delimiters).

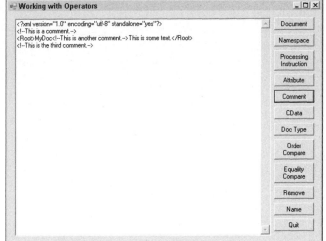

Figure 9-5:
Use com-
ments as
needed to
document
the XML
data.

Working with XCData

A CDATA section in an XML file lets you include data that's normally invalid in XML. For example, many developers use CDATA sections to include binary data. In some cases, the data would be legitimate XML, but the document designer simply wants to process it in another way, rather than using the XML parser. The important consideration with CDATA sections is that the XML parser doesn't review them in any way, so you can place any kind of data there. Listing 9-6 shows the XCData object used to create CDATA sections.

Listing 9-6   Defining CData Elements

```
private void btnCData_Click(object sender, EventArgs e)
{
   // Create the XML Document if necessary.
   if (NewDoc == null)
      CreateDocument();

   // Add the CData.
   NewDoc.Element("Root").Add(
      new XElement("CDataElement",
         new XCData("This is a CData Entry!")));

   // Display the document.
   DisplayDocument();
}
```

The example begins by creating a basic document. It then adds a new element, named `CDataElement`, to the root node of that document. The content of `CDataElement` is a CDATA section. The `XCData` object accepts anything you want to provide as input. The data could include binary information or you could save objects. What you store is unimportant to the XML parser.

If you've followed the examples to this point, you should know that the `XElement` object is a kind of container. The examples have shown a number of ways to create and use `XElement` objects to obtain specific effects; Listing 9-6 is just another one of those examples. A good rule of thumb for working with `CDATA` sections is to place them in a separate element. Using this approach makes it considerably easier to access the `CDATA` section later when you must process the content. Figure 9-6 shows the output from this example.

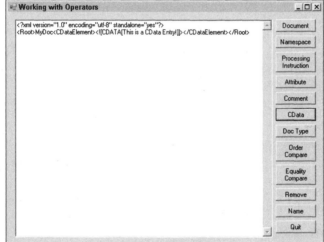

Figure 9-6:
Most applications don't process CDATA sections.

Working with XDocumentType

Most developers associated the `<!DOCTYPE>` tag with HTML files. You can also find them in XML files, where they perform essentially the same task they perform in HTML files: telling the parser which standard to use to interact with the document. The short tutorial at `http://www.w3schools.com/TAGS/tag_doctype.asp` provides additional information about working with the `<!DOCTYPE>` tag.

Most XML documents don't include the `<!DOCTYPE>` tag. They rely on the processing instruction to determine how to interact with the document instead. However, it's important to know that the `<!DOCTYPE>` tag exists and how to create it when necessary. Listing 9-7 shows how to add a `<!DOCTYPE>` tag to your XML file.

Listing 9-7   Providing a Document Type

```
private void btnDocumentType_Click(object sender,
                                   EventArgs e)
{
    // Create the XML Document if necessary.
    if (NewDoc == null)
        CreateDocument();

    NewDoc.AddFirst(
        new XDocumentType(
            "MyDocType", "MyPubID",
            "MySysID", "ThisInternalSubset"));

    // Display the document.
    DisplayDocument();
}
```

The example begins with a basic document. Because the `<!DOCTYPE>` tag must appear as the first item in the file after the XML processing instruction, the code uses the `AddFirst()` method to add it. A `<!DOCTYPE>` tag can include four items:

- Document type (name)
- Public identifier
- System identifier
- Internal document type subset

The only item you must include is the document type (or name). This value generally is the same as the root node name. For example, if the document type is `MyDocType`, the root node name is also `MyDocType`. However, you don't necessarily have to follow this protocol. The other three items are optional and their values depend on the document type you want to create. Figure 9-7 shows the output of this example.

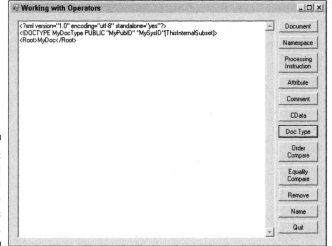

Figure 9-7:
Providing
a docu-
ment type
enhances
processing.

Microsoft provides limited processing capability for the document type.
The default XML parser ignores this value completely. You must create an
`XmlReader` of your own to perform Document Type Definition (DTD) processing for an XML file. LINQ to XML doesn't perform any validation using the DTD
specified by the `<!DOCTYPE>` tag, but you can perform this processing manually. You shouldn't rely on a DTD for security; the article at `http://msdn2.`
`microsoft.com/en-us/library/bb669138.aspx` explains why this is
a problem. The blog entry at `http://blogs.msdn.com/mikechampion/`
`archive/2006/06/30/652896.aspx` explains that full DTD processing
wasn't even a goal of the Visual Studio team, so it isn't surprising that you'll
need to do a lot of legwork when it comes to using DTD with LINQ to XML.

Working with
XNodeDocumentOrderComparer

If you were beginning to wonder where the query part of LINQ to XML
comes into play, the `XNodeDocumentOrderComparer` is the first part of the
answer. You use this object to determine where two nodes appear in relation
to each other in the document hierarchy. Listing 9-8 shows how to use this
particular query feature.

Listing 9-8 Performing an Order Comparison

```
private void btnOrderComp_Click(object sender,
                                EventArgs e)
{
   // Create the XML Document if necessary.
   if (NewDoc == null)
      CreateDocument();

   // Add elements to use for comparison.
   NewDoc.Element("Root").Add(
      new XElement("First", "Hello"),
      new XElement("Second", "Hello"),
      new XElement("Third", "Goodbye"));

   // Create the comparer.
   XNodeDocumentOrderComparer Comp =
      new XNodeDocumentOrderComparer();

   // Obtain the nodes.
   XElement First =
      NewDoc.Element("Root").Element("First");
   XElement Second =
      NewDoc.Element("Root").Element("Second");

   // Perform the comparison.
   int Result = Comp.Compare(First, Second);

   // Display the result.
   if (Result == 0)
      txtResult.Text = "First is the Same as Second";
   else if (Result < 0)
      txtResult.Text = "First is Before Second";
   else
      txtResult.Text = "Second is Before First";
}
```

The example begins by creating the basic document and adding three elements to the root node. The elements appear in a specific order as shown in the code: First, Second, and Third.

The next step is to create an XNodeDocumentOrderComparer object, Comp. This is the object that performs the comparison. To make the code a little easier to read, the example also creates two XElement comparison objects, First and Second.

At this point, the code performs the comparison. The Comp.Compare() method accepts two XElement inputs and compares their order in the document. The output is an int value, Result, that shows the order of First compared to Second. A simple if statement serves to perform the comparison. As you might expect, the output from this example is

```
First is Before Second
```

The principle use of this comparer is to determine the location of one element when compared to another. You can use this information to infer the document's structure or to decide on the best placement for a new element in the document. In some cases, you can use this technique to look for errors or even as part of the method for verifying the document.

Working with XNodeEqualityComparer

The XNodeEqualityComparer helps you check the equality of two nodes, whatever those nodes might be. The nodes need not have the same reference, but they do require the same content. Consequently, when checking an element, the name and value of both elements must be the same. Listing 9-9 shows an example of using the XNodeEqualityComparer object.

Listing 9-9   Performing an Equality Comparison

```csharp
private void btnEqualityComp_Click(object sender,
                                   EventArgs e)
{
   // Create the XML Document if necessary.
   if (NewDoc == null)
      CreateDocument();

   // Add elements to use for comparison.
   NewDoc.Element("Root").Add(
      new XElement("One", "Hello"),
      new XElement("Two", "Hello"),
      new XElement("Three", "Goodbye"));

   // Create the comparer.
   XNodeEqualityComparer Comp =
      new XNodeEqualityComparer();

   // Obtain the nodes.
   XElement First =
      NewDoc.Element("Root").Element("One");
   XElement Second =
      NewDoc.Element("Root").Element("One");

   // Perform the comparison.
   bool Result = Comp.Equals(First, Second);
```

(continued)

Listing 9-9 *(continued)*

```
    // Display the result.
    if (Result)
        txtResult.Text = "First Equals Second";
    else
        txtResult.Text = "First Doesn't Equal Second";

    // Obtain another node.
    XElement Third =
        NewDoc.Element("Root").Element("Two");

    // Perform the comparison.
    Result = Comp.Equals(First, Third);

    // Display the result.
    if (Result)
        txtResult.Text = txtResult.Text +
            "\r\nFirst Equals Third";
    else
        txtResult.Text = txtResult.Text +
            "\r\nFirst Doesn't Equal Third";
}
```

The example begins by creating a basic document. The code then adds three elements to the root node named One, Two, and Three. Note that One and Two have the same values but different names. Three differs in both name and value from the other two.

The next step is to create an XNodeEqualityComparer object, Comp. You use Comp to perform the comparison between two nodes. Using XElement objects, First and Second, makes the code easier to read, but you don't have to perform this extra step in your own code. The example shows an equal comparison first, so it sets both XElement objects to the same element, One.

The comparison is next. The output of the Comp.Equals() method is a bool that's true when the two nodes compare and false when they don't. The code checks the output in Result using a simple if statement.

At this point, the code creates another XElement object, Third, from the Two element. The code uses the Comp.Equals() method to perform another comparison and places the output in Result. Another if statement places the results on screen. Here are the results.

```
First Equals Second
First Doesn't Equal Third
```

As you might expect, the first comparison succeeds because you're looking at the same node. The second comparison fails because Two has a different name than One. As mentioned, both the name and the value must be the same for the comparison to succeed.

Working with Remove

This chapter has already shown a number of ways to add elements and attributes to a document. In some cases, you need to remove elements and attributes as well. The Remove() operator acts differently than Add() because you don't supply the name of the element or attribute you want to remove as input to the Remove() method. As shown in Listing 9-10, the Remove() method appears as one of the methods for the object you want to remove.

Listing 9-10   Removing a Node

```
private void btnRemove_Click(object sender, EventArgs e)
{
    // Create the XML Document if necessary.
    if (NewDoc == null)
        CreateDocument();

    // Add elements to use for comparison.
    NewDoc.Element("Root").Add(
        new XElement("One", "Hello"),
        new XElement("Two", "Hello"),
        new XElement("Three", "Goodbye"));

    // Remove an element.
    NewDoc.Element("Root").Element("Two").Remove();

    // Display the document.
    DisplayDocument();
}
```

The code begins by creating a basic document and attaches three new elements to the root node using the Add() method. These new nodes appear as an argument to the Add() method.

The next step is to remove an element. In this case, the code removes the Two element. The code begins by accessing the Two element using NewDoc. Element("Root").Element("Two") and then calls the Two element's Remove() method. Figure 9-8 shows the output from this example.

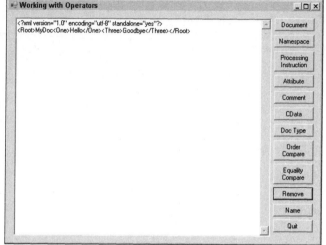

Figure 9-8:
LINQ to
XML also
provides the
means to
remove ele-
ments and
attributes.

Working with XName

Namespaces aren't very useful if you can't access them. The XName object helps you access both local name and namespace information for any element that defines them. Listing 9-11 shows an example of how this operator works.

Listing 9-11   Defining a Name

```
private void btnName_Click(object sender, EventArgs e)
{
    // Create an XML element.
    XElement ThisElement =
        new XElement(
            "{http://www.johnmuellerbooks.com/}First",
            new XAttribute(
                XNamespace.Xmlns + "NewNS",
                "http://www.microsoft.com"),
            "Hello");

    // Display the XML document on screen.
    txtResult.Text =
        ThisElement.ToString();

    // Get the element name.
    XName ThisName = ThisElement.Name;
```

```
        // Display the name on screen.
        txtResult.Text = txtResult.Text +
            "\r\n\r\nLocal Name: " + ThisName.LocalName +
            "\r\nNamespace: " + ThisName.Namespace +
            "\r\nNamespace Name: " + ThisName.NamespaceName;

        // Get the second namespace name.
        ThisName = ThisElement.Attribute(
            XNamespace.Xmlns + "NewNS").Name;

        // Display the second namespace on screen.
        txtResult.Text = txtResult.Text +
            "\r\n\r\nSecond Local Name: " + ThisName.LocalName +
            "\r\nSecond Namespace: " + ThisName.Namespace +
            "\r\nSecond Namespace Name: " +
                ThisName.NamespaceName +
            "\r\nAttribute Value: " +
                ThisElement.Attribute(
                    XNamespace.Xmlns + "NewNS").Value; ;
}
```

The code begins by creating an XElement, ThisElement. ThisElement has
two namespaces attached to it. The first is an XML namespace. Notice that
this example doesn't rely on the XNamespace object. The code places the
namespace within curly brackets instead. The second is a named namespace.
As you might expect, the code adds this namespace using an attribute. Now
that the element is complete, the code displays it. Note that you don't use the
Document property when working with an element — you simply display the
element as a whole.

Displaying the namespace information comes next. The code begins by creating an XName object, ThisName, and setting it equal to the ThisElement.
Name property. The Name property always contains the XML namespace
information. The output contains

✔ LocalName: The local name of the node. This is the name of the node
  without the namespace decoration attached.

✔ Namespace: The actual namespace value. This is the fully qualified
  namespace value.

✔ NamespaceName: The namespace URI. In most cases, the Namespace
  and NamespaceName properties are the same. (You'll see that they are
  the same for this example when you view the output.)

Now we need to look at the named namespace. It's in an attribute, so it
doesn't work the same as the XML namespace, as shown in the code. The
example uses ThisElement.Attribute() to obtain the named namespace.

The name you supply must include both `XNamespace.Xmlns` and `"NewNS"`. The output of the `LocalName`, `Namespace`, and `NamespaceName` properties may surprise you. As shown in Figure 9-9, the `LocalName` property is as expected, but you see the `XNamespace.Xmlns` value in the `Namespace` and `NamespaceName` properties. To obtain the namespace URI, you must use the `ThisElement.Attribute(XNamespace.Xmlns + "NewNS").Value` property instead.

Figure 9-9:
Retrieving names correctly is important.

Creating the Simple XML File Example

Working with XML in memory will help you understand how XML works with LINQ to XML, but it doesn't do anything useful. The example in this section begins discussing some practical elements, such as loading and saving XML as a file. Chapter 10 provides some additional practical XML examples — you'll discover how useful LINQ to XML becomes when you need to work with a Word document. You'll find this example in the `\Chapter 09\ SimpleXML` folder of the source code for this book.

Creating the project

You create an XML manipulation program the same way you create any other program. Of course, you want to ensure that all the references you need are in place, including `System.Xml.Linq.DLL`. After you add the appropriate references, add the required `using` statements. This example requires that you provide the following `using` statements:

```
using System.Xml;
using System.Xml.Linq;
using System.IO;
```

Building an XML document

Before you can work with the XML document, you need to create one. Listing 9-12 shows the XML document creation code used for this example.

Listing 9-12   Creating the XML Document

```
// Holds the XML document.
XDocument ThisDoc;

private void btnCreate_Click(object sender, EventArgs e)
{
   // Define the new XML document.
   ThisDoc = new XDocument(

      // Add the declaration.
      new XDeclaration("1.0", "utf-8", "yes"),

      // Add a list of contacts.
      new XElement("Contacts",

         // Each contact has specific elements.
         new XElement("Contact",
            new XElement("Name", "Jane Newton"),
            new XElement("Address1", "123 First St."),
            new XElement("Address2", "Suite 3"),
            new XElement("City", "Anywhere"),
            new XElement("State", "WI"),
            new XElement("ZIP", "99999-9999")),

          // A second contact.
         new XElement("Contact",
            new XElement("Name", "George Banes"),
            new XElement("Address1", "99 North Rd."),
            new XElement("Address2", "First Floor"),
            new XElement("City", "Somewhere"),
            new XElement("State", "CA"),
            new XElement("ZIP", "88888-8888"))));

   // Display the result.
   wbResult.DocumentText =
      ThisDoc.Declaration.ToString() +
      ThisDoc.Document.ToString();

   // Enable the Save button.
   btnSave.Enabled = true;
}
```

The interesting feature of this example is that it creates the entire XML document, `ThisDoc`, using a single line of code. You can create XML documents of any length and complexity using a single line of code. The problem with this approach is that it does make debugging more difficult because the debugger can't show you what is happening with individual elements when they all appear in a single line of code.

After the code creates the XML document, it displays it on the screen. This approach does work, but the results may not appear as you expect. Figure 9-10 shows that you see only the two contact entries and none of the tags supporting them (Figure 9-11).

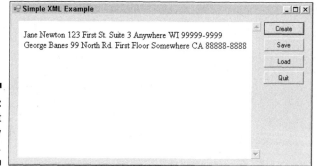

Figure 9-10: The output shows only the names.

Figure 9-11: The source shows the true document information.

Saving an XML document

The document created in the "Building an XML document" section still resides in memory. It's time to put the XML file on disk. The application stores this file in the same folder as the application executable using the code shown in Listing 9-13.

Listing 9-13   Saving an XML Document

```
private void btnSave_Click(object sender, EventArgs e)
{
    // Save the document where you need it.
    ThisDoc.Save(Application.StartupPath +
        @"\Test.XML", SaveOptions.None);

    // Reload the document.
    wbResult.Navigate(
        Application.StartupPath + @"\Test.XML");
}
```

The `ThisDoc` object includes the `Save()` method, which lets you save the document to disk without writing a lot of code. All you need to supply is a string that includes the file path and filename. The `Save()` method also includes some special save options that appear as part of the `System.Xml.Linq.SaveOptions` enumeration.

The `System.Xml.Linq.SaveOptions` enumeration provides the means to save an XML document in a specific way. These options are mutually exclusive, which means you can combine them to achieve specific results. The following lists describes each of these options.

- ✔ None: Causes the application to indent the XML while serializing it. This option makes the XML easily readable by humans but also adds to the disk storage requirements because the document now contains additional white space.

- ✔ DisableFormatting: Saves the document with all insignificant white space intact, which means the resulting document contains all the formatting you provided while creating it.

After the code saves the file to disk, it can display the information correctly in the `WebBrowser` control. In this case, the code relies on the `Navigate()` method to reload the XML file. Figure 9-12 shows the results of the loading process. The result is an XML file that looks the same as if you had loaded it using Internet Explorer.

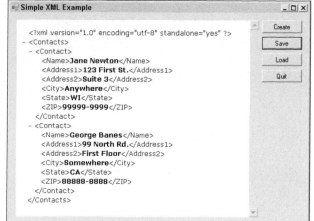

Figure 9-12:
The XML
looks closer
to the
anticipated
output.

Loading an XML document

The final task to perform in this example application is loading the XML document from disk. As before, XDocument makes this task straightforward, as shown in Listing 9-14.

Listing 9-14   Loading an XML Document from Disk

```
private void btnLoad_Click(object sender, EventArgs e)
{
   // Verify that the file exists.
   if (File.Exists(
      Application.StartupPath + @"\Test.XML"))
   {
      // Load the document.
      ThisDoc = XDocument.Load(
         Application.StartupPath + @"\Test.XML");

      // Display the document.
      wbResult.Navigate(
         Application.StartupPath + @"\Test.XML");
   }
   else
      // Display an error message.
      MessageBox.Show(
         "The Test.XML file doesn't exist. " +
         "Click Create!");
}
```

The code begins by checking for the existence of the file using the `File.Exists()` method. When the file doesn't exist, the example displays an error message and then exits.

When the file does exist, the code loads it using the static `XDocument.Load()` method. This method actually creates a new `XDocument` based on the content of the file. Notice that you don't have to do anything special to load the XML document and you don't have to worry about creating a `TextReader` to do it. Everything takes place in the background. As with the `Save()` method, you also have access to some special load options.

The `System.Xml.Linq.LoadOptions` enumeration provides the means to load an XML document in a specific way. These options are mutually exclusive, which means you can combine them to achieve specific results. These options are

- None
- PreserveWhitespace
- SetBaseUri
- SetLineInfo

The example ends by displaying the file in `wbResult`. It relies on the `Navigate()` method to perform this task. You see output similar to Figure 9-12.

Part III
Extending LINQ to New Horizons

In this part . . .

*I*f you think LINQ is amazing now, wait until you see what you can do with additional providers and a few new techniques. LINQ can work with just about any data type there is, including a few that you may not have heard about before.

Chapter 10 shows you how to access Office 2007 files using LINQ. It's astonishing to discover that you can access any part of the document, manipulate it, and save it back. The user sees the changes, but only you know how they were made.

Chapter 11 adds to your LINQ to SQL knowledge by showing you a few new techniques. Even though you can use these techniques only with SQL Server, you'll find that LINQ greatly increases the flexibility of your applications.

Chapter 12 helps you use a third-party provider to access Active Directory. Yes, LINQ even helps you bring the vast Active Directory database under control. Chapter 13 expands on the third-party provider theme by showing you how to work directly with COM+ applications, RDF files, and MySQL.

Chapter 10

Using LINQ with Office 2007

In This Chapter

▶ Considering the structure of Office 2007 documents

▶ Interacting with Office 2007 using LINQ

▶ Performing the required setup

▶ Developing an Office 2007 document application

*Y*ou can use LINQ for an interesting array of application types, including Microsoft's new Office Open XML (OOXML) file format in Office 2007. As the name implies, OOXML uses XML files to store document data. Microsoft relies on other methods to organize the data as well, so one of the first issues this chapter tackles is a quick look at the file structure.

These new OOXML file formats have a different file extension than before. For example, Word users will find that Word 2007 now supports DOCM for documents with macros and DOCX for documents without macros. In both cases, the file content actually appears as a series of specially constructed XML files. The only difference is that one has macros and the other doesn't, so you can use either form with LINQ. Naturally, you have to follow a certain process when working with the files, so this chapter discusses process concerns as well.

The remainder of the chapter helps you discover OOXML as it relates to LINQ. You discover that you can easily query an Office 2007 document for information, modify the information as needed, and save the changes back to disk. Queries can include all kinds of interesting information — everything from document content to custom properties. Consequently, you could even build your own custom reader for OOXML — a task that required major code when working with previous versions of Office. To interact with Office 2007 documents using LINQ, you need a special library, and this chapter tells you how to obtain and install it. Finally, you see how to create an application that interacts with OOXML.

Getting ready for working with OOXML

You probably need to work through a few issues before beginning to work with OOXML. The first issue is your Office suite. Not everyone has Office 2007 installed. Using a converter, you can read and write Office 2007 files using Office 2000 and Office 2003 (download it at `http://www.microsoft.com/downloads/details.aspx?FamilyId=941b3470-3ae9-4aee-8f43-c6bb74cd1466`).

Another concern is standardization. OOXML recently passed as an International Standards Organization (ISO) standard, but the standard is still subject to review (as of this writing). If you want to see what all the hubbub is about, check out the article at `http://www.infoworld.com/article/08/03/14/Microsoft-OOXML-SDK-renews-standards-debate_1.html`. You'll also find OOXML as an ECMA standard (see `http://www.ecma-international.org/publications/standards/Ecma-376.htm` for details). The bottom line is that many other applications may find a use for OOXML in the near future, so discovering this format and how to interact with it using LINQ could save you considerable time and effort.

Understanding the Office Document Structure

One of the most interesting aspects of the Office 2007 document format is that you can see everything. Unlike the binary files in earlier versions of the product, you can take the OOXML files apart, look at them in detail, make changes, put them back together again, and expect it all to work without problem. When you think about it, this is one of the first acts of file format simplification Microsoft has embarked upon. This chapter looks at a particular Word document, but the same concepts apply to any Office 2007 document. You'll find this example in the `\Chapter 10\SampleDocument` folder of the source code for this book.

The Word document in question, `Sales Letter to Joe Smythe.DOCX`, is a simple letter, so there isn't anything fancy about it. If you want to see the structure of any Office 2007 document you own, simply create a copy of it and then change the file extension of the copy to ZIP. Open the ZIP file with your favorite ZIP application (the example uses WinZIP, but any application will do). You see a series of XML files in the ZIP file, as shown for `Sales Letter to Joe Smythe.DOCX` in Figure 10-1.

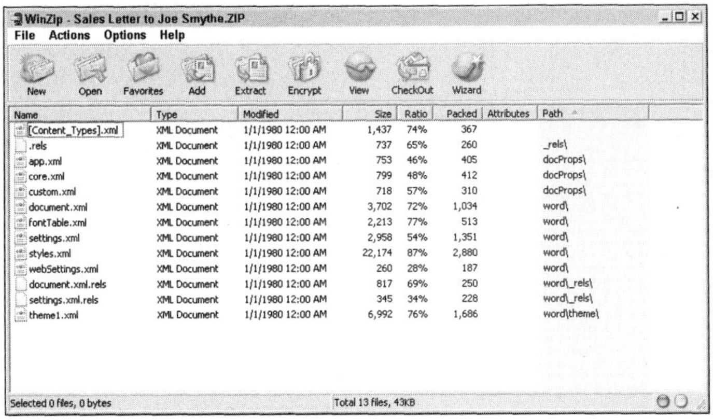

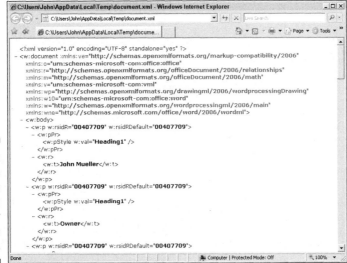

Figure 10-1:
OOXML files
are a kind
of ZIP file
containing
multiple
XML files.

The listing of files in Figure 10-1 shows a basic setup. All the files are in XML format. The files with an XML extension normally contain data of some type. Some of the data files, such as fontTable.xml, contain data for the application (a list of fonts used in the document in this case). Other data files, such as document.xml, contain the content for your document. Try opening one of the data files and you'll see the data for your document, such as the document.xml file shown in Figure 10-2.

Figure 10-2:
Data files
contain
information
about your
document in
XML form.

The `rels` files contain schemas for the various document areas, as shown in Figure 10-3. A *schema* defines the structure of the document — what Office expects to see in a given element. Each of the elements provide a relationship identifier, schema type (a URI pointing to the information), and a target in the document file, such as `docProps/custom.xml`, that combines a folder and filename. Normally, you won't need to work with the `rels` files, but it's good to know how they're used in the document.

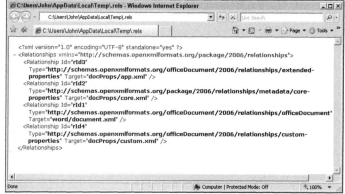

Figure 10-3:
Relationships files contain the schemas used to define document structure.

When you work with an OOXML document in Visual Studio, you need to drill down through the document layers to locate the various pieces of information. To an extent, LINQ can help by approaching the drill down process as working with collections. However, the real value of LINQ comes into play when you start working with the data. Trying to locate a specific piece of information is cumbersome when using pure XML techniques because Office tends to bury the data, as you can see in Figure 10-2.

Study Figures 10-1 through 10-3 carefully. The most common problem that developers experience is not strictly following the document format. Small things, such as capitalization, matter. For example, when working with custom properties, the `Properties` element appears in initial caps, but individual `property` elements are in lowercase. Using the wrong case will cause the application to give you an ambiguous, "Could not open file" error message even when the rest of the data format is correct. It's possible to spend hours trying to locate something as simple as the wrong capitalization.

Understanding LINQ Interaction with Office

LINQ interacts with Office 2007 documents at several levels. You use both LINQ to Object and LINQ to XML providers when working with the document.

Reading data may not even require any use of XML. However, in many cases, you convert the document parts to XML format to make it easier to add new data. The point is that you usually follow a specific process when working with Office 2007 documents as described in the following steps.

1. Load the Office 2007 document.

2. Locate the XML document that you want to work with (often described as a `Part` object).

3. Navigate to the portion of the XML document you want to work with.

4. Retrieve the XML found in the target portion of the document or work with the data it contains as you would with an object.

5. Interact with the XML or the data object by making a query using LINQ.

6. (Optional) Retrieve a specific XML data structure and modify it as needed.

7. (Optional) Save the XML to the in-memory component of the document.

8. (Optional) Save the modified document to disk.

Using the 2007 Office System: Microsoft SDK for Open XML Formats product significantly reduces the work you must perform because it makes the Office 2007 document appear as a single entity to LINQ, rather than as a collection of XML files stored in a ZIP file. However, it's important to keep the actual structure of the document in mind because some issues don't become noticeable until you consider the way Microsoft has put these documents together. In addition, the debugger tends to provide more useful information when you understand the underlying OOXML file format (which I describe in the "Understanding the Office Document Structure" section of the chapter).

One of the best ways to start studying the structure of the document you want to use with your application is to create a test document, add all the features you intend to use with that document, and then save the document to disk. Change the file extension to ZIP and then use a product such as WinZIP to extract all the components. Now it's time to open the various XML files using your favorite XML. If you don't have a good XML editor in your toolkit, consider downloading Microsoft's free offering at `http://www.microsoft.com/downloads/details.aspx?familyid=72d6aa49-787d-4118-ba5f-4f30fe913628`. This product provides everything you need to understand the structure of the XML documents in an OOXML file. Figure 10-4 shows an example of the output from XML Notepad 2007 when working with the `custom.xml` file.

As you can see from Figure 10-4, XML Notepad provides a graphical view of the hierarchy of the XML file. You can also use it to try changes to the various XML files, put the document back together, and see the results by opening the file in the Office application. Make sure you add any modifications to the ZIP file and then rename the ZIP file with the original document extension before you try to open it.

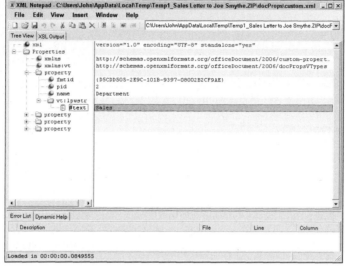

Figure 10-4:
Use an XML file editor to view the document files in new ways.

Obtaining the Required Library

Before you can do any work with Office 2007 documents, you need a special library. Yes, you could work with the documents as ZIP files containing a group of XML files, but that's the hard way to approach the task. Consequently, this chapter assumes that you've downloaded the 2007 Office System: Microsoft SDK for Open XML Formats file (`OpenXMLSDK.MSI`) found at `http://www.microsoft.com/downloads/details.aspx?FamilyId=AD0B72FB-4A1D-4C52-BDB5-7DD7E816D046`.

After you download the file, right-click the `OpenXMLSDK.MSI` file and choose Install from the context menu. (Note that you can also use this file to repair a corrupted setup by choosing the Repair option.) The program starts a wizard you use to install the program. The following steps lead you through the installation:

1. **Click Next.**

   You see the License Agreement page.

2. **Read the licensing agreement and choose I Agree. Click Next.**

   You see the Select Installation Folder page.

3. **Click Disk Cost to see a summary of the amount of space the files will require on each of your drives.**

4. **Click Browse when you want to choose a new installation location.**

5. **Choose an installation location (or simply accept the default location) and click Next.**

   You see a Confirm Installation page.

6. **Click Next.**

   If you're working on Vista or Windows Server 2008, you see the User Access Control (UAC) dialog box. Click Continue to give the system permission to perform the installation. The wizard performs the Software Development Kit (SDK) installation. Eventually, you see an Installation Complete page.

7. **Click Close.**

   The installation is complete.

At this point, a new set of files is in the `\Program Files\2007 Office System Developer Resources\OpenXMLSDK\1.0.0531` folder of your hard drive if you used the default installation options. The `ReadMe.HTM` file contains important information about the release of the SDK that you're using (the examples in this chapter rely on the 1.0.0531 version). The most important information in this file is known issues with the library. For example, the current release can't create new Word documents — it can only manipulate the content of the document. Even if you create a new Word document, Office 2007 won't be able to open it.

Immediately below the main folder are the `doc` and `lib` folders. The `doc` folder contains a help file that documents the SDK. The `lib` folder contains the `DLL` you use to create applications and an XML file that supplies information to IntelliSense. Surprisingly enough, Microsoft doesn't make entries in the Start menu for any of the files in the `SDK` folder, so if you want to view the ReadMe file or examine the help file, you need to locate them on the hard drive using Windows Explorer.

Creating the Office 2007 Document Example

The example in this section works with `Sales Letter to Joe Smythe.DOCX` described in the "Understanding the Office Document Structure" section of the chapter. The techniques described in this example work with any Word document that you want to use and the same concepts apply to any Office 2007 document. In fact, when other vendors begin providing OOXML support, you may find that the example also provides useful information for these other applications because OOXML provides a standard base from which to begin working with the document files.

The example performs a seemingly simple task — reading and writing document properties. You could just as easily use the approach in this example to read and write document content or work with any other part of the document. Working with the properties provides an easy way to examine OOXML without writing a lot of data manipulation code. You'll find this example in the \ `Chapter 10\ReadWriteDocument` folder of the source code for this book.

Creating the project

You begin an OOXML document application as you do any other application — with a project. The example uses a standard Windows form as a starting point. After you create the basic application, use the following steps to add the required support for working with OOXML:

1. **Right-click the project entry in Solution Explorer and choose Add Reference from the context menu.**

   You see the Add Reference dialog box shown in Figure 10-5.

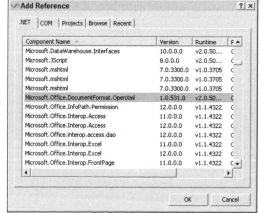

Figure 10-5:
Add the references required for an OOXML application.

2. **Highlight the Microsoft.Office.DocumentFormat.OpenXml. Click OK.**

   Visual Studio adds the `Microsoft.Office.DocumentFormat.OpenXml` reference to your application. If you don't see the `Microsoft.Office.DocumentFormat.OpenXml` entry, it means that you didn't install the 2007 Office System: Microsoft SDK for Open XML Formats SDK properly. See the "Obtaining the Required Library" section for details.

   Your project should already have the `System.Xml.dll` and `System.Xml.Linq.dll` references. However, you'll want to double-check in the `References` folder of Solution Explorer to ensure they're in place. Add them using the same technique you used for the `Microsoft.Office.DocumentFormat.OpenXml` entry when necessary.

3. **Open the code file for your project and type the following statements.**

```
using Microsoft.Office.DocumentFormat.OpenXml;
using Microsoft.Office.DocumentFormat.OpenXml.
        Packaging;
using System.Xml.Linq;
using System.IO;
```

The `Microsoft.Office.DocumentFormat.OpenXml` and `Microsoft.Office.DocumentFormat.OpenXml.Packaging` references provide access to the special 2007 Office System: Microsoft SDK. The `System.Xml.Linq` reference provides the means to make queries against the Office 2007 document. Because the data you need resides in a file and you need to verify certain aspects of that file, as well as read and write it, you also need the `System.IO` reference.

At this point, your project has all the basics configured. Make sure you check out the example program to see how these prerequisites fit with your project plans.

Understanding the custom properties

This example works with the custom properties in the `docProps\custom.xml` file of the document (see Figure 10-1 for details of the document folder arrangement). Figure 10-6 shows how the `custom.xml` file is configured.

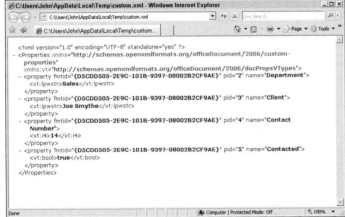

Figure 10-6:
The custom. xml file holds all the custom properties.

The file contains some basic information about the custom properties in the document. The root node is `Properties`. Note that `Properties` contains two namespaces — these namespaces are extremely important. The first namespace, `http://schemas.openxmlformats.org/officeDocument /2006/custom-properties`, defines the general layout of the file. The second namespace, `http://schemas.openxmlformats.org/office Document/2006/docPropsVTypes`, defines the data types in the files. If you use the wrong namespace for a particular task, Word will simply tell you that it can't load the file, leaving you wondering (often for hours) what went wrong.

The `property` elements tell you the format identifier, property identifier, and property name. These attributes belong to the first namespace. The child element contains the property value. The element includes the data type of the value and the value itself. This child element belongs to the second namespace.

Word provides several kinds of properties and it's easy to confuse them. Custom properties appear on the Custom tab of the document's Properties dialog box, as shown in Figure 10-7. The custom properties are configurable. You can choose one of the suggested values in the Name list or create one of your own. Custom properties can use one of four data types: text, date, number, or yes/no. Any properties you create appear in the Properties list.

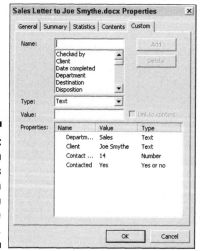

Figure 10-7:
Custom properties appear on the Custom tab of the document.

It's easy to confuse custom properties with core properties. The core properties appear on the Summary tab of the document's Properties dialog box, as shown in Figure 10-8. Because the structure of the `core.xml` file is different from the `custom.xml` file, any code you write for one will not work with the other. Unfortunately, the two names are similar enough that you could easily mistake one for the other and spend still more time trying to figure out why your code can't access any of the expected values.

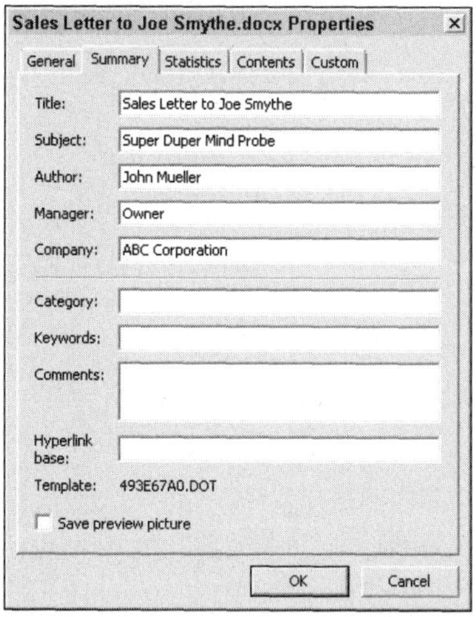

Figure 10-8:
Avoid confusing the core properties with the custom properties.

When you add a custom property to your document, what you really do is add a new entry to the `custom.xml` file. An application can read this file and interact with the custom properties outside Word. You can use this information to discover specific facts about the document without reading the document itself. An application could manipulate these custom properties in certain ways to make it easier to locate a particular document or group of documents. The application could also perform statistical analysis or other tasks with the document. Listing 10-1 shows the custom properties for the example document. (Note that most of the entries are so long that they appear on multiple lines in the book even though they appear on a single line in the source code file.)

Listing 10-1   Custom Property XML

```
<?xml version="1.0" encoding="UTF-8" standalone="yes"?>
<Properties
   xmlns="http://schemas.openxmlformats.org/office
       Document/2006/custom-properties"
   xmlns:vt="http://schemas.openxmlformats.org/
       officeDocument/2006/docPropsVTypes">
   <property fmtid=
       "{D5CDD505-2E9C-101B-9397-08002B2CF9AE}" pid="2"
       name="Department">
       <vt:lpwstr>Sales</vt:lpwstr>
```

(continued)

Listing 10-1 *(continued)*

```
    </property>
    <property fmtid=
        "{D5CDD505-2E9C-101B-9397-08002B2CF9AE}" pid="3"
        name="Client">
        <vt:lpwstr>Joe Smythe</vt:lpwstr>
    </property>
    <property fmtid=
        "{D5CDD505-2E9C-101B-9397-08002B2CF9AE}" pid="4"
        name="Contact Number">
        <vt:i4>14</vt:i4>
    </property>
    <property fmtid=
        "{D5CDD505-2E9C-101B-9397-08002B2CF9AE}" pid="5"
        name="Contacted">
        <vt:bool>true</vt:bool>
    </property>
</Properties>
```

The code begins with the `Properties` root node, which includes a list of schemas used to define the document types as attributes. Each of the properties appears in a separate `property` element. This document has four custom properties:

- ✔ Department
- ✔ Client
- ✔ Contact Number
- ✔ Contacted

Each `property` element contains a format identifier, property identifier, and name as attributes. The child element contains the type of the data:

- ✔ **vt:lpwstr:** Text
- ✔ **vt:filetime:** DateTime
- ✔ **vt:i4:** Number
- ✔ **vt:bool:** Yes or No

The child elements define the kind of data that the property holds. The element value is the value of the property. Consequently, to view these custom properties, you must look through the individual property, the value type, and finally the property value itself.

Office 2007 also supports a new `vt:r8` property type that provides support for double (real) numbers. Although a property with a decimal value might prove interesting, you lose backward compatibility with older versions of Office, even when the copy of Office has access to the Office 2007 converter. Word will simply tell you that some of the new features won't appear in Office

2000 or Office 2003, even though you can see them in Office 2007. Avoid using incompatible data types whenever possible to maximize the flexibility of your application.

Reading document properties

Many applications will begin with a need to read the properties in the document. Remember that you need to drill down into the `custom.xml` file, and then into the `Properties` collection, and finally locate the specific `property` element that you need. Listing 10-2 shows a basic example of how you can access properties in a Word document.

Listing 10-2   Reading the Document Properties

```
private void btnRead_Click(object sender, EventArgs e)
{
   // Verify the document exists.
   if (File.Exists("Sales Letter to Joe Smythe.docx"))
   {
      // Create a custom properties object.
      TextReader PropStream;

      // Open the document.
      WordprocessingDocument WD =
         WordprocessingDocument.Open(
            "Sales Letter to Joe Smythe.docx", false);

      // Locate the part needed for this example.
      OpenXmlPackage CustFileProps =
         WD.CustomFilePropertiesPart.OpenXmlPackage;
      IEnumerable<IdPartPair> Parts =
         from ThisPart
            in CustFileProps.Parts
         where ThisPart.OpenXmlPart.Uri.OriginalString
            == "/docProps/custom.xml"
         select ThisPart;

      // Obtain the data from the
      // /docProps/custom.xml part.
      if (Parts.Count() != 0)
         PropStream =
            new StreamReader(
               Parts.ElementAt(0).
                  OpenXmlPart.GetStream());

      // When the Parts object is null, there aren't any
      // custom properties.
```

(continued)

Listing 10-2 *(continued)*

```
        else
        {
            MessageBox.Show("The document doesn't contain" +
                            " any custom properties.");
            return;
        }

        // Read the custom property data into memory.
        XDocument PropDoc = XDocument.Load(PropStream);

        // Query the custom property data.
        IEnumerable<XElement> Props =
            from ThisProp in PropDoc.Document.Element(
                XName.Get("Properties",
                    "http://schemas.openxmlformats.org/" +
                    "officeDocument/2006/custom-properties"))
                .Elements()
            select ThisProp;

        // List the properties.
        txtResult.Text = "Custom Properties:\r\n";
        foreach (var ThisProp in Props)
            txtResult.Text = txtResult.Text + "\r\n" +
                ThisProp.Attribute(
                    XName.Get("name", "")).Value +
                ":\r\n" +
                ThisProp.Elements().ElementAt(0).Value
                + "\r\n";


        // Close the file.
        PropStream.Close();
        WD.Close();
    }

    // Display an error message when the document
    // doesn't exist.
    else
        MessageBox.Show(
            "The document, Sales Letter to Joe Smythe.docx, "
            + "doesn't exist in the application folder.");
}
```

The code begins by checking for the existence of the file. LINQ can help with a lot of tasks, but it still needs a file to begin doing anything for you.

The first step in locating the information you need is to open the document using the `WordprocessingDocument.Open()` method. The first argument contains the path and filename of the file you want to use. The second argument determines whether the application opens that file as read/write. Because this portion of the example only reads the file, it sets the read/write value to `false`.

Now that you have an open ZIP file, you need to locate `custom.xml`. The SDK calls the `custom.xml` file a part because it's part of the overall document. The parts are a collection in the `WD.CustomFilePropertiesPart.OpenXmlPackage.Parts` property. The output of a LINQ query of these parts is an `IEnumerable<IdPartPair>` object. Notice how the query locates the right part by checking the `ThisPart.OpenXmlPart.Uri.OriginalString` entry and comparing it to `/docProps/custom.xml`. Look again at Figure 10-1 and you'll see that `/docProps/custom.xml` is the full path to the `custom.xml` file that contains the data needed by the application.

At this point, `Parts` contains a pointer to the `custom.xml` file. Unfortunately, this file is optional — the document won't include it when there aren't any custom properties. Consequently, the code checks to verify whether the file is present using `Parts.Count() != 0`. Don't make the mistake of using `Parts != null` for the check because `Parts` will always have a value.

It's time to look inside the `custom.xml` file. You can use a number of techniques to perform this task, but the example application begins by creating a `StreamReader` object, `PropStream`, using the `Parts.ElementAt(0).OpenXmlPart.GetStream()` method. The application has access to the document content now.

The next step is to create an XML document you can use to interact with the data inside the `custom.xml` file. All you need, in this case, is a call to the `XDocument.Load(PropStream)` method.

The final major step is to perform another query against the `XDocument` object, `PropDoc`. The `Properties` element contains two namespaces, but you need only the structural namespace to access the data structure. The query creates an `IEnumerable<XElement>` object, `Props`, using the `PropDoc.Document.Element()` method, which requires the name of the element you want and the namespace in which that element exists.

All that remains is to output the data using a `foreach` statement. The output shown in Figure 10-9 consists of the `name` attribute and the underlying property value. To obtain the attribute, you again use the `XName.Get()` method and supply it with the name of the attribute and its namespace. It may seem odd that this example doesn't have a namespace for the name attribute. However, you specify the namespace as part of the `Properties` element — the namespace flows down to the child elements and their attributes. Unless you use a different namespace for an element or attribute, you don't need to provide a namespace value for the `XName.Get()` method.

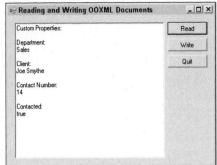

Figure 10-9:
The output
shows the
four proper-
ties supplied
with the
default
document.

Notice that the code ends with two calls. The first closes the data stream and the second closes the document. If you don't make these two calls, Windows may insist that the document is open, and you won't be able to access it again until after you reboot the machine. In some rare cases, the file could actually experience data loss, so make sure you close the files before you exit the application.

Writing document properties

Writing properties to the document comes next. This example doesn't show how to start from scratch. What it shows instead is how to add a property to an existing document. If you wanted to add a property to a document that doesn't include custom properties, you'd begin by creating a new document using the techniques shown in Chapter 9. Listing 10-3 shows how to write properties to an existing `custom.xml` file.

Listing 10-3   Writing Properties to a Document

```
private void btnWrite_Click(object sender, EventArgs e)
{
    // Define the required namespaces.
    XNamespace CustProp =
        "http://schemas.openxmlformats.org/" +
        "officeDocument/2006/custom-properties";
    XNamespace DocPropVTypes =
        "http://schemas.openxmlformats.org/" +
        "officeDocument/2006/docPropsVTypes";

    // Verify the document exists.
    if (File.Exists("Sales Letter to Joe Smythe.docx"))
    {
        // Create a custom properties object.
```

```
TextReader PropStream;

// Open the document.
WordprocessingDocument WD =
   WordprocessingDocument.Open(
      "Sales Letter to Joe Smythe.docx", true);

// Locate the part needed for this example.
OpenXmlPackage CustFileProps =
   WD.CustomFilePropertiesPart.OpenXmlPackage;
IEnumerable<IdPartPair> Parts =
   from ThisPart
      in CustFileProps.Parts
   where ThisPart.OpenXmlPart.Uri.OriginalString
      == "/docProps/custom.xml"
   select ThisPart;

// Obtain the data from the
// /docProps/custom.xml part.
if (Parts.Count() != 0)
   PropStream =
      new StreamReader(
         Parts.ElementAt(0).
            OpenXmlPart.GetStream());

// When the Parts object is null, there aren't any
// custom properties.
else
{
   MessageBox.Show("The document doesn't contain" +
                   " any custom properties.");
   return;
}

// Read the custom property data into memory.
XDocument PropDoc = XDocument.Load(PropStream);

// Add a new property.
XElement DocProperties =
   PropDoc.Element(CustProp + "Properties");
DocProperties.Add(
   new XElement(CustProp + "property",
      new XAttribute("fmtid",
         "{D5CDD505-2E9C-101B-9397-08002B2CF9AE}"),
      new XAttribute("pid", "22"),
      new XAttribute("name", "NewValue")));

// Add data to the new property.
XElement NewProp =
   PropDoc.Element(CustProp + "Properties")
```

(continued)

Listing 10-3 *(continued)*

```
            .Elements().Last();
    NewProp.Add(
        new XElement(
            DocPropVTypes + "lpwstr", "NewContent"));

    // Save the new property.
    TextWriter SaveStream =
        new StreamWriter(
            Parts.ElementAt(0).OpenXmlPart.GetStream());
    PropDoc.Save(SaveStream,
        SaveOptions.DisableFormatting);

    // Close the file.
    SaveStream.Close();
    PropStream.Close();
    WD.Close();

    // Display a success message.
    MessageBox.Show("New Property Written!");
}

// Display an error message when the document
// doesn't exist.
else
    MessageBox.Show(
        "The document, Sales Letter to Joe Smythe.docx, "
        + "doesn't exist in the application folder.");

}
```

The example begins in the same way that the reading example in Listing 10-2 does. The application checks for the file, opens it, and gains access to the custom.xml file. This example differs at the point where the application loads the document into an XDocument object, PropDoc.

The first task the code must perform is to create the property element. This is a structural element, so the code uses the structural namespace, CustProp. The fmtid attribute is always the same value, so you never need to change this line of code. The pid attribute is usually the next number in line, but you can use any unique number. The example uses 22 in the interest of making the code simple. Normally, you'd access the pid attribute of the previous property element and increment its value by 1. Finally, you add the name attribute and the name of the custom property.

Theoretically, you can add the child element as part of the initial construction process, but it's easier to add it later. The example adds a new element with a type of `lpwstr` and a value of `NewContent`. This element is a type element, not a structural element, so it uses the `DocPropVTypes` namespace. Notice how the code adds this namespace to the element — you must use this technique if you want the resulting file to load.

The code ends by saving the updated XML to the file. Note that you must create a `TextWriter` to perform this task. In addition, the output can't contain white space, so you need to use the `SaveOptions.DisableFormatting` enumeration. Remember to close both data streams and the file when writing new property values (as shown in Listing 10-3). If you click Read on the sample application at this point, you'll see that the file contains the new property as shown in Figure 10-10.

Figure 10-10:
Reading
the docu-
ment after
you add
the custom
property
shows the
new
property.

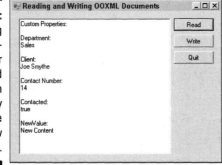

Chapter 11

Advanced LINQ to SQL Server

. . . .

In This Chapter

▶ Defining LINQ query and update issues for SQL Server

▶ Performing database interaction and modification

▶ Handling concurrency issues

. . . .

SQL Server is a complex database product, and two chapters can't discuss the product completely. In fact, most database developers probably have a shelf full of books precisely because a single book can't discuss the topic completely. This chapter discusses some specific advanced LINQ to SQL Server topics. The goal for this chapter is to end up with an application that can perform some level of modification to a database using LINQ queries as the source of the modification data.

You can probably skip this chapter if you plan to use LINQ only as a means for querying SQL Server (as described in Chapter 8). This book views querying SQL Server as a separate task from interacting with the data in SQL Server. This chapter considers interactions in the following three categories:

✔ Inserting

✔ Updating

✔ Deleting

To accomplish the data modification goal, you must consider the framework in which the application makes the modifications. Balancing record safety, which often slows the application down to unusable speeds, with application performance, which can sacrifice reliability factors such as record safety, is important. Fortunately, LINQ helps you achieve these seemingly incompatible goals by providing a level of automated concurrency resolution and by helping you optimize the manner in which those checks occur.

You can address performance at many levels — concurrency checks are just one level. This chapter also considers some of the performance enhancements you can use with LINQ to SQL Server. By optimizing what LINQ checks, how it resolves any issues it finds, and also improving the way LINQ makes queries, you can create an application that handles data safely and works quickly, with a lot less code than you have used when working with other techniques.

Considering SQL Server Issues

SQL Server is a multiuser environment, so you have a few additional issues to consider when using LINQ in this environment than when you work in a single-user application environment. LINQ handles a few of these situations for you (which is a surprise because Microsoft isn't normally very good about handling issues like this). Automation is always nice, but you still need to monitor the situation and ensure that LINQ handles the multiuser requirements correctly.

The following sections describe two major SQL Server multiuser issues that you'll encounter when working with LINQ. Don't forget that you still need to think about the other multiuser issues that you normally consider when working with SQL Server. In addition, these sections don't consider minor multiuser issues you may never see when working with LINQ; this is simply a discussion of the most common problems.

Understanding concurrency problems

The most basic of all multiuser issues is concurrency. A *concurrency* problem occurs whenever two parties attempt to modify the same data at the same time. If Party A reads the data, and then Party B does the same, both Party A and Party B have the same data in memory. Let's say that both parties decide to modify the data in some way. Party A submits its changes first, so now Party B has outdated information. When Party B attempts to submit its changes to the data, the data is in conflict — there's a concurrency problem. SQL Server can solve it in one of three ways:

- ✔ Discard the Party A changes and use those provided by Party B
- ✔ Discard the Party B changes and keep those provided by Party A
- ✔ Attempt to consolidate the changes from both parties

Understanding the problem and its resolution

The answer to concurrency problems comes in two parts: detection and resolution. Fortunately, the classes you create using SQLMetal (see the "Generating the Northwind entity classes and XML mapping files" section of Chapter 8 for details) automatically detect concurrency problems. The classes that SQLMetal creates inherit the `DataContext` class. Whenever the class you create with SQLMetal detects a conflict, it fires a `ChangeConflictException` exception. Your code can catch this exception and handle it according to company policy.

The question is how the detection occurs. The `DataContext` class provides the `SubmitChanges()` method. This one method executes any insert, update, or delete changes found in your code. It's during this method that the `DataContext` class detects conflicts and fires the `ChangeConflictException` exception. Consequently, the `try...catch` block appears as part of the `SubmitChanges()` method. Because of the way concurrency detection works, you should never see a `ChangeConflictException` exception when performing a query or insert (unless something tries to insert precisely the same record that you're inserting).

Seeing concurrency checks and resolution in action

Resolution occurs after the application detects the conflict. You have many options in resolving the conflict, one of which is not to do anything about it. The `ChangeConflicts` collection of the class you derive from `DataContext` includes the `ResolveAll()` method that tells the code to perform a resolution based on the policy you select. Listing 11-1 shows an example of simple detection and resolution taking place. You'll find this example in the `\Chapter 11\SimpleDataError` folder of the source code for this book.

Listing 11-1   A Simple Conflict Detection and Resolution

```
private void btnTest_Click(object sender, EventArgs e)
{
    //Define the XML mapping source.
    XmlMappingSource MS;
    MS = XmlMappingSource.FromUrl(
        @"C:\Northwind\Northwindmap.XML");

    // Create the DataContext object.
    Northwind DB = new Northwind(
        @"Data Source=MAINVISTA;Initial Catalog=Northwind;"
        + "Integrated Security=True", MS);

    // Obtain the target customer.
    Customer Cust = (from ThisCust in DB.Customers
                    where ThisCust.CustomerID == "ALFKI"
                    select ThisCust).Single<Customer>();

    // Obtain the postal code and save it.
    String Postal = Cust.PostalCode;
```

Listing 11-1 *(continued)*

```
    // Update the postal code locally.
    Cust.PostalCode = "12345";

    try
    {
        // Save the change to the database.
        DB.SubmitChanges();

        // Display the old and new postal code.
        MessageBox.Show(
            "Old Postal Code: " + Postal +
            "\r\nNew Postal Code: " + Cust.PostalCode,
            "Success!", MessageBoxButtons.OK,
            MessageBoxIcon.Information);
    }

    // Detect any concurrency problems.
    catch (ChangeConflictException CCE)
    {
        // Display the conflict information.
        MessageBox.Show(CCE.Message);

        // Resolve the conflict.
        DB.ChangeConflicts.ResolveAll(
            RefreshMode.KeepChanges);
    }
}
```

The code begins by creating a mapping source, MS, and then instantiating the Northwind object (derived from DataContext) DB. The example retrieves a single Customer object, Cust, with a CustomerID value of ALFKI. None of this code is much different from the examples in Chapter 8.

At this point, the code saves the current Cust.PostalCode property value and then changes that value to 12345. The change affects only the local copy of the record — the record on the server remains unchanged, so you don't have to place this code within the try...catch structure. In fact, it's better if you don't so that you can ensure that the one item that does affect the database on the server is the one that you monitor.

The next step is to use the DB.SubmitChanges() method to update the database. When the code is successful, you see a dialog box showing the old and new PostalCode property value as shown in Figure 11-1. (The original value you see may differ from the one in the screenshot if you have made changes to the Northwind database.) At this point, the record in the database matches the local copy.

Figure 11-1:
A view of
the old and
new postal
code.

Your application could always experience a concurrency conflict before it displays the message shown in Figure 11-1. When this problem happens, the code goes to the `catch` portion of the `try...catch` structure. It catches the `ChangeConflictException`, `CCE`, and displays the `CCE.Message` property, which tells the user about the problem. The code ends by using the `RemoveAll()` method. You have three choices of actions as defined in the `RefreshMode` enumeration:

✔ `KeepCurrentValues`: The application keeps the current values in the database and ignores the changes that the application requested.

✔ `KeepChanges`: The application forces the database to modify the values to match those provided by the application.

✔ `OverwriteCurrentValues`: Instead of using either of the values completely, the application performs a field-by-field comparison between the two changes. When a field in the updated record is unchanged from its initial value, the application supplies the new value from the application. For example, if Party A changes the `PostalCode` field but not the `Region` field, and Party B changes both the `PostalCode` and `Region` fields, the application would retain the `PostalCode` field change made by Party A but change the `Region` field to the update provided by Party B. The result is a combination of the changes made by both Party A and Party B.

Defining alternatives to ResolveAll()

Most applications will rely on some form of `ResolveAll()` to handle conflicts. However, you do have other choices. The following list describes the methods you can use in place of or in combination with `ResolveAll()` to handle a particular concurrency problem:

✔ `Clear()`: Clears all concurrency issues without handling them.

✔ `Remove()`: Removes the specified concurrency issue without handling it. You can still call `ResolveAll()` to handle the remaining concurrency issues after using this method. It's also possible to remove multiple concurrency issues from the list by calling this method multiple times.

Using entity class attributes to modify concurrency detection

Microsoft provides another method of determining how your application detects concurrency conflicts. When you view a property inside the `Northwind.CS` file (the file that SQLMetal created for you in Chapter 8), the property uses a default set of attributes. These default attributes tell the application to always check every field for potential concurrency conflicts. You can change that behavior using the `Column` attribute. The named parameters of interest are

✔ `IsVersion`: When set to `true`, the entity class that has the attribute set is used as the sole check for concurrency issues. For example, when working with the Customers database, setting the `[Column(IsVersion=true)]` attribute on `CustomerID` would tell the application to check for concurrency problems using only the `CustomerID` column.

✔ `UpdateCheck`: This attribute is active only when none of the columns has the `IsVersion` attribute set to `true`. You can use any of the three values to modify the way the application uses the column to check for concurrency problems:

  • `Always`: The application always checks this column for potential conflicts, even when the column has no changes.

  • `Never`: The application never checks this column for potential conflicts, even when the column has changes.

  • `WhenChanged`: The application first determines whether the column has a change. If the column has a change, the application uses it as part of the concurrency check.

Modifying the concurrency checks using the `Column` attribute means modifying the SQLMetal generated file. Consequently, you won't want to regenerate the file using SQLMetal or all your changes will disappear. Use the `Column` attribute only after your database design is complete and there is no possibility of additional changes.

Overcoming performance issues

The most reliable computer in the world is one in which security is so intense that no one can use it. Unfortunately, *reliable* and *secure* aren't the only words associated with database use. A database that isn't fast has no purpose in today's corporate environment. Consequently, you must balance reliability, security, and speed to create a database application that performs well. These three elements form a triangle that helps you visualize the performance environment. Increase speed and you'll reduce both reliability and security. Increase security and you change the reliability and speed.

Using Column attributes

LINQ to SQL generally performs better than other query methods because Microsoft has built some optimization directly into the technology. When you create a LINQ query, you tell LINQ what you want, not how to get it. It's up to LINQ to find the best method of accomplishing the task given the requirements you provide. In addition, the entity class file provides LINQ to SQL with cues as to how to work with the database. It would almost seem as if everything is already handled, but the weak point in this scenario is that entity class file. In the "Using entity class attributes to modify concurrency detection" section of the chapter you discover that modifying the `IsVersion` and `UpdateCheck` attributes affect concurrency. Not surprisingly, they also affect performance.

When possible, use the `IsVersion` attribute to ensure that the primary key field for your table doesn't have a conflict. LINQ won't check for conflicts with other fields in the record. Although this approach doesn't work when you must ensure that no one overwrites someone else's record, it does work in situations where an overwrite may result in the same data being entered twice or a minor edit later, such as with a contact database. When using the `IsVersion` attribute is out of the question, use the `UpdateCheck` attribute to modify the way LINQ verifies each field — check only those fields that actually require a check to save some time.

Relying on standard database performance tricks

All the database performance tricks you normally use also work with LINQ. For example, making your query specific and returning only the records you need help improve performance. If you don't include the `Select` operator with your query, LINQ returns the entire data set, as if you used as `SELECT *` query in SQL Server. Consequently, you should always include a `Select` operator as part of your query.

Performing database updates only as needed

Keep network traffic to a minimum whenever possible by using the `SubmitChanges()` method sparingly. You have a balance to maintain when working with LINQ to SQL. Frequent updates mean a significant number of network calls, one for each table in a request. A simple act such as getting the `Customer` table performs eight or more network calls. When working with the `Customer` table, you notice that it contains entries for `Orders` and `CustomerCustomerDemos` of type `Entity`. Every time you load the Customer table, you also load the following tables:

- ✔ `Orders`
- ✔ `CustomerCustomerDemo`

If you then interact with the `Orders` table, you also load the `Order Details` table. A seemingly simple query can suddenly unleash a flurry of application-stopping network traffic.

Using eager loading

LINQ normally uses a lazy loading strategy, where it loads what it needs, when it needs it. A lazy loading strategy provides the benefit of using system resources more efficiently, but it also loads items inconsistently, which can result in application delays. When you plan to work with a number of tables, try using an eager loading strategy to reduce the effect of loading multiple tables on your network and the application. To perform this task, you create a loading strategy, as shown here:

```
// Create the DataContext object.
Northwind DB = new Northwind(
   @"Data Source=MAINVISTA;Initial Catalog=Northwind;"
   + "Integrated Security=True", MS);

// Define the data load options.
DataLoadOptions ThisLoad = new DataLoadOptions();
ThisLoad.LoadWith<Customer>(CustLoad => CustLoad.Orders);
ThisLoad.LoadWith<Order>(OrdLoad => OrdLoad.OrderDetails);

// Add the load options to the DataContext.
DB.LoadOptions = ThisLoad;
```

This code creates a `DataContext` object as the previous examples have done. It then creates a `DataLoadOptions` object, `ThisLoad`. Each `LoadWith<T>()` method calls tells the code to load the required tables as part of creating the connection. This `DataContext` is ready to create queries that show customer orders and the order details without making a lot of extra network calls at inopportune times. A complete order request can consume upward of seventeen network requests per record, but using eager loading can reduce that number to five network requests per record — a significant savings, but only if you load the records carefully.

Creating the Database Modification Example

The LINQ to SQL provider is simple in some respects. It doesn't provide the functionality required for complex database applications. For example, you might find it difficult to create a new stored procedure (sproc) using LINQ to SQL. However, LINQ to SQL does make it possible to perform some essential database tasks such as manipulating records. Chapter 8 shows you how to query the database. The examples in this section demonstrate the techniques for inserting, updating, and deleting records from a table. The example relies on the Customers table in the Northwind database. You'll find this example in the \Chapter 11\ModifyDB folder of the source code for this book.

Performing an insert

Inserting records is one of the first tasks you perform with a table because the table is useless without data. When inserting a record, you need to

1. Check for the primary key
2. Verify that the record doesn't already exist
3. Create a new record object
4. Fill the new record with data
5. Add the record to the table

This process is pretty much set in stone. Even if you weren't working with LINQ, you'd follow the same set of steps. Listing 11-2 shows how you'd implement these steps using LINQ.

Listing 11-2 Inserting a New Record

```
private void btnInsert_Click(object sender, EventArgs e)
{
    //Define the XML mapping source.
    XmlMappingSource MS;
    MS = XmlMappingSource.FromUrl(
        @"C:\Northwind\Northwindmap.XML");

    // Create the DataContext object.
    Northwind DB = new Northwind(
        @"Data Source=MAINVISTA;Initial Catalog=Northwind;"
        + "Integrated Security=True", MS);

    // Check for the example customer. If the check fails,
    // then Cust is null.
    Customer Cust =
        (from ThisCust in DB.Customers
         where ThisCust.CustomerID == "EXMPL"
         select ThisCust).SingleOrDefault<Customer>();

    // Create the record only when it doesn't exist
    // already.
    if (Cust == null)
    {
```

Listing 11-2 *(continued)*

```
        // Create the record.
        Cust = new Customer()
        {
            CustomerID = "EXMPL",
            Address = "1234 Anywhere",
            City = "Nowhere",
            CompanyName = "ABC Foods Inc.",
            ContactName = "Jane Smith",
            ContactTitle = "Owner",
            Country = "USA",
            Fax = "(619)555-1212",
            Phone = "(619)555-1234",
            PostalCode = "99999",
            Region = "WI"
        };

        // Insert the record locally.
        DB.Customers.InsertOnSubmit(Cust);

        try
        {
            // Save the change to the database.
            DB.SubmitChanges();

            // Display the old and new postal code.
            MessageBox.Show("Inserted Record EXMPL");
        }

        // Detect any concurrency problems.
        catch (ChangeConflictException CCE)
        {
            // Display the conflict information.
            MessageBox.Show(CCE.Message);

            // Resolve the conflict.
            DB.ChangeConflicts.ResolveAll(
                RefreshMode.KeepChanges);
        }
    }
    // Otherwise, tell the user the record exists and exit.
    else
        MessageBox.Show("The EXMPL Record Already Exists");
}
```

As usual, the code begins by creating a mapping source and instantiating a `DataContext` object. The first step is to verify that the record you want to add doesn't already exist by checking for the key field, which is `CustomerID` in this case. The record for this example is `EXMPL`. If that record already exists, you can't add another one.

Notice that the query uses `SingleOrDefault<Customer>()` to obtain a single record. Previous examples used `Single<Customer>()` as shown here:

```
Customer Cust = (from ThisCust in DB.Customers
                 where ThisCust.CustomerID == "EXMPL"
                 select ThisCust).Single<Customer>();
```

You can obtain a slight performance benefit by using `Single<Customer>()`, but at the cost of an exception when LINQ can't find the record. The resulting exception doesn't tell you about the problem, unfortunately, as shown in Figure 11-2. What you see instead is an `InvalidOperationException` message and a detailed message that says the Sequence Contains No Elements, which is hardly helpful.

Figure 11-2: Using Single inappropriately results in exceptions.

InvalidOperationException was unhandled	✕
Sequence contains no elements	
Troubleshooting tips:	
Get general help for this exception.	
Search for more Help Online...	
Actions:	
View Detail...	
Copy exception detail to the clipboard	

Using `SingleOrDefault<Customer>()` provides you with a default output from the query of a `null` record that you can validate using an `if` statement. In fact, that's the next step the code takes. When the `EXMPL` record doesn't exist, the code creates a new `Customer` record, `Cust`, and fills it with data. As with all changes, the new record is local at this point. LINQ reminds you of the fact that the data is local by using the `InsertOnSubmit()` method to add the new record to `Customers`. If you want to add multiple records to the table, you create an array of `Customer` objects and then add them to the table using the `InsertAllOnSubmit()` method.

At this point, the code is ready to add the record to the database. To perform this task, you use the `SubmitChanges()` method. Because this call actually sends the data to the database, you must place it within a `try...catch` structure as shown. The `try...catch` structure contains error handling, the most important of which is handling potential conflict resolution.

Performing an update

Updates are normally the next step in working with a table. You update records to show changes that occur after the initial entry or to correct errors in the original entry. When updating a record, you need to

1. Check for the primary key

2. Verify that the record exists

3. Modify the existing record's data

4. Update the record in the table

Most applications add other steps. For example, you'll usually check the data for potential errors and verify that the data meets specific requirements such as being in a particular range. This example doesn't consider these additional needs. Listing 11-3 shows the basic four steps used to update a record.

Listing 11-3   Updating an Existing Record

```
private void btnUpdate_Click(object sender, EventArgs e)
{
    //Define the XML mapping source.
    XmlMappingSource MS;
    MS = XmlMappingSource.FromUrl(
        @"C:\Northwind\Northwindmap.XML");

    // Create the DataContext object.
    Northwind DB = new Northwind(
        @"Data Source=MAINVISTA;Initial Catalog=Northwind;"
        + "Integrated Security=True", MS);

    // Obtain the target customer.
    Customer Cust =
        (from ThisCust in DB.Customers
         where ThisCust.CustomerID == "EXMPL"
         select ThisCust).SingleOrDefault<Customer>();

    // If the customer exists, perform the update.
    if (Cust != null)
    {

        // Update the contact name and title locally.
        Cust.ContactName = "Sara Smith";
        Cust.ContactTitle = "Buyer";

        try
        {
            // Save the change to the database.
            DB.SubmitChanges();

            // Display the old and new postal code.
            MessageBox.Show(
                "Contact Information for EXMPL Changed");
        }
```

```
        // Detect any concurrency problems.
        catch (ChangeConflictException CCE)
        {
            // Display the conflict information.
            MessageBox.Show(CCE.Message);

            // Resolve the conflict.
            DB.ChangeConflicts.ResolveAll(
                RefreshMode.KeepChanges);
        }
    }

    // Otherwise, display an error message.
    else
        MessageBox.Show("The EXMPL Record Doesn't Exist");
}
```

The code for obtaining the record is the same as when you insert a record. However, in this case, you want the record to contain something. If the record is null, you can't update it. The example handles this requirement using a simple if statement. Notice that the example code still uses the SingleOrDefault<Customer>() method because you can't be sure whether the record exists in the table.

Data modification always begins locally. In this case, the example updates the contact information. The code then enters a try...catch structure and performs the remote update using DB.SubmitChanges(). Notice that you don't use any special method to perform an update. LINQ automatically marks the record as dirty (having changes) and updates it for you. This act differs from an insertion or deletion because LINQ can't know that the record is inserted or deleted until you tell it to perform the task using a special method call. As with all database changes, you must provide error handling that considers conflict resolution as a minimum.

Performing a delete

Record deletions occur when the data in a record is no longer needed. The data is either outdated or so hopelessly damaged that you want to start the record over. When deleting a record, you need to

1. Check for the primary key

2. Verify that the record exists

3. Mark the record as deleted

4. Delete the record from the table

As with other operations shown in this example, a real world application will have other checks when performing a deletion. You want to ensure that any child records are also deleted and that the deletion won't have any undesired side effects. In addition, in many applications, you place the deleted record in an archive, rather than delete it entirely. Listing 11-4 shows the basic delete operation performed by this example.

Listing 11-4   Deleting an Existing Record

```
private void btnDelete_Click(object sender, EventArgs e)
{
    //Define the XML mapping source.
    XmlMappingSource MS;
    MS = XmlMappingSource.FromUrl(
        @"C:\Northwind\Northwindmap.XML");

    // Create the DataContext object.
    Northwind DB = new Northwind(
        @"Data Source=MAINVISTA;Initial Catalog=Northwind;"
        + "Integrated Security=True", MS);

    // Obtain the target customer.
    Customer Cust =
        (from ThisCust in DB.Customers
         where ThisCust.CustomerID == "EXMPL"
         select ThisCust).SingleOrDefault<Customer>();

    // If the customer exists, delete it.
    if (Cust != null)
    {

        // Delete the record.
        DB.Customers.DeleteOnSubmit(Cust);

        try
        {
            // Save the change to the database.
            DB.SubmitChanges();

            // Display the old and new postal code.
            MessageBox.Show("Deleted Record EXMPL");
        }

        // Detect any concurrency problems.
        catch (ChangeConflictException CCE)
        {
            // Display the conflict information.
            MessageBox.Show(CCE.Message);
```

```
        // Resolve the conflict.
        DB.ChangeConflicts.ResolveAll(
            RefreshMode.KeepChanges);
    }
}

// Otherwise, display an error message.
else
    MessageBox.Show("The EXMPL Record Doesn't Exist");
}
```

The code begins by creating the required database connection and locating the customer record. As with an update, you can't delete a record that doesn't exist, so a `null` return value causes the application to display an error message an exit the event handler.

Deleting a record is easier than any other task you can perform. You already know which record you want to delete because you queried the database for it and have a local copy of it. Consequently, all the code must do is call the `DeleteOnSubmit(Cust)` method to mark the record for deletion. When the code calls `DB.SubmitChanges()`, SQL Server removes the record from the table. As with all the other examples, you must perform this last task within a `try...catch` structure to provide conflict error handling as a minimum.

Using Concurrency Checks and Resolving Errors

The "Understanding concurrency problems" section of the chapter discusses many of the issues you must consider when detecting and resolving concurrency issues. However, the basic detection and resolution scenario has a few more twists and turns to it. LINQ provides techniques for checking into the details of concurrency problems. It then lets you handle those concurrency problems at a detailed level. This section describes two detail levels you can use when working with concurrency issues:

- **Object:** Use the object level when you want to work with one object at a time. In most cases, an object will equate to a record. Consequently, you can decide on a record-by-record basis how to resolve conflicts. The object can refer to other database entities depending on how you create the enumeration used to process the database data.

- **Member:** Use the member level when you want to work with a single element of the sequence at a time. In most cases, this means a single field of the record. This option helps you ensure that database requirements such as relational integrity remain in effect. You could use this feature to reject changes to key fields, for example, and leave other changes in place.

Understanding optimistic versus pessimistic concurrency

The default concurrency model used for LINQ is optimistic. The term *optimistic* refers to how LINQ handles record usage. It assumes that only one caller will request a record for modification at a time but that many people could request the record for viewing. When you use optimistic concurrency, you let other people use a record even if someone else is modifying it. The reason for using optimistic concurrency is to make the record available to more people. Nothing would be worse than to have a contact database with some records inconveniently locked. Eventually, users would rely on their own address books and forget the one on the network because their personal address book is always available.

Unfortunately, optimistic concurrency doesn't always work. For example, you wouldn't want to use optimistic concurrency in a bank. Imagine the chaos that would occur when one person's changes to a record are lost after someone else overwrites them. *Pessimistic* concurrency takes the view that you need to lock every record for

every change. In fact, you can create a transaction while making the change to ensure that all changes take place or none of them do — perfect for a bank.

The `System.Transactions` namespace contains the classes you use to implement pessimistic concurrency. You use precisely the same techniques for using transactions with LINQ that you do with any application. The only difference is that you use these transactions with the LINQ query, rather than standard code. Complete coverage of transactions is outside the scope of this book. You can find a discussion of the `System.Transactions` namespace at `http://msdn2.microsoft.com/en-us/library/system.transactions.aspx`. The article at `http://www.devsource.com/c/a/Languages/Managing-Database-Transactions-with-the-TransactionScope/` provides you with a good overview of using transactions with technologies such as LINQ.

Resolving conflicts at the object level

As mentioned, object level concurrency checks let you work at the record level of the database in most cases. The example in this section performs a few new tasks. First, it retrieves multiple records and performs a batch change on them. Second, it shows how you could use record-by-record conflict resolution to ensure that any record that can change does change. The example bypasses problem records and displays them on the screen. Listing 11-5 shows the code for this example. You'll find this example in the `\Chapter 11\ObjectConcurrency` folder of the source code for this book.

Listing 11-5 Handling Concurrency at the Object Level

```csharp
private void btnTest_Click(object sender, EventArgs e)
{
    //Define the XML mapping source.
    XmlMappingSource MS;
    MS = XmlMappingSource.FromUrl(
        @"C:\Northwind\Northwindmap.XML");

    // Create the DataContext object.
    Northwind DB = new Northwind(
        @"Data Source=MAINVISTA;Initial Catalog=Northwind;"
        + "Integrated Security=True", MS);

    // Obtain a list of customers in Oregon.
    IQueryable<NWind.Customer> Cust =
        from ThisCust in DB.Customers
        where ThisCust.Region == "OR"
        select ThisCust;

    // Update the Country field locally.
    foreach (Customer ThisCust in Cust)
        ThisCust.Country = "United States";

    try
    {
        // Save the change to the database.
        DB.SubmitChanges(ConflictMode.ContinueOnConflict);

        // Show a success message.
        txtResult.Text = txtResult.Text + "Success!";
    }

    // Detect any concurrency problems.
    catch (ChangeConflictException CCE)
    {
        // Resolve each conflict individually.
        foreach (ObjectChangeConflict ThisConflict
            in DB.ChangeConflicts)
        {
            // Show the conflict.
            txtResult.Text = txtResult.Text +
                "\r\nConflict: " +
                ((Customer)ThisConflict.Object).CustomerID +
                "\r\n" + CCE.Message;

            // Resolve the conflict.
            ThisConflict.Resolve(RefreshMode.KeepChanges);
        }
    }
}
```

The example begins with the usual tasks of creating a mapping source and a data context. The example then shows how to create a query to extract multiple records from the database. In this case, the code relies on the `IQueryable<NWind.Customer>` object, `Cust`. Notice that the example uses `IQueryable` rather than `IEnumerable`. The query retrieves the records of all customers who live in Oregon. You can use any combination of `where` operators to create a list of records from any location or matching any other criteria. No matter what criteria you use, the output is a collection of records.

The application uses a `foreach` statement to move through the records individually. In each case, the code changes USA to United States in the `ThisCust.Country` field. It's important to realize that the change occurs only locally. The entries in the database remain the same while this loop does its work to the local sequence.

At this point, the code calls `DB.SubmitChanges()` to perform the updates on SQL Server. Notice the use of `ConflictMode.ContinueOnConflict`, which lets the application continue processing records even when a concurrency or other conflict occurs. The default settings stop all processing the moment the application sees the first conflict, which isn't the best way to perform batch processing. Using this approach lets you see all problem records at one time.

The `try...catch` structure for this example differs from those you've seen in other examples in this chapter. The exception handler begins with a `foreach` structure that extracts each `ObjectChangeConflict` object in the `DB.ChangeConflicts` collection. Each of these entries will normally represent a failed record change. It's important to note that a record be associated with multiple conflicts. Consequently, the `foreach` loop may process the same record more than once.

In this case, the example tracks each of the failures and displays them in a text box. The output includes the `CustomerID` value. Note that you must cast the object as a `Customer` type before you can extract the information; otherwise the application won't compile. The output also includes the failure message provided as part of the exception.

The example ends by telling each object to handle the error by keeping the changes provided by the application. Note that the code uses the `ThisConflict.Resolve()` method to handle the conflict, rather than relying on `ResolveAll()`. You use `ResolveAll()` only when you want to handle all the errors in a particular way — this technique is oriented toward handling the errors individually, so you use `Resolve()` instead.

Resolving conflicts at the member level

Sometimes conflicts require precise control. You may want to retain some data and force updates of other data. For example, you probably don't want to update the key field of a record when that update is in conflict. Otherwise, the relations between records could become damaged and you'd spend your weekend cleaning them up. The example in this section takes the example in the "Resolving conflicts at the object level" section of the chapter another step. The exception handler works with data at the member level in this case. Because the application performs essentially the same task, Listing 11-6 shows only the exception handler. You'll find this example in the \Chapter 11\MemberConcurrency folder of the source code for this book.

Listing 11-6   Handling Concurrency at the Member Level

```
// Detect any concurrency problems.
catch (ChangeConflictException CCE)
{
   // Resolve each conflict individually.
   foreach (ObjectChangeConflict ObjConflict
      in DB.ChangeConflicts)
   {

      // Resolve each member individually.
      foreach (MemberChangeConflict MemConflict
         in ObjConflict.MemberConflicts)
      {
         // Show the conflict.
         txtResult.Text = txtResult.Text +
            "\r\nConflict: " +
            ((Customer)ObjConflict.Object).CustomerID +
            "\r\n" + CCE.Message;

         // Resolve specific members.
         if (MemConflict.Member.Name.Equals("Country"))
            MemConflict.Resolve(
               RefreshMode.OverwriteCurrentValues);
         else
            MemConflict.Resolve(RefreshMode.KeepChanges);
      }
   }
}
```

The exception handler begins as before by extracting a record object from DB.ChangeConflicts as a ObjectChangeConflict object, ObjConflict. In this case, ObjConflict acts as input to another foreach loop where the code extracts each of the members (fields) of the record individually. The MemberChangeConflict object, MemConflict, contains the conflict information for a specific member. The foreach loop could end up processing multiple members for each record, so you need to consider both object (record) and member requirements.

The conflict output information for this example is the same as the ObjectConcurrency example: CustomerID and the precise conflict error message. However, note that you must now use the MemConflict. Resolve() method to handle the concurrency problem. To resolve concurrency issues at the object or member level, use the object at the same level. In this case, you use MemConflict, rather than ObjConflict, because you're working at the member level.

Chapter 12

LINQ to Active Directory

In This Chapter

▶ Locating specific Active Directory objects

▶ Specifying the Active Directory variables

▶ Getting and installing the LINQ to Active Directory provider

▶ Designing a simple Active Directory application

▶ Defining the LINQ to Active Directory provider limitations

*I*f you work in a corporate environment, you know how much Active Directory means to your organization. You use Active Directory to store just about every piece of important information for your organization — everything from user names and rights to application settings. In short, Active Directory is more than a simple database; it's the source of information for most activities in your organization.

Unfortunately, Active Directory relies on your knowledge of the Lightweight Directory Access Protocol (LDAP), a query language in its own right. The language is complex enough that some people have put together tutorials for it and others have compiled lists of LDAP resources such as the one found at `http://labmice.techtarget.com/activedirectory/AD_ldap.htm`.

This chapter helps you discover a new way of working with Active Directory without relying on LDAP directly. Instead of using LDAP, you depend on a special LINQ to Active Directory provider that translates queries that you already understand into LDAP syntax. Yes, you're still relying on LDAP, but you aren't formulating the LDAP requests. The techniques shown in this chapter help you create consistent requests with reliable results.

As part of working with LINQ to Active Directory, this chapter shows you how to set up your system to use LINQ to Active Directory, create an application prototype, and develop a simple application. No solution is completely foolproof or absolutely right for every situation, so this chapter also helps you understand some of the potential problems you'll encounter when working with LINQ to Active Directory. The point of LINQ to Active Directory is providing you with another tool to use with Active Directory, not the only tool.

Working with Specific Active Directory Objects

Unlike many of the databases that you work with, Active Directory is special for two reasons. First, it uses a hierarchical model. Most databases today rely on the relational model of tables and relationships between those tables. Second, unlike any other database you use, Active Directory is composed exclusively of objects. These objects have attributes (another term for properties) that you use to store data. When working with Active Directory in an application, you modify these objects and their properties using code.

This chapter works with a common object, the user. An administrator is accustomed to seeing the user object in the Active Directory Users and Computers console. You choose the Users folder, double-click an account within that folder, and see the user Properties dialog box shown in Figure 12-1.

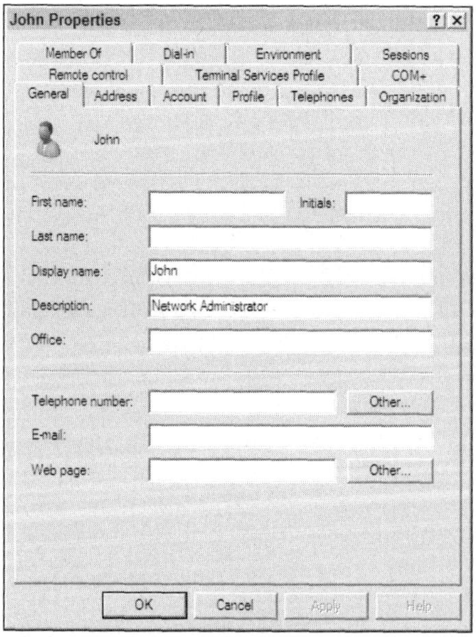

Figure 12-1:
The user object appears in a Properties dialog box for the administrator.

Using the user Properties dialog box completely hides the complexity of Active Directory from the administrator but tends to make it difficult for you as a developer to interact with Active Directory. You can obtain a little better view of Active Directory using the Active Directory Service Interface Editor (ADSI Edit) utility. This tool appears in the Administrative Tools folder of the Control Panel.

When you start the application, you see a blank screen. You must first create a connection to the domain controller using LDAP. Note the LDAP connection string because it is the same string you need later to create a connection using the example application. Right-click the ADSI Edit entry in the ADSI Edit utility and choose Connect To from the context menu. The LDAP connection string for your server appears in the Path field. Click OK to create the connection.

At this point, you can begin drilling down into the Active Directory database as shown in Figure 12-2. Note the rightmost column in Figure 12-2, Distinguished Name. This information is important when creating applications because it provides a full path to the particular object you want to work with. You use distinguished names for a number of tasks, so it's important to know how to find the distinguished name using ADSI Edit.

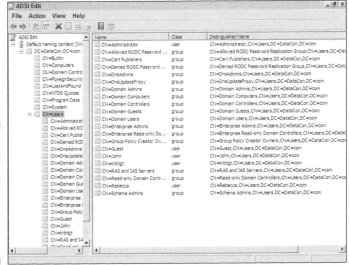

Figure 12-2: ADSI Edit provides a view of the Active Directory objects on your server.

Each of the CN= values shown in Figure 12-2 is an object. When you right-click an object and choose Properties from the context menu, you see a listing of attributes (properties) for that object, as shown in Figure 12-3. As you scroll through the list, you discover that each of these objects has a considerable number of attributes and you can interact with any of them within your application. Not all of these attributes are visible to the administrator, so you can't always count on the administrator knowing you've made a required change.

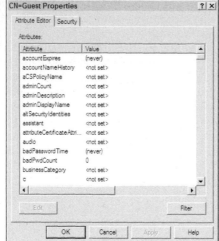

Figure 12-3:
Each object
has a
number of
attributes
associated
with it.

Using ADSI Edit to explore Active Directory before you write your first application is a great idea because ADSI Edit will help you familiarize yourself with the objects as they appear to Active Directory. In addition, you begin to understand how Active Directory organizes information and what you must do to see that information in your application.

Defining Active Directory Variables

It may seem archaic, but you always access Active Directory through COM objects. .NET Framework doesn't provide a direct Active Directory access mechanism but does encapsulate much (but not all) of the functionality in the `System.DirectoryServices` namespace. Using LINQ actually adds another layer because now you're using the LINQ to Active Directory provider to encapsulate both the `System.DirectoryServices` namespace and the remaining COM object functionality you require. The results are worth the effort, however, because working with Active Directory using COM can be a painful experience and the learning curve is extreme. Using LINQ to Active Directory is almost simple.

Unfortunately, as you see when working with the example program in the "Creating the Simple Active Directory Query Example" section of the chapter, you can't quite escape without knowing a little about how the `System.DirectoryServices` namespace and the COM object interface work. While the `System.DirectoryServices` namespace is straightforward, you have to know which COM interface to use. All .NET applications rely on the `IADs*` COM interfaces. You'll also see a lot of information about the `IDirectoryObject` interfaces, but these interfaces are used only by C++ developers.

You have a number of options for defining the information you want to work with in Active Directory. The technique used by this example is the easiest: you simply access one of the `IADs*` COM interfaces. In this case, the example uses the `IADsUser` interface, which provides a considerable amount of information about the user. There are too many `IADs*` interfaces to mention, but the Visual Studio documentation contains a complete list of them.

Just knowing about the interfaces is enough. The LINQ to Active Directory provider hides the implementation details from view. All you need to know is which `IADs*` interface you want to use. The example program provides you with pointers. You may want to look at the `IADs*` interface information because the `IADs*` interface often provides access to additional Active Directory attributes that you won't see in the object's attribute list when using ADSI Edit. In short, research is a must when working with Active Directory.

Obtaining the LINQ to Active Directory Provider

Before you can begin creating new Active Directory applications, you must have a new provider. This provider adds to the capabilities provided by LINQ to Object and LINQ to XML. In many respects, it works similarly to LINQ to SQL by providing mappings to existing technologies. (See Chapter 8 for details about LINQ to SQL.) You find the LINQ to Active Directory provider at `http://www.codeplex.com/LINQtoAD`.

The developer of the LINQ to Active Directory provider warns that this isn't a Microsoft supported product. Although the developer does provide some support, Microsoft doesn't, so you use this provider at your own risk and without any support. You need to test any application that uses this provider thoroughly before you move the application to a production environment. Always use a test server, not your production server, for application testing; otherwise you may have a nasty surprise when the library fails to perform some task as expected. Use the following steps to download and install the provider on your system:

1. **Click the Releases tab on the CodePlex Web site.**

   You see the LINQ to Active Directory RTW page of the Web site.

2. **Click the LINQtoAD.zip link.**

   The Web site displays a licensing agreement.

3. **Read the licensing agreement and click I Accept if you agree with it.**

   The file download begins. Note the location of the download on your hard drive. The filename is LINQtoAD CodePlex Release.ZIP.

4. **UnZIP the file on your hard drive.**

   The LINQ to Active Directory provider is in code form, not a compiled product. It consists of the provider and a demonstration application. Make sure you spend time working with the demonstration application because it shows how to use all the LINQ to Active Directory features. This product also shows you how to build a provider — you can use it as a model for creating your own provider at some point.

5. **Load the LINQ to Active Directory provider into Visual Studio by double-clicking the LinqToAD.SLN file.**

6. **Unless you're using precisely the same source control as the developer of this provider, you'll see a message saying that Visual Studio couldn't find the source control provider. Click Yes to remove source control from the project.**

   You see the project entries in Solution Explorer shown in Figure 12-4. Figure 12-4 also shows the demonstration program opened. The demonstration program helps you understand how this provider works.

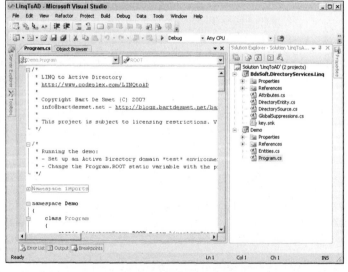

Figure 12-4: The LINQ to Active Directory provider project includes the provider and a demo.

7. **Select Release in the Solution Configurations drop-down list box.**

   You want a release build, not a debug build, unless you want to track how the provider works in your debugger.

8. Choose Build⇨BdsSoft.DirectoryServices.Linq.

You see the Save File As dialog box shown in Figure 12-5. This feature saves the configuration without source control and to match your machine setup.

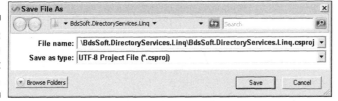

Figure 12-5:
Save the new project settings.

9. Choose a location to save the CSProj file. Click Save.

Visual Studio builds the LINQ to Active Directory provider. The `BdsSoft.DirectoryServices.Linq\bin\Release` folder will contain a `BdsSoft.DirectoryServices.Linq.dll` file and an `Interop.ActiveDs.dll` file that provide support for working with Active Directory.

At this point, you can choose to add the LINQ to Active Directory provider to the Global Assembly Cache (GAC). Doing so makes the assembly easier to access — you use the same technique you use for any other .NET Framework assembly. This chapter assumes that you're using a local copy of the required file. Use the following steps to add the assembly to the GAC:

1. Choose Start⇨Programs⇨Microsoft Visual Studio 2008⇨Visual Studio Tools. Right-click the Visual Studio 2008 Command Prompt and choose Run As Administrator from the context menu.

You see a command prompt that has the path information required to access Visual Studio command line utilities.

2. Change directories to the LINQ to Active Directory assembly folder using the CD command.

The command you type depends on the location of the code on your system. In most cases, you use a command such as `CD \LINQtoAD CodePlex Release\BdsSoft.DirectoryServices.Linq\bin\ Release`.

3. Type GACUtil /i BdsSoft.DirectoryServices.Linq.DLL and press Enter.

The Global Assembly Cache Utility (GACUtil) adds the assembly to the GAC. If you see the dreaded "Failure adding assembly to the cache: Access denied." error message, you probably didn't open the command prompt using administrative privileges as described in Step 1.

Creating the Simple Active Directory Query Example

The example in this section demonstrates how to set up a project to work with Active Directory using the LINQ to Active Directory provider. If you haven't already downloaded, built, and installed this provider, you need to do so using the instructions in the "Obtaining the LINQ to Active Directory Provider" section of the chapter before you try to create this example. You'll find this example in the \Chapter 12\SimpleAD folder of the source code for this book.

Performing the project setup

Active Directory applications can rely on any of the Visual Studio templates. It's possible to use Active Directory in many different circumstances, so keep your options open when you choose a project type. The example uses a standard Windows form as a starting point. After you create the basic application, use the following steps to add the required support for working with LINQ to Active Directory:

1. **Right-click the project entry in Solution Explorer and choose Add Reference from the context menu.**

2. **Select the Browse tab and locate the Release folder for the BdsSoft. DirectoryServices.Linq.DLL file. Highlight both DLL files.**

   You see the Add Reference dialog box shown in Figure 12-6.

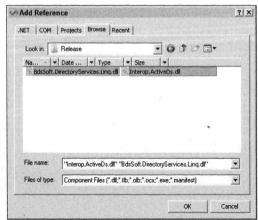

Figure 12-6:
Create a reference for the LINQ to Active Directory provider.

3. **Click OK.**

   Visual Studio adds references for the LINQ to Active Directory provider to the `References` folder in Solution Explorer.

4. **Right-click the project entry in Solution Explorer and choose Add Reference from the context menu.**

   You see the Add Reference dialog box shown in Figure 12-7.

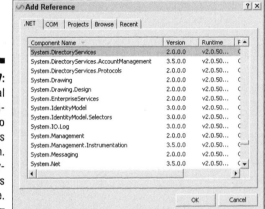

Figure 12-7: A minimal application also requires the System. Directory- Services namespace.

5. **Select the .NET tab and locate the System.DirectoryServices entry. Click OK.**

   Visual Studio adds the required `System.DirectoryServices` reference. Depending on your application needs, you may also need to add references to `System.DirectoryServices.AccountManagement` and `System.DirectoryServices.Protocols`. The example application doesn't require these namespaces.

6. **Open the code file for your project and type the following statements:**

```
using System.DirectoryServices;
using ActiveDs;
using BdsSoft.DirectoryServices.Linq;
```

   The `System.DirectoryServices` namespace offers access to the native Active Directory features provided by .NET Framework. Most of these resources aren't directly usable by LINQ, but you need them to use the LINQ to Active Directory provider successfully. The `BdsSoft. DirectoryServices.Linq` namespace gives you access to the LINQ to Active Directory provider.

Active Directory applications tend to have complex setup requirements because Active Directory is a complex database. Not only is Active Directory a hierarchical database, it's also a database of complex objects — each of which has different requirements. The example in this section provides basic Active Directory access functionality. You can perform tasks such as querying the Active Directory objects and processing some data types.

Defining an Active Directory object class

As mentioned, Active Directory is a complex hierarchical database consisting of specialized objects. These objects have no predefined form — they can contain any number of properties. Yes, Active Directory does come with predefined objects, such as Users, but even these objects include a considerable number of properties. Before you can begin working with a particular object, you must define an object class for it that tells LINQ what you want from Active Directory. Listing 12-1 shows a typical Active Directory object class.

Listing 12-1   Creating an Object Class

```
[DirectorySchema("user", typeof(IADsUser))]
public class User : DirectoryEntity
{
    // When working with a directory entry in
    // read-only mode, you need only implement
    // the standard get/set methods.
    [DirectoryAttribute("name")]
    public String Name { get; set; }

    [DirectoryAttribute("description")]
    public String Description { get; set; }

    [DirectoryAttribute("distinguishedName")]
    public String DistinguishedName { get; set; }

    // When working with a directory entry in
    // read/write mode, you must define a local
    // variable, and implement the specialized
    // get/set methods shown here.
    private String _manager;

    [DirectoryAttribute("manager")]
    public String Manager
    {
        get
        {
            return _manager;
```

```
        }
        set
        {
            _manager = value;

            // This call registers the change
            // with the local variable.
            OnPropertyChanged("Manager");
        }
    }
}
```

The first thing you should notice is that this class doesn't define properties for every Active Directory object attribute. Even if you created an object class that defines a property for every potential common attribute, it's likely that your Active Directory implementation will include a few nonstandard attributes, which means you'd have to define properties for these attributes in your code. Generally, you want to create an object class that contains properties for just the attributes you want to interact with to keep things simple.

All the attributes for the object class come from the LINQ to Active Directory provider, so you won't find them in your MSDN help. The `DirectorySchema` attribute requires two inputs. The first is the name of the Active Directory schema. This is the name of the schema as it appears in ADSI Edit and other Active Directory utilities. The second input is the data type of the schema as defined by the `IADs` COM interface you want to use. Because this example works with the user schema, it uses the `IADsUser` data type.

The object class derives from the `DirectoryEntry` class provided by the LINQ to Active Directory provider. You can call your class anything you want, but it pays to stick with a name that helps you remember its purpose, which is why the example relies on `User` as the class name.

Your object class will contain two kinds of properties. When you plan to use a property for read-only tasks, you can use the shortcut method of creating the property. However, even though you can write information to this property, the application won't save it to Active Directory. Note that the property has a `DirectoryAttribute` attribute that defines the name of the attribute that you want to interact with in Active Directory.

The second property type lets you both read and write Active Directory attribute values. In this case, you must use the formal property declaration method. The major difference is that you add a call to `OnPropertyChanged()` with the name of the property that has changed. This calls signals the `DirectorySource` object (described in the "Reading user information" section of the chapter) to save the change. If you don't include the

`OnPropertyChanged()` method call, it will appear that the change has occurred in your local code, but the change won't take effect in Active Directory because your code won't have the required coupling in place.

Creating a root node pointer

Active Directory is a hierarchical database, and in many respects it has the same structural features as the registry or an XML file. With this in mind, you need a pointer to the location that you want to work with in Active Directory. The most common starting point is the Active Directory root node, so that's the starting point used in this example. Listing 12-2 shows how to obtain a pointer to the Active Directory root node.

Listing 12-2   Obtaining an Active Directory Pointer

```
// Create a pointer to the root of Active Directory.
DirectoryEntry Root;

public frmMain()
{
    InitializeComponent();

    // Define the Active Directory root.
    Root = new DirectoryEntry(txtServerName.Text);
}
```

In most cases it's best to use a global object for the pointer. The application defines a `DirectoryEntry` object, `Root`, for this purpose. The `Directory Entry` class is part of the `System.DirectoryServices` namespace, so you can find full documentation for this object as part of your Visual Studio help.

The example assumes that you have administrator access to the domain controller, so it relies on Windows authentication. Consequently, the only input that the example provides is the LDAP URI for the server. In this case, this value is `LDAP://WinServer`. You must change this value in the Server Name field of the example application as explained in the "Reading user information" section of the chapter; otherwise the example won't work.

If you need to use something other than Windows authentication or don't have administrator privileges on the domain controller, the application must also supply credentials to access the domain controller. For example, you can provide a name and password as credentials when necessary.

Reading user information

A good place to start when working with Active Directory is reading information so that you can test your connection. In fact, at least some of the applications you write won't require anything more than read access for configuration information. This example shows how to read user information. Obviously, Active Directory has considerably more information to offer. Listing 12-3 shows how to read the user information.

Listing 12-3   Reading the User Information

```
private void btnRead_Click(object sender, EventArgs e)
{
   // Create a directory source for working with
   // the users.
   DirectorySource<User> Users =
      new DirectorySource<User>(Root,
                                   SearchScope.Subtree);

   // Obtain a list of users.
   DirectoryQuery<User> UserList =
      (DirectoryQuery<User>)Users.Select(
          ThisUser => ThisUser);

   // Display the list of users.
   txtResult.Text = "User List:\r\n\r\n";
   foreach (User ThisUser in UserList)
      txtResult.Text = txtResult.Text +
          ThisUser.Name + "\r\n" +
          ThisUser.Description + "\r\n" +
          ThisUser.DistinguishedName + "\r\n" +
          ThisUser.Manager + "\r\n\r\n";
}
```

The example begins by creating a `DirectorySource` object, `Users`. You can create a `DirectorySource` object in a number of ways. The example shows how to create one for searching for users within Active Directory. In this case, you provide two inputs: the `Root` pointer object shown in Listing 12-1 and a `SearchScope` enumeration value (the child elements of the Active Directory tree in this case).

Now that you have an Active Directory connection, you can create a query for it. The example simply selects all available users. It places these objects in a `DirectoryQuery` object, `UserList`. Both the `DirectorySource` and `DirectoryQuery` classes appear as part of the LINQ to Active Directory provider, so you won't find them listed in the Visual Studio help.

At this point, the code uses a `foreach` loop to build the application output. This information includes the user name, description, distinguished name, and manager's name, as shown in Figure 12-8. Note that the manager name appears as a distinguished name in the output. Even though you see just the manager name when working with the various Active Directory utilities, the manager name is always a distinguished name internally. This is an important consideration when you build applications to change the manager name (or any other Active Directory attribute that has an internal presentation that doesn't match the presentation of the Active Directory utilities). Always check the Active Directory values to ensure that you understand what Active Directory requires.

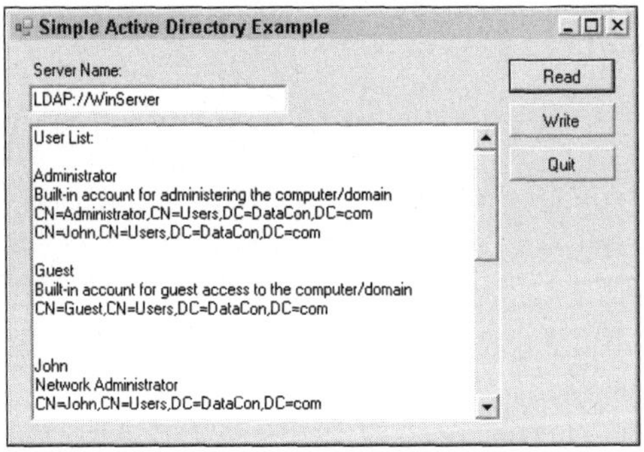

Figure 12-8:
The application output shows the user information of interest.

> **Simple Active Directory Example**
>
> Server Name:
> LDAP://WinServer
>
> User List:
>
> Administrator
> Built-in account for administering the computer/domain
> CN=Administrator,CN=Users,DC=DataCon,DC=com
> CN=John,CN=Users,DC=DataCon,DC=com
>
> Guest
> Built-in account for guest access to the computer/domain
> CN=Guest,CN=Users,DC=DataCon,DC=com
>
> John
> Network Administrator
> CN=John,CN=Users,DC=DataCon,DC=com
>
> Read
> Write
> Quit

Writing user information

After you know you can access Active Directory and understand the format of the information it requires, you can start writing information to it from your application. This example changes the manager information for the Guest account. It relies on a manager named John, but you can use the name of any account that you've configured. Listing 12-4 shows the code for this portion of the example.

Listing 12-4 Writing Data to Active Directory

```
private void btnWrite_Click(object sender, EventArgs e)
{
   // Create a directory source for working with
   // the users.
   DirectorySource<User> Users =
      new DirectorySource<User>(Root,
                                SearchScope.Subtree);

   // Obtain a list of users.
```

```
DirectoryQuery<User> UserList =
    (DirectoryQuery<User>)Users.Select(
        ThisUser => ThisUser);

// Locate the manager to use for the Guest account.
String Manager = "";
foreach (User ThisUser in UserList)
    if (ThisUser.Name == "John")
        Manager = ThisUser.DistinguishedName;

// Locate the Guest account and change the manager.
foreach (User ThisUser in UserList)
    if (ThisUser.Name == "Guest")
        ThisUser.Manager = Manager;

// Update the information in Active Directory.
Users.Update();

// Display a success message.
MessageBox.Show("Manager for Guest Account Updated");
}
```

As with reading data from Active Directory, you must create a `DirectorySource` object and create a `DirectoryQuery` object based on the query you want to perform. The example retrieves a list of all the users on the server, but you can obtain just the information you need using a combination of the `Where()` method and a lambda expression. When you're finished, you should have a listing of the object you want to manipulate.

The next step is to retrieve the manager information. It's always easier to retrieve this information from Active Directory than to try and create it yourself. Note how the example uses a combination of the `Name` property and the `DistinguishedName` property to obtain the `Manager` value. Because this information comes directly from Active Directory, you know that it already appears in the correct form. You must use an existing account for the `Manager String`. If you don't have a `John` user account on your system, be sure to modify the name to a name that does exist and recompile the code before you test this example.

At this point, the code locates the `Guest` account and assigns the `Manager` value to it. As with many LINQ tasks, the change affects only the local copy of the data. To modify the data on the server, the application calls the `Users.Update()` method. When you click the example application's Read button again, you see a manage account value for the `Guest` account as shown in Figure 12-9.

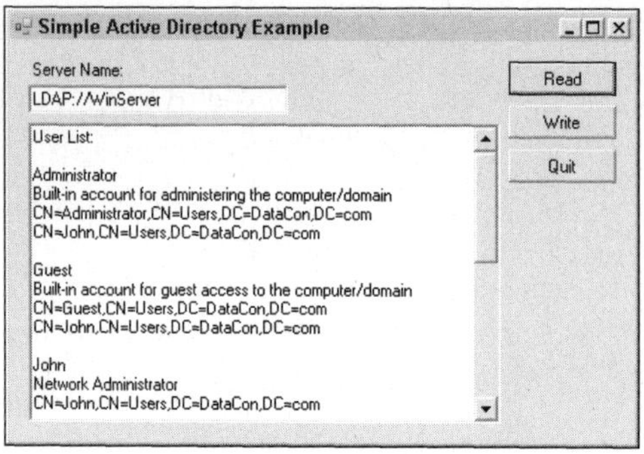

Figure 12-9:
The Guest
account
now has a
manager
assigned to
it.

Figure 12-9:
The Guest
account
now has a
manager
assigned to
it.

Understanding the Limitations of Active Directory Interaction

The LINQ to Active Directory provider isn't perfect. This chapter has already pointed out a few potential flaws. Even with these flaws, however, using LINQ to Active Directory makes life for the developer considerably easier than you might expect. This section provides a couple of additional issues that you need to consider when working with the LINQ to Active Directory provider.

Some LINQ methods aren't implemented

The current LINQ to Active Directory provider has limitations. It doesn't implement all the methods that you've used with the generic providers. For example, the `Count<T>()` method doesn't work. In every case where a method isn't implemented, the provider does return a `NotImplemented Exception`, as shown in Figure 12-10.

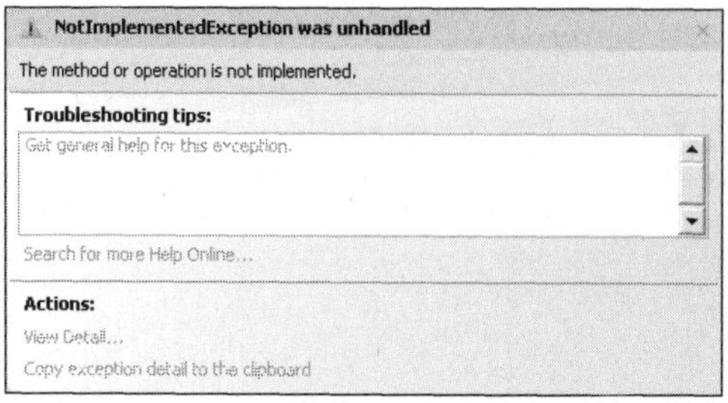

Figure 12-10:
Although
the provider
doesn't sup-
port LINQ
completely,
it does tell
you about
the problem.

The point is that you must test your applications carefully when using the LINQ to Active Directory provider. Make sure you include appropriate error handling with the application and handle all exceptions that you may encounter, even if you think that the method will work properly.

You'll find that using specific data types, rather than relying on `var`, will usually help you get better results when using the LINQ to Active Directory provider because the compiler doesn't have to guess about anything. In addition, you may find that your application runs slightly faster when using specific data types.

Defining the need for LDAP patience

The Achilles' heal of working with Active Directory is LDAP — you can't get away from it. Even when working with the LINQ to Active Directory provider, you must contend with issues such as creating an LDAP URI for the connection and working with distinguished names. It's in your best interest to spend time working with the various administrator tools on test machines before you begin writing Active Directory code. Even small mistakes can have costly consequences on a production system.

The best way to approach Active Directory is to assume that you'll make a mistake. Copy as much as you can directly from Active Directory as shown in the example in this chapter. When you can't copy, have a friend or two verify your code. Creating the right URIs and distinguished names appears simple, but it can become deceptively complex. Never test a new Active Directory application or an application update on a production machine because you'll almost certainly regret doing so in the long run.

Chapter 13

Other LINQ to Strategies

In This Chapter

▶ Considering what makes a LINQ solution viable

▶ Developing a COM+ application

▶ Developing an RDF application

▶ Developing a MySQL application

The previous chapters of this book have shown you what appears to be a considerable number of LINQ solutions, but these examples only skim the surface of what LINQ can do. As was shown in Table 1-1, you can find a significant number of LINQ to solutions on the Internet. In fact, you saw two of these LINQ to solutions in Chapters 11 and 12, where you discovered how to work with Office 2007 and Active Directory, respectively. You can probably use LINQ in more places than anticipated or even expected. This chapter examines a few more of the possibilities.

More important than the existing solutions are the solutions you need for your particular needs. Most organizations have custom applications and may wonder whether LINQ will work for them. The interesting thing about LINQ is that it's expandable without resorting to using extreme amounts of low-level code. Yes, you must have good coding skills to write a provider of your own, but as the LINQ to Active Directory example in Chapter 12 shows, you can write a provider using standard C# programming techniques. This chapter also explores some of the issues you must consider before you attempt to write a provider of your own.

Understanding the Qualifications for a LINQ to Solution

Given the right provider, you can use LINQ to technology to connect to just about anything. Many developers will likely create their own provider using the techniques shown with the LINQ to Active Directory example in Chapter 12.

Microsoft even provides instructions for creating your own LINQ to provider at `http://msdn2.microsoft.com/en-us/library/bb546158.aspx`. The Microsoft example is complete, but it's also a typical Microsoft example in that it's so complex that only a developer with a lot of experience will understand it. This is the example to use, though, if you need a high-performance, fully functional provider that does everything. Fortunately, you don't have to rely on this one complex example as your own solution. Microsoft provides a considerable number of examples at `http://msdn2.microsoft.com/en-us/library/bb397965.aspx`. (Visual Basic developers will want to look at the examples at `http://msdn2.microsoft.com/en-us/library/bb397978.aspx`.)

A simpler solution than starting from scratch for creating providers is to rely on a kit that automates some of the coding requirements. For example, the LINQExtender kit, at `http://www.codeplex.com/LinqExtender`, can help you create a new provider in a relatively short time. (Make sure you get the latest version of the LINQExtender kit to ensure you get good results.) However, using a kit can have the downside of performance penalties because you're adding yet another processing level to the resulting application. Most users won't even notice the difference, though, and the time saved by developers using LINQ is a big benefit. To see how someone else has faired using the LINQExtender kit, check out the LINQ to Flickr solution at `http://www.codeplex.com/LINQFlickr`. The article at `http://dotnetslackers.com/articles/csharp/CreatingCustomLINQProviderUsingLinqExtender.aspx` provides complete details on using LINQExtender to build a solution of your own.

The question remains of whether your application will work properly with LINQ. Although LINQ doesn't have many requirements and you can overcome many of them through data conversion or careful programming, an application does need to meet some criteria to work well with LINQ. The following list provides an overview of these basic requirements:

✔ **Structured:** A structure lets you interact with the data in an orderly manner. It doesn't matter whether the data is in a hierarchical format, such as XML, or in a tabular format, such as SQL Server. In fact, the data need not even appear in a single file — you could process the data from a group of files on a hard drive if desired. However, in all these cases, the data has an identifiable structure. Many binary files, such as those used to store graphics, have an identifiable structure, so you aren't even limited to data that appears in human readable form.

✔ **Repetitious:** A single instance of a data element doesn't require a query because you already know what that single instance entails. To use LINQ successfully, you must be able to define a sequence of repeated data elements. Not every data element need contain every property (such as with XML), but the data element must have a specific structure of both required and optional properties that's repeated as a sequence. It's possible to overcome this requirement with careful programming. For example, you could use LINQ on a sentence by breaking it into individual words. Don't be afraid to break down data into constituent elements as needed to obtain the required results.

✓ **Accessible:** After seeing everything that LINQ can do, it might be tempting to use it on so-called hidden data. LINQ can't find data that you can't see yourself. It helps you organize data and it can locate data that you know resides in a certain sequence, but as good as LINQ is, it can't produce data out of thin air. The issue of accessibility also affects data that's layers deep within a data source. In most cases, such as the Office 2007 example in Chapter 10, you must drill down into the data source before you can use LINQ effectively.

Whether you create a custom provider or use the LINQExtender kit depends on your data and application requirements. The LINQExtender kit tends to work best when the data is relatively simple, such as a table from a database or a single XML file, and when the processing requirements aren't real time. The performance hit isn't significant, but it could be noticeable in some situations. If you do use a custom provider, it's essential that you provide enough time in your provider schedule to accommodate data and application complexities. Even though LINQ does make it possible for advanced users to create providers, writing a provider is normally a task accomplished by skilled developers working for third-party vendors who have lots of resources. Think challenging (not impossible) when you create a provider of your own.

Accessing COM+ Using LINQ

Some people may think that it's impossible to access COM+ using a new technology such as LINQ. In fact, some may wonder whether most organizations use COM+ at all — they view it as an old technology that has gone by the wayside.

COM+ is alive and well. You may be surprised to learn that some .NET and a few SQL Server features won't work without it. The COM+ functionality on your system resides in the Component Services console shown in Figure 13-1. (If you don't see the Component Services console in the Administrative Tools folder of the Control Panel, choose Start⇨Run, type **COMExp.MSC** in the Open field of the Run dialog box, and click OK.) As shown in the figure, you must drill down a few levels to find the COM+ applications on your system, but they're definitely there and in use much of the day. Consequently, making LINQ work with COM+ may not be such a wasted effort as originally thought.

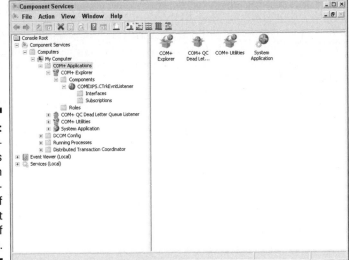

Figure 13-1:
COM+
applications
abound on
your sys-
tem, even if
you aren't
aware of
them.

COM+ is an older technology and you may find that you have to jump through a few hoops to get COM+ and LINQ to work together. Fortunately, you have a number of options when you want to access COM+ from LINQ. The two most useful options are

✔ Accessing COM+ as a Web service

✔ Using the same interoperability features as you always have with COM+ components

COM+ for Vista and Windows Server 2008 developers

COM+ has a few different requirements for Vista and Windows Server 2008 developers. The first requirement is that you must install all the IIS 6 features for your Internet Information Server (IIS) setup; otherwise, COM+ will insist that you don't have IIS installed. The IIS 6 features are an optional install, so you must install them separately. You still use the IIS 7 tools to manage your setup, but the IIS 6 tools must also be in place.

Microsoft has changed the security for COM+ in Vista and Windows Server 2008. These operating systems use the role-based security provided by COM+ and require that you install a Secure Sockets Layer (SSL) certificate on the server. (Don't confuse COM+ role-based security with role-based security in .NET — you implement COM+ role-based security using the Component Services console.) Fortunately, you can use the self-signed certificate for testing.

However, using SSL does mean that you must use the HTTPS protocol and not the HTTP protocol to access your WSDL file.

The new security requirements can open a host of problems for your application — creating an application is definitely easier when using Windows XP (or earlier) and Windows Server 2003 (or earlier). The most common security problem is that you'll see an "HTTP Error 500.24 — Internal Server Error" message. Use the following procedure to get rid of this message. (If you need additional help with IIS 7 configuration, please see my book *Microsoft IIS 7 Implementation and Administration,* published by Sybex.)

1. Open the Internet Information Services (IIS) Manager console.

2. Highlight your COM+ application in the Connections pane.

3. Double-click the Authentication icon.

4. Right-click ASP.NET Impersonation and choose Disable from the context menu.

You'll also probably see a "System.Runtime. Remoting.RemotingException: Requested Service not found" error message. Unfortunately,

you probably won't find help anywhere on how to fix this problem because it doesn't tell you anything about the issue in this case. Your application resides in the `\Windows\ System32\com\SoapVRoots\ <Application Name>` folder of your system. This folder contains at least one file (and I hope three). The important file is `web.config` (the other two, less important, files are `Default. aspx` and `Default.disco` — we don't use them in this example). In this file you should see a `<Service>` element entry similar to the one shown at the end of this sidebar.

The `<wellknown>` element always appears on a single line, even though it appears on multiple lines in this book. For some odd reason, Vista and Windows Server 2008 leave out the `<wellknown>` element and you have to create it yourself using information you obtain about your component from the `\Windows\ assembly` folder of your system. Make absolutely certain that you use `GACUtil` to register your component or you can't use it as a Web service. Failure to register the component is one of the major sources of error for COM+ Web services.

```
<service>
    <wellknown mode="SingleCall"
            type="COMPLusAccess.COMPLusAccess, COMPlusAccess,
                Version=1.0.0.30391, Culture=neutral,
                PublicKeyToken=d39e7a5f9adaf1cf"
            objectUri="COMPLusAccess.COMPLusAccess.soap" />
    <activated type="COMPLusAccess.COMPLusAccess,
    COMPlusAccess" />
</service>
```

The following sections describe these two options from a LINQ development perspective. You'll find code for the COM+ component used in these sections in the `\Chapter 13\COMPlusAccess` folder of the source code for this book. Here's the essential code for this COM+ component (all it does is break a string into individual words and place those works in an array):

```
public string[] CreateArray(string Input)
{
    return Input.Split(new char[] {' '});
}
```

COM+ accessed as a Web service

The easiest way to work with COM+ applications is to configure the COM+ application as a Web service. Interestingly enough, this feature has been around for a long time, so the technology is stable. You can find an article about configuring your COM+ application as a Web service at `http://www.informit.com/articles/article.aspx?p=332883`. The process isn't complex — it requires only that you change a few settings — and it does offer some interesting benefits such as making your COM+ application visible through a firewall.

COM+ applications that you configure as a Web service rely on the Simple Object Access Protocol (SOAP) for connectivity. Consequently, you configure Visual Studio to use a Web Reference. Type the WSDL file location for your COM+ application, now a Web service. For example, you might type `http://localhost/TestCOMPlus/COMPlusAccess.COMPlusAccess.soap?WSDL` for a COM+ application on your local machine. (Remember to use the HTTPS version of the URL, `https://localhost/TestCOMPlus/COMPlusAccess.COMPlusAccess.soap?WSDL`, when working with Vista and Windows Server 2008.) Figure 13-2 shows the COM+ application access as a Web service. After you can access your COM+ application as a Web service, you can use the XML techniques described in Chapter 9 to interact with it.

Visual Studio 2008 gotchas for the COM+ developer

Microsoft has changed some features in Visual Studio and .NET Framework that makes COM+ development interesting. The instructions in the original article at `http://www.informit.com/articles/article.aspx?p=332883` still work, but you must make a few concessions for Visual Studio 2008. The first change is to open the `AssemblyInfo.CS` file in the `Properties` folder of Solution Explorer. Modify the following two assembly attributes so that they contain an asterisk in the build field:

```
[assembly: Assembly
    Version("1.0.0.*")]
[assembly: AssemblyFile
    Version("1.0.0.*")]
```

You must also set the `[assembly: ComVisible(true)]` attribute to `true`. Without these two changes, the assembly will never work in COM+. Registration won't take place correctly unless the build number changes between compilations and you must make the assembly COM visible.

After you make these changes, open the project's Properties window using the Project⇨project Properties command. On the Signing page, select Sign the Assembly and create a new key by choosing <New...> in the drop-down list box.

COM+ projects work best when you have fewer assembly references. The References folder of Solution Explorer requires references to `System` and `System.Enterprise Services` as a minimum. Add only the references you must have to implement your code and remove any extra references that your code doesn't require.

Now, here's the most important bit of information. Make sure you don't select the Register for COM Interop option on the Build page of the project Properties window. Instead of letting Visual Studio perform the registration automatically, use the Register Assembly (RegAsm) utility to perform the task. Open a Visual Studio command line in Administrator mode (right-click the Start⇨Programs⇨Microsoft Visual Studio 2008⇨Visual Studio Tools⇨Visual Studio 2008 Command Prompt entry and choose Run as Administrator from the context menu). Type **RegAsm <DLL filename> /TLB** and press Enter. Make sure you use the resulting TLB file when registering your component with COM+. It's also essential that you register your component in the Global Assembly Cache (GAC) using the Global Assembly Cache Utility (GACUtil) application. Type **GACUtil /i <DLL filename>** and press Enter to register the component.

```
AssemblyVersion
    ("1.0.0.*")]
[assembly: Assembly
    FileVersion("1.0.0.*")]
```

You must also set the `[assembly: Com Visible(true)]` attribute to `true`. Without these two changes, the assembly will never work in COM+. Registration won't take place correctly unless the build number changes between compilations and you must make the assembly COM visible.

After you make these changes, open the project's Properties window using the Project⇨project Properties command. On the Signing page, select Sign the Assembly and create a new key by choosing <New...> in the drop-down list box.

COM+ projects work best when you have fewer assembly references. The References folder of Solution Explorer requires references to `System` and `System.Enterprise Services` as a minimum. Add only the references you must have to implement your code and remove any extra references that your code doesn't require.

Now, here's the most important bit of information. Make sure you don't select the Register for COM Interop option on the Build page of the project Properties window. Instead of letting Visual Studio perform the registration automatically, use the Register Assembly (RegAsm) utility to perform the task. Open a Visual Studio command line in Administrator mode (right-click the Start⇨Programs⇨Microsoft Visual Studio 2008⇨Visual Studio Tools⇨Visual Studio 2008 Command Prompt entry and choose Run as Administrator from the context menu). Type **RegAsm <DLL filename> /TLB** and press Enter. Make sure you use the resulting TLB file when registering your component with COM+. It's also essential that you register your component in the Global Assembly Cache (GAC) using the Global Assembly Cache Utility (GACUtil) application. Type **GACUtil /i <DLL filename>** and press Enter to register the component.

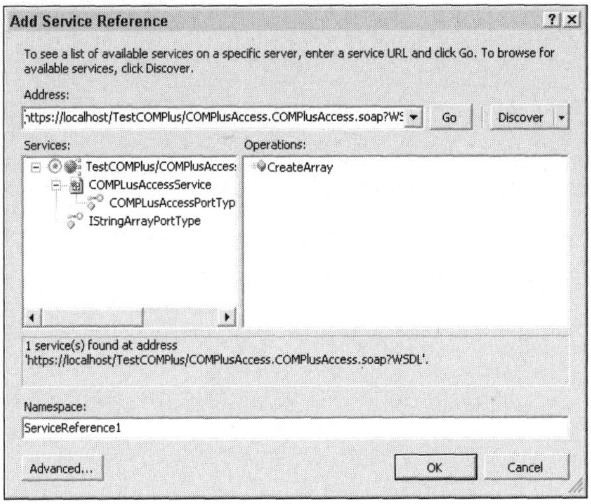

Figure 13-2:
Access
your COM+
application
as a Web
service.

The code for calling COM+ as a Web service doesn't look much different from any other LINQ query you create. The big difference is that you're calling an enumeration on another machine. Listing 13-1 shows the LINQ query for this example. You'll find this example in the `\Chapter 13\COMPlusTest` folder of the source code for this book.

Listing 13-1 Defining a Web Service LINQ Query

```
private void btnTest_Click(object sender, EventArgs e)
{
   // Create the service object. Make sure that the
   // service object points to the correct URL, which
   // relies on HTTPS for Vista and Windows Server 2008.
   COMPLusAccessPortTypeClient ThisCall =
      new COMPLusAccessPortTypeClient();

   // Address any required security procedure. Uncomment
   // this line when using Vista or Windows Server 2008.
   ServicePointManager.CertificatePolicy =
      new CertPolicy();

   // Create the query.
   var Output =
      from ThisEntry in
         ThisCall.CreateArray(
            "The quick brown fox " +
            "jumped over the lazy dog.")
      where ThisEntry.Length > 3
      orderby ThisEntry
```

```
        orderby ThisEntry.Length
        select ThisEntry;

    // Display the results.
    txtResult.Text = "Output:\r\n";
    foreach (String ThisOut in Output)
        txtResult.Text = txtResult.Text + "\r\n" + ThisOut;
}
```

The code begins by creating a service object that provides access to the Web service. Precisely how this service object works depends on your Web service setup and Visual Studio configuration. For example, you can configure the Web service to provide asynchronous calls. This example uses a simple, generic, default Web service setup. To change this configuration, right-click the Web service reference in the Service References folder of Server Explorer and choose Configure Service Reference from the context menu. The resulting dialog box contains all of the configuration options for your Web service (a topic outside the scope of this book). You need to consider any unique characteristics of your Web service, however, when you put the application together. LINQ tends not to work well with asynchronous calls, so you want to avoid them whenever possible.

The next LINQ step is to create the query. Note that you don't call the service object first. If you can set up your Web service to provide direct data access (as contrasted to the often convoluted XML data structures provided by many Web services), you can make the Web service method call as part of your LINQ query as shown. The query also works fine with lambda expressions — the approach you use is a matter of personal preference.

After the code obtains the data from the Web service, it uses a `foreach` loop to display it on the screen. There isn't anything different here from what you've done in the past. Figure 13-3 shows the output for this example.

Figure 13-3:
A Web
service
query can
work the
same as any
other query
you make.

Working with older versions of Windows is different from working with Vista and Windows Server 2008 because of the additional security requirements for these newer operating systems. The ServicePointManager. CertificatePolicy = new CertPolicy(); line of code addresses the security needs of these newer Windows versions. You normally comment out this line of code when working with older versions of Windows.

The ServicePointManager line of code sets the application to use a certificate policy manager that you create. You must create a special class to perform an SSL exchange with these newer setups. Listing 13-2 shows a very simple class you can use for testing (your real world class should include security checks and methods for validating user information you provide to the server).

Listing 13-2   Performing SSL Verification

```
public class CertPolicy : ICertificatePolicy
{
    // The only call you need to implement is
    // CheckValidationResult() as shown here.
    public Boolean CheckValidationResult(
        ServicePoint srvPoint,
        X509Certificate certificate,
        WebRequest request,
        int certificateProblem)
    {
        // Supply the username and password. If you don't
        // supply a valid username and password, the
        // call will fail.
        request.Credentials =
            new NetworkCredential(
                "Your Name", "Your Password");

        // Return True to force the application to accept
        // the certificate.
        return true;

    }
}
```

The CheckValidationResult() method accepts a number of inputs, including an integer value that defines a certificate issue. Unfortunately, the help provided with Visual Studio doesn't really define what these Security Support Provider Interface (SSPI) status codes are all about. In most cases, you'll need to work through potential issues in your application and trap those errors.

The two important tasks are to supply credentials as needed and to verify the X509Certificate object that the server provides. This example takes a shortcut by setting the credentials to a known value — your credentials. Simply replace the strings in the example with your name and password.

After the example sets the appropriate credentials, it returns a value of true. Returning true means that you've verified the X509Certificate object and found it acceptable. Make certain you check the details of any X509Certificate object you work with in your application.

The SSL technique shown in this example doesn't just work for COM+ applications. You can use this approach for any application where you need to use SSL to communicate with a Web server. Some Web services use this approach and you'll find it useful also when making requests from a standard Web page. The concepts are the same in both cases. You provide the credentials required to access the Web service or Web site and accept the X.509 certificate that the Web service or Web site presents. In some cases, you also need to provide a client-side X.509 certificate during this check.

COM+ accessed using interop functionality

Accessing COM+ components as a Web service has the advantage of letting you access the component anywhere. However, the extra access layers build a little latency into the connections and tend to produce a slight, but noticeable, performance hit. Using an interop approach to COM+ components does provide better performance than using a Web service when working on a local network. You add the COM+ reference to your application using the COM tab of the Add Reference dialog box shown in Figure 13-4.

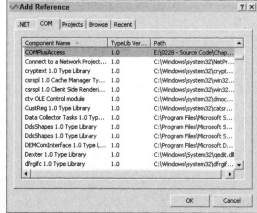

Figure 13-4:
Add a COM+ component to your application using the COM tab.

This technique doesn't work for managed COM+ components. If you attempt to use this approach for managed components, Visual Studio will detect the managed environment and tell you to add the component to your application as a .NET component. No matter which approach you use to add the component to your application, you end up with a reference to it in the References folder in Solution Explorer. Accessing the component is similar to working with it as a Web service. Listing 13-3 shows an example of performing this task. You'll find this example in the \Chapter 13\COMPlusTest2 folder of the source code for this book.

Listing 13-3   Defining an Interop LINQ Query

```
private void txtTest_Click(object sender, EventArgs e)
{
   // Create the object reference.
   COMPLusAccess.COMPLusAccess ThisComp =
      new COMPLusAccess.COMPLUSACCESS();

   // Define the query.
   var ThisQuery = ThisComp.CreateArray(
      "The quick brown fox jumped over the lazy dog.").
      Where(Entry => Entry.Length > 3).
      OrderBy(Entry => Entry).
      OrderBy(Entry => Entry.Length);

   // Display the results.
   txtResult.Text = "Output:\r\n";
   foreach (String ThisOut in ThisQuery)
      txtResult.Text = txtResult.Text + "\r\n" + ThisOut;
}
```

In this case, the code begins by instantiating the object. It then accesses the CreateArray() method using lambda expressions. The output technique is the same as shown in Listing 13-1 and appears the same as Figure 13-3.

Creating the Resource Description Format (RDF) Files Example

RDF files appear almost everywhere on the Internet because they provide descriptions of content that content providers hope people will use. For example, the MusicBrainz Web site (http://musicbrainz.org/) relies on RDF to present you with information about your favorite music by employing RDF in the background. The information you see on the Web site is also accessible by your .NET application as RDF. To discover more about how MusicBrainz works as an RDF resource, see the article at http://wiki.musicbrainz.org/RDF. The following sections describe RDF in further detail and present a LINQ to RDF example. You'll find this example in the `\Chapter 13\RDFExample` folder of the source code for this book.

A quick overview of RDF

RDF employs a subject-predicate-object format or a triple to present information to the application. The subject defines the resource, the predicate defines an attribute or a trait, and the object defines the content of that attribute or trait. For example, if you say that a rose has a green stem, the subject is *rose,* the predicate is *has a*, and the object is *green stem.*

You find a number of forms of RDF on the Internet, so it's important to understand how the host site presents the RDF information when creating your application. Some Web sites, such as MusicBrainz, present RDF in XML format. However, many other Web sites use a newer form of RDF that relies on a non-XML format called Notation 3 (N3). This chapter doesn't provide a full treatment of RDF as a technology. You can find additional information about RDF at the following:

- **Wikipedia:** `http://en.wikipedia.org/wiki/Resource_Description_Framework`
- **World Wide Web Consortium (W3C) basic RDF standards:** `http://www.w3.org/RDF/` and `http://www.w3.org/TR/1999/REC-rdf-syntax-19990222/`
- **W3C RDF Schema (RDFS) specification:** `http://www.w3.org/TR/2000/CR-rdf-schema-20000327/`
- **W3C Web Ontology Language (OWL) specification:** `http://www.w3.org/2004/OWL/`
- **W3Schools RDF tutorial:** `http://www.w3schools.com/rdf/default.asp`
- **W3C Notation 3 reference:** `http://www.w3.org/DesignIssues/Notation3`
- **W3C Notation 3 primer:** `http://www.w3.org/2000/10/swap/Primer.html`
- **Mozilla RDF reference:** `http://www.mozilla.org/rdf/doc/`

A quick overview of SPARQL

This RDF example relies on a special query method, the Simple Protocol and RDF Query Language (SPARQL). The SemWeb.Sparql.DLL file that comes with the LINQ to RDF provider (`\Program Files\LinqToRdf`) encapsulates the functionality you need to implement SPARQL in a .NET application. You create a query by posting information to the host site. In SPARQL terminology, this Web site acts as an ontology host. Essentially, it's your means of communicating with the RDF data — the ontology host is a kind of listener. Consequently, your client application calls the ontology host, which then provides access to the RDF data. In many respects, SPARQL is a kind of Web service that provides access without relying on a single product definition (such as using COM+ on IIS as in the "Accessing COM+ Using LINQ" section of the chapter). You can discover more about how SPARQL works at the following:

- **W3C Opens Data on the Web with SPARQL:** `http://www.w3.org/2007/12/sparql-pressrelease`
- **SPARQL Query Language for RDF**: `http://www.w3.org/TR/rdf-sparql-query/`
- **SPARQL Tutorial:** `http://jena.sourceforge.net/ARQ/Tutorial/`
- **SPARQLer:** `http://sparql.org/`
- **GovTrack.us (see queries through a Web page):** `http://www.govtrack.us/sparql.xpd`
- **Introducing SPARQL: Querying the Semantic Web:** `http://www.xml.com/pub/a/2005/11/16/introducing-sparql-querying-semantic-web-tutorial.html`
- **SPARQL Protocol and Query Language: SPARQL Frequently Asked Questions:** `http://thefigtrees.net/lee/sw/sparql-faq`
- **Search RDF data with SPARQL:** `http://www-128.ibm.com/developerworks/library/j-sparql/`

Starting the project

The example in this section started with information from a couple of blog entries: `http://blogs.msdn.com/hartmutm/archive/2006/07/10/661512.aspx` and `http://blogs.msdn.com/hartmutm/archive/2006/07/24/677200.aspx`. Don't download the provider source code found on the blog because it's based on Visual Studio 2005 and the LINQ preview. I hope the author will update this provider because it works with the XML RDF format. In the meantime, working with the XML form of RDF is very much like working with any XML document (see Chapter 9 for details), as shown in Figure 13-5.

Working with N3 does require a provider because it presents the RDF information in human readable form. The nature of N3 is part of the reason the example in this chapter focuses on N3 rather than the XML form. The provider you want to download for this example (which relies on N3) appears at `http://code.google.com/p/linqtordf/` (click the Downloads tab). Make sure you get the latest edition. You can discuss the LINQ to RDF provider at `http://groups.google.com/group/linqtordf-discuss/`.

Figure 13-5: Working with the XML form of RDF is like working with any XML document.

Configuring the project

This example isn't designed to show you how to work with RDF or create complex SPARQL syntax — that's a topic for another book or those resources you saw in the "A quick overview of RDF" and "A quick overview of SPARQL" sections of the chapter. This example begins with the `Contacts.N3` file shown in Figure 13-6. This file contains the class declarations for the RDF file. In some respects, it looks like a conversational form of an XML file.

If you can't see the N3 files on your system, you need to add a Multipurpose Internet Mail Extensions (MIME) type for the extension to your IIS configuration. Use the `text/plain` type for the N3 file so you can view it directly in the browser. In IIS 7 you can add this MIME type directly to the folder that holds the RDF data so that you don't have to worry about people using the N3 extension in other folders. It also helps to enable directory browsing for text scenarios (but it isn't absolutely required).

The data for this example appears in the `ContactData.N3` file shown in Figure 13-7. As shown in the figure, this second file contains a list of contacts that include entries for all the properties defined in the class.

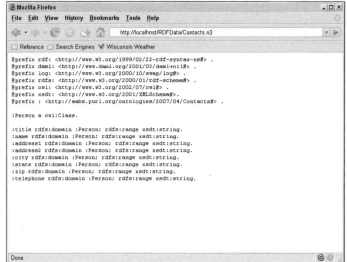

Figure 13-6:
The first file
contains
a listing of
RDF class
elements.

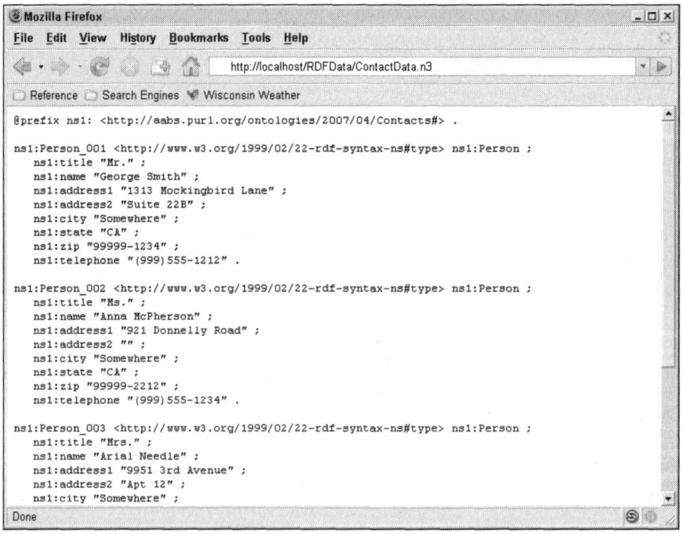

Figure 13-7:
The second
file contains
the contact
informa-
tion for the
example.

You place the entire RDFData folder found in the \Chapter 13 folder of the source code for this book in the \inetpub\wwwroot folder of your system. The application you write won't access this folder directly. It instead relies on some ASP.NET connectivity. If you have a heavy-duty RDF requirement, the author of the LINQ to RDF provider documentation recommends that you look into a Java solution.

Now that you have two data files to use, it's time to create the solution used to access them. The following section describes the two projects required to create a complete LINQ to RDF solution.

Defining the client project

Begin by creating the user application. The project includes all the forms the user relies on to interact with the RDF files. The following steps help you configure the client project:

1. **Right-click the client project entry and choose Add Reference from the context menu.**

   You see the Add Reference dialog box.

2. **Click the Browse tab. Highlight the SemWeb.DLL and LinqToRdf.DLL files located in the \Program Files\LinqToRdf folder of your hard drive. Click OK.**

   Visual Studio adds the required references to your project.

3. **Open the AssemblyInfo.CS file and add a reference to LinqToRdf.**

4. **Type the following attribute into the AssemblyInfo.CS file:**

   ```
   [assembly: Ontology(
    BaseUri =
     "http://aabs.purl.org/ontologies/2007/04/Contacts#",
    Name = "Contacts",
    Prefix = "Contacts",
    UrlOfOntology =
    "http://aabs.purl.org/ontologies/2007/04/Contacts#")]
   ```

   The attribute tells the LINQ to RDF provider what to call the ontology you create in `Contacts.N3` and provides the base URI for that ontology so you don't have to type it every time you need it in the remaining ontology-specific code.

5. **Open the application code file and add a reference to LinqToRdf.**

   At this point, the client project is configured for use.

Defining the host project

Now it's time to add a Web project to the RDF solution. The example uses the name RDFHost for this project. The Web project provides a means for posting the query to the SPARQL host. The following steps help you configure the host project:

1. **Right-click the host project entry and choose Add Reference from the context menu.**

   You see the Add Reference dialog box.

2. **Click the Browse tab. Highlight the SemWeb.Sparql.DLL file located in the \Program Files\LinqToRdf folder of your hard drive. Click OK.**

   Visual Studio adds the required references to your project. At this point, the host project is configured for use.

Creating the host application

You should create the host application first so that you can test the required connectivity. The host application includes a form you use to make the query. The actual form of the host application, Default.ASPX, consists of a means for submitting a query. Listing 13-4 shows the code you'll use to create the form for the example (note that all the PREFIX lines should appear on a single line in your code, even if they appear on multiple lines in the book).

Listing 13-4   Creating a Host Query Form

```
<body>
    <form action="/RDFHost/SparqlQuery.yada"
            method="post">
        <input type="hidden" name="outputMimeType"
                value="text/xml" />
        <textarea name="query" rows="20" cols="80">
PREFIX rdf: <http://www.w3.org/1999/02/22-rdf-syntax-ns#>
PREFIX daml: <http://www.daml.org/2001/03/daml+oil#>
PREFIX log: <http://www.w3.org/2000/10/swap/log#>
PREFIX rdfs: <http://www.w3.org/2000/01/rdf-schema#>
PREFIX owl: <http://www.w3.org/2002/07/owl#>
PREFIX xsdt: <http://www.w3.org/2001/XMLSchema#>
PREFIX :
    <http://aabs.purl.org/ontologies/2007/04/Contacts#>

SELECT *
WHERE {
 ?p a :Person;
 :city "Somewhere"
}
        </textarea>
        <p>
            <input type="submit" />
        </p>
    </form>
</body>
```

You may wonder where you obtain all this information. The form always begins by specifying that the application should post the data to whatever location you chose for the host URL. Don't worry too much about this entry for now; the entries used to create the host URL appear later in this section.

A hidden control determines the output MIME type for the data. You include this control to tell the host application what output to provide. In this case, the output is of the `text/xml` MIME type.

The `<textarea>` element defines the query itself. The `PREFIX` entries are the same as those that you use in your class declarations N3 file; `Contacts. N3` for the example. The `SELECT * WHERE {?p a :Person; :city "Somewhere"}` entry defines the query. It tells the host to retrieve all `ContactData.N3` file entries where the name of the city is Somewhere. You can modify this query as needed for testing.

Finally, a `submit` button posts the query defined on the form to the host. Click Submit Query and you'll see host output. More importantly, the check ensures that the host is working.

At this point, you need to open the `Web.CONFIG` file and make some changes to it that define the required connectivity to the host. The first step is to add a `sparqlSources` section definition, as shown here:

```
<!--Add the sparqlSources section to create
    a connection to the host.-->
<section
   name="sparqlSources"
   type="System.Configuration.NameValueSectionHandler,
         System, Version=2.0.0.0, Culture=neutral,
         PublicKeyToken=b77a5c561934e089"/>
```

This entry simply tells .NET that there's a new section called `sparqlSources` that will provide key/value pair handling. The next step is to configure the `sparqlSources` section:

```
<sparqlSources>
  <add
    key="/RDFHost/SparqlQuery.yada"
    value="n3:C:\inetpub\wwwroot\RDFData\ContactData.n3"/>
</sparqlSources>
```

The `<sparqlSources>` element adds a new key/value pair to the list of handlers for this Web site. When the user requests the `/RDFHost/SparqlQuery. yada` Web page, the application will obtain data from the physical location shown in the value. It's essential that you provide the Web page location and physical file location on your machine, which means that you'll probably have to change this code at some point.

The form of the `value` attribute in this example shows a physical hard drive location. However, you don't have to use this format. You can use any of the `SemWeb.Store.CreateForInput()` methods described at `http:// occams.info/code/semweb/semweb-current/apidocs/SemWeb/ Store.html`. This includes XML-formatted information. One of the more interesting supported data stores is MySQL. Make sure you check out this Web site (`http://occams.info/code/semweb/semweb-current/apidocs/`) for additional details about the `SemWeb.Sparql.DLL` file

You now have a data source. However, there's the matter of the `SparqlQuery.yada` file described earlier as a host source. The project doesn't include this file and you don't need to create it. Theoretically, you can use an existing file extension, such as `SparqlQuery.aspx`, but there's a possibility that the server will refuse to use the handlers required to make LINQ to RDF work, so using a nonexisting file extension is best. The query against the `SparqlQuery.yada` file actually sends data to the host. You specify this requirement as part of a special entry in the `<handlers>` element, as shown here. (You find the `<handlers>` element under `configuration\system.webServer`.)

```
<!--Add a handler for the SPARQL host.-->
<add name="SparqlHost"
    path="SparqlQuery.yada"
    verb="*"
    type="SemWeb.Query.SparqlProtocolServerHandler,
        SemWeb.Sparql"
    resourceType="Unspecified"
    requireAccess="Execute"
    preCondition="integratedMode" />
```

Because you're calling on an executable file as part of the query, you must also change the execute permissions for handlers. Add the `accessPolicy` attribute, as follows:

```
<!--You must change the accessPolicy to include
    Excecute permissions or the application
    will fail.-->
<handlers accessPolicy="Read, Execute, Script">
```

This entry tells .NET that any request for the `/RDFHost/SparqlQuery.yada` resource is sent to the `SemWeb.Query.SparqlProtocolServer Handler` class, which is part of the `SemWeb.Sparql.DLL` file. At this point, right-click the host project entry and choose Build from the context menu to build the host application. After you successfully build the host application, publish it to your Web server.

Now comes the time for your first test. Before you can do anything, you must turn the published application into a Web application. Open the Internet Information Services (IIS) Manager, drill down to the application, right-click the application entry, and choose Convert to Application. Follow the prompts to create the Web application and make sure to test the application to ensure that you can access it without any security problems. Go to the host Web site, which is `http://localhost/RDFHost/` for this example. You see a query page, as shown in Figure 13-8.

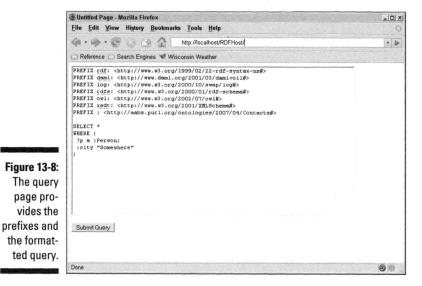

Figure 13-8:
The query
page pro-
vides the
prefixes and
the format-
ted query.

When you click Submit Query, you should see the query output shown in
Figure 13-9. If you see any kind of error message, you know that a setting or
some of the host code is wrong. The usual culprit is a Web.CONFIG entry, so
that's the best place to start.

Figure 13-9:
The test
shows that
the host is
ready to
receive
queries.

Creating the application class definition

It's important to remember that your application is interacting with what amounts to a non-Microsoft Web service. Consequently, the application has no idea of what the data looks like in `Contacts.N3` — and neither does LINQ. Therefore, you must define a class definition to provide access to the RDF data. Before you get the idea that this is an extra requirement, this manual process is taking the place of the class building that SQLMetal (see Chapter 8) normally performs for you, so there isn't anything new here. The only difference is that you're writing the code by hand. Listing 13-5 shows the `Contacts.N3` file class definition code.

Listing 13-5   Defining the Ontology Class

```
// This class defines the data elements
// within the ContactData.N3 file. Each
// element you want to display must have
// an associated property.
[OwlResource(OntologyName = "Contacts",
            RelativeUriReference = "Person")]
public class Person : OwlInstanceSupertype
{
    [OwlResource(OntologyName = "Contacts",
                RelativeUriReference = "title")]
    public String Title { get; set; }

    [OwlResource(OntologyName = "Contacts",
                RelativeUriReference = "name")]
    public String Name { get; set; }

    [OwlResource(OntologyName = "Contacts",
                RelativeUriReference = "address1")]
    public String Address1 { get; set; }

    [OwlResource(OntologyName = "Contacts",
                RelativeUriReference = "address2")]
    public String Address2 { get; set; }

    [OwlResource(OntologyName = "Contacts",
                RelativeUriReference = "city")]
    public String City { get; set; }

    [OwlResource(OntologyName = "Contacts",
                RelativeUriReference = "state")]
    public String State { get; set; }

    [OwlResource(OntologyName = "Contacts",
                RelativeUriReference = "zip")]
```

```
    public String ZIP { get; set; }

    [OwlResource(OntologyName = "Contacts",
                 RelativeUriReference = "telephone")]
    public String Telephone { get; set; }
}
```

The code isn't that special. All you're really doing is telling LINQ what to expect from your RDF class. What is important is the `OwlResource` attribute, which provides that mapping between your application and the N3 files. If you don't include this attribute, the code will appear to work, but you'll receive a `null` data set as a return value. Consequently, if your host test (see Figure 13-9) works, this is the first place you should look for potential application problems.

Reading RDF files

It's finally time to read the data file. The reading process isn't complex or difficult. You won't notice much of a difference from working with other LINQ queries in the book. Listing 13-6 shows the code required for this portion of the example.

Listing 13-6   Reading the Example Data File

```
private void btnTest_Click(object sender, EventArgs e)
{
    // Define the data store. The data store includes the
    // location of the data and the kind of store to use.
    TripleStore TS = new TripleStore();
    TS.EndpointUri =
        "http://localhost/RDFHost/SparqlQuery.yada";
    TS.QueryType = QueryType.RemoteSparqlStore;

    // Define the query. You must provide a class that
    // defines the elements that the output contains.
    var Output = from Entry
                 in new RDF(TS).ForType<Person>()
                 select Entry;

    // Display the result.
    txtResult.Text = "Query Results:\r\n\r\n";
    foreach (var ThisEntry in Output)
        txtResult.Text = txtResult.Text +
            ThisEntry.Name + "\r\n" +
            ThisEntry.Address1 + "\r\n" +
            ThisEntry.Address2 + "\r\n" +
            ThisEntry.City + ", " +
            ThisEntry.State + "   " +
            ThisEntry.ZIP + "\r\n" +
            ThisEntry.Telephone + "\r\n\r\n";
}
```

The first task is to create a `TripleStore` object, which equates to working with a `DataContext` object in SQL Server. The `TripleStore` object, `TS`, includes the data location (where to post the query) and the location of the data store (local or remote).

After the code defines the data store location, it performs the query. The LINQ query isn't any different than other LINQ queries in the book, except you must define the type of the N3 data. This is the `Person` class found in Listing 13-5.

The application finishes by displaying the data. The individual entries, `ThisEntry`, provides full IntelliSense support. Consequently, you see all the properties you define in the `Person` class. If you don't define properties for every entry in `Contacts.N3` as part of the `Person` class, then `ThisEntry` will show only those elements you do define. Figure 13-10 shows the output from this example.

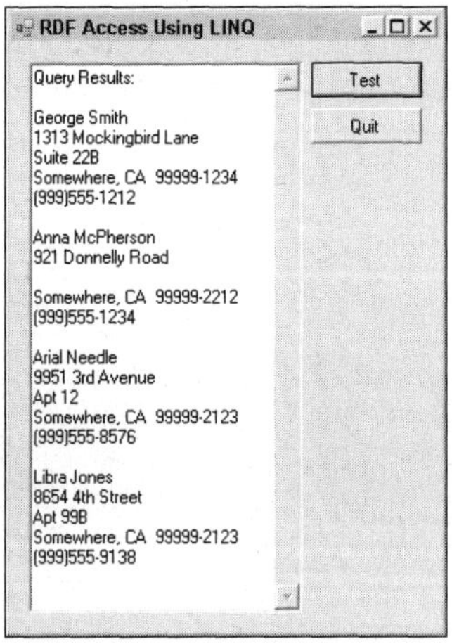

Figure 13-10: The application output shows the content of the N3 data file.

Creating the MySQL Example

Some people probably felt that Microsoft had left a huge part of the database community out of the picture by providing support only for SQL Server in the DB LINQ (LINQ to MySQL) provider. As a result of the efforts of several developers, you can also interact with MySQL, Oracle, and PostgreSQL (as well as other potential candidates) using the LINQ Provider for MySql, Oracle, and PostgreSQL. You can read about this provider at `http://code2code.net/DB_Linq/`. The provider is available at `http://code.google.com/p/dblinq2007/downloads/list` (make sure you get the latest version of the product). Unlike the LINQ to Active Directory provider, this provider is even community supported. If you have provider usage questions, you can get help with them at `http://groups.google.com/group/dblinq`.

One of the interesting bits of information about the LINQ Provider for MySql, Oracle, and PostgreSQL is that one of the supporters, Miguel de Icaza, is considering porting it to Mono (http://www.mono-project.com/Main_ Page). *Mono* is the .NET Framework substitute for Linux and other systems that don't support .NET Framework directly. You can also use Mono with Microsoft's new Windows Server 2008 Server Core version, which doesn't provide .NET Framework support. Theoretically, you could have a .NET Framework solution that relies on LINQ working in a Windows environment that doesn't support .NET Framework or SQL Server by relying on Mono, so moving the LINQ Provider for MySql, Oracle, and PostgreSQL to Mono is a big deal.

The following sections describe how to create a MySQL application using the Northwind database, which appears in other areas of this book. This example assumes that you know how to work with MySQL and won't provide much in the way of MySQL usage information. You'll find this example in the \Chapter 13\MySQLExample folder of the source code for this book.

Getting the MySQL ADO.NET connector

.NET Framework doesn't come with built-in support for MySQL, so you need ADO.NET support for your LINQ application that relies on MySQL. The LINQ to MySQL provider includes the ADO.NET connection, MySQL.Data.DLL. This connection is probably fine for development work, but you should obtain the latest connector for your production needs.

You can obtain the MySQL ADO.NET connector at http://www.mono-project.com/MySQL. Click the MySQL Connector/Net link and choose the most current connector version from the list in the left pane (version 5.2.1 as of this writing). Make sure you download the Windows Binaries file to obtain a compiled version of the connector. Even though the Web site urges you to register your product, you can bypass the registration process by clicking the No thanks, just take me to the downloads! link at the bottom of the page.

Compiling the DbLinq.DLL and DbLinq.MySQL.DLL files

After you download the DB LINQ ZIP file, extract its contents to a new folder. You must compile the library before you can use it. The following steps help you perform this task:

1. **(Optional) Replace the copy of MySql.Data.DLL in the \dblinq2007\ DbLinq\bin folder with the latest version, if desired.**

2. **Open the DbLinq.SLN file in the \dblinq2007 folder using Visual Studio 2008.**

The DB LINQ provider doesn't work with older versions of Visual Studio.

3. **Right-click the DbLinq folder in Solution Explorer and choose Build from the context menu.**

   Visual Studio compiles the `DbLinq.DLL` file. You find it in the `\dblinq 2007\DbLinq\bin` folder of your hard drive.

4. **Right-click the DbLinq.MySQL folder in Solution Explorer and choose Build from the context menu.**

   Visual Studio compiles the DbLinq.MySQL.DLL file. You find it in the `\dblinq2007\DbLinq.MySql\bin\Debug` or `\dblinq2007\DbLinq.MySql\bin\Release` folder depending on the kind of build you create.

5. **Place the MySql.Data.DLL, DbLinq.DLL, and DbLinq.MySQL.DLL files in one place for use with the MySQL project.**

Configuring the database

You must have a database to work with for the example. The DB LINQ creators thoughtfully provided a version of the Northwind database to use. The scripts required to create this database appear in the `\dblinq2007\ Example\DbLinq.MySql.Example\sql` folder. Run each of these scripts in turn using the MySQL utility.

Defining the MySQL project

Before you begin this section, you need to know the location of the `MySql. Data.DLL`, `DbLinq.DLL`, and `DbLinq.MySQL.DLL` files. You create references to these files as part of defining the project. The following steps help you create a DB LINQ project:

1. **Create a new application using the desired template.**

   The example uses the standard Windows Forms Application template.

2. **Add any required design elements.**

3. **Right-click the project entry in Solution Explorer and choose Add Reference from the context menu.**

   You see the Add Reference dialog box.

4. **Click the Browse tab, highlight the MySql.Data.DLL, DbLinq.DLL, and DbLinq.MySQL.DLL files, and click OK.**

   Visual Studio adds the three references to your system.

5. **Right-click the project entry in Solution Explorer and choose Add Reference from the context menu.**

6. **Click the .NET tab, highlight System.Data.Linq, and click OK.**

7. **Right-click the project entry in Solution Explorer and choose Add⇨Existing Item from the context menu.**

You see the Add Existing Item dialog box.

8. **Highlight the Northwind.CS, AllTypes.CS, and DbLinq_EnumTest.CS files in the \dblinq2007\Example\DbLinq.MySql.Example\nwind folder of your hard drive and click OK.**

These three files are the equivalent of the files you created using the SQLMetal utility in the "Generating the Northwind entity classes and XML mapping files" section of Chapter 8. The DB LINQ provider comes with a version of SQLMetal for other database types that you must compile. You see it in Solution Explorer when you load the DB LINQ provider project.

9. **Open the code file for your project and type the following statements:**

```
using nwind;
using DbLinq;
using DbLinq.MySql;
using MySql.Data.MySqlClient;
```

These additions provide access to the DB LINQ provider, the MySQL connector, and the Northwind entity classes. At this point, your application is configured and ready to go.

Developing the query code

Creating the code for this example is similar to working with the LINQ to SQL example. You create a data context, make the query, and process the output. The example doesn't require a mapping file to work properly. The output processing, however, requires a little more work, as shown in Listing 13-7.

Listing 13-7   Performing a MySQL Query

```
private void btnTest_Click(object sender, EventArgs e)
{
    // Create the Data Context object.
    Northwind DB = new Northwind(
        new MySqlConnection(
            "server=localhost;user id=ODBC;"+
            "password=;database=Northwind"));

    // Define the query.
```

(continued)

Listing 13-7 *(continued)*

```
var ThisQuery = from Cust in DB.Customers
                select Cust;

// Build a table from the data.
DataTable ThisTable = new DataTable();
ThisTable.Columns.Add("Customer ID");
ThisTable.Columns.Add("Company Name");
ThisTable.Columns.Add("Contact Name");

// Move the data from the results to the table.
foreach (var ThisRow in ThisQuery)
{
    // Create the data row.
    DataRow AddRow = ThisTable.NewRow();

    // Add the data.
    AddRow["Customer ID"] = ThisRow.CustomerID;
    AddRow["Company Name"] = ThisRow.CompanyName;
    AddRow["Contact Name"] = ThisRow.ContactName;

    // Place the data in the table.
    ThisTable.Rows.Add(AddRow);
}

// Display the results.
dgResult.DataSource = ThisTable;
}
```

The string for the data context is slightly different. The connection requires that you provide a server name, user name, password, and database name. MySQL doesn't support Windows authentication.

The query is the same as any query you create using LINQ to SQL. In fact, you could possibly move the queries from one environment to the other without changes in at least most cases.

Unfortunately, you can't simply assign the output, `ThisQuery`, to the `dgResult.DataSource` property as you can with LINQ to SQL. The output is blank when you do, even when the query is successful. You have to build a table from scratch and work with the data directly. Consequently, the DB LINQ provider doesn't provide quite as much automation as LINQ to SQL. However, the important point is that it does work.

As shown in Listing 13-7, you transfer the data by building a `DataTable` much as you would with any other complex data query. The example uses a `foreach` loop to extract the individual rows from `ThisQuery` and place them in `ThisRow`. The code then builds individual `DataRow` objects, `AddRow`, and places them in `ThisTable` using the `ThisTable.Rows.Add()` method call.

Part IV
The Part of Tens

"Please answer the following survey questions about our company's performance with either, 'Excellent', 'Good', 'Fair', or 'I'm Really Incapable of Appreciating Someone Else's Hard Work.'"

In this part . . .

This part of the book is all about tens. In Chapter 14 you discover ten new ways to make the LINQ application development process easier. Chapter 15 moves from development to LINQ application support. You find out about ten new ways to keep both users and support staff happy, which makes less work for you.

Everyone likes to have tools and resources that make things easier. Chapter 16 discusses ten tools or resources you can use to make working with LINQ significantly easier. Even though LINQ has only recently appeared in the marketplace, third parties are already working feverishly to make your job easier. Check out these tools and resources when you have a special need for creating better applications.

Chapter 14

Ten Ways to Improve LINQ Development

In This Chapter

▶ Simplifying code using LINQ tools

▶ Creating self-documenting code using LINQ

▶ Performing code pattern analysis

▶ Defining a code snippet database

▶ Using LINQ to find other development resources

▶ Understanding data format using LINQ

▶ Discovering usage trends

▶ Creating your own LINQ library

▶ Trading useful LINQ queries with others

▶ Performing compilation and code analysis

Throughout this book, you see a myriad of ways in which you can use LINQ to create applications. Of course, knowing you can use a technology and understanding that it will improve your development experience are two different things. By now, you know that LINQ can help you produce shorter code, but this chapter helps you discover why shorter code doesn't translate into harder to read code. LINQ is quite easy to read, and because it uses the same form with every query, it provides a solid method for creating self-documenting code. Anyone who sees one LINQ query can easily read most other LINQ queries of the same complexity. The first question that this chapter answers, therefore, is whether LINQ provides something of value to you as an individual developer — it answers the questions of whether easy to use and easy to read translate into meaningless technology.

The first question begs a second question, the one that most developers ask about coding efficiently and maximizing potential. This chapter also helps you get the most out of LINQ. After you begin working with LINQ, you may discover a need to make LINQ do more. It's easy to get excited about the capabilities that LINQ provides and equally easy to become frustrated when you discover that you don't have all the resources you need. For example, many providers still rely on beta code and others are still in the construction phase. You may want to help things along by helping other developers do more with LINQ. This chapter discusses these needs too.

When you begin asking questions about your development environment, you also begin looking for ways to quantify needs and progress that you make in honing that environment to meet specific requirements. The third issue that this chapter discusses, then, is how to quantify the LINQ advantage. Yes, you still have many intangible benefits to consider, but the tips in this chapter help you quantify many LINQ elements so that you can garner support for LINQ from other people (say a boss who doesn't understand coding but does understand productivity gains).

Using LINQ Tools to Simplify Coding

LINQ reminds me of the game Othello — minutes to learn, a lifetime to master. It's easy to put some amazing queries together on your first day working with LINQ. The second day is even better. However, you eventually start creating queries so complex that the simplicity of LINQ is overshadowed by the intricacies of the task you want to perform. The intricacies become real especially fast when working with LINQ to SQL because you normally want to use multiple data sources for your query. After you get to the point of complexity saturation in your LINQ experience, you won't find it surprising that other developers create tools that make writing queries easier.

Getting the VLinq add-in application

This section discusses a tool called Visual LINQ (VLinq) query build for LINQ to SQL. You use this Visual Studio add-in application in essentially the same way as you use Query Builder in Microsoft Access. The difference is that the output is a LINQ to SQL query rather than a SQL statement. The main page for VLinq is `http://code.msdn.microsoft.com/vlinq/`. You download VLinq (`VLinqSetup.MSI`) at `http://code.msdn.microsoft.com/vlinq/Release/ProjectReleases.aspx`. In addition to the application, you can obtain

- Quick reference guide
- Detailed user documentation
- How to use VLinq video
- VLinq source code

It's a good idea to download all these resources immediately, except for the source code, which you can download later should you want to personalize VLinq for your own purposes. The quick reference guide and detailed user documentation appear in DOCX format (the new Word 2007 document storage method), so you need the converter found at `http://www.microsoft.com/downloads/details.aspx?FamilyId=941b3470-3ae9-4aee-8f43-c6bb74cd1466` if you're working with Office 2000 or 2003. Beside these sources, you should review the blog entry at `http://blogs.msdn.com/mitsu/archive/2008/04/02/visual-linq-query-builder-for-linq-to-sql-vlinq.aspx` for a quick walkthrough of VLinq.

Creating a VLinq query

After you download VLinq, install it by right-clicking the MSI file and choosing Install from the context menu. The installation process creates a new add-in application for your Visual Studio setup. The following steps provide an overview of how to use VLinq to build a LINQ to SQL query. You'll find this example in the `\Chapter 14\VLinqExample` folder of the source code for this book:

1. **Create a new project in Visual Studio.**

   You can use any project type that supports database connectivity.

2. **Add a new data source to your application by right-clicking Data Connections in Server Explorer and choosing Add Connection from the context menu.**

3. **Use the Add Connection dialog box to add a new database connection to your application.**

   Visual Studio adds a new data source to your application. Figure 14-1 shows an example of the Add Connection dialog box. This dialog box shows a standard SQL Server connection. You can also create connections to MDF files by using the Microsoft SQL Server Database File data source. No matter what kind of connection you create, always click Test Connection to ensure the connection works as anticipated.

4. **Right-click the project entry in Solution Explorer and choose Add⇨New Item from the context menu. Select the Data folder.**

   You see the Add New Item dialog box shown in Figure 14-2. Note that the dialog box contains a new VLinq Queries item. Use this item to add a new LINQ to SQL query to your application. However, before you can add the VLinq Queries item, you must add a LINQ to SQL Classes item.

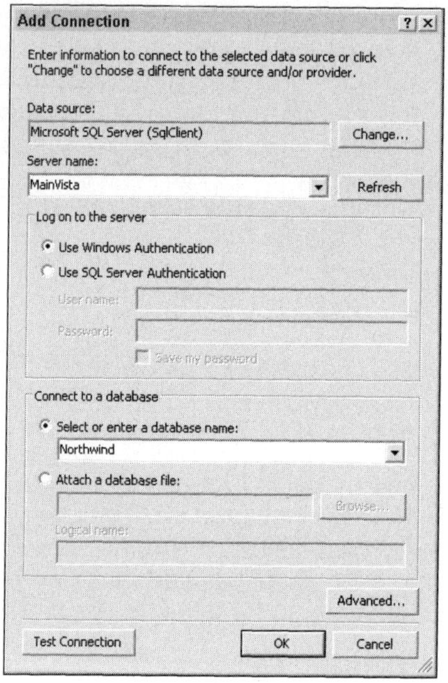

Figure 14-1:
Create a
connection
to the data-
base.

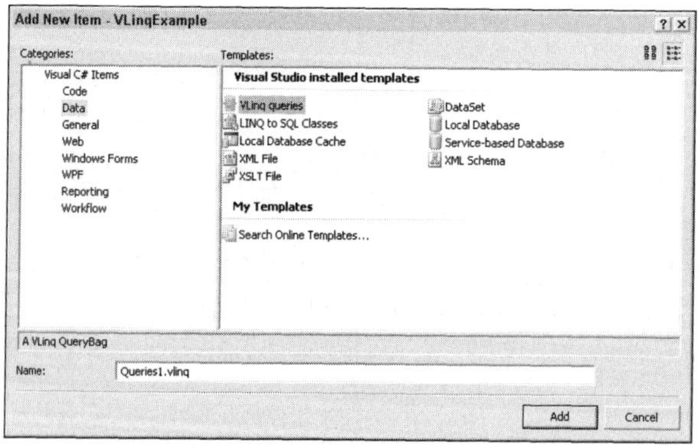

Figure 14-2:
Add a VLinq
query to
your appli-
cation.

5. **Highlight LINQ to SQL Classes. In the Name field, type a name for the item and then click Add.**

Visual Studio displays a LINQ to SQL Classes designer like the one shown in Figure 14-3. In this case, the screen shows the setup for the example application. Simply drag and drop database objects from Server Explorer onto the design area as needed.

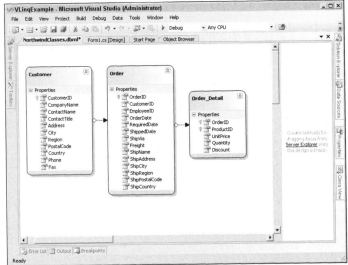

Figure 14-3:
Create a
LINQ to SQL
class design
for your
application.

6. **Choose Build⇨Build Solution.**

   Visual Studio compiles your application. If you don't perform this step, it will appear that you don't have any data sources when you use the VLinq designer.

7. **Right-click the project entry in Solution Explorer and choose Add⇨New Item from the context menu. Select the Data folder.**

8. **Highlight VLinq Queries. In the Name field, type a name for the query and then click Add.**

   Visual Studio adds a new VLINQ file to Solution Explorer.

9. **Double-click the VLINQ file to open it.**

   Visual Studio displays a blank designer interface.

10. **In the Properties window, click the ellipses (...) button of the Connection String property.**

    You see the Connection String dialog box shown in Figure 14-4. The screen shows a sample connection.

Figure 14-4:
Define a
VLinq con-
nection.

Connection string...

○ Custom connection string:

● Visual studio Connection: mainvista\sql2005.Northwind.dbo ▼

Ok   Cancel

11. Provide connection information for VLinq to use and then click OK.

In most cases, you use the Visual Studio Connection option. You select the connection you want to use by clicking the down arrow next to the option, as shown in Figure 14-4.

12. Click Create a New Query.

The VLinq designer displays a query that contains the standard operators. The display appears in red and you see a Validation Errors indicator on the right side of the designer area because you haven't created a query yet. Don't worry about any validation errors until you complete your query.

13. Click the plus sign (+) next to *from*.

You see a series of query option buttons, as shown in Figure 14-5. These buttons help you create the from portion of the query.

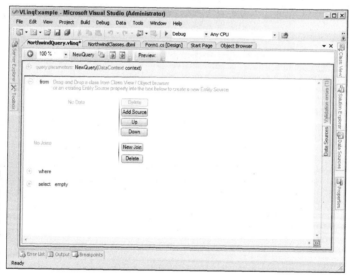

Figure 14-5:
Define the *from* elements of your query.

14. Click Add Source.

You see the New Source dialog box shown in Figure 14-6. When you expand the entries, you should see the tables or other database objects you selected in Step 5 (refer to Figure 14-3). If you don't see the information shown in Figure 14-6, close the New Source dialog box, compile your application, and then click Add Source again.

15. Highlight the data source you want to use and then click OK.

The VLinq designer adds the data source to the query.

16. Repeat Steps 14 and 15 for each data source you want to use.

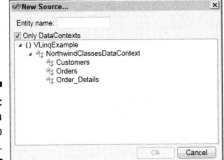

Figure 14-6:
Add a data
source to
your query.

17. **Use the remaining buttons to configure the other operators for your query.**

Figure 14-7 shows an example of what you can do with this tool. The documentation, videos, and other sources of information provided in this section help you discover the purpose of each button.

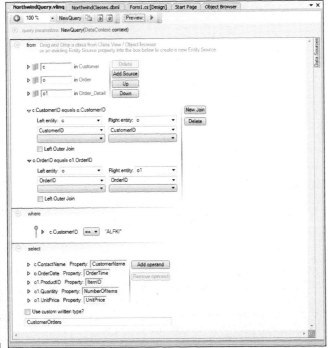

Figure 14-7:
The VLinq
designer
provides a
graphical
environment
for creating
LINQ to SQL
queries.

18. **Compile the application.**

19. **Click Launch Data/SQL Preview.**

You see the Preview pane shown in Figure 14-8. This pane lets you see the data output of the query, the SQL used to create the query, and the C# or Visual Basic code used to define the query. Figure 14-8 shows the C# code.

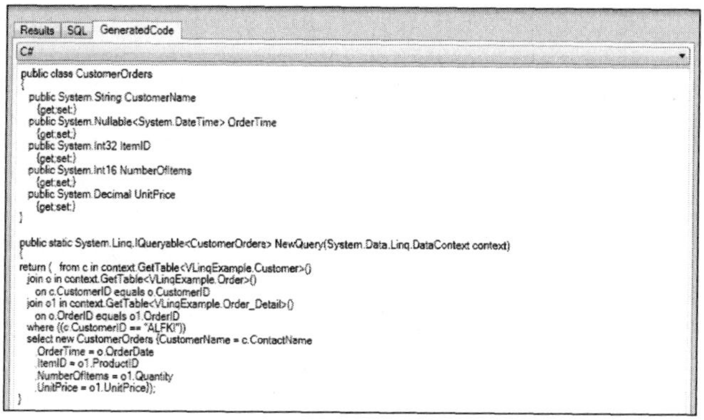

Figure 14-8:
The output
of this pro-
cess is a
query you
can use in
your code.

Using a VLinq query in an application

When you complete the task of creating your query and ensure that it produces the output you want, you can build an application that tests it. Listing 14-1 shows the code for this example.

Listing 14-1   Using a VLinq Query

```csharp
private void btnTest_Click(object sender, EventArgs e)
{
    // Create the DataContext object.
    DataContext DB2 = new DataContext(
        @"Data Source=MAINVISTA;Initial Catalog=Northwind;"
        + "Integrated Security=True");

    // Create the query.
    var ThisQuery = NorthwindQuery.NewQuery(DB2);

    // Display the results.
    dgResults.DataSource = ThisQuery;
}
```

Even though the query is significantly more complex than some of the other examples in the book (compare this example with those in Chapter 8), the code to use it is significantly less complex. Notice that the example doesn't rely on a mapping file or any special code files. The VLinq designer performs this work for you.

All you need is a connection to the data source to create the query. In this case, you use the `DataContext` class to create the data context for the query and you don't even need a custom class to make things work. The `NewQuery()` method of the `NorthwindQuery` class you create with VLinq accepts this generic data context to create the query. You can then add the result, `ThisQuery`, to the `DataSource` property of a `DataGridView` control. Figure 14-9 shows the output from this application.

Using LINQ to Create Self Documenting Code

Ask four people what they mean by self-documenting and you'll likely receive four different answers. The truth is that the term *self-documenting* is used in a number of ways. LINQ helps you create self-documenting code by using a simple set of operators to create queries. In many cases, your query will consist of just five simple words: `from`, `in`, `where`, `orderby`, and `select`, as shown here.

```
var ThisQuery =
    from StringValue
    in QueryString
    where StringValue.Length > 3
    orderby StringValue.Length
```

```
select StringValue;
```

Anyone who knows the meaning of these five terms already has a significant understanding of the form of your query. In addition, the operators break the query into manageable pieces. Consequently, even if you don't understand a particular operator argument, you can work with it as an individual element, making the problem of understanding it considerably smaller.

The values you choose for objects within each of the arguments helps make them easier to understand as well. You have direct control over the name of the temporary variables used for each query, which makes it possible to use something specific, rather than the generic variable name that you might ordinarily use. The temporary variables should reflect the use of the variable for this specific query, rather than of the data source that the application queries.

Many of your queries will use a single data source. However, some situations will call for data from multiple data sources. In these cases, use the `join` syntax shown here to make your queries clearer:

```
var Squares =
    from QueryA in ArrayA
    join QueryB in ArrayB
    on QueryA equals QueryB
    let TheSquare = QueryA * QueryB
    where TheSquare > 4
    select new { QueryA, QueryB, TheSquare };
```

It's possible to obtain the same results when using two `from` operators, but using the `join` operator instead makes the multiple data source nature of the query clear. Always use the `on` operator when using the `join` operator. Use the `let` operator whenever possible to enhance the performance of the query and to make calculated values more obvious. Return calculated values as part of the query output when necessary to further reduce the cost of performing the query.

There's a temptation to add comments to a query in a way that prevents the code from compiling. Because the query appears on multiple lines, some developers will place comments on a particular line and then find that their code won't compile. It's even possible to stare right at the problem and miss it because you're accustomed to working with comments on a line-by-line basis. Remember that the query you create is a single line of code, even though you place it on multiple lines for readability. Here's an example of comments that will and won't work.

```
// This comment works because it appears before the query.
var ThisQuery =
    from StringValue
    in QueryString

    // This comment won't work because it appears within
    // the query.

    where StringValue.Length > 3
    select StringValue;
// This comment works because it appears after the query.
```

In addition to the issues described in this section, you need to follow all the usual programming best practices. The requirement of using easily under-stood variable names doesn't end simply because you're using LINQ. In fact, due to the compact nature of LINQ queries, the requirement increases. Using good programming practices will help you create LINQ queries that are essentially self-documenting — making your job as a developer significantly easier.

Analyzing Code Patterns

Many developers look at the XML documentation feature of C# or Visual Basic .NET as just that — a means of creating documentation. Of course, cre-ating documentation is the primary purpose of this feature, but you can use it for a number of other tasks, especially when you bring LINQ into the pic-ture. All you need to do is provide judicious comments throughout the appli-cation. To use this feature, you use a triple comment marker like the one shown here (Visual Basic .NET developers use ' ' ' instead).

```
/// <summary>
/// Twiddles bits and causes the screen to blink.
/// </summary>
/// <param name="sender">Contains sender object.</param>
/// <param name="e">Contains sender arguments.</param>
```

After you complete enough code that you want to begin looking for patterns, you enable the XML documentation feature by choosing Project⇨ <ProjectName> Properties. Select the Build page and you'll see the XML Documentation File option shown in Figure 14-10, where you provide the name of the XML file you want to use.

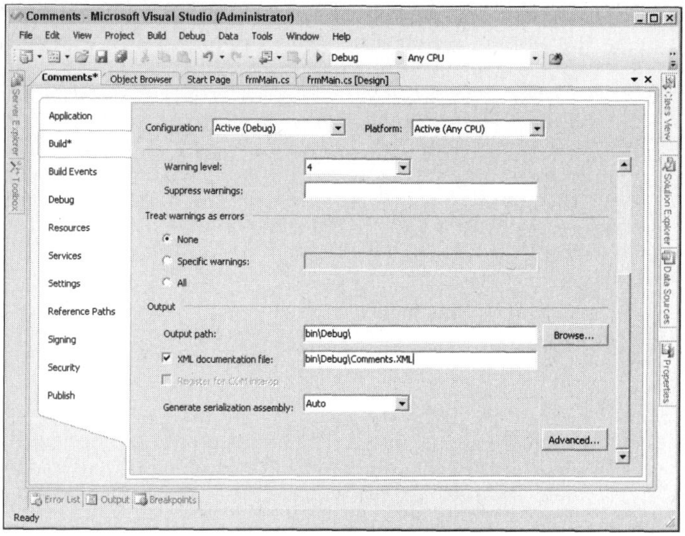

Figure 14-10:
Create an
XML file that
contains all
your com-
ments.

After you compile your application, you see a new XML file containing all the comments you made in a format that's easy for LINQ to parse (as shown in Figure 14-11).

Figure 14-11:
The XML
file Visual
Studio
produces
contains
all the
application
comments.

To use this XML file for analysis, simply load it and use the techniques described in Chapter 9 to interact with it. You can begin asking questions such as how often you actually use the `EventArgs` object send to event handlers in your application. To give you a better idea of how this would work,

Listing 14-2 shows a query that accesses the information. You'll find this example in the \Chapter 14\Comments folder of the source code for this book.

Listing 14-2   Reading XML Comments for an Application

```
private void btnCheckComments_Click(object sender,
        EventArgs e)
{
   // Load the XML file.
   XDocument ThisDocument =
      XDocument.Load(Application.StartupPath +
                     @"\Comments.XML");

   // Create the query.
   var ArgNotUse =
      from ThisEntry in ThisDocument.DescendantNodes()
      where ThisEntry.NodeType == XmlNodeType.Element
      where ((XElement)ThisEntry).Name == "param"
      let EntryValue = ((XElement)ThisEntry).Value
      where EntryValue.Contains("Not Used")
      select new
      {
          ThisEntry.Parent.Attribute("name").Value,
          EntryValue
      };

   // Display the result.
   txtResults.Text = "Arguments Not in Use:\r\n";
   foreach (var CommentEntry in ArgNotUse)
      txtResults.Text = txtResults.Text +
         "\r\n" + CommentEntry.Value +
         "\r\n" + CommentEntry.EntryValue + "\r\n";
}
```

This example adds to the Chapter 9 examples. In this case, you know where the file is located on your system, so you load it using the information in the Application.StartupPath property.

The query requires a little time to understand, but remember to take the query apart using the operators as a starting point. The first task is to divide the file into nodes using the ThisDocument.DescendantNodes() method so that you can check each node in turn. The next step is to accept only elements using the ThisEntry.NodeType == XmlNodeType.Element argument.

Of course, you don't want all the elements, just those that contain parameter information. To check for just parameters, you must first cast ThisEntry to an XElement type and then check the resulting object's Name property for the param keyword.

At this point, you have a list of parameters, but you don't know whether the application is using them. This is where your keyword in a comment comes into play. All the parameters that aren't used in the application have the words *Not Used* as part of the comment. Consequently, the last `where` operator checks for these words using the `Contains("Not Used")` method.

This query requires the use of a `let` operator because the output array can't have two elements with the same name. If the code had used `((XElement) ThisEntry).Value` as an output, then two elements would have the name `Value`, which won't work. Using the `let` operator helps you work around problems such as this one. Figure 14-12 shows the output from the example application.

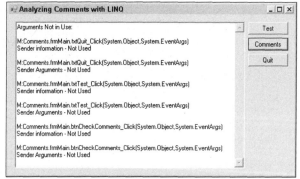

Figure 14-12: Using LINQ and XML documentation together helps you discover application patterns.

The idea behind this technique is mapping your application and understanding how you use code to achieve specific goals. It isn't the same as mapping the flow of your application. Consider this more of a block diagram approach to understanding the construction of your application. The output you obtain is useful because you can literally begin to interact with the design of your application — to ask it questions about how you've put it together.

This is also a handy way to find code that you've already constructed. You may remember that you created a method to twiddle bits, but you may not remember what you called it. Using the LINQ approach and the documentation XML file, you can simply ask the application about any methods that twiddle bits and have it present you with a list.

Querying a Code Snippet Database

Code snippets are an essential developer productivity tool. You already use them even if you haven't created any of your own because Visual Studio

comes packed with them. Type certain keywords and you'll find that Visual
Studio adds essential code for you automatically (depending on the language). If you haven't already started your own code snippet database, you
can discover how to perform this task at `http://msdn2.microsoft.com/`
`en-us/library/ms165394(VS.80).aspx`. The default Visual Studio snippets appear in a number of folders, including the following (look in the sub-
folders too):

✔ `\Program Files\Microsoft Visual Studio 9.0\VB\Snippets`

✔ `\Program Files\Microsoft Visual Studio 9.0\VC#\Snippets`

✔ `\Program Files\Microsoft Visual Studio 9.0\Xml\1033\`
`Snippets`

✔ `\Program Files\Microsoft SQL Server\100\Tools\Binn\`
`VSShell\Xml\1033\Snippets`

Most developers eventually create a code snippet database. Even if the snippet is a shell, it beats writing everything from scratch. Instead of facing a
blank editor, the developer with a code snippet database has the start of
every application (even those that don't exist yet as concepts). The problem
is that a code snippet database can quickly become large and unwieldy.

It's important to remember that your code snippets exist as groups of files in
XML format (despite having a `SNIPPET` file extension). Consequently, you
can locate code snippets anywhere on your system using a combination of
LINQ and the `FileSystem` object. After you locate all `SNIPPET` files, you
can open each in turn and examine them as you would any other XML file.
You can find a complete code snippet file reference at `http://msdn2.`
`microsoft.com/en-us/library/ms171418(VS.80).aspx`. Figure 14-13
shows a typical `SNIPPET` file (`\Program Files\Microsoft Visual`
`Studio 9.0\VB\Snippets\1033\application\CheckForUpdates.`
`snippet`).

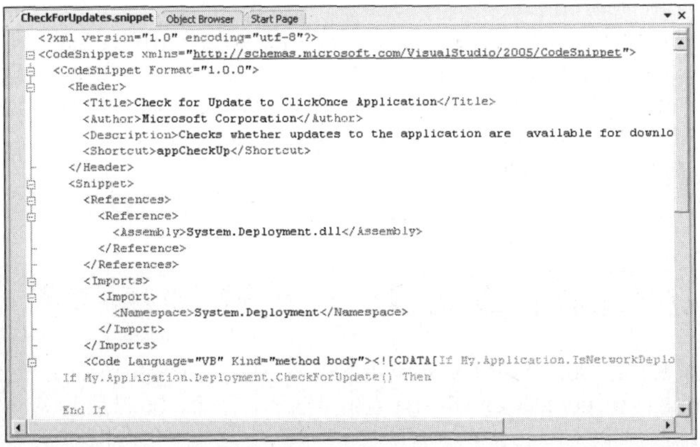

Figure 14-13:
Code snip-
pets are
essential
parts of the
developer
toolkit for
Visual
Studio.

Locating Other Development Resources

LINQ is everywhere it seems, and yet you may find that you can't easily locate the information you need to use LINQ without help because some resources aren't indexed properly, don't appear in existing search engines, or rely on older terminology that Microsoft has updated. Using LINQ to locate resources on your local drive is easy. All you need is a `FileSystem` query that locates the correct file types and then a LINQ to Object or LINQ to XML query to delve inside the file as needed. Extending this technique to the mapped drives for your network is relatively easy, so you can also search shared information sources for your organization.

Getting other kinds of information is also relatively easy, but you'll need another helper, such as Google Web Services (`http://code.google.com/`). For example, you can perform a site search on MSDN (by adding `site:msdn2.microsoft.com` to your query string). In some cases, combining LINQ with Google Web Services to search MSDN provides superior results to searching your local help file. All your help file contents do appear online, so this kind of search doesn't rob you of any useful information. (If you have an interest in Google Web Services, see my book, *Mining Google Web Services,* published by Sybex.)

Now that you have access to local, organization-shared, and online resources, you might think you have everything you need. Don't forget to use LINQ to search any code bases you can access, online versions of magazines you like, other Web services that might contain useful information, newsgroups, and just about everything else you can imagine.

You can go too far with these kinds of searches, so remember to keep your searches under control to remain productive. A search is only useful when it saves you time. Consequently, waiting all day for LINQ to search your local resources, network resources, MSDN resources, other online sources, and even that magazine you remember reading once is probably not efficient. This is where your search plan comes into play. You'll want to create an application that searches one area at a time and then asks whether you want it to go on — you could very well have everything you need on your local machine.

Using LINQ to Query Data Formats

You have an amazing number of data formats on your system. At one time developers relied on books such as "File Formats for Popular PC Software" to interact with the data files on their hard drive. The older data formats depend heavily on binary formatting. Interestingly enough, you can use LINQ to query binary data, but it does take a little effort to get the query right.

Fortunately for the modern developer, XML is becoming the popular alternative to binary data formats. Chapter 10 demonstrates that you can take any Office 2007 document apart, parse the information, analyze it, make changes as necessary, and put it back together. The next time the reader opens the file, the changes appear without any apparent damage to the file (because there isn't any).

Developers spend a considerable amount of time trying to interact with data files. A number of my personal programming projects have involved obtaining data from a Point of Sale (POS) terminal, massaging it into a form that a database will accept, and then sending the translated data to the database.

When you discover that a data file appears in XML format, all you need to do is load it and begin analyzing it with LINQ to XML. It won't take long to begin seeing patterns within the file that will help you write an application to interact with it. Even if the file is in binary form, you should still consider working with it using LINQ. The point of using LINQ to help you perform the analysis is that you can discover more about the file in a shorter time by concentrating on the specifics of the file format, rather than how to access the file. Let LINQ take care of the background details (such as reading that XML file) for you.

Finding Usage Trends

Many applications create log files. In fact, most installation programs include logging capability. But if you've ever tried to work through one of those log files, you know that they can be large, difficult to read, and hard to understand. In some cases, you can't find the source of a problem for all the data you must trudge through. LINQ is a perfect way to scrutinize log files for data you need to make the application better.

One of the reasons to provide logging with an application is to see usage trends. This is an uncommon use for logging, however, because it takes so much time to analyze the files. Using LINQ, you can cut through some of that data to find just the details you need. The full data remains available for future queries, but LINQ helps you cut it down to size for whatever current analysis you need to perform.

Using proper logging and query techniques, you can begin to look for potential sources of code bloat in your applications. Some custom applications have features that someone requested long ago and that only they used. The person is gone, but the feature remains — using resources, increasing interface complexity, and adding to management headaches. By comparing what the user employs against the list of application features, you can probably eliminate much of the dead wood in your application without a lot of effort. You'll have to handle the corporate politics on your own.

Developing a LINQ Library

Organizations tend to seek the same kinds of data more than once. The reasons for this repetition are many. The weekly, monthly, and annual reports you create are one source of repeated queries. Users also tend to want the same kinds of data for various needs such as customer interaction and project updates. External requirements also play a role in creating a constraint for repetitious queries — government agencies and other monitoring require updates of the same information you provided the week or month before. If you find yourself using the same LINQ query more than once, consider placing it in a library for the same reasons that you place any other repeated code in a library. In general, storing LINQ queries in libraries will reduce update complexity and potential errors.

Some queries also fall into patterns. You may not query the same data source each time, but the form of the query doesn't vary. For example, your organization may have a number of customer databases. Each database uses the same tables, views, and other constructs and the information varies only by the customer content. Theoretically, you could place all these databases into a single huge database and query it, but for reasons of complexity, security, or privacy you must maintain the separate databases. This is a perfect example of a LINQ query that belongs in a library. By passing a reference to the particular customer database you need, you can reuse the query and reduce your workload as well.

Queries can vary by other operator arguments as well. For example, you may need to perform a number of searches on a parts catalog database that vary only by the `where` operator information. Placing the query in a method that accepts a `where` argument as input and then storing the resulting method in a library makes sense because you spend less time maintaining and updating the LINQ query for any number of search conditions. The same concept holds true for the `orderby` operator, and you can even combine various `where` and `orderby` scenarios into a single method.

LINQ query libraries tend not to work well where both the data source and the `where` and/or `orderby` operator arguments are subject to change. The reason is simple: It's easier to use LINQ to create a new query at this point. The resulting method will contain a skeleton query that you'll find difficult to maintain and even harder to understand later. In addition, the result is brittle because you don't have a well-defined query scenario to work with.

Sharing LINQ Queries with Others

One of the best ways to improve LINQ is by sharing your knowledge with other people. This book contains many references to Web sites, blogs, applications, and other resources provided by people in the development community. The number of these resources increases every day as people begin to realize just how flexible LINQ makes queries. As you begin to work with LINQ and realize that you have a unique take on how this product works, consider sharing your findings with others. The same need to share holds true for providers and tools that you create.

Make sure that you share your findings with me. If you decide to share your LINQ queries, library, or provider publicly, please feel free to contact me at JMueller@mwt.net. I'll consider the best resources I receive for inclusion in articles, my blog, or an update of this book. Please don't send me your unfinished ideas or untested code.

Analyzing Compiler and IDE Output

Adding debugging messages to your application is a time honored way to locate information. However, a long debugging session can prove frustrating when you have a large amount of data to work with. It's possible to copy data from any of the IDE windows and place it in a text file. Save this file to disk and you can use LINQ to examine its contents. For example, you can use this approach to determine whether you're wasting time checking the same information in the Immediate window. You can use it also to determine whether there are patterns in the Error List window. The important issue is to use LINQ to help you find patterns, special issues, potential data errors, and other issues that aren't immediately apparent when you view a long list of compiler and other IDE output.

One thing that LINQ can't help you find is the missing item. It won't tell you that your application is failing because you left out some important exception handling. LINQ also won't tell you that you really need to use a particular IDE feature to solve a problem. The omitted item isn't LINQ's forte. To overcome this problem, keep a checklist of items you should check. LINQ will tell you which items you've already tried, so you can check those items off the list. The items that remain are the ones that you should try to fix the problem.

Always keep notes. Talk with other developers about the issues that you find cause the most problems for you as you work with applications. The notes that you maintain translate into checklists that you can use with LINQ to improve the development process. The bottom line is to work out ways to make yourself more efficient — to write better code, to find unavoidable bugs faster, and to locate application inefficiencies, such as features that no one is using.

Chapter 15

Ten Ways to Reduce Application Support Costs

In This Chapter

▶ Defining queries that automatically change to meet user needs

▶ Developing reports using LINQ

▶ Creating user-specific searches using LINQ

▶ Combining LINQ with other user-related technologies

▶ Using LINQ to make application help easier and faster

▶ Tracking user support with LINQ

▶ Using LINQ with multiple data sources

▶ Avoiding data duplication with better searches

▶ Automating application support tasks

▶ Managing applications using LINQ queries

*B*esides making life easier for yourself, as described in Chapter 14, LINQ can make life easier for both the support staff at your organization and the users who rely on your application. Making things easier on these two groups has a tendency to further reduce your burden as well, so a win for this group is a win for you. The bottom line is that support costs tend to eat up developer time and increase hostility toward your programming efforts, so it's always a good idea to focus some attention in this area.

The question is how to reduce support costs without increasing application complexity through additional user aids. This chapter examines support costs from a number of angles — all of which make your development process easier. The following list points out some of the ways in which LINQ can make life easier for everyone:

✔ Program automation that adjusts to user needs

✔ Self-help in creating output (reports or other kinds of end data)

✔ Searches that make it possible to locate information with little effort

✔ Application help that provides what the user needs and wants

✔ Noninvasive application management strategies

This chapter describes how you can use LINQ to make some of these benefits a reality in your application development environment. The actual implementation is up to you. The examples throughout the book provide tips on how you can make these techniques a reality in your application.

Creating Self-Modifying Queries

At one time, applications used hard-coded queries that didn't change to match conditions because the system hardware lacked sufficient computing power and the developer lacked adequate tools to perform the task any other way. Today, applications can self-modify their operation based on the numerous input sources that systems provide. Self-modifying LINQ queries automatically change the arguments for one or more operators depending on one of these factors:

✔ **Environmental:** You may choose to automatically modify a query so that it always provides 30 days worth of results from the current date. An application may automatically modify path information for data sources depending on the system configuration. It's possible to use LINQ to detect most of these requirements by querying the system before performing the target query. In other words, one query acts as input for another query.

✔ **Security:** A query should always consider the security requirements of the data, the application, and the user. An external query should have fewer access rights than an internal query. Applications shouldn't create queries that divulge information that the application has no need to know. Users should gain access to only the data to which they have rights. A LINQ application should also log queries, especially if you provide the user with rights to make flexible queries. Monitoring the queries that a user makes is as important to security as putting barriers in the way of incorrect or improper queries.

✔ **User:** Queries should consider the needs of the user. For example, if you're providing access to an online resource, the query should provide data output at the level the user requires. To an extent, the application should also provide the user with input needed to make a knowledgeable query. For example, by querying a database for acceptable values first, a LINQ-based application can present a list of acceptable choices to the user making incorrect choices less likely. An application can also provide administrator-controlled user selection criteria, where the administrator can configure the application to meet specific user needs.

✔ **Context:** Considering context in an application is admittedly difficult in some cases. A few contexts, such as whether the user is making a local or online query, are easy to detect. However, the application can't know whether a particular customer in a database requires special handling unless the database provides the required information. When the database does provide the required information, it's up to the developer to use that information to modify the query arguments such that the query returns the information that fits that particular customer context. The same holds true for any query scenario: The data source should provide useful information to the LINQ query that the LINQ query in turn uses to modify the query to fit the needs of a particular query target.

Although creating self-modifying queries may seem daunting, sometimes all you need is good programming techniques. For example, you can meet many environmental objectives simply by using existing .NET Framework features. You might not know where an application resides on the hard drive, but you don't have to know that information because .NET Framework provides it to you in the `Application.StartupPath` property. In fact, you should consider the `Application`, `Environment`, `FileSystem`, `File`, `Directory`, and other built-in classes best friends when writing a LINQ application because they help you design self-modifying queries that don't rely on any input.

Using LINQ to Create Reports

Reports are the bane of most developers because they involve complexity issues that developers simply don't learn to handle in school. The concept of what makes a good report is often in the eye of the beholder — no amount of cold, hard science is going to make reports easier to create, and art often doesn't answer the question either. One user may want a single report that's crowded with facts, while another wants several simple reports that include the same information.

LINQ can't help you design a pretty report. You can't ask it whether the company logo with the blue background or the austere black and white logo is the best choice for a particular report. In fact, ask any two people at your company the same question and you're likely to get two different answers, so the artistic choices you make are up to you. However, LINQ can make it possible to produce a complex or simple report using the same template. All you need to do is add code that builds the LINQ query based on user input.

Consider this scenario. The user interface includes one of several data source selections that you provide. When the user chooses a data source, the application uses a LINQ query to obtain a list of fields for that data source and fills in a list box containing them. The user chooses fields from the list by moving them from an available list box to a report list box. As the user moves these fields, the application builds a `select` operator for the query. The output is an array that you process in a `foreach` loop using the same techniques as many of the examples in this book use.

This first phase takes care of the content. The application must now accommodate the conditions used for selecting records. When the user selects a particular field for limiting the content, a LINQ query automatically queries the database for acceptable values for that field. As the user makes these selections, the application creates `where` operators and adds them (and their associated arguments) to the report query.

Finally, the user selects one or more fields to use to order the data. Again, the user simply selects the fields you supply courtesy of a LINQ query. As the user makes field selections, the application creates `orderby` operators and adds them to the report query. The report query executes at this point and the report data is ready for presentation on the screen, all without any concrete programming on your part. Everything relies on a LINQ query.

Locating report ideas online

A look at a single organization will likely turn up hundreds of reports, all of which view the same corporate data in different ways. Although LINQ can help you collect and organize the data used in a report, it can't help you create a beautiful report — one that everyone will enjoy seeing and using. A developer can spend considerable time putting together a report that has all the right information but isn't in a form that users can readily identify and employ to make business decisions.

Fortunately, you don't have to go it alone. Other people have the same problems putting reports together that you do, so sometimes the best way to approach this issue is to look for a solution online. One such example is the blog entry at `http://tiredblogger.wordpress.com/2007/07/16/using-linq-as-a-activereports-datasource/`. In this case, the author tells you how to use LINQ as a data source for ActiveReports

(see `http://www.datadynamics.com/Products/ProductOverview.aspx?Product=ARNET3` for details about ActiveReports).

Some developers aren't even sure which report writing tool to use. One reporting tool isn't the same as every other reporting tool, so the tool you choose has to fit your skill set and the needs of your organization. If you're in this boat, you might want to check out report source conversations such as the one at `http://weblogs.asp.net/pwilson/archive/2003/09/03/26193.aspx` before you make a decision on how to incorporate LINQ into the picture. No matter which reporting tool you use, however, you still have to remember that LINQ provides substance, not style. When you find that you don't have the skills required to create a beautiful report, try some of the online sources at your disposal for ideas.

Addressing User Search Needs

Most users aren't concerned about your variables or the data source that you use to obtain the information they need. In fact, it's better that they don't know about these issues. What the user needs is a subset of the available information ordered in a particular way. You can address this need by providing a method that accepts one or more inputs for the `where` operator and one or more inputs for the `orderby` operator.

The standard methods of dealing with this need are to provide a completely freeform fill-in-the-blank kind of interface or a Draconian select-the-item interface. In many cases, the fill-in-the-blank options are hard coded, which means that the interface won't automatically update itself to show new entries in the data source. Some user interfaces combine the two approaches.

When you must provide a specific set of search items for security or other reasons, consider using a LINQ query to fill the list box or other display element with data directly from the data source. Using this approach reduces the risk that the form you create becomes outdated when the hard-coded search options are no longer applicable. Outdated form entries cause considerable grief for both users and support staff because the user often knows that an option is available even if it doesn't appear on the screen. Of course, eventually their grief becomes your grief as you find yourself updating an application you thought was complete.

In some cases, you can also combine standard and user-specific search selections. Using a combo box lets the user input a search choice when the standard selections won't work. You can capture these user-specific additions and serialize them to an XML file in the user's data area on the hard drive. This technique ensures that the user's choices remain an option for that user and that the user won't have to re-create the choice later.

Finding XML serialization resources on the Internet

XML serialization is becoming more popular as developers realize how powerful it is. Besides the amazing array of Microsoft resources for XML serialization on MSDN, it's easy to find good third-party exchanges on the topic of XML serialization on the Internet. You can find a discussion of the topic of serialization at `http://www.15seconds.com/issue/020903.htm`. The article at `http://www.codeproject.com/KB/XML/cardfileserialization demo.aspx` provides an interesting example of XML serialization in use. This is one of the few examples online that isn't specific to ASP.NET. If you're building a Web application, you may also want to review the article at `http://www.4guysfromrolla.com/webtech/012302-1.shtml`.

Creating User-Friendly Mashups

One of the most amazing features of LINQ is that you can use it to create what appears as a single data source from multiple data sources. The common term for this approach to working with data is a *mashup* — it often appears as the term used to describe combining information from multiple Web services, but it can also apply to other uses of multiple data sources as well.

The Internet abounds with examples of mashups (see the Web site at `http://www.programmableweb.com/mashups` for some details on mashups), but one of the more interesting examples appears at `http://blogoscoped.com/archive/2003_06_21_index.html#105620701911984896`. This one is interesting because it's a useful Web application of the sort that someone in the business community can truly appreciate. The output shown at `http://www.authorama.com/` helps the viewer locate free books that they can download and view offline.

Most of the mashups you see online include some incredibly complex programming because the author had to consider the Web service requirements for each of the Web services, plus any local data used to cement the mashup into a cohesive unit. Because LINQ providers hide the details of the Web service and present you with a simple data source, you can easily combine these Web services with local sources to create mashups.

For the developer, the best part about mashups is that they offer an opportunity to create unique views of data to use in reports or as part of a research effort in an organization. You may find that the data you need is already available — all you need to do is combine the right sources into a mashup. The Web site at `http://www.programmableweb.com/mashups` provides numerous examples of existing mashups. You can use these ideas either directly or as a source for your own mashups.

Making Help More Accessible

Help files are a problem for most users, support staff, and developers alike. When you can get the user interested in looking at the help file, they often complain that the help file doesn't contain the help they need or that the help is incomplete. Users generally don't care about how your application works or the clever programming employed to complete a task. All that the users know is that they need to type a letter and your application is preventing them from completing that task. Consequently, anything you can do to help users focus on the letter and not on your application will make your life happier.

It's easy to diagnose the source of help-related problems. Choose an application at random and you find that some context-sensitive help works and some doesn't because the context-sensitive help depends on hard-coded entries made by the developer. Help indexes contain only the words that the developer or other documentation specialist decided the user would need. Even looking at the contents of a help file usually leaves the user wondering where to go next. The search routines used for help files commonly provide results that have nothing to do with the task at hand.

LINQ has the potential for revolutionizing how help works. Instead of implementing help using the standard methods, a developer could rely on user activity to build a LINQ query that would then go to the help file and locate information based on the help context. Instead of presenting the user with a single help screen that probably doesn't contain the required information, the application could present a list of help topics based on what task the user is performing at the time. Of course, such an approach would require that you create a log of user activity and then use that log as input to the where operators of the LINQ query.

You can use LINQ also to combine sources of help information. For example, the output of the LINQ query might include both standard application help information and information from a commonly asked question database maintained by support staff. It's even possible to couple this information with online sources by providing the results of a Google search (using the Google Web Service) or the Microsoft Knowledge Base. The point is that most applications provide a simple, static, local database that's based on archaic help techniques. LINQ makes it possible for an application to provide significantly more information without a lot of extra programming on your part.

Organizing and Querying Support Requests and Responses

Every support team has experts. Unfortunately, the experts are often working on solving issues for which they have no expertise. The expert on the user interface is solving database problems, while the database expert is solving a user interface problem, all because the support system serves users on a first come, first served basis. Part of the problem is discovering which support staff member has the most expertise in solving a particular problem. The other part of the problem is queuing the requests in such a manner that the user receives optimal support response times without getting frustrated over support staff answers. The problem resolves into one of discovering these bits of information:

✔ Which support staff member has the formal training required to solve the problem?

✔ Who has worked on this issue in the past?

✔ Is this a known issue that the support staff can answer using a help file?

✔ When does a support problem actually require developer support?

✔ Is this a new problem that requires special handling?

You can probably come up with additional questions for your organization. The problem is that when the user calls, there usually isn't time to locate a particular expert or consider who has the best chance of solving the issue quickly unless you have some means to organize the requests and the required responses. Using one or more databases and LINQ queries, you can locate the right support personnel, ask the right questions, and provide the correct responses in a timely manner.

The likely scenario for this LINQ application is that you query a list of support staff members based on the target area of the request. Once the support person is selected, he or she would create another LINQ query for searching a support database with the right questions. The support person would then use another LINQ query to locate the proper response for the user. Another LINQ query would show whether this is a new issue, and the support person could make appropriate support database entries to support the request and the response.

Developing Fast Searches from Multiple Sources

This book has talked a lot about combining data from multiple sources using LINQ. It's true that you can possibly combine information from any number of disparate sources no matter what format the data uses into a single LINQ query. The problem is one of time. You must consider the amount of time required to satisfy a particular query when building your application. Most importantly, you must consider the issue of time from the user's perspective. Perhaps the user doesn't have a high-speed broadband connection — the user might actually rely on a dial-up connection (as rare as you might think dial-up has become, it still plays a major part in some user connections).

LINQ answers the questions of where to look, what to find, how to order it, and what to provide as output — but LINQ can't answer the questions of when or how much. The question of when depends on the strategy you use to optimize the query, and the question of how much depends on the user's requirements. Leave the question of how much to the user. If the user complains about slow query times, yet continues to ask for the entire database, you might want to leave that issue to someone who can guide the user into asking for less information. However, you can control the optimization of the query by considering the following issues:

- ✔ **Local caching of data:** You can't be sure that an online or remote data source will answer a query quickly. Caching the data locally means that the user will get significantly faster response times but you have to weigh the benefits of this option against the age of the data. The user won't thank you for providing old data. Consequently, when using a caching strategy, you must also consider the need to age the data so that the local cache doesn't become filled with old information.

- ✔ **Provide search levels:** The users might know that the data they need appears locally. Just as the Visual Studio help setup lets you optimize the search routine to favor local or online help, you must give the users this option as well. Perhaps the users only need to know locally accessible information and searching online is a waste of time.

- ✔ **Get only what you need:** A major problem with most searches is that the search requests too much data. As a result, the search uses network bandwidth inefficiently. Not only does it require more time to obtain the data, but the additional bandwidth usage slows every other network activity. The smart approach is to request only the data you actually need, which means requesting only the records you need and only the fields you need from each record.

- ✔ **Display partial results:** A long running query can fill the user with a sense of dread. The user eventually stops the query and starts it all over again, thinking that the first attempt failed. Meanwhile, the server that holds the data may continue the original request. The second request simply adds to the server load and slows things even more. Displaying a partial result shows the user that the query is indeed working but is just taking a while to complete. Seeing the partial result lets the user make an intelligent decision about waiting for the query to complete in its entirety.

- ✔ **Perform pre-queries:** Nothing says that you must create a huge LINQ query that performs the entire task at one time. It's interesting to see a 200 data source query with 50 `where` operators and 20 `orderby` operators work, but such a query would be inconceivably slow. Several other sections in this chapter have mentioned the need to perform a query, ask the user to do something with the output, and then perform the next query in the sequence. Such an approach can make a long query appear considerably more responsive as well as save processing cycles by refining each query step.

Developing queries using tools

Chapter 14 discusses the VLinq query tool. You can find an amazing assortment of LINQ query tools on the Internet considering that LINQ hasn't been around for very long. One such tool, LINQPad (`http://www.linqpad.net/`), provides a unique user interface that makes it possible for less skilled users to create reasonable LINQ queries. In some cases, you can use such a tool to work with an administrator to create and optimize LINQ queries for your applications. Even though you have the skill required to write the application, the administrator probably has a better grasp of what the query must accomplish. Using a tool that the administrator understands can help you work together to write the perfect LINQ query.

Testing continues on how LINQ queries affect performance. A tool won't necessarily provide you with an optimized query, but it can help you produce the query you need. Once you have the query in hand and know the results you want, you begin optimizing it. Something as simple as modifying the order of entries in the `where` operator can produce interesting results, so performance testing is essential. The article at `http://codebetter.com/blogs/steve.hebert/archive/2008/02/06/linq-to-objects-relating-data-structure-organization-to-where-clause-optimization.aspx` describes the results of some `where` operator modification. The results are eye opening and interesting. In short, after you create the query you need using a tool and the administrator's help, take time to optimize the query for best performance.

✔ **Use specific data types:** Normally, LINQ optimizes data types for you and you don't have to do anything more than use `var` to accomplish your query goals. In rare circumstances, you can obtain better performance by specifying a particular data type for the query results. This may mean performing a cast to convert the LINQ output to the proper type. The only way you can determine whether this approach helps is to rely on application performance testing.

✔ **Reuse query data:** In some cases, the user will view the same data in multiple ways. Consequently, using the local application data will provide the best response times for second and subsequent searches. You can save the data in an application cache and simply use another LINQ query to reorder and reselect the data as needed.

These are all the things you can do. It's important to realize that LINQ performs query optimization in the background. You'll probably notice at least a small performance gain simply by using LINQ, rather than relying on older query techniques. The actual performance gains depend on how you use LINQ and the optimization provided by the LINQ provider.

Helping Users Locate Existing Resources

Many shrink-wrap applications contain some method of locating existing resources — everything from graphics files to new document templates. For example, when working with Microsoft Word, you can tell the application to search online and locate a new template that contains just the right settings for the calendar you want to build. Getting the prebuilt template saves considerable time and effort. In addition, you know that the result will appear in a certain way — you don't have to experiment with a custom template to obtain a particular result.

In an organization with a custom application, prebuilt resources can also lend a consistent appearance to application output and ensure that the output meets company requirements. For example, you might add a list of standard forms to your application and define those forms in such a way that the user knows that the information is both correct and complete when submitting the form. A resource could also include graphics, sound bites, and other data that the user needs to create a particular output, say a presentation.

Anyone who has spent much time working in a large organization knows that multiple versions of the same item tend to appear because one person didn't know that someone else had already created the item. These repeated resources cost the organization significant amounts of time and money to maintain and make it impossible to provide a consistent look to the organization's data.

Using LINQ in an application helps you create an environment in which a user can locate existing resources no matter where they appear within the organization. The result is less repeated work on the part of users and less frustration as well. In addition, you obtain a consistent look and feel to presentations, reports, and other forms of data output.

The need to search for these resources begs the question of why they aren't located in a central place. Given a perfect organization with no politics and users who absolutely adhere to every policy, you could possibly expect to centralize resources and have every user find them without having to search. Unfortunately, most organizations consist of little fiefdoms that will share data — but only if you come to their area to get it. They want control over the data and want to control it in a way that places their stamp on the data. Using LINQ to search for these resources is the next best choice.

Performing Support Task Automation

The support staff that works with your application will want to automate as many support functions as possible. As with many areas of IT, management has shrunk the size of support staff, so they must do their work more efficiently. To accomplish this task, you must make the resources for them to interact with your application more accessible. This support happens on a number of levels, all of which you can augment with LINQ:

- **Usable help:** Users require a different level of help for an application than does the support staff. Yes, the support staff needs to know everything that the user needs to know. Whether user or support staff, everyone needs to know the purpose of that button on the dialog box. However, support staff often need additional information. For example, support staff need to know about application update plans and known application problems. They also need to know where to find detailed technical information about the application — information that the user wouldn't ordinarily need, such as the purpose of each of the settings in the CONFIG file. Support staff also require information about the application's environmental factors and issues surrounding use of third-party applications. You can make all this information searchable using LINQ.

- **User event data:** User events signal some type of user activity. Obviously, you don't want to inundate the support staff with every user activity. The normal use of an application doesn't interest the support staff unless it points to some kind of usage problem. However, unexpected events such as an application failure or activities that the user performs outside the normal range of expected activities are events of interest. Even these events can prove difficult for the support staff to view, so you need to provide some means of searching through the data and providing the support staff with alerts when needed. LINQ can help your application locate and report these events quickly.

- **Application settings information:** If you've ever had to search an entire network looking for the one wrong setting that affects everyone else on the network, you know the need for this particular support help. Just as a developer might search through application settings to find unused features or settings that contain incorrect information, support staff sometimes needs to locate a particular setting so that they can change it and fix an application error. In general, you should use LINQ to locate configuration files, delve into the contents of the target files, and report settings information to the support staff.

- **Application update status and notification:** Nothing is worse for the support staff than to know that you're working on a solution for an application problem and not to know the status for that fix. From the developer's perspective, nothing is worse than having the support staff constantly hounding you for update information. A good solution for the problem is to make the status information for an update available using LINQ. The LINQ query can act as a database view, where the support staff knows the update status without delving into the grisly details of the update.

Improving Application and System Management

Developers often miss opportunities to improve their applications because the source of the required information is buried. As you write applications and send them off to users, administrators configure the applications and help determine how the user interacts with them. All these activities generate changes in your application. Some of the changes are available today in the form of CONFIG file entries. At some point in an application's roll out, you should be able to query all the CONFIG files for your applications on the network. Because CONFIG files are in XML format, you can user LINQ to XML to read them and extract the configuration details.

The information you find in the CONFIG files can be extremely helpful when it comes time to make changes to your application. For example, you might notice that most of the CONFIG files disable a particular feature. Perhaps this information points to a feature that's too hard to use, commonly misunderstood by users, or not needed. At least the configuration setting provides you with some useful information about the application and how people are using it.

Working with the CONFIG file

Some developers are stuck in an ancient history mode — they still rely on the registry to hold their application settings. Yes, you can use the registry to hold application settings, but doing so involves some unnecessary risks. The most serious risk is that the registry is notoriously difficult to fix after a configuration problem. Using the registry also makes it difficult to move user settings to a new machine, and even administrators find it hard to interact with the settings the way they should. Using CONFIG files solves these problems because CONFIG files are external — they don't rely on the registry. You can use a simple text editor to modify a CONFIG file, and moving the CONFIG file to another machine is a snap. In addition, CONFIG files are exceptionally easy for an administrator to modify from a remote location.

A major issue that developers face is figuring out how to interact with the CONFIG file. Using

the registry feels familiar because it has been around for so long. The CONFIG file is relatively new and working with it means discovering new skills. Fortunately, you can find a wealth of self-help resources on the Internet. For example, the article at http://www.codeproject.com/KB/dotnet/config.aspx goes through the basics step-by-step. The article at http://www.developer.com/net/net/article.php/3396111 describes customized configuration settings that let you add your own settings. Some developers are scared away from CONFIG files by supposed security issues — you can read how to overcome common problems at http://www.devx.com/dotnet/Article/32493. The best part about the CONFIG file format is that it's richer than the registry in potential setting options. You can read about them at http://msdn.microsoft.com/en-us/library/1fk1t1t0.aspx.

Another way to look at this data is whether the administrator understands how to work with it. You may find that all the CONFIG files contain a common configuration error. The error may cause subtle but noticeable application problems. A little training might significantly reduce the support calls that a company experiences for a particular application and move it from the unreliable to reliable category. The CONFIG file entry can also point out reasons why an application misbehaves on a particular machine. The administrator may forget to turn off logging or have the logging level set too high, which can cause the application to work slowly.

In some cases, a CONFIG file can point to a problem in communication. You may receive a request for a particular feature and know that the feature already exists in the application. A configuration error may make that feature unusable, and relying on the CONFIG file entries can help you locate the source of the problem.

The CONFIG file is a given for .NET applications today. However, you can add other recording features. Logging user activity and interactions with the application are also important. You don't want to spy on the user, but understanding how the user interacts with the application in important. Trying to retrace the precise set of steps that causes a bug to appear can be difficult without using logging mechanisms. It's also important to use logging when you suspect that an application error is actually the result of user errors — the log may point out the need for additional training, a change in the user interface, or the need to rethink a particular feature. All these log entries are accessible with LINQ, which make it possible for you to perform detailed analysis without digging through those logs one line at a time.

Chapter 16

Ten LINQ Resources

In This Chapter

▶ Using the Microsoft Developer Network

▶ Discovering blogs as a helpful source of information

▶ Relying on third-party Web site support

▶ Relying on third-party newsletter and blog support

▶ Obtaining additional LINQ to Object projects

▶ Finding additional LINQ to SQL projects

▶ Getting hold of additional LINQ to XML projects

▶ Acquiring help with other LINQ to project types

▶ Getting help with C# development projects

▶ Finding help with Visual Basic development projects

*I*t's always helpful to know where you can go for additional information and tools and enhancements when creating your LINQ applications. This book already contains a number of useful resources in other chapters. For example, you discover the VLinq Visual Studio add-in in Chapter 14. Chapter 10 describes XML Notepad, a tool you can use with any XML file, and tells you where to locate it online.

All the tools listed in this book provide some helpful way of increasing your productivity, and you should at least try them when creating your first several LINQ applications. You might be surprised to find that they really do help you produce better application with less effort and in less time than coding everything by hand.

Before you visit any of the Web sites in this chapter, make sure you know the latest information about LINQ itself. The first place you should go is the main LINQ Web page at `http://msdn2.microsoft.com/en-us/data/cc299380.aspx`. This Web site is where Microsoft posts the latest LINQ information and updates, tells you about Webcasts, and helps you discover new LINQ providers that you can use in your applications. This chapter is the place to look after you've discovered the current state of LINQ from the Microsoft perspective.

General questions wanted

Sometimes it's hard to know what to ask or your question is of such a nature that you need generalized help before you can get down to specific needs. In both cases, you want to v isit a Web site that offers generalized help rather than specific help. (People on a specific help site can sometimes get frustrated by the developer who has general needs, so you'll probably get better help on a general site.) Three of the better general question Web sites are Tek-Tips Forums at `http://www.tek-tips.com/index.cfm`, C# Corner at `http://www.c-sharpcorner.com/`, and VB Forums at `http://www.vbforums.com/`.

This chapter is *my* list of ten helpful resources; I might have missed your favorite. Since I'm always looking for something better, please be sure to write me about your favorite resource at `JMueller@mwt.net`. I can't guarantee that I'll use the information you provide, but I do guarantee I'll at least check it out. It's amazing to see how many sources people provide me over time — many of which prove indispensable at some point.

Starting with the Microsoft Developer Network

The Microsoft Developer Network (MSDN) has always provided the baseline material for all Microsoft development products. You'll find a whole warehouse of information there — more than any one human being can probably read in a lifetime. Consequently, you need to sift the information carefully or you'll quickly become lost in the MSDN labyrinth. The main MSDN site for working with LINQ is at `http://msdn2.microsoft.com/en-us/netframework/aa904594.aspx`. The links on this site provide you with news, resources, and access to other information such as samples. You'll also want to check out these other locations on MSDN:

- ✔ Comparing LINQ and Its Contemporaries: `http://msdn2.microsoft.com/en-us/library/aa479863.aspx`

- ✔ Language-Integrated Query (LINQ): `http://msdn2.microsoft.com/en-us/library/bb397926.aspx`

- ✔ LINQ: .NET Language-Integrated Query: `http://msdn2.microsoft.com/en-us/library/bb308959.aspx`

- ✔ MSDN Code Gallery: `http://code.msdn.microsoft.com/Project/ProjectDirectory.aspx?TagName=LINQ`

Finding your own MSDN resources fast

Trying to find something on MSDN can be difficult, especially considering the fact that Microsoft constantly moves things around, seemingly to annoy the developers who use the site. The MSDN materials typically appear at two domains: `msdn.microsoft.com` and `msdn2.microsoft.com`. As a result, you can perform what is known as a site search with Google and locate information faster. Simply begin with your keywords at the main Google search site at `http://www.google.com/`, type the word *site* followed by a colon (:) and then the domain you want to use (`msdn.microsoft.com` or `msdn2.microsoft.com`). For example, if you want to find everything Microsoft has to offer on their newer MSDN site for LINQ, you would type **LINQ site:msdn2.microsoft.com** in the Google Web page's search field.

Site searches work well for a number of other Microsoft resources. For example, you may have spent hours looking for a download, only to find that Microsoft has moved it yet again. To find the download fast, type the filename, followed by **site:download.microsoft.com** in the Google Web page's search field. You'll be amazed at how fast you can find whatever you need.

Let's say that you do find an interesting link on Google, but Microsoft insists that the link no longer exists. Google usually provides a special link called Cached. You see it at the end of the link description. Simply click this link and you'll see the cached version that Google provides of the Microsoft Web page.

If you're still stumped in finding that lost Microsoft Web page, you can rely on another resource. Go to the Internet Archive Wayback Machine site at `http://web.archive.org/collections/web/advanced.html`. Type the URL you want in the Find This URL field, choose the dates you want to see (optional), and click Go Wayback. The Web site shows you an archived copy of the Web page in question. In many cases, you can go back to Google with the title of the article or other MSDN resource you want and find the latest version of that Web page on MSDN. If you get too many hits, try enclosing your search terms in quotes. For example, if you want to find the article entitled, "Working with Range Variables and Let Statements in LINQ," you type **"Working with Range Variables and Let Statements in LINQ" site:msdn2.microsoft.com** in the Google Web page's search field. A test of this search term during the writing of this chapter returned one result and it contained only the article in question.

✔ Parallel LINQ: Running Queries on Multi-Core Processors: `http://msdn2.microsoft.com/en-us/magazine/cc163329.aspx`

This list represents only generic LINQ information. The remaining sections of this chapter provide specific LINQ information links that you can use to discover more about specific LINQ technologies. Microsoft provides considerable resources for specific providers. The remaining sections of the chapter also include some third-party links you can use.

Getting Tips from the Microsoft Blogs

Microsoft wants you to know how to work with LINQ. In the past, you'd find much of the information you need on the MSDN Web site at `http://msdn2.microsoft.com`. The MSDN Web site is still a good place to go, but many Microsoft developers complained that it was a bit too formal (the articles are pretty difficult to understand in some cases) and there wasn't any opportunity to interact with the authors. The Microsoft blogs (`http://blogs.msdn.com`) provide a friendlier environment for obtaining information where you can actually correspond with the author. Here are some of the blogs you'll definitely want to visit when working with LINQ:

- Beth Massi — Sharing the goodness that is VB: `http://blogs.msdn.com/bethmassi/default.aspx`

- Brian Jones: Open XML Formats: `http://blogs.msdn.com/brian_jones/`

- Charlie Calvert's Community Blog: `http://blogs.msdn.com/charlie/`

- Dan Fernandez's Blog: `http://blogs.msdn.com/danielfe/`

- Hartmut Maennel's Blog: `http://blogs.msdn.com/hartmutm/default.aspx`

- LukeH's WebLog: `http://blogs.msdn.com/lukeh/default.aspx`

- Microsoft XML Team's WebLog: `http://blogs.msdn.com/xmlteam/default.aspx`

- Mircea Trofin's Blog: LINQ Framework Design Guidelines: `http://blogs.msdn.com/mirceat/`

- Mitsu's Blog: `http://blogs.msdn.com/mitsu/default.aspx`

- Man vs Code: `http://blogs.msdn.com/aconrad/default.aspx`

- The Wayward WebLog: `http://blogs.msdn.com/mattwar/default.aspx`

- Wriju's BLOG: `http://blogs.msdn.com/wriju/default.aspx`

Most of these blogs are generic — they all discuss programming issues of some kind. Consequently, you'll find a mix of topics in each blog. The author may discuss the file system on one day and LINQ on another. Each has LINQ-specific entries that you can search for using the search features on the blog. Charlie Calvert's Community Blog is the best place to go for a wealth of general LINQ information.

You can depend on finding certain kinds of LINQ information on some blogs. If you need to consider design guidelines, visit Mircea Trofin's Blog. For tough problem resolution, such as how to convert LINQ to Representative

State Transfer (REST), Man vs Code is a great place to visit and leave a question. At least two of the entries on the Hartmut Maennel's Blog show how to create a provider. If you need more provider advice, check out The Wayward WebLog. For those of you who want help with specific VB.NET questions, look to the Beth Massi blog. Finally, if you want to see some truly extreme LINQ programming, check out LukeH's WebLog.

If you don't think that you're getting enough interaction with Microsoft through a blog, Microsoft employees often frequent the Microsoft forums as well. Uploading a message to the correct forum can net you some professional help or at least some knowledgeable help from another forum member. Most developers rely on the MSDN forum (`http://forums.microsoft.com/MSDN/`) for basic questions about LINQ. You can see a general listing of forums at `http://forums.microsoft.com/`. There isn't a LINQ-specific forum as of the time of this writing, but you can expect Microsoft to add one later. Don't forget to try the language-specific forums for Visual Basic .NET (`http://forums.microsoft.com/MSDN/default.aspx?ForumGroupID=10`) and C# (`http://forums.microsoft.com/MSDN/default.aspx?ForumGroupID=9`).

Finding Help in Third-Party Web Sites

When you work with a Microsoft resource, you get the Microsoft view of LINQ, which is fine, but it's also biased. For example on a Microsoft Web site, you won't find out that some LINQ queries fail due to, ahem, bugs in Microsoft's software. In addition, you're unlikely to find a workaround for that bug unless Microsoft finally owns up to it and publishes a fix in the Microsoft Knowledge Base. Third-party developers also have a different view of LINQ than Microsoft does and you'll find some interesting ideas if you scout around to the right places. With this in mind, you'll definitely want to check out these third-party sites:

- Barry Gervin's Software Architecture Perspectives: LINQ Resources: `http://www.objectsharp.com/cs/blogs/barry/archive/2005/09/13/3395.aspx`

- DevelopersDex: `http://www.developersdex.com/`

- DevSource: `http://www.devsource.com/`

- Hooked on LINQ: `http://www.hookedonlinq.com/`

- Microsoft LINQ Resource Center: `http://www.deitel.com/ResourceCenters/Programming/MicrosoftLINQ/tabid/2659/Default.aspx`

- Programmer's Heaven: `http://www.programmersheaven.com/`

- ✔ The Code Project: `http://www.codeproject.com/`
- ✔ Working with Range Variables and Let Statements in LINQ: `http://www.developer.com/net/net/article.php/3731096`

Many of these third-party Web sites also provide a newsletter. For example, you can subscribe to the DevSource newsletter, which gives you the latest DevSource content at `http://www.eweek.com/newsletter-manage/`. A few of the Web sites also have discussion forums and other resources you can use to discover more about LINQ. Even though LINQ is a relatively new technology, you have a wealth of information at your disposal.

Don't forget to check sites that offer computer courses. For example, Learning Tree (`http://www.learningtree.com/courses/506.htm`) now includes LINQ in some of their courses. Taking a course can be an expensive way to discover new information about LINQ, but it can also save you time. Whether a course makes sense for you depends on how fast you have to get a LINQ application up and running — courses often make it possible to fulfill those need-it-yesterday requirements.

Finding Help in Third-Party Newsletters and Blogs

Third-party newsletters are helpful because they provide you with tidbits of information and tips on how to get the most out of a Microsoft technology. In addition, newsletters often provide a forum for you to voice questions or concerns and get a published response from the author.

One of my favorite newsletters is VB Helper (`http://lists.topica.com/lists/VBHelper`). The author, Rod Stephens, has a weekly newsletter packed with great code examples and a few helpful tips. If you want to see archives of just the Visual Basic .NET material that Rod provides, check out `http://lists.topica.com/lists/VBNetHelper/read`. You can even ask Rod questions by submitting them at `http://lists.topica.com/lists/VBHelperQA`.

A few of the newsletters that you might want to check out are part of news services. For example, TechRepublic puts out a newsletter on SQL Server (`http://search.techrepublic.com.com/search/SQL%20Server%20Newsletter.html`). This newsletter contains a number of interesting articles on LINQ to SQL. TechRepublic also provides Webcasts and other resources you should consider adding to your toolbox. Another such Web site is Programmer's Heaven (`http://www.programmersheaven.com/`), which puts out a weekly newsletter containing an assortment of articles and product reviews.

Groups that sponsor a particular technology can also provide good newsletters. For example, the ASPAlliance has a newsletter that contains LINQ topics. You can find this newsletter at `http://aspalliance.com/news letter/`. If you belong to a group or know of a group that focuses on a particular technology, don't be surprised to find that they also have a newsletter packed with useful information for your field of interest.

Authors are another good source of newsletters, especially when the author has a large organization. The Deitel Buzz Online (`http://www.deitel.com/newsletter/`) newsletter caters mainly to the books written by the Deitels, but you can still find an interesting assortment of LINQ material for the less skilled developer. Deitel products tend to take a very slow, ordered approach to training, so you might find that their newsletter provides helpful information for those difficult LINQ strategies in your application.

Newsletters are nice, but they're also a one-way communication. As with the Microsoft blogs, third-party blogs can contain a wealth of information, only some of which is LINQ specific. Following is a list of a few third-party blogs that contain some LINQ topics:

- B# .NET Blog: `http://community.bartdesmet.net/blogs/bart/default.aspx`

- Barry Gervin's Software Architecture Perspectives: `http://www.objectsharp.com/cs/blogs/barry/default.aspx`

- Jeffrey Richter's Blog: `http://www.wintellect.com/cs/blogs/jeffreyr/default.aspx`

- Jon Skeet: Coding Blog: `http://msmvps.com/blogs/jon.skeet/default.aspx`

- Oakleaf Systems: `http://oakleafblog.blogspot.com/`

- Panopticon Central: `http://www.panopticoncentral.net/`

- Saqib Ullah: `http://geekswithblogs.net/technetbytes/Default.aspx`

- Scott Hanselman's ComputerZen.com: `http://www.hanselman.com/blog/`

- ScottGu's Blog: `http://weblogs.asp.net/scottgu/default.aspx`

- The EntitySpaces Team Blog: `http://www.entityspaces.net/blog/default.aspx`

Using Other Sources for LINQ to Objects Projects

LINQ to Objects forms the basis of most of your LINQ applications. Yes, you'll probably add other providers to the mix, but when all is said and done, LINQ to Objects will always provide the features required to get the most out of LINQ. After all, almost everything you work with in a programming language today is an object, property, method, or event. Consequently, you'll want to know the most you can about the LINQ to Objects provider. The following list provides some resources you'll want to check as you use LINQ to Objects in your application:

- Data Points: Standard Query Operators with LINQ: http://msdn2.microsoft.com/en-us/magazine/cc337893.aspx

- LINQ to Objects: http://msdn2.microsoft.com/en-us/library/bb397919.aspx

- LINQ to Objects — 5-Minute Overview: http://www.hookedonlinq.com/Default.aspx?Page=LINQtoObjects5MinuteOverview

- LINQ to Objects: Play with OS Component: http://blogs.msdn.com/wriju/archive/2007/04/26/linq-to-object-play-with-os-component.aspx

Using Other Sources for LINQ to SQL Server Projects

Most business applications rely on a database connection of some type to retrieve information the user needs. LINQ to SQL provides the LINQ connection to SQL Server. Using LINQ to SQL relieves you of much of the burden of having to maintain the connection yourself. In addition, LINQ to SQL tends to reduce the complexity of working with SQL Server. The following list provides you with some additional resources you'll want when working with LINQ to SQL:

- Introducing LINQ to Relational Data: http://msdn2.microsoft.com/en-us/library/cc161164.aspx

- LINQ to SQL: http://msdn2.microsoft.com/en-us/library/bb386976.aspx

- LINQ to SQL: .NET Language-Integrated Query for Relational Data: http://msdn2.microsoft.com/en-us/library/bb425822.aspx

- LINQ to SQL In Disconnected/N-Tier scenarios: http://jonkruger.com/blog/2008/02/10/linq-to-sql-in-disconnectedn-tier-scenarios-saving-an-object/

✔ LINQ to SQL Samples: `http://msdn2.microsoft.com/en-us/vbasic/bb688085.aspx`

✔ Object Relational Designer (O/R Designer): `http://msdn2.microsoft.com/en-us/library/bb384429.aspx`

✔ The ADO.NET Entity Framework Overview: `http://msdn2.microsoft.com/en-us/library/aa697427(VS.80).aspx`

LINQ to SQL works fine with most newer versions of SQL Server, even SQL Server Express. You don't need to purchase an expensive version of SQL Server for your test setup. Simply download a copy of SQL Server Express from `http://msdn2.microsoft.com/en-us/express/bb410792.aspx` or a SQL Server 2008 Trial Edition from `http://www.microsoft.com/sqlserver/2008/en/us/trial-software.aspx`. You can also use your existing copy of SQL Server 2000 and above. LINQ to SQL doesn't work with other SQL products such as MySQL — you must obtain a special provider for these other databases or use LINQ to Entities or LINQ to ADO.NET to work with them.

Using Other Sources for LINQ to XML Projects

XML may be the most prevalent data storage technology today, at least when it comes to application configuration, Web services, localized application storage, and user-specific data. You may eventually see XML replace much of the storage for enterprise databases as well, but that day may not occur for a while yet. Even so, XML appears in many places on your hard drive and the files don't always have an XML extension. Sometimes XML appears bundled with other application storage, such as when working with an Office 2007 document. No matter where you find XML, the LINQ to XML provider gives you a way to interact with that data without a lot of extra effort. The following list provides resources that you'll want to add to your LINQ to XML toolbox:

✔ LINQ to XML: `http://msdn2.microsoft.com/en-us/library/bb387098.aspx`

✔ LINQ to XML Overview: `http://msdn2.microsoft.com/en-us/library/bb387061.aspx`

✔ Overview of LINQ to XML in Visual Basic: `http://msdn2.microsoft.com/en-us/library/bb384460.aspx`

✔ Programming Guide (LINQ to XML): `http://msdn2.microsoft.com/en-us/library/bb387087.aspx`

Working with XML files correctly

XML often requires special handling in your application. It's easy to look at XML as specially formatted text, but you must also approach it as you would any other database, which means considering the data schema when you make changes. In addition, the XML file may make use of an XSD file or require translation with XSLT. These other files place requirements on the content of the XML file. Be sure you understand the technologies that XML relies on before you begin making changes to any XML file. The following resources provide additional information about XML as a technology:

✔ W3C Schools: `http://www.w3schools.com/xml/`

✔ XML namespace tutorial: `http://www.zvon.org/index.php?nav_id=172&ns=34`

✔ XML Schema 2001 Reference: `http://www.zvon.org/xxl/xmlSchema2001Reference/Output/index.html`

✔ XML Schema Reference (draft 2000/10): `http://www.zvon.org/xxl/xmlSchemaReference/Output/index.html`

✔ Annotated XML Specification: `http://www.xml.com/axml/axml.html`

✔ Microsoft XML Developer Center: `http://msdn2.microsoft.com/en-us/xml/default.aspx`

Considering Other LINQ to Sources Projects

The basic LINQ to technologies that come with .NET Framework are just the tip of the iceberg. This book has shown you a number of alternative LINQ to providers, including LINQ to Active Directory and LINQ to RDF. The Internet contains a host of other LINQ to technologies, many of which appear in Table 1-1. In addition to the Web sites you find in Table 1-1 and in the chapters that discuss alternative LINQ to providers, you'll also want to check out these other LINQ to sources of information. These resources may be the answer to your next project using third-party technologies:

✔ Advanced Basics: Office 2007 Files and LINQ: `http://msdn2.microsoft.com/en-us/magazine/cc337894.aspx`

✔ LINQ to ADO.NET: `http://msdn2.microsoft.com/en-us/library/bb399360.aspx`

✔ LINQ to DataSet: `http://msdn2.microsoft.com/en-us/library/bb386977.aspx`

✔ LINQ to DataSet Overview: `http://msdn2.microsoft.com/en-us/library/bb399399.aspx`

- ✔ **LINQ to DataSet Samples:** `http://msdn2.microsoft.com/en-us/vbasic/bb688086.aspx`

- ✔ **LINQ to Entities:** `http://msdn2.microsoft.com/en-us/library/bb386964.aspx`

- ✔ **Map LINQ: Create Dynamic Maps with Visual Basic 9.0 and WPF:** `http://msdn2.microsoft.com/en-us/magazine/cc185721.aspx`

- ✔ **The IQueryable tales — LINQ to LDAP:** `http://community.bartdesmet.net/blogs/bart/archive/2007/04/05/the-iqueryable-tales-linq-to-ldap-part-0.aspx`

- ✔ **Walkthrough: Creating an IQueryable LINQ Provider:** `http://msdn2.microsoft.com/en-us/library/bb546158.aspx`

One of the problems with other LINQ to providers is that the authors may not keep them updated. Make sure you verify that the LINQ to provider you download will work with the version of .NET Framework you're using. For example, a number of the current LINQ to providers work with the beta version of Visual Studio 2008 as of this writing, but the authors have promised to update them to the released version of Visual Studio 2008. Even so, you must make sure that the provider you're using will work with Visual Studio 2008 and .NET Framework 3.5 as anticipated before you begin writing a large project. Contact the provider author whenever possible to ask about potential updates.

Getting Help with Visual Basic Projects

Even though much of the emphasis of LINQ to technologies is on C#, Visual Basic is also a great LINQ to technology language and you shouldn't avoid using it. The amazing thing about Visual Basic is that it tends to provide extremely readable code and can simplify the LINQ to experience, in some cases, so this is an excellent language for some LINQ application needs. With this in mind, you'll want to check out the Visual Basic .NET resources in the following list:

- ✔ **101 Visual Basic LINQ Samples:** `http://msdn2.microsoft.com/en-us/vbasic/bb688088.aspx`

- ✔ **"How Do I" Videos — Visual Basic:** `http://msdn2.microsoft.com/en-us/vbasic/bb466226.aspx`

- ✔ **LINQ Sample Applications in Visual Basic:** `http://msdn2.microsoft.com/en-us/library/bb397978.aspx`

- ✔ **Visual Basic 9.0 Language Enhancements:** `http://msdn2.microsoft.com/en-us/netframework/aa463382.aspx`

Getting Help with C# Projects

Microsoft and many others have focused on C# as the language of choice when working with LINQ. Yes, you can use LINQ in other languages. In fact, it's theoretically possible to use LINQ in any .NET languages that can work with .NET Framework 3.5. That said, you'll find many providers and example applications written in C#. The Internet also abounds in articles and other resources that use C# as the basis for LINQ applications. The following list is just a small sample of the links that form the wealth of C# documentation you can find for working with LINQ on the Internet:

- 101 C# LINQ Samples: `http://msdn2.microsoft.com/en-us/vcsharp/aa336746.aspx`

- C# 3.0 Language Enhancements: `http://msdn2.microsoft.com/en-us/netframework/aa336745.aspx`

- LINQ C# Samples: `http://msdn2.microsoft.com/en-us/library/bb397965.aspx`

- LINQ Query Expressions (C# Programming Guide): `http://msdn2.microsoft.com/en-us/library/bb397676.aspx`

- The Evolution of LINQ and Its Impact on the Design of C#: `http://msdn2.microsoft.com/en-us/magazine/cc163400.aspx`

Index

• A •

access simplification design goal, 14
accessPolicy attribute, 290
Active Directory
  CN values, 255
  interaction limitations, 268–269
  LDAP (Lightweight Directory Access
    Protocol), 253, 269
  object class, 262–264
  overview, 253
  provider, downloading and installing,
    257–259
  required support for working with, 260
  root node pointer, 264
  simple query example, 260–264
  user information, reading, 265–266
  user information, writing, 266–267
  variables, 256–257
Active Directory Service Interface Editor
    (ADSI Edit) utility, 254
Add() method, 190, 193, 201
add-in application, VLinq tool, 302–303
administrator-controlled user selection
    criteria, 322
ADO.NET
  dataset behaviors, 134
  MySQL ADO.NET connector, 295
ADSI Edit (Active Directory Service
    Interface Edit) utility, 254
AdventureWorks database, 160
Aggregate keyword
  support, 71
  Visual Basic example, 83–84
Aggregate operator, 127–128
aggregation operators, 42, 127–128
All operator, 130–131

Amazon, 12
And keyword, 77
AndAlso keyword, 77
anonymous data types, 49
Any operator, 130–131
API, XML, 184–185
application and system management,
    333–334
application class definition, RDF example,
    292–293
application errors, 148
applications
  about this book, 3
  Console, 94
  settings information, support task
    automation, 332
  update status and notification, 332
  Windows, 94
array elements, 27
AsDataView() method, 144
AsEnumerable operator, 114–115
ASP Alliance newsletter, 341
AsQueryable operator, 114–115
attributes
  accessPolicy, 290
  Column, 238
  fmtid, 230
  name, 230
  pid, 230
  value, 289
  XML document, 191
authentication, Windows, 172
automation
  automatic properties, language
    extensions, 56
  support task, 331–332
Average operator, 127–128
axis manipulation, 186

• B •

backward compatibility, 15
binary data, 194
binary expressions, 19
BinaryExpression type, 20, 66
Bindable Sources, 12
blogs, 338–341
bool data type, 65
break points, 31, 96
btnTest_Click() method, 53

• C •

C# programming language
  as language of choice, 16
  Visual Basic differences, 69–72
caching, 329
calculations
  let keyword, 28–29, 39–40, 81
  multiple-source queries, 38–39
Calvert, Charlie (blog resource), 338
Capacity property, 60
carriage return, 30
case-sensitivity, 216
Cast operator, 114–115
Changed event, 186
CheckValidationResult() method, 280
child elements
  document properties, 224
  namespaces, 189–190
classes
  ConstraintCollection, 135
  DataColumnCollection, 135
  DataContext, 158–159, 309
  DataOut, 178
  DataRelation, 135
  DataRelationCollection, 135
  DataRowCollection, 135
  DataTableCollection class, 134
  DataView, 135
  defined, 134
  DirectoryEntity, 263
  DirectoryEntry, 263
  DirectoryQuery, 265
  DirectorySource, 265

  entity, 167
  ExtendedProperties, 135
  Extensions, 184
  partial methods, 62–63
  PMethodTest, 63–64
  XNode, 184
  XObjectChange, 186
  XObjectChangeEventArgs, 186
Clear() method, 237
CN values, Active Directory, 255
code. See also listings
  code pattern analysis, 311–314
  self-documenting, 309–311
Code Project Web site, 340
code snippets, 314–315
collection initializers
  custom object collection, 59–60
  defined, 49
collections, dataset, 134–135
Column attribute, 238
columns
  attributes, for performance issues, 239
  DataColumnCollection class, 135
  table, 139, 149
COM+ technology
  accessed as Web service, 276, 278–281
  accessed using interop functionality,
    281–282
  overview, 273
  registration, 277
  for Vista and Windows server developers,
    274–275
  WSDL file location, 276
combo boxes, 109–111
command line switches, SQL Server, 167
commands, 2
comments, 192–193
Community Technology Preview
    (CTP), 157
Comp.Compare() method, 198
Comp.Equals() method, 200
Component Services console, 273
Concat operator, 113–114, 179
concatentation operators, 42, 113–114
concurrency problems, SQL server
  detection, 234–235
  entity class attributes, 238

member level, 247, 251–252
object level, 247–250
optimistic versus pessimistic concurrency, 248
resolution, 235–238
ResolveAll operator, 237
ConditionalExpression type, 20
CONFIG files, 333–334
connectivity
  connectivity issues, SQL server, 168–170
  dataset, 139–141
  ODBC (Open DataBase Connectivity), 134
consistency, LINQ performance, 10–11
Console application, 94
constant expressions, 19
ConstantExpression type, 20, 66
ConstraintCollection class, 135
constructors, 63
Contains operator, 130–131
context factors, self-modifying queries, 323
conversion operators, 114, 128
converting data type operators, 42
CopyToDataTable operator, 146–148
core.xml file, 222
Count operator, 127–128
CreateDataSet.CS file, 136
CreateDocument() method, 187
CreateDS() method, 139
CreateDT() method, 138
CreateQuickData() method, 138, 154
CRM (Customer Relationship Management), 12
CTP (Community Technology Preview), 157
custom.xml file, 221, 223

• D •

data files, Office 2007 document structure, 215
data filtering operators, 42
data formats, 316–317
data manipulation
  design goals, 14
  System.Data.Linq namespace, 20–21
data partitioning operators, 43

data source access simplification design goal, 14
data source extensibility design goal, 15
data structures, LINQ overview, 9–10
data translation design goal, 14, 18
data types
  anonymous, 49
  bool, 65
  conversion operators, 42
  optimization techniques, 330
  Variant, 48
database configuration, MySQL, 296
database connection, VLinq tool, 303–304
databases. *See also* datasets; tables
  installing on SQL Server, 162–164
  ODBC (Open DataBase Connectivity), 134
  updates, 239–240
DataColumnCollection class, 135
DataContext class, 158–159, 309
DataOut class, 178
DataRelation class, 135
DataRelationCollection class, 135
DataRowCollection class, 135
datasets. *See also* databases; tables
  adding to projects, 149
  application errors, 148
  collections, 134–135
  connectivity, 139–141
  ConstraintCollection class, 135
  content, 150–151
  CopyToDataTable operator, 146–148
  DataColumnCollection class, 135
  DataRelationCollection class, 135
  DataRowCollection class, 135
  DataTable operators, 142
  DataTableCollection class, 134
  DataView class, 135
  ExtendedProperties class, 135
  filtered output example, 142–146
  filtering data in, 143–145
  multiple tables, 152–156
  operators, 141–142
  overview, 133
  resources for, 344–345
  test table definition example, 136–138
  typed, 148–152
  uses for, 134

`DataTable` operators, 142
`DataTableCollection` class, 134
`DataView` class, 135
`DB.SubmitChanges()` method, 236, 245
debugger
    simple query application, 31–33
    SQL server and, 173–175
    support design goals, 15
    Visual Studio 2005, 96–97
debugging messages, 319
decimal values, 224
declarative languages, 18–19
`DefaultIfEmpty` operator, 116–118, 179
deferred evaluation, 73–74
deferred operators
    defined, 108
    role of, 112–113
Deitel Buzz Online newsletter, 341
deleting table records, 245–247
design goals, 14–15
DevelopersDex Web site, 338
DevSource Web site, 339
`Dim` keyword, 70
`DirectoryEntity` class, 263
`DirectoryEntry` class, 263
`DirectoryQuery` class, 265
`DirectoryServices` namespace, 256
`DirectoryServices.Linq` namespace, 261
`DirectorySource` class, 265
`DisableFormatting` property, 207
`DisplayDocument()` method, 187
`Distinct` keyword
    support, 71
    Visual Basic example, 84–85
`Distinct` operator, 123–124, 141, 153
DLinq applications, 92
`DocPropVTypes` namespace, 231
`<!DOCTYPE>` tag, 195–196
document structure (Office 2007), 214–216
Document Type Definition (DTD), 197
documents, Office 2007
    application creation example, 220–221
    properties, 221–225
    properties, reading, 225–228
    properties, writing, 228–231
documents, XML

comments and text, 192–193
creation, 187, 205–206
equality comparison, 199–201
loading, 208–209
names, 202–203
nodes, removing, 201
order comparison, 198–199
saving, 207
type, 195–197
dot notation syntax, 67–68
DTD (Document Type Definition), 197
dynamic queries, 51

• *E* •

ECMA standard, 214
efficiency, LINQ overview, 10–11
element operators, 42, 108, 128–129
`ElementAt` operator, 128–129, 179
`ElementAtOrDefault` operator, 128–129, 179
`Empty` operator, 116–117
entity classes, 167
EntitySpaces Team Blog, 341
environmental factors, self-modifying queries, 322
equality comparison, XML documents, 199–201
equality operators, 42, 129–130
errors, application, 148
evaluation
    deferred, 73–74
    Lambda expressions, 52
`EventArgs` event, 312
events
    `Changed`, 186
    `EventArgs`, 312
    `KeyDown`, 111
    `KeyPress`, 110–111
Excel, 12
`Except` operator, 123–124, 141, 154–155, 179
expression trees
    defined, 50
    how to create, 64–66
expressions
    binary, 19
    `BinaryExpression` type, 20, 66

`ConditionalExpression` type, 20
constant, 19
`ConstantExpression` type, 20, 66
`InvocationExpression` type, 20
`LambdaExpression` type, 20
`ListInitExpression` type, 20
`MemberExpression` type, 20, 66
`MemberInitExpression` type, 20
`MethodCallExpression` type, 20
named parameter, 19–20
`NewArrayExpression` type, 20
`NewExpression` type, 20
`ParameterExpression` type, 20, 66
query, 67–68
`System.Linq.Expressions`
    namespace, 19–20
`TypeBinaryExpression` type, 20
`UnaryExpression` type, 20
`ExtendedProperties` class, 135
extensibility design goal, 15
extension methods
  special characters, 61–62
  uses for, 49
`Extensions` class, 184
extensions, language
  anonymous data types, 49
  automatic properties, 56
  collection initializers, 49, 58–60
  discussed, 47
  dynamic queries, 51
  expression trees, 50, 64–66
  extension methods, 49, 61–62
  `IEnumerable` interface, 50, 54–55
  `IEnumerable<T>` interface, 50, 54–55
  `IQueryable` interface, 51
  Lambda expressions, 50–53
  object initializers, 49, 57–58
  partial methods, 49, 62–64
  query expressions, 50, 67–68
  `var` keyword, 48

• F •

Fernandez, Dan (blog resource), 338
`File.Exists()` method, 209

`FileSystem` queries, 316
filtering
  data in datasets, 143–145
  data operators, 42
  with Lambda expressions, 52–53
  operators, 115–116
  queries, 34, 76
  `where` keyword, 25, 101
`FilterStrings()` method, 53
`First` operator, 128–129
`FirstOrDefault` operator, 128–129
Flickr, 12
`fmtid` attribute, 230
`foreach` loop, 30, 55, 266
`ForeignKeyConstraint` object, 135
formats, 316–317
formatting, `DisableFormatting`
    property, 207
`from` keyword
  overview, 24–25
  Visual Basic example, 72–73
  Visual Studio 2005 project definition,
    95–96
`FromReader()` method, 172
`FromStream()` method, 172
`FromUrl()` method, 172
`FromXml()` method, 172

• G •

GAC (Global Assembly Cache), 259
GACUtil (Global Assembly Cache Utility),
    259, 277
generation operators, 42, 116–117
Geo (geospatial data), 12
Gervin, Barry (blog resource), 341
Google searches, 327
Google Web services, 316
`GroupBy` operator, 118–119
grouping
  data operators, 42
  operators, 118–119
  queries, 35–36
`GroupJoin` operator, 120
guest accounts, 267

• H •

hard-coded queries, 322
help files. *See also* resources
  accessibility, 326–327
  support task automation, 332
hidden data, 273
Hooked on LINQ Web site, 339
host application, RDF file example, 288–291
HTTP protocol, 275

• I •

IADs interface, 257, 263
IComparable interface, 141–142, 153
icons, about this book, 5–6
IDirectoryObject interface, 257
IEnumerable interface, 50, 54–55, 108
IEnumerable<T> interface, 50, 54–55
IIS (Internet Information Server), 274–275
IL (Intermediate Language) output, 49
imperative languages, 18
Imports statement, 30
in keyword, 25, 33
IndexArray variable, 99–100
indexes, 12
IndexValue variable, 99, 103–104
InsertAllOnSubmit() method, 243
InsertOnSubmit() method, 243
installation
  Active Directory provider, 257–259
  databases on SQL server, 162–164
  LINQ support for Visual Studio 2005,
    92–93
  VLinq tool, 303
instantiation, object initializers, 58
IntelliSense support design goal, 15
interaction limitations, Active Directory,
  268–269
interfaces
  ADSI Edit, 254
  IADs, 257, 263
  IComparable, 141–142, 153
  IDirectoryObject, 257
  IEnumerable<T>, 50, 54–55

  IEnumerable, 50, 54–55, 108
  IQueryable, 51, 65
  SSPI (Security Support Provider
    Interface), 280
Intermediate Language (IL) output, 49
International Standards Organization
  (ISO), 214
Internet Information Server (IIS), 274–275
interpretation design goal, 18
Intersect operator, 123–124, 141, 155,
  179
InvocationExpression type, 20
IQueryable interface, 51
ISO (International Standards
  Organization), 214
IsVersion parameter, 238–239

• J •

JavaScript Object Notation (JSON), 13
Javascript scripts, 13
join keyword
  multiple-source application code, 37
  overview, 27–28
  Visual Basic example, 79–81
  Visual Studio 2005 example, 98–100
Join operator, 120
join operators, 42, 120
Jones, Brian (blog resource), 338
JSON (JavaScript Object Notation), 13

• K •

KeyDown event, 111
KeyPress event, 110–111
keywords. *See also* operators
  And, 77
  Aggregate, 71
  AndAlso, 77
  combining with operators, 23
  Dim, 70
  Distinct, 71, 84–85
  from, 24–25, 72–73, 95–96
  in, 25, 33
  join, 27–28, 37, 79–81, 98–100
  let, 28–29, 39–40, 81–82, 103–104

mapping to methods, 43–45
orderby, 26–27, 78–79, 102–103
select, 25
Skip, 71, 85–86
Take, 71, 87–88
var, 24, 33, 48
where, 25–26, 44, 75–77, 100–101

• L •

Lambda expressions
  defined, 50
  evaluations, 52
  filtering tasks with, 52–53
  multiple parameters, 51
  in Visual Basic, 88–90
LambdaExpression type, 20
language extensibility design goal, 15
language extensions
  anonymous data types, 49
  automatic properties, 56
  collection initializers, 49, 58–60
  discussed, 47
  dynamic queries, 51
  expression trees, 50, 64–66
  extension methods, 49, 61–62
  IEnumerable interface, 50, 54–55
  IEnumerable<T> interface, 50, 54–55
  IQueryable interface, 51
  Lambda expressions, 50–53
  object initializers, 49, 57–58
  partial methods, 49, 62–64
  query expressions, 50, 67–68
  var keyword, 48
languages
  LINQ supported, 16
  OSQL (Object-Oriented Structured Query
      Language), 162
Last operator, 128–129, 179
LastOrDefault operator, 128–129, 179
LDAP (Lightweight Directory Access
      Protocol), 11, 253, 269
let keyword
  calculations, 28–29, 39–40, 81
  Visual Basic example, 81–82
  Visual Studio 2005 example, 103–104

libraries
  accessing, 10
  query, 318
  searching, 10
Lightweight Directory Access Protocol
      (LDAP), 11, 253, 269
linefeed, 30
LINQ overview, 9–10
LINQ to Active Directory provider. *See*
      Active Directory
LINQ to DataSet provider. *See* datasets
LINQ to MySQL provider. *See* MySQL
LINQ to Object provider. *See* objects
LINQ to RDF provider. *See* RDF files
LINQ to solutions provider, 12–14
LINQ to SQL Server provider. *See* SQL
      server
LINQ to XML provider. *See* XML
LINQ Web site, 92
LINQExtender kit, 272–273
LINQPad tool, 330
LISP (List Processing), 50
listings
  Active Directory root node pointer, 264
  Active Directory user information,
      reading, 265
  Active Directory user information,
      writing, 266–267
  Aggregate keyword, 83
  aggregation operators, 127–128
  calculated values, 40, 81
  CData operator elements, 194
  code patterns, 313
  collection initializers, 59–60
  collections, unique values in, 84
  comments, 192–193
  concatenation operator, 113
  conversion operators, 114
  datasets, content definition, 150–151
  datasets, filtered, 144–145
  Distinct operator, 153
  document properties, reading, 225–226
  document properties, writing, 228–230
  document type, 196
  element operators, 129
  equality comparison, 199–200

listings *(continued)*
Except operator, 154–155
extension methods, 61–62
filtering operators, 115–116
from keyword, 73, 95
generation operators, 116–117
grouping operators, 118–119
host query form, 288
IEnumerable<T> interface, 54–55
interop query, 282
join keyword, 98–99
Lambda expressions, 52–53
Lambda functions, 89–90
let keyword, 103–104
multiple query sources, 79–80
MySQL queries, 297–298
namespaces, 188–189
nodes, removing, 201
object class, 262–263
object initializers, 57–58
Object Relational Designer tool, 177
Office 2007 document properties, 223–224
order comparison, 198
orderby keyword, 102
partial methods, 63–64
partitioning operators, 120–121
projection operators, 121–122
qualifier operators, 131
queries, alternative multiple-source example, 38
queries, filtering, 34, 76
queries, grouping, 35
queries, multiple-source application code, 37
query application code, 30
query expressions, 67–68
RDF files, reading, 293
records, deletions, 246–247
records, inserting, 241–242
records, updates, 244–245
set operators, 123–124
Skip keyword, 85–86
sorting operators, 125
SQL server concurrency issues, 235–236
SSL verification, 280
tables, copying queries to, 146–147
Take keyword, 87
test tables, 136–138
Web services, 278–279
where keyword, 44, 101
XML attributes, 191
XML document creation, 187, 205–206
XML document names, 202–203
XML documents, loading, 208–209
XML documents, saving, 207
ListInitExpression type, 20
loading strategies, overcoming performance issues, 240
loading XML documents, 208–209
LocalName variable, 203
log files, 317–318
LongCount operator, 127–128
Lucene technology, 13

• *M* •

Man versus Code blog, 338
manipulation
  design goals, 14
  System.Data.Linq namespace, 20–21
Mansfield, Richard (*XML All-in-One Desk Reference For Dummies*), 184
mashups, 326
Massi, Beth (blog resource), 338
Max operator, 127–128
member level concurrency problems, 247, 251–252
MemberChangeConflict object, 252
MemberExpression type, 20, 66
MemberInitExpression type, 20
MemConflict object, 252
message boxes, 63–64
MethodCallExpression type, 20
methods
  Add(), 190, 193, 201
  AsDataView(), 144
  btnText_Click, 53
  CheckValidationResult(), 280
  Clear(), 237
  Comp.Compare(), 198

`Comp.Equals()`, 200
`CreateDocument()`, 187
`CreateDS()`, 139
`CreateDT()`, 138
`CreateQuickData()`, 138, 154
`DB.SubmitChanges()`, 236, 245
`DisplayDocument()`, 187
extension, 49
`File.Exists()`, 209
`FilterStrings()`, 53
`FromReader()`, 172
`FromStream()`, 172
`FromUrl()`, 172
`FromXml()`, 172
`InsertAllOnSubmit()`, 243
`InsertOnSubmit()`, 243
mapping keywords to, 43–45
`MethodCallExpression` type, 20
`Navigate()`, 207, 209
`OnPropertyChanged()`, 263–264
partial, 49, 62–64
`Save()`, 207, 209
`SpecialCharChount()`, 62
static, 138
`SubmitChanges()`, 235, 239
`ToString()`, 187
`WordProcessingDocument.Open()`, 226
`XDocument.Load()`, 209
`XName.Get()`, 227
Microsoft Developer Network (MSDN), 336–337
Microsoft IIS 7 Implementation and Administration (Mueller), 275
Microsoft LINQ Resource Center Web site, 339
MIME (Multipurpose Internet Mail Extensions), 285
`Min` operator, 127–128
Mining Google Web Services (Mueller), 316
missing items, 319
monitoring queries, 322
Mono system, 295
Mozilla Web site, 283
MSDN (Microsoft Developer Network), 336–337

Mueller, John
Microsoft IIS 7 Implementation and Administration, 275
Mining Google Web Services, 316
Web site, 319
Multipurpose Internet Mail Extensions (MIME), 285
multisets, SQL server, 178
MySQL
ADO.NET connector, 295
database configuration, 296
DbLinq.DLL and DbLinq.MySQL.DLL compilation, 295–296
project definition example, 296–297
query code development example, 297–298

• N •

`name` attribute, 230
`Name` property, 203
named parameter expressions, 19–20
names, XML document, 202–203
`Namespace` variable, 203
`NamespaceName` variables, 203
namespaces
child elements, 189–190
defining, 188–189
`DirectoryServices`, 256
`DirectoryServices.Linq`, 261
`DocPropVTypes`, 231
expression types, 20
`System.Data.Linq`, 20–21
`System.Data.Linq.Mapping`, 21
`System.Data.SqlClient`, 21
`System.Data.SqlClient.Implementation`, 22
`System.DirectoryServices`, 256
`System.Linq`, 19
`System.Linq.Expressions`, 19–20
`System.Xml.Linq`, 22
URI, 203
`Navigate()` method, 207, 209
.NET Framework providers, 4
`NewArrayExpression` type, 20
`NewExpression` type, 20

newsletter resources, 340–341
NHibernate solution, 13
nodes
   local name, 203
   removing, 201
nondeferred operators
   defined, 108
   role of, 125–126
Northwind database example, SQL server
   and, 160–164
Notation 3 (N3) format, 283
note taking, 319

• *O* •

Oakleaf Systems blog, 341
object class, Active Directory, 262–264
object initializers
   data structure, 57
   defined, 49
   instantiation, 58
object level concurrency problems,
   247–250
object mapping design goal, 15
Object Relational (O/R) Designer tool, 158,
   175–177
Object-Oriented Structured Query
   Language (OSQL), 162
objects
   aggregation operators, 127–128
   concatenation operators, 113–114
   conversion operators, 128
   deferred operators, 108, 112–113
   element operators, 128–129
   elements, 108
   equality operators, 129–130
   filtering operators, 115–116
   ForeignKeyConstraint, 135
   grouping operators, 118–120
   joining operators, 120
   MemberChangeConflict, 252
   MemConflict, 252
   nondeferred operators, 126–127
   operators, 117
   partitioning operators, 120–121
   projection operators, 121–122

PropStream, 227
qualifier operators, 130–131
resources for, 342
sequences, 108
set operators, 123–124
simple object query example, 109–111
sorting operators, 124–125
StreamReader, 227
UniqueConstraint, 135
XObjectChange class, 186
XObjectChangeEventArgs class, 186
ODBC (Open DataBase Connectivity), 134
Office 2007
   custom properties, 221–225
   document application creation example,
      220–221
   document properties, reading, 225–228
   document properties, writing, 228–231
   document structure, 214–216
   library, obtaining, 218–219
   LINQ interaction with, 216–217
   OOXML (Office Open XML), 213–214
   overview, 213
OfType operator, 114–116
on operator, 310
OnPropertyChanged() method, 263–264
OOXML (Open Office XML), 213–214
Open DataBase Connectivity (ODBC), 134
operators. *See also* keywords
   Aggregate, 127–128
   aggregation, 42, 127–128
   All, 130–131
   Any, 130–131
   AsEnumerable, 114–115
   AsQueryable, 114–115
   Average, 127–128
   Cast, 114–115
   combining with keywords, 23
   Concat, 113–114, 179
   concatenation, 42, 113–114
   Contains, 130–131
   conversion, 42, 114, 128
   CopyToDataTable, 146–148
   Count, 127–128
   data type conversion, 42
   dataset, 141–142

DataTable, 142
Default, 128–129
DefaultIfEmpty, 116–118, 179
deferred, 108, 112–113
defined, 23
Distinct, 123–124, 141, 153
element, 42, 108, 128–129
ElementAt, 128–129, 179
ElementAtOr, 128–129, 179
Empty, 116–117
equality, 42, 129–130
Except, 123–124, 141, 154–155, 179
filtering, 115–116
filtering data, 42
First, 128–129
FirstOrDefault, 128–129
generation, 42, 116–117
GroupBy, 118–120
grouping, 118–119
grouping data, 42
Intersect, 123–124, 141, 155, 179
join, 42
Join, 120
joining, 120
Last, 128–129, 179
LastOrDefault, 128–129, 179
LongCount, 127–128
Max, 127–128
Min, 127–128
nondeferred, 108, 125–126
object, 117
OfType, 114–116
on, 310
or (||), 61
OrderBy, 124–125
OrderByDescending, 124–125
partitioning, 120–121
partitioning data, 43
projection, 43, 121–122
qualifier, 130–131
quantifier, 43
Range, 116–117
Remove, 184, 201
Repeat, 116–117
ResolveAll, 237
Reverse, 124–125, 179

Select, 121–122, 239
SelectMany, 121–122
SequenceEqual, 129–130, 141
set, 43, 123–124
SetField, 144–145
Single, 128–129
SingleOrDefault, 128–129
Skip, 120–121, 179
SkipWhile, 120–121, 179
sorting, 124–125
sorting data, 43
SQL server, 178–179
standard query operators, 41–43
Sum, 127–128
Take, 120–121, 179
TakeWhile, 120–121, 179
ThenBy, 124–125
ThenByDescending, 124–125
ToArray, 128
ToDictionary, 128
ToList, 128
ToLookup, 118–119, 128
Union, 123–124, 141, 156, 180
Where, 115–116
XAttribute, 184, 191–192
XCData, 184, 194–195
XComment, 184, 192–193
XContainer, 184
XDeclaration, 185–187
XDocument, 185–187
XDocumentType, 185, 195–197
XElement, 185–187
XName, 185, 202–204
XNamespace, 185, 188–190
XNodeDocumentOrderComparer, 185,
    197–199
XNodeEqualityComparer, 185, 199–200
XProcessingInstruction, 185, 190
XText, 185, 192–193
or operator, 61
O/R (Object Relational) Designer tool, 158,
    175–177
Oracle database, 295
order comparison, XML documents,
    198–199

orderby keyword
  overview, 26–27
  Visual Basic example, 78–79
  Visual Studio 2005 example, 102–103
OrderBy operator, 124–125
OrderByDescending operator, 124–125
Orders property, 159
organization, about this book, 3–4
OSQL (Object-Oriented Structured Query
    Language), 162
output
  IL (Intermediate Language), 49
  orderby keyword, 26–27

● *P* ●

Panopticon Central blog, 341
ParameterExpression type, 20, 66
partial methods
  class descriptions, 62–63
  defined, 49
partitioning data operators, 43
partitioning operators, 120–121
patterns, code, 311–314
performance, blog resources, 11
performance issues, overcoming
  loading strategies, 240
  overview, 238
  using column attributes, 239
permissions, 290
pid attribute, 230
PMethodTest class, 63–64
policies, 290
POS (Point of Sale), 317
PostgreSQL database, 295
prebuilt templates, 331
prefixes, 289–291
pre-queries, 329
presentations, 331
problems, performance issues, 11–12
processing instruction, XML, 190
product support, design goals, 15
Programmer's Heaven Web site, 339, 341
project definition
  MySQL example, 296–297
  RDF file example, 285–288

SQL server, 170–171
Visual Studio 2005, 94–95
projection operators, 43, 121–122
properties
  Capacity, 60
  DisableFormatting, 207
  ExtendedProperties class, 135
  Name, 203
  Office 2007 document, 221–225
  Orders, 159
  selector, 32
PropStream object, 227
protocols
  HTTP, 275
  LDAP, 11, 253, 269
  SOAP, 276
providers
  about this book, 5
  defined, 4
  LINQ to solutions, 12–14
  .NET Framework, 4
public identifiers, 196

● *Q* ●

qualifier operators, 130–131
quantifier operators, 43
queries
  alternative multiple-source example,
      38–39
  calculated values, 38–39
  DirectoryQuery class, 265
  dynamic, 51
  FileSystem, 316
  filtering, 34, 76
  grouping, 35–36
  hard-coded, 322
  libraries for, 318
  monitoring, 322
  multiple-source application code, 37–38
  output variables, 33
  pre-queries, 329
  query testing, 17
  reusing, 330
  selector and source for, 32
  self-modifying, 322–323

simple query application code, 29–30
standard query operators, 41–43
WebQueries, 13
query expressions
defined, 50
dot notation syntax comparison, 67–68
QueryString array, 72–73, 104

• R •

Range operator, 116–117
RDF (Resource Description
    Framework) files
  application class definition example,
    292–293
  class element listing, 286
  client project definition example, 287
  discussed, 1
  host application example, 288–291
  host project definition example, 287–288
  overview, 282–283
  project configuration example, 285–288
  reading, 293–294
  resources, 283
  SPARQL file, 283–284
  XML form of, 284
reading
  document properties, 225–228
  RDF files, 293–294
  user information, Active Directory,
    265–266
real numbers, 224
records, table
  deletions, 245–247
  inserting, 241–243
  updates, 243–245
reference guide, VLinq tool, 303
RegAsm (Register Assembly), 277
rels files, 216
Remove operator, 184, 201
Repeat operator, 116–117
reports, 323–324
Representative State Transfer (REST),
    338–339
requests and responses, 327–328
ResolveAll operator, 237

Resource Description Framework
    (RDF) files
  application class definition example,
    292–293
  class element listing, 286
  client project definition example, 287
  discussed, 1
  host application example, 288–291
  host project definition example, 287–288
  overview, 282–283
  project configuration example, 285–288
  reading, 293–294
  resources, 283
  SPARQL file, 283–284
  XML form of, 284
resources
  blogs, 338–341
  for datasets, 344–345
  MSDN, 336–337
  newsletters, 340–341
  for objects, 342
  RDF files, 283
  for SQL server, 342–343
  third-party Web sites, 339–340
  for Visual Basic, 345
  for XML, 343–344
responses and requests, 327–328
REST (Representative State Transfer),
    338–339
result sets, 108
Reverse operator, 124–125, 179
Richter, Jeffrey (blog resource), 341
root node pointer, Active Directory, 264
rows
  DataRowCollection class, 135
  table, 142

• S •

safety, LINQ design goals, 15
Save() method, 207, 209
saving XML documents, 207
schema, 216
script files, 162
SDK (Software Development Kit), 219

search selections
  fast searches from multiple sources, 328–330
  Google searches, 327
  overview, 325
  search levels, 329
searching libraries, 10
Secure Sockets Layer (SSL), 274–275, 280
security factors, self-modifying queries, 322
Security Support Provider Interface (SSPI), 280
`select` keyword, 25
`Select` operator, 121–122, 239
`SelectMany` operator, 121–122
`selector` property, 32
self-documenting code, 309–311
self-modifying queries, 322–323
`SequenceEqual` operator, 129–130, 141
sequences, 108
serialization, XML, 325
Server Management Studio (SQL), 163
server, SQL
  command line switches, 167
  concurrency problems, 234–238
  configuring Visual Studio for, 160
  connectivity issues, 168–170
  database modification example, 240–244
  debugger output, 173–175
  installing databases on, 162–164
  multisets, 178
  Northwind database example, 160–164
  Object Relational Designer tool, 158, 175–177
  operators, 178–179
  overview, 157, 233
  performance issues, overcoming, 238–240
  PostgreSQL database, 295
  project definition, 170–171
  query example, 168–172
  resources for, 342–343
  Server Management Studio, 163
  SQLMetal command line tool, 158, 165–167
  uses for, 158–159

Service Reference folder, 279
set operators, 43, 123–124
`SetField` operator, 144–145
SharePoint solution, 13
sharing resources, 319
Simple Object Access Protocol (SOAP), 276
Simple Protocol and RDF Query Language (SPARQL), 283–284
SimpleDB solution, 13
`Single` operator, 128–129
`SingleOrDefault` operator, 128–129
sites. *See* Web sites
Skeet, Jon (blog resource), 341
`Skip` keyword
  support, 71
  Visual Basic example, 85–86
`Skip` operator, 120–121, 179
`SkipWhile` operator, 120–121, 179
`SNIPPET` files, 315
SOAP (Simple Object Access Protocol), 276
Software Development Kit (SDK), 219
sorting
  data operators, 43
  operators, 124–125
  `orderby` keyword, 26–27
source code. *See* listings
SPARQL (Simple Protocol and RDF Query Language), 283–284
special characters, 61–62
`SpecialCharCount()` method, 62
specialized topics, about this book, 3
sproc (stored procedure), 240
SQL server
  command line switches, 167
  concurrency problems, 234–238
  configuring Visual Studio for, 160
  connectivity issues, 168–170
  database modification example, 240–244
  debugger output, 173–175
  installing databases on, 162–164
  multisets, 178
  Northwind database example, 160–164
  Object Relational Designer tool, 158, 175–177
  operators, 178–179

overview, 157, 233
performance issues, overcoming, 238–240
PostgreSQL database, 295
project definition, 170–171
query example, 168–172
resources for, 342–343
Server Management Studio, 163
SQLMetal command line tool, 158, 165–167
uses for, 158–159
SQL (Structured Query Language)
discussed, 18
  `System.Data.SqlClient` namespace, 21
  `System.Data.SqlClient.Implementation` namespace, 22
SQLMetal command line tool, 158, 165–167
SSL (Secure Sockets Layer), 274–275, 280
SSPI (Security Support Provider Interface), 280
statements, 30
static methods, 138
Stephens, Rod (VB Helper newsletter), 340
stored procedure (sproc), 240
`StreamReader` object, 227
Streams solution, 13
strings
  `FilterStrings()` method, 53
  number of characters used in, 26
  `QueryString` array, 72–73, 104
  `ToString()` method, 187
`StringValue` variable, 99
Structured Query Language (SQL)
discussed, 18
  `System.Data.SqlClient` namespace, 21
  `System.Data.SqlClient.Implementation` namespace, 22
`SubmitChanges()` method, 235, 239
`Sum` operator, 127–128
support
  requests and responses, 327–328
  support task automation, 331–332
syntax, dot notation, 67–68
system identifiers, 196
system management, 333–334
`System.Data.Ling` namespace, 20–21

`System.Data.Linq.Mapping` namespace, 21
`System.Data.SqlClient` namespace, 21
`System.Data.SqlClient.Implementation` namespace, 22
`System.DirectoryServices` namespaces, 256
`System.Linq` namespace, 19
`System.Linq.Expressions` namespace, 19–20
`System.Xml.Linq` namespace, 22

• T •

tables. *See also* databases; datasets
  columns, 139, 149
  copying queries to, 146–148
  `DataTableCollection` class, 134
  intersection, 155
  multiple, 152–156
  records, deletions, 245–247
  records, inserting, 241–243
  records, updates, 243–245
  results output, 139
  rows, 142
  test table definition example, 136–138
`Take` keyword
  support, 71
  Visual Basic example, 87–88
`Take` operator, 120–121, 179
`TakeWhile` operator, 120–121, 179
TechRepublic newsletter, 340
templates, 331
text, XML document creation, 192–193
`TextReader` variable, 209
`ThenBy` operator, 124–125
`ThenByDescending` operator, 124–125
third-party Web site resources, 339–340
`ToArray` operator, 128
`ToDictionary` operator, 128
`ToList` operator, 128
`ToLookup` operator, 118–119, 128
`ToString()` method, 187
`try...catch` structure, 237
type safety design goal, 15
type, XML document, 195–197
`TypeBinaryExpression` type, 20
typed datasets, 148–152

• U •

UAC (User Access Control), 219
UnaryExpression type, 20
Union operator, 123–124, 141, 156, 180
UniqueConstraint object, 135
UpdateCheck parameter, 238
updates
  database, 239–240, 243–245
  table records, 244–245
URI, namespace, 203
usage trends, 317–318
User Access Control (UAC), 219
user documentation, VLinq tool, 303
user events, support task automation, 332
user factors, self-modifying queries, 322
user information, Active Directory
  reading, 265–266
  writing, 266–267
user-specific search selections, 325
using statement, 30

• V •

value attribute, 289
var keyword
  limitations, 48
  support, 24, 33
variables
  Active Directory, 256–257
  IndexArray, 99–100
  IndexValue, 99, 103–104
  LocalName, 203
  Namespace, 203
  NamespaceName, 203
  StringValue, 99
  TextReader, 209
Variant data type, 48
VB Helper newsletter (Stephens), 340
Vista developers, COM+ technology for, 274–275
Visual Basic
  Aggregate keyword, 83–84
  C# differences, 69–72
  deferred evaluation, 73–74

Distinct keyword, 84–85
from keyword example, 72–73
join keyword example, 79–81
Lambda expressions in, 88–90
let keyword example, 81–82
orderby keyword example, 78–79
resources for, 345
Skip keyword, 85–86
supported keywords, 71–72
Take keyword, 87–88
where keyword example, 75–77
Visual LINQ (VLinq) tool
  add-in application, 302–303
  database connection, 303–304
  graphical environment in, 307
  how to use, 303–307
  installation, 303
  queries, in applications, 308–309
  query creation, 303–307
  query elements, 306
  reference guide, 303
  user documentation, 303
Visual Studio 2005
  debugger functionality, 96–97
  from keyword example, 95–96
  join keyword example, 98–100
  let keyword, 103–104
  LINQ support installation, 92–93
  obtaining LINQ support for, 92
  orderby keyword example, 102–103
  overview, 91
  project definition, 94–95
  where keyword example, 100–101
Visual Studio 2008, 16
VLinq (Visual LINQ) tool
  add-in application, 302–303
  database connection, 303–304
  graphical environment in, 307
  how to use, 303–307
  installation, 303
  queries, in applications, 308–309
  query creation, 303–307
  query elements, 306
  reference guide, 303
  user documentation, 303

• W •

Wagner, Richard (*XML All-in-One Desk Reference For Dummies*), 184
Web services
  COM+ technology accessed as, 276, 278–281
  Google, 316
  LINQ and, 17
  X.509 certificate, 281
Web sites
  Code Project, 340
  DevelopersDex, 338
  DevSource, 339
  Hooked on LINQ, 339
  LINQ, 92
  Microsoft LINQ Resource Center, 339
  Mozilla, 283
  Mueller, John, 319
  Programmer's Heaven, 339, 341
  third-party Web site resources, 339–340
  W3C, 283
Webcasts, 340
Web.CONFIG file, 289
WebQueries, 13
where keyword
  overview, 25–26
  support, 44
  Visual Basic example, 75–77
  Visual Studio 2005 example, 100–101
Where operator, 115–116
white space, 207
Wikipedia Web site, 283
Windows application, 94
Windows authentication, 172
Windows Presentation Foundation (WPF), 92
Windows Server developers, COM+ technology for, 274–275
WinFX Runtime components, 92, 94
WinZIP application, 214
WMI (Windows Management Instrumentation), 13
WordProcessingDocument.Open() method, 226

World Wide Web Consortium (W3C) Web site, 283
WPF (Windows Presentation Foundation), 92
writing data
  to Active Directory, 266–267
  document properties, 228–231
WSDL file location, COM+ technology, 276
W3C (World Wide Web Consortium) Web site, 283–284

• X •

XAttribute operator, 184, 191–192
XCData operator, 184, 194–195
XComment operator, 184, 192–193
XContainer class, 186
XContainer operator, 184
XDeclaration operator, 185–187
XDocument operator, 185–187
XDocument.Load() method, 209
XDocumentType operator, 185, 195–197
XElement operator, 185–187
X.509 certificate, Web services, 281
XML
  API, 184–185
  attributes, 191–192
  axis manipulation, 186
  classes of concern for, 184–185
  comments, 192–193
  configuring Visual Studio for, 183
  core.xml file, 222
  custom.xml file, 221, 223
  document creation, 187, 205–206
  document names, 202–203
  documents, loading, 208–209
  documents, saving, 207
  DTD (Document Type Definition), 197
  equality comparison, 199–201
  FromXml() method, 172
  LINQ and XML interaction, 182–183
  nodes, removing, 201
  order comparison, 198–199
  overview, 181
  processing instruction, 190

XML *(continued)*
  resources for, 343–344
  serialization, 325
  simple file creation example, 204–206
  `System.Xml.Linq` namespace, 22
  text, 192–193
*XML All-in-One Desk Reference For
    Dummies* (Wagner and Mansfield), 184
`XName` operator, 185, 202–204
`XName.Get()` method, 227
`XNamespace` operator, 185, 188–190
`XNode` class, 184, 186
`XNodeDocumentOrderComparer`
    operator, 185, 197–199

`XNodeEqualityComparer` operator, 185,
    199–200
`XObject` class, 186
`XObjectChange` class, 186
`XObjectChangeEventArgs` class, 186
`XProcessingInstruction` operator,
    185, 190
`XText` operator, 185, 192–193
XtraGrid solution, 13

• Z •

ZIP application, 214

USINESS, CAREERS & PERSONAL FINANCE

0-7645-9847-3

0-7645-2431-3

Also available:
- Business Plans Kit For Dummies
  0-7645-9794-9
- Economics For Dummies
  0-7645-5726-2
- Grant Writing For Dummies
  0-7645-8416-2
- Home Buying For Dummies
  0-7645-5331-3
- Managing For Dummies
  0-7645-1771-6
- Marketing For Dummies
  0-7645-5600-2

- Personal Finance For Dummies
  0-7645-2590-5*
- Resumes For Dummies
  0-7645-5471-9
- Selling For Dummies
  0-7645-5363-1
- Six Sigma For Dummies
  0-7645-6798-5
- Small Business Kit For Dummies
  0-7645-5984-2
- Starting an eBay Business For Dummies
  0-7645-6924-4
- Your Dream Career For Dummies
  0-7645-9795-7

OME & BUSINESS COMPUTER BASICS

0-470-05432-8

0-471-75421-8

Also available:
- Cleaning Windows Vista For Dummies
  0-471-78293-9
- Excel 2007 For Dummies
  0-470-03737-7
- Mac OS X Tiger For Dummies
  0-7645-7675-5
- MacBook For Dummies
  0-470-04859-X
- Macs For Dummies
  0-470-04849-2
- Office 2007 For Dummies
  0-470-00923-3

- Outlook 2007 For Dummies
  0-470-03830-6
- PCs For Dummies
  0-7645-8958-X
- Salesforce.com For Dummies
  0-470-04893-X
- Upgrading & Fixing Laptops For Dummies
  0-7645-8959-8
- Word 2007 For Dummies
  0-470-03658-3
- Quicken 2007 For Dummies
  0-470-04600-7

OOD, HOME, GARDEN, HOBBIES, MUSIC & PETS

0-7645-8404-9

0-7645-9904-6

Also available:
- Candy Making For Dummies
  0-7645-9734-5
- Card Games For Dummies
  0-7645-9910-0
- Crocheting For Dummies
  0-7645-4151-X
- Dog Training For Dummies
  0-7645-8418-9
- Healthy Carb Cookbook For Dummies
  0-7645-8476-6
- Home Maintenance For Dummies
  0-7645-5215-5

- Horses For Dummies
  0-7645-9797-3
- Jewelry Making & Beading For Dummies
  0-7645-2571-9
- Orchids For Dummies
  0-7645-6759-4
- Puppies For Dummies
  0-7645-5255-4
- Rock Guitar For Dummies
  0-7645-5356-9
- Sewing For Dummies
  0-7645-6847-7
- Singing For Dummies
  0-7645-2475-5

NTERNET & DIGITAL MEDIA

0-470-04529-9

0-470-04894-8

Also available:
- Blogging For Dummies
  0-471-77084-1
- Digital Photography For Dummies
  0-7645-9802-3
- Digital Photography All-in-One Desk Reference For Dummies
  0-470-03743-1
- Digital SLR Cameras and Photography For Dummies
  0-7645-9803-1
- eBay Business All-in-One Desk Reference For Dummies
  0-7645-8438-3
- HDTV For Dummies
  0-470-09673-X

- Home Entertainment PCs For Dummies
  0-470-05523-5
- MySpace For Dummies
  0-470-09529-6
- Search Engine Optimization For Dummies
  0-471-97998-8
- Skype For Dummies
  0-470-04891-3
- The Internet For Dummies
  0-7645-8996-2
- Wiring Your Digital Home For Dummies
  0-471-91830-X

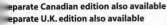

Separate Canadian edition also available
Separate U.K. edition also available

ilable wherever books are sold. For more information or to order direct: U.S. customers visit www.dummies.com or call 1-877-762-2974.
 customers visit www.wileyeurope.com or call 0800 243407. Canadian customers visit www.wiley.ca or call 1-800-567-4797.

SPORTS, FITNESS, PARENTING, RELIGION & SPIRITUALITY

0-471-76871-5

0-7645-7841-3

Also available:
- Catholicism For Dummies
0-7645-5391-7
- Exercise Balls For Dummies
0-7645-5623-1
- Fitness For Dummies
0-7645-7851-0
- Football For Dummies
0-7645-3936-1
- Judaism For Dummies
0-7645-5299-6
- Potty Training For Dummies
0-7645-5417-4
- Buddhism For Dummies
0-7645-5359-3

- Pregnancy For Dummies
0-7645-4483-7 †
- Ten Minute Tone-Ups For Dummies
0-7645-7207-5
- NASCAR For Dummies
0-7645-7681-X
- Religion For Dummies
0-7645-5264-3
- Soccer For Dummies
0-7645-5229-5
- Women in the Bible For Dummies
0-7645-8475-8

TRAVEL

0-7645-7749-2

0-7645-6945-7

Also available:
- Alaska For Dummies
0-7645-7746-8
- Cruise Vacations For Dummies
0-7645-6941-4
- England For Dummies
0-7645-4276-1
- Europe For Dummies
0-7645-7529-5
- Germany For Dummies
0-7645-7823-5
- Hawaii For Dummies
0-7645-7402-7

- Italy For Dummies
0-7645-7386-1
- Las Vegas For Dummies
0-7645-7382-9
- London For Dummies
0-7645-4277-X
- Paris For Dummies
0-7645-7630-5
- RV Vacations For Dummies
0-7645-4442-X
- Walt Disney World & Orlando
For Dummies
0-7645-9660-8

GRAPHICS, DESIGN & WEB DEVELOPMENT

0-7645-8815-X

0-7645-9571-7

Also available:
- 3D Game Animation For Dummies
0-7645-8789-7
- AutoCAD 2006 For Dummies
0-7645-8925-3
- Building a Web Site For Dummies
0-7645-7144-3
- Creating Web Pages For Dummies
0-470-08030-2
- Creating Web Pages All-in-One Desk
Reference For Dummies
0-7645-4345-8
- Dreamweaver 8 For Dummies
0-7645-9649-7

- InDesign CS2 For Dummies
0-7645-9572-5
- Macromedia Flash 8 For Dummies
0-7645-9691-8
- Photoshop CS2 and Digital
Photography For Dummies
0-7645-9580-6
- Photoshop Elements 4 For Dummies
0-471-77483-9
- Syndicating Web Sites with RSS Feed
For Dummies
0-7645-8848-6
- Yahoo! SiteBuilder For Dummies
0-7645-9800-7

NETWORKING, SECURITY, PROGRAMMING & DATABASES

0-7645-7728-X

0-471-74940-0

Also available:
- Access 2007 For Dummies
0-470-04612-0
- ASP.NET 2 For Dummies
0-7645-7907-X
- C# 2005 For Dummies
0-7645-9704-3
- Hacking For Dummies
0-470-05235-X
- Hacking Wireless Networks
For Dummies
0-7645-9730-2
- Java For Dummies
0-470-08716-1

- Microsoft SQL Server 2005 For Dummi
0-7645-7755-7
- Networking All-in-One Desk Referen
For Dummies
0-7645-9939-9
- Preventing Identity Theft For Dummie
0-7645-7336-5
- Telecom For Dummies
0-471-77085-X
- Visual Studio 2005 All-in-One Desk
Reference For Dummies
0-7645-9775-2
- XML For Dummies
0-7645-8845-1